westermann

Dieter Smolka / Francis Corke

Great Speeches

Erklärung der Abkürzungen und Symbole:

Abbreviations:

AmE	American English
BrE	British English
coll.	colloquial
e.g.	*exempli gratia,* for example
fig.	figurative, metaphorical meaning
here	special meaning in this context
i.e.	id est, that is to say; *d.h., das heißt*
infml.	informal English
lit.	literary English
sb.	somebody
sth.	something

Symbol:

▶: Suggested Teaching and Learning Methods

Orthography: *Globalization or Globalisation, emphasize or emphasise, summarize or summarise* are examples of a group of words that are generally spelled with a "z" in American English and with an "s" in British English. The American spelling is gaining acceptance around the world. Even some Abitur assignments tend to use the American English spelling, e.g. *summarize.* In this textbook the American or British English spelling is employed according to the speaker, the source or the context of the particular speech. With a few exceptions, e.g. *summarize,* the assignments which follow each speech, employ the British English spelling.
Here are some examples:

American English	**British English**
to analyze	to analyse
to criticize	to criticise
to emphasize	to emphasise
to globalize	to globalise
to realize	to realise
to recognize	to recognise

westermann GRUPPE

Druck A[1] / Jahr 2019
Alle Drucke der Serie A sind im Unterricht parallel verwendbar.

Coverfoto: © smolaw11 / stock.adobe.com
Layout: Harald Thumser, Frankfurt am Main
Realisation: Satz und Grafik Walter Laß e.K., Meitingen
Druck und Bindung: westermann druck GmbH, Braunschweig

ISBN 978-3-425-**04974**-8

Table of Contents

Introduction

They are exceptional.
They are famous, exciting, excellent and outstanding.
They are passionate, moving and brimming with emotions.
They are classics. They are modern and revolutionary.
They are motivational.
They are infuriating and enraging.
They made history and have changed the world.
They share knowledge, personal experiences and wisdom.

They deal with the problems facing the world today:
The American Dream, Civil Rights and Human Dignity, War and Peace, Violence and Terror, the Earth in Danger, Global Warming and Climate Change, Global Migration and Global Solidarity, Education, the United Nations: Peacekeeping in a World of Conflicts, the Digital Age, the Media, School Shootings and Gun Control in the USA, and the Future UK – EU Relationship.

This textbook *Great Speeches* features forty-three famous speeches by outstanding speakers. The annotations facilitate understanding. Additional material and standardised, as well as creative and thought-provoking assignments are offered to support a comprehensive analysis and evaluation of these exceptional speeches. A variety of teaching and learning methods are suggested to complement the learning process.

The textbook is recommended for upper-intermediate and advanced learners studying in the *Oberstufe* and preparing for their *Abitur* examination. The speeches encourage and empower any speaker, and offer useful tips for public speaking.

Bear in mind that, when delivered well, a speech can be very powerful, and can even transform the world-view of the attentive listener.

We would like to thank Bethany Creamer, Shayaan Khan, Scarlett Milner-Stopps, Jack Nason, Catriona Kopschina, and Andrew Shearn for their great help and assistance in proofreading the manuscript. We would also like to extend our sincere thanks to Westermann Gruppe and the head of the Foreign Languages department, Ulrich Steppat, as well as a number of other colleagues who have contributed to the realisation of this work. Working together has been a pleasure.

Enjoy the speeches and feel free to express your own ideas and opinions in a carefully crafted speech – in class, at school, or in public.

Dieter Smolka and Francis Corke

A American Dream or American Nightmare?

"We Must Do These Things Together as One Nation and One People."

President Barack Obama: The Second Inaugural Address on January 21, 2013

RELATED TOPICS

THE AMERICAN DREAM · CLIMATE CHANGE · THE CONSTITUTION · THE DECLARATION OF INDEPENDENCE · DEMOCRACY · DIGNITY · EDUCATION · THE FOUNDING CREED · FREEDOM · FUTURE GENERATIONS · GLOBAL WARMING · GOD · HISTORY · HUMAN RIGHTS · IMMIGRATION · INEQUALITY · INJUSTICE · JUSTICE · LIBERTY · NATIONHOOD · RACE RELATIONS · SEGREGATION · SLAVERY · SOCIAL SECURITY · UNALIENABLE RIGHTS

Barack Obama served as the 44th President of the United States. His story is the American story – American values, a middle-class upbringing in a strong family, hard work and education as a means to get ahead, and the conviction that a life so blessed should be lived in the service of others.

President Obama was born in Hawaii on August 4, 1961 to a mother from Kansas, and a Kenyan father. He was raised with the help of his grandfather, who served in Patton's army, and his grandmother, who worked her way up from the secretarial pool to middle management at a bank.

After working his way through college with the help of scholarships and student loans, Barack Obama moved to Chicago, where he worked with a group of churches to help rebuild communities devastated by the closure of local steel plants.

He went on to attend law school, where he became the first African-American president of the Harvard Law Review. Upon graduation, he returned to Chicago to help lead a voter registration drive, and to teach constitutional law at the University of Chicago, during which time he played an active role in his local community.

He was elected the 44th President of the United States on November 4, 2008, and was sworn in on January 20, 2009. He and his wife, Michelle, are the proud parents of two daughters, Malia and Sasha.

From: *The White House* https://www.whitehouse.gov/about-the-white-house/presidents/barack-obama/
Speech transcript: https://obamawhitehouse.archives.gov/the-press-office/2013/01/21/inaugural-address-president-barack-obama

THE PRESIDENT Barack Obama:

Vice President Biden, Mr. Chief Justice,
members of the United States Congress, distinguished guests, and fellow citizens:

Each time we gather to inaugurate a President, we bear witness to the enduring strength of our Constitution. We affirm the promise of our democracy. We recall that what binds this nation together is not the color of our skin, or the tenets of our faith, or the origins of our names. What makes us exceptional – what makes us American – is our allegiance to an idea articulated in a declaration made more than two centuries ago:
"We hold these truths to be self-evident, that all men are created equal; that they are endowed by their Creator with certain unalienable rights; that among these are life, liberty, and the pursuit of happiness."

WE CONTINUE A NEVER-ENDING JOURNEY

Today, we continue a never-ending journey to bridge the meaning of those words with the realities of our time. For history tells us that while these truths may be self-evident, they've never been self-executing; that while freedom is a gift from God, it must be secured by His people here on Earth. The patriots of 1776 did not fight to replace the tyranny of a king with the privileges of a few or the rule of a mob. They gave to us a republic, a government of, and by, and for the people, entrusting each generation to keep safe our founding creed.

And for more than two hundred years, we have.

Through blood drawn by lash and blood drawn by sword, we learned that no union founded on the principles of liberty and equality could survive half-slave and half-free. We made ourselves anew, and vowed to move forward together.

A GREAT NATION MUST CARE FOR THE VULNERABLE

Together, we determined that a modern economy requires railroads and highways to speed travel and commerce, and schools and colleges to train our workers.

Together, we discovered that a free market only thrives when there are rules to ensure competition and fair play.

Together, we resolved that a great nation must care for the vulnerable, and protect its people from life's worst hazards and misfortunes.

United States Congress: the legislative body of government, consisting of the Senate and the House of Representatives.

to inaugurate a President *in das Amt des Präsidenten einführen*
we bear witness to the enduring strength *wir werden Zeugen der unvergänglichen Stärke*
the Constitution *see* ADDITIONAL NOTES
to affirm to confirm; *bestätigen*
to recall to remember; *sich erinnern*
to bind to unite
the tenets of our faith set of beliefs; *die Grundlagen unseres Glaubens*
allegiance loyalty, commitment; *Treue*
declaration Declaration of Independence
endowed by their Creator *von ihrem Schöpfer ausgestattet*
unalienable rights *unveräußerliche Rechte*

to bridge with *in Einklang bringen mit*

self-evident clear; *selbstverständlich*
self-executing to perform a skilful action without help; *selbst ausführend*
secured obtained, protected
the patriots of 1776 *see* ADDITIONAL NOTES

the founding creed: the principles of the constitution; *die Gründerprinzipien*

through blood drawn by lash and blood drawn by sword *durch das Blut von Peitschenhieben und Schwertern;* "blood drawn by the lash" is an allusion to Abraham Lincoln's second inaugural address in 1865.
half-slave and half-free an allusion to Abraham Lincoln's famous address, his "House Divided" speech, from his campaign for the Senate in 1858
to speed to speed up, to enable

to thrive to do well, to prosper

hazards dangers, threats

to relinquish to give up
succumbed to the fiction *dem Irrglauben verfallen sein*
society's ills the problems/troubles of society
constants in our character unchanging traits; *beständige Charaktermerkmale*

Through it all, we have never relinquished our scepticism of central authority, nor have we succumbed to the fiction that all society's ills can be cured through government alone. Our celebration of initiative and enterprise, our insistence on hard work and personal responsibility, these are constants in our character.

WE MUST DO THESE THINGS TOGETHER, AS ONE NATION AND ONE PEOPLE

fidelity loyalty, faithfulness
challenges *Herausforderungen*
to preserve to protect, to secure; *erhalten, bewahren*
ultimately basically, fundamentally; *im Grunde, prinzipiell*
muskets and militias *Musketen und Milizen*

But we have always understood that when times change, so must we; that fidelity to our founding principles requires new responses to new challenges; that preserving our individual freedoms ultimately requires collective action. For the American people can no more meet the demands of today's world by acting alone than American soldiers could have met the forces of fascism or communism with muskets and militias. No single person can train all the math and science teachers we'll need to equip our children for the future, or build the roads and networks and research labs that will bring new jobs and businesses to our shores. Now, more than ever, we must do these things together, as one nation and one people.

THIS WORLD WITHOUT BOUNDARIES

steeled our resolve *unsere Entschlossenheit gestärkt*
resilience *Widerstandsfähigkeit, Belastbarkeit, Resilienz*
youth and drive *Jugend und Elan*
capacity for risk *Risikofreudigkeit*
we will seize it we will achieve it, we will make the most of it

This generation of Americans has been tested by crises that steeled our resolve and proved our resilience. A decade of war is now ending. An economic recovery has begun. America's possibilities are limitless, for we possess all the qualities that this world without boundaries demands: youth and drive; diversity and openness; an endless capacity for risk and a gift for reinvention. My fellow Americans, we are made for this moment, and we will seize it – so long as we seize it together.

THE SAME CHANCE TO SUCCEED AS ANYBODY ELSE

prosperity *Wohlstand*
to liberate to set free
the brink of hardship at risk of poverty
the bleakest poverty extreme poverty; *trostlose Armut*

For we, the people, understand that our country cannot succeed when a shrinking few do very well and a growing many barely make it. We believe that America's prosperity must rest upon the broad shoulders of a rising middle class. We know that America thrives when every person can find independence and pride in their work; when the wages of honest labor liberate families from the brink of hardship. We are true to our creed when a little girl born into the bleakest poverty knows that she has the same chance to succeed as anybody else, because she is an American; she is free, and she is equal, not just in the eyes of God but also in our own eyes.

outworn outdated; *überholt*
the needs of our time *Erfordernisse unserer Zeit*
to harness to profit from, to utilize
to remake *erneuern*
to revamp to update

We understand that outworn programs are inadequate to meet the needs of our time. So we must harness new ideas and technology to remake our government, revamp our tax code, reform our schools, and empower our citizens with the skills they need to work harder, to learn more, to reach higher. But while the means will change, our purpose endures: a nation that rewards the effort and determination of every single American. That is what this moment requires. That is what will give real meaning to our creed.

We, the people, still believe that every citizen deserves a basic measure of security and dignity. We must make the hard choices to reduce the cost of health care and the size of our deficit. But we reject the belief that America must choose between caring for the generation that built this country and investing in the generation that will build its future. For we remember the lessons of our past, when twilight years were spent in poverty and the parents of a child with a disability had nowhere to turn.

We do not believe that, in this country, freedom is reserved for the lucky, or happiness for the few. We recognize that no matter how responsibly we live our lives, any one of us, at any time, may face a job loss, or a sudden illness, or a home swept away in a terrible storm. The commitments we make to each other through Medicare and Medicaid and Social Security, these things do not sap our initiative, they strengthen us. They do not make us a nation of takers; they free us to take the risks that make this country great.

We, the people, still believe that our obligations as Americans are not just to ourselves, but to all posterity.
We will respond to the threat of climate change, knowing that the failure to do so would betray our children, and future generations.

Some may still deny the overwhelming judgment of science, but no one can avoid the devastating impact of raging fires and crippling drought and more powerful storms.

WE WILL PRESERVE OUR PLANET,
COMMANDED TO OUR CARE BY GOD

The path towards sustainable energy sources will be long, and sometimes difficult. But America cannot resist this transition, we must lead it. We cannot cede to other nations the technology that will power new jobs and new industries, we must claim its promise. That's how we will maintain our economic vitality and our national treasure – our forests and waterways, our croplands and snow-capped peaks.

That is how we will preserve our planet, commanded to our care by God. That's what will lend meaning to the creed our fathers once declared.

but while the means will change *auch wenn sich die Mittel ändern*
our purpose endures our aims are still valid and important
creed belief, principles

when twilight years were spent in poverty *wenn man seinen Lebensabend in Armut verbringen musste*
the parents of a child with a disability had nowhere to turn *die Eltern eines Kindes mit einer Behinderung hatten niemanden, an den sie sich wenden konnten*
may face a job loss may lose a job, be confronted with unemployment
Medicare *die öffentliche und bundesstaatliche Krankenversicherung innerhalb des Gesundheitssystems der USA für ältere oder Bürger mit Behinderungen*
Medicaid *ein steuerfinanziertes Gesundheits-Fürsorgeprogramm für Bürger mit geringem Einkommen*
to sap our initiative to weaken our drive/ambition/resolve
a nation of takers *eine Nation von Sozialhilfeempfängern*
obligations as Americans are not just to ourselves, but to all posterity *wir haben nicht nur Verpflichtungen uns gegenüber, sondern auch gegenüber unseren Nachkommen*
threat danger; *Bedrohung, Gefährdung*
to betray *verraten*
devastating impact *verheerende Auswirkungen*
crippling drought *lähmende Dürre*
sustainable renewable; *nachhaltig*
transition change; *Wandel*
to cede to other nations *anderen Ländern überlassen*
we must claim its promise *vielversprechende Entwicklungen (Technologien) für uns in Anspruch nehmen*
commanded to our care by God *den Gott uns zur Fürsorge anvertraut hat*
That's what will lend meaning to the creed our fathers once declared *so erlangt die Überzeugung unserer Gründungsväter Bedeutung.*

perpetual never-ending, endless
tempered by strengthened by
unmatched in skill and courage *einzigartig an Erfahrung, Können und Mut*
seared by the memory *gezeichnet durch die Erinnerung*
vigilant against aware of, alert to; *wachsam*
heirs *Erben*
to turn sworn enemies into the surest of friends *aus Erzfeinden enge Freunde machen*
to resolve differences peacefully to solve problems peacefully; *Differenzen friedlich beilegen*
suspicion mistrust, distrust; *Misstrauen*

We, the people, still believe that enduring security and lasting peace do not require perpetual war. Our brave men and women in uniform, tempered by the flames of battle, are unmatched in skill and courage. Our citizens, seared by the memory of those we have lost, know too well the price that is paid for liberty. The knowledge of their sacrifice will keep us forever vigilant against those who would do us harm. But we are also heirs to those who won the peace and not just the war; who turned sworn enemies into the surest of friends – and we must carry those lessons into this time as well.

We will defend our people and uphold our values through strength of arms and rule of law. We will show the courage to try to resolve our differences with other nations peacefully – not because we are naïve about the dangers we face, but because engagement can more durably lift suspicion and fear.

WE WILL SUPPORT DEMOCRACY

alliances *Bündnisse*
to have a stake in to have an interest in, to have a role to play in
conscience *Gewissen*
to compel to force
the marginalized *Randgruppen*
advance (*here:*) *Verbreitung*
creed belief, principles

America will remain the anchor of strong alliances in every corner of the globe. And we will renew those institutions that extend our capacity to manage crises abroad, for no one has a greater stake in a peaceful world than its most powerful nation. We will support democracy from Asia to Africa, from the Americas to the Middle East, because our interests and our conscience compel us to act on behalf of those who long for freedom. And we must be a source of hope to the poor, the sick, the marginalized and, the victims of prejudice – not out of mere charity, but because peace in our time requires the constant advance of those principles that our common creed describes: tolerance and opportunity, human dignity and justice.

forebears ancestors
Seneca Falls Declaration (1848) *see* Additional Notes
Selma *see Additional Notes*
Stonewall (1969) *see Additional Notes*
King a reference to Martin Luther King Jr., *see Additional Notes*
inextricably inseparably, completely

We, the people, declare today that the most evident of truths – that all of us are created equal – is the star that guides us still; just as it guided our forebears through Seneca Falls, and Selma, and Stonewall; just as it guided all those men and women, sung and unsung, who left footprints along this great Mall, to hear a preacher say that we cannot walk alone; to hear a King proclaim that our individual freedom is inextricably bound to the freedom of every soul on Earth.

OUR JOURNEY IS NOT COMPLETE

It is now our generation's task to carry on what those pioneers began. For our journey is not complete until our wives, our mothers, and our daughters can earn a living equal to their efforts. Our journey is not complete until our gay brothers and sisters are treated like anyone else under the law – for if we are truly created equal, then surely the love we commit to one another must be equal as well.

Our journey is not complete until no citizen is forced to wait for hours to exercise the right to vote.
Our journey is not complete until we find a better way to welcome the striving, hopeful immigrants who still see America as a land of opportunity – until bright young students and engineers are enlisted in our workforce, rather than expelled from our country.
Our journey is not complete until all our children, from the streets of Detroit to the hills of Appalachia, to the quiet lanes of Newtown, know that they are cared for and cherished and always safe from harm.

expelled (*here:*) deported; *abgeschoben*

VALUES OF LIFE, LIBERTY AND THE PURSUIT OF HAPPINESS

That is our generation's task – to make these words, these rights, these values of life and liberty and the pursuit of happiness, real for every American. Being true to our founding documents does not require us to agree on every contour of life. It does not mean we all define liberty in exactly the same way or follow the same precise path to happiness. Progress does not compel us to settle centuries-long debates about the role of government for all time, but it does require us to act in our time.

every contour of life every aspect of life

For now decisions are upon us and we cannot afford delay. We cannot mistake absolutism for principle, or substitute spectacle for politics, or treat name-calling as reasoned debate. We must act, knowing that our work will be imperfect.

We must act, knowing that today's victories will only be partial and that it will be up to those who stand here four years and forty years and four-hundred years hence to advance the timeless spirit once conferred to us in a spare Philadelphia Hall.

decisions are upon us we have to make decisions
we cannot afford delay we must start immediately; *wir können keine Verzögerungen/Aufschiebungen dulden*
to substitute spectacle for politics *Politik durch Theater ersetzen*
name-calling *Beschimpfungen*

a spare Philadelphia Hall a reference to Independence Hall in Philadelphia, Pennsylvania, where the Second Continental Congress met on July 4, 1776 to write The Declaration of Independence

My fellow Americans, the oath I have sworn before you today, like the one recited by others who serve in this Capitol, was an oath to God and country, not to party or faction. And we must faithfully execute that pledge during the duration of our service.

pledge oath, promise; *Versprechen, Gelöbnis*

CARRY INTO AN UNCERTAIN FUTURE THAT PRECIOUS LIGHT OF FREEDOM

But the words I spoke today are not so different from the oath that is taken each time a soldier signs up for duty or an immigrant realizes her dream. My oath is not so different from the pledge we all make to the flag that waves above us and that fills our hearts with pride.

They are the words of citizens and they represent our greatest hope. You and I, as citizens, have the power to set this country's course. You and I, as citizens, have the obligation to shape the debates of our

obligation duty, responsibility

defence (*AmE*), defense (*BrE*), protection

awesome overwhelming , tremendous, great

dedication commitment; *Leidenschaft, Hingabe*

time – not only with the votes we cast, but with the voices we lift in defence of our most ancient values and enduring ideals.

Let us, each of us, now embrace with solemn duty and awesome joy what is our lasting birth right. With common effort and common purpose, with passion and dedication, let us answer the call of history and carry into an uncertain future that precious light of freedom.

Thank you. God bless you, and may He forever bless these United States of America.

ASSIGNMENTS

A) Listening and Reading Comprehension

SQ3R reading method / think-pair-share / think: take notes / pair: discuss your ideas with your partner / share: share your ideas with another pair, with the class / presentation / feedback

1. Watch the video of President Obama's Second Inaugural Address on YouTube: https://www.youtube.com/watch?v=BzC135ql_wA&feature=youtu.be
2. Read the speech transcript and highlight the important statements and significant keywords.
3. Barack Obama talks about the principles of the *Declaration of Independence*. What does he think of these principles?
4. How does he want American citizens to preserve our planet?
5. What advice does Obama give to the audience, and what appeal does he make to them?
6. Summarise Barack Obama's main arguments.

B) Analysis

1. Analyse the structure of Barack Obama's speech.
2. Analyse the keywords Obama uses in his speech.
3. Obama uses repetition and personal pronouns to reinforce the underlying message of his speech, and to build an emotional momentum. Please analyse some examples.
4. Examine the rhetorical devices Obama uses to support his message.
5. Obama uses the image of a journey a couple of times in his speech. Why does he use it? And why is the journey still incomplete?
6. The *Declaration of Independence* and the *Constitution of the United States* are the most important documents in American political history. In which parts of his speech does Obama refer to these documents? What is the intended effect of referring to these documents?
7. Obama's positive regard for Abraham Lincoln, the 16th President, is quite obvious. In his address, he refers to him twice. Firstly, he alludes to the *Gettysburg Address*, secondly, he directly cites Lincoln's 1858 *House Divided* speech, which he delivered at the Illinois State Capitol. Why does Barack Obama refer to Abraham Lincoln so many times?
8. Political leaders in the US often plan to refer to God at the beginning and end of their speeches. It is a standard feature of American political speeches to conclude one's speech by asking God to bless the people in attendance, and the country as a whole. Analyse the effects of Obama's religious references.

C) Comment, Evaluation, Creative Writing

▶ *creative writing / presentation / peer support and feedback / discussion / speech / evaluation*

1. Creative Writing:
   a) Write a letter to the former President and respond to his speech from your own point of view.
   b) Write an article for a newspaper and discuss one topic Obama emphasises.
   c) Imagine you are an influential politician; write and give a speech in response to Obama's speech.
2. "You and I, as citizens, have the power to set this country's course. You and I, as citizens, have the obligation to shape the debates of our time – not only with the votes we cast, but with the voices we lift in defence of our most ancient values and enduring ideals." Discuss and explain your opinion.
3. "We are true to our creed when a little girl born into the bleakest poverty knows that she has the same chance to succeed as anybody else, because she is an American; she is free, and she is equal, not just in the eyes of God but also in our own eyes." Explain, discuss and evaluate this statement.
4. "That is our generation's task – to make these words, these rights, these values – of life, and liberty, and the pursuit of happiness – real for every American. Being true to our founding documents does not require us to agree on every contour of life; it does not mean we will all define liberty in exactly the same way, or follow the same precise path to happiness." Do you agree or disagree with Obama's statement? Give reasons for your answer.
5. Obama refers to historical movements, including: the women's rights supporters who gathered at Seneca Falls in 1848, the civil rights marchers who protested against the mistreatment of African-Americans, and were beaten by state troopers and police officers in Selma, Alabama in 1965, and the LGBT-people who protested against discrimination during the Stonewall riots in 1969. Obama also pays tribute to the people who participated in the March on Washington in 1963, specifically mentioning Martin Luther King Jr. Why are these social movements particularly important, according to Obama?
6. Compare Barack Obama's *Inaugural Address* to Donald Trump's *Inaugural Address.*
7. Read and evaluate the poem "One Today" by Richard Blanco, written for the 57th Presidential Inauguration, which took place on January 21, 2013.

D) Creative Activities

1. Imagine you are a journalist interviewing the former US President Barack Obama. Prepare an interview with your partner and act it out in your English class.
2. "I Have a Dream." Imagine that you are a member of Barack Obama's speech writing team. Write a "dream"-based speech for Obama's next visit to Germany, then give the speech to your class.

E) Mediation: Abschiedsrede des Bundestagspräsidenten Prof. Dr. Norbert Lammert am 5. September 2017 im Deutschen Bundestag:

„Autoritäre Regime brauchen kein bürgerschaftliches Engagement. Sie mögen es nicht, sie behindern es, und wenn es nicht anders geht, verbieten sie es. Die Demokratie braucht es. Und wir wissen aus noch nicht ganz so lange zurückliegenden Phasen der deutschen Geschichte, dass auch Demokratien ausbluten können, dass sie ihre innere Kraft verlieren, wenn sie die Unterstützung der Menschen verlieren, für die es sie gibt. Die Demokratie steht und fällt mit dem Engagement ihrer Bürgerinnen und Bürger. Das ist die wichtigste Lektion, die ich in meinem politischen Leben gelernt habe, und dieser Einsicht und dieser Verantwortung werde ich verpflichtet bleiben."

From: *Bundestag* https://www.bundestag.de/parlament/praesidium/reden/2017/006/525764

Tasks:

a) Give the gist of Norbert Lammert's speech in English.
b) Write a personal response to Lammert's speech for an English newspaper, evaluating the significance of the speech to a democratic society.
c) Write an inspiring conversation between Barack Obama and Norbert Lammert about democratic values.

"Ask Not What Your Country Can Do for You – Ask What You Can Do for Your Country."

John Fitzgerald Kennedy's Inaugural Address on January 20, 1961

RELATED TOPICS

THE AMERICAN DREAM · AMERICAN HERITAGE · THE COLD WAR · THE CONSTITUTION · THE DECLARATION OF INDEPENDENCE · DEMOCRACY · EDUCATION · THE FOUNDING CREED · FREEDOM · FUTURE GENERATIONS · HISTORY · HUMAN RIGHTS · IMMIGRATION · INEQUALITY · JUSTICE · LIBERTY · NATION · PEACE · POVERTY · RACE RELATIONS · SEGREGATION · SOCIAL SECURITY · TYRANNY · UNALIENABLE RIGHTS · UNITED NATIONS

John F. Kennedy was born on May 29, 1917, in Brookline, Massachusetts, U.S.; he was assassinated in Dallas and died on November 22, 1963, in Dallas, Texas. He was the 35th president of the United States (1961–63) and he faced a number of foreign crises, but managed to secure such achievements as the Nuclear Test-Ban Treaty and the Alliance for Progress. Kennedy's administration lasted only 1,037 days.

On January 20, 1961, President John F. Kennedy was sworn into office, and delivered his famous Inaugural Address. He spoke of the need for all Americans to be active citizens. "Ask not what your country can do for you, ask what you can do for your country." He also asked the nations of the world to join together to fight what he called the "common enemies of man: tyranny, poverty, disease, and war itself." JFK, as Kennedy is often known, started a new phase of the Cold War, one that led to the most dangerous event of his presidency, the Cuban Missile Crisis.

Kennedy used his Inaugural Address to issue a warning about the imminent possibility of nuclear war. He also emphasized the U.S. intentions to protect freedom and democracy, and argued that cooperating with the Soviet Union would prevent a nuclear war, and would help to build a more peaceful world.

The Cold War: The 1950s and 1960s were characterized by severe tension between the United States and the Soviet Union, commonly called the Cold War. The Cold War was not an actual military conflict fought with armies and weapons, but a conflict of ideas, threats, and competition.

Cold War rhetoric dominated the 1960 presidential campaign. Senator John F. Kennedy and Vice President Richard M. Nixon both promised to strengthen American military forces, and took a tough stance against the Soviet Union, and Communist regimes around the world. Kennedy warned of the Soviet Union's growing arsenal of intercontinental ballistic missiles, and pledged to renew American nuclear forces.

Many people believed and hoped that Kennedy could make his presidency one of peace and progress. John F. Kennedy wanted to inspire the nation, and to send a message abroad, in which he described the challenges of the Cold War, and expressed his hope for peace in the Nuclear Age.

Based on: *Encyclopaedia Britannica* https://www.britannica.com/biography/John-F-Kennedy
and on the *JFK Presidential Library and Museum* https://www.jfklibrary.org/

THE PRESIDENT John F. Kennedy:

[1] Vice President Johnson, Mr. Speaker, Mr. Chief Justice, President Eisenhower, Vice President Nixon, President Truman, Reverend Clergy, fellow citizens:

[2] We observe today not a victory of party but a celebration of freedom – symbolizing an end as well as a beginning – signifying renewal as well as change. For I have sworn before you and Almighty God the same solemn oath our forebearers prescribed nearly a century and three-quarters ago.

MAN HOLDS IN HIS MORTAL HANDS THE POWER TO ABOLISH ALL FORMS OF HUMAN POVERTY AND ALL FORMS OF HUMAN LIFE

[3] The world is very different now. For man holds in his mortal hands the power to abolish all forms of human poverty and all forms of human life. And yet the same revolutionary beliefs for which our forebearers fought are still at issue around the globe – the belief that the rights of man come not from the generosity of the state but from the hand of God.

[4] We dare not forget today that we are the heirs of that first revolution. Let the word go forth from this time and place, to friend and foe alike, that the torch has been passed to a new generation of Americans – born in this century, tempered by war, disciplined by a hard and bitter peace, proud of our ancient heritage – and unwilling to witness or permit the slow undoing of those human rights to which this nation has always been committed, and to which we are committed today at home and around the world.

THE SURVIVAL AND THE SUCCESS OF LIBERTY

[5] Let every nation know, whether it wishes us well or ill, that we shall pay any price, bear any burden, meet any hardship, support any friend, oppose any foe, to assure the survival and the success of liberty.

[6] This much we pledge – and more.

[7] To those old allies whose cultural and spiritual origins we share, we pledge the loyalty of faithful friends. United there is little we cannot do in a host of cooperative ventures. Divided, there is little we can do – for we dare not meet a powerful challenge at odds and split asunder.

a victory of party (*here:*) The Democratic Party's victory
signifying renewal symbolizing a revival
I have sworn ... the same solemn oath our forebearers prescribed *ich habe den gleichen feierlichen Eid geschworen, den unsere Vorfahren festgelegt haben*
forebearers ancestors, forefathers; *Vorväter*
man holds in his mortal hands *der Mensch hält in seinen vergänglichen Händen*
at issue *relevant*, open to debate
the heirs *die Erben*
The American Revolution (1775-83); the conflict arose from growing tensions between residents of Great Britain's thirteen North American colonies and the colonial government which represented the British Crown
friend and foe alike *Freund und Feind gleichermaßen*
torch *Fackel*
tempered by war *gehärtet durch Krieg*
disciplined by a hard and bitter peace *geprägt durch einen schwierigen Frieden*
our ancient heritage *Vermächtnis unserer Vorfahren*
unwilling to witness or permit the slow undoing of those human rights *nicht bereit, tatenlos einer schleichenden Aushöhlung jener Menschenrechte zuzusehen*
to which this nation has always been committed *denen diese Nation immer verpflichtet war*
to assure to guarantee, to ensure
this much we pledge – and more *nicht weniger geloben wir – und mehr*
in a host of cooperative ventures *in einem ganzen Verbund gemeinsamer Wagnisse*
venture undertaking
we dare not meet a powerful challenge at odds and split asunder *denn keiner mächtigen Herausforderung könnten wir uneins und entzweit entgegentreten*

[8] To those new states whom we welcome to the ranks of the free, we pledge our word that one form of colonial control shall not have passed away merely to be replaced by a far more iron tyranny. We shall not always expect to find them supporting our view. But we shall always hope to find them strongly supporting their own freedom – and to remember that, in the past, those who foolishly sought power by riding the back of the tiger ended up inside it.

[9] To those people in the huts and villages of half the globe struggling to break the bonds of mass misery, we pledge our best efforts to help them to help themselves, for whatever period is required – not because the communists may be doing it, not because we seek their votes, but because it is right. If a free society cannot help the many who are poor, it cannot save the few who are rich.

CONVERT OUR GOOD WORDS INTO GOOD DEEDS

[10] To our sister republics south of our border, we offer a special pledge – to convert our good words into good deeds – in a new alliance for progress – to assist free men and free governments in casting off the chains of poverty. But this peaceful revolution of hope cannot become the prey of hostile powers. Let all our neighbors know that we shall join with them to oppose aggression or subversion anywhere in the Americas. And let every other power know that this Hemisphere intends to remain the master of its own house.

[11] To that world assembly of sovereign states, the United Nations, our last best hope in an age where the instruments of war have far outpaced the instruments of peace, we renew our pledge of support – to prevent it from becoming merely a forum for invective – to strengthen its shield of the new and the weak – and to enlarge the area in which its writ may run.

THE QUEST FOR PEACE

[12] Finally, to those nations who would make themselves our adversary, we offer not a pledge but a request: that both sides begin anew the quest for peace, before the dark powers of destruction unleashed by science engulf all humanity in planned or accidental self-destruction.

[13] We dare not tempt them with weakness. For only when our arms are sufficient beyond doubt can we be certain beyond doubt that they will never be employed.

[14] But neither can two great and powerful groups of nations take comfort from our present course – both sides overburdened by the cost of modern weapons, both rightly alarmed by the steady spread

iron tyranny JFK's use of this phrase was a reference to what Winston Churchill had previously called the Iron Curtain of communism; it is obvious that JFK was mainly referring to the Soviet Union.
those who foolishly sought power by riding the back of the tiger ended up inside it (*metaphorical:*) the nations which accept tyrannical domination by a foreign power may lose all their independence; *jene, die in ihrem Streben nach Macht fälschlich auf dem Rücken des Tigers reiten wollten, endeten in seinem Bauch, d.h. in einer Katastrophe*
huts and villages a reference to underdeveloped nations, like Vietnam, where the U.S. was supporting anti-communist forces; Kennedy considered Vietnam a strategically important country in the global struggle between communism and the free world
half the globe refers to large parts of the world - in the context of JFK's speech, it identifies the poverty in these areas
become the prey of hostile powers *zur Beute feindlicher Mächte werden*
instruments of war the deployment of the atom bomb in World War II left an enduring fear that the world would destroy itself in a nuclear war
to have far outpaced have developed much faster than
invective criticism, attack, insult
to enlarge the area in which its writ may run *den Geltungsbereich ihrer Regeln weiter ausdehnen*

adversary enemy
request appeal, plea
both sides both democratic and communist countries
unleashed by science *von der Wissenschaft entfesselt;* a reference to nuclear weapons
to engulf all humanity (*here:*) *alle menschliche Existenz in den Abgrund reißen*

of the deadly atom, yet both racing to alter that uncertain balance of terror that stays the hand of mankind's final war.

[15] So let us begin anew – remembering on both sides that civility is not a sign of weakness, and sincerity is always subject to proof. Let us never negotiate out of fear. But let us never fear to negotiate.

LET BOTH SIDES EXPLORE WHAT PROBLEMS UNITE US

[16] Let both sides explore what problems unite us instead of belaboring those problems which divide us.

[17] Let both sides, for the first time, formulate serious and precise proposals for the inspection and control of arms – and bring the absolute power to destroy other nations under the absolute control of all nations.

[18] Let both sides seek to invoke the wonders of science instead of its terrors. Together let us explore the stars, conquer the deserts, eradicate disease, tap the ocean depths and encourage the arts and commerce.

[19] Let both sides unite to heed in all corners of the earth the command of Isaiah – to "undo the heavy burdens and let the oppressed go free."

[20] And if a beachhead of cooperation may push back the jungle of suspicion, let both sides join in creating a new endeavor, not a new balance of power, but a new world of law, where the strong are just and the weak secure and the peace preserved.

[21] All this will not be finished in the first one hundred days. Nor will it be finished in the first one thousand days, nor in the life of this Administration, nor even perhaps in our lifetime on this planet. But let us begin.

[22] In your hands, my fellow citizens, more than mine, will rest the final success or failure of our course. Since this country was founded, each generation of Americans has been summoned to give testimony to its national loyalty. The graves of young Americans who answered the call to service surround the globe.

A STRUGGLE AGAINST THE COMMON ENEMIES OF MAN: TYRANNY, POVERTY, DISEASE AND WAR

[23] Now the trumpet summons us again – not as a call to bear arms, though arms we need – not as a call to battle, though embattled we are – but a call to bear the burden of a long twilight struggle, year in

to alter to change

balance of terror that stays the hand of mankind's final war *das Gleichgewicht des Schreckens bewahrt die Menschheit vor dem finalen Atomkrieg*

belaboring those problems *auf den Problemen herumreiten;*
to belabor: to emphasise

bring the absolute power to destroy other nations under the absolute control of all nations *die unbeschränkte Macht, andere Nationen zu vernichten, der unbeschränkten Kontrolle durch alle Nationen (United Nations) unterstellen; this is a reference to the United Nations*

to eradicate to extinguish, to get rid of

to tap to explore

commerce business; *Handel, Handelsverkehr*

if a beachhead of cooperation may push back the jungle of suspicion *wenn es mit einem Brückenkopf der Verständigung gelingt, den Dschungel des Misstrauens zurückzudrängen*

endeavor (*AmE*), endeavour (*BrE*), effort, enterprise

rejoicing in hope, patient in tribulation rejoicing in hope [because of our confidence in Christ], steadfast and patient in distress and suffering: from the Bible, Romans 12:12
to forge to build
alliance cooperation

and year out, "rejoicing in hope, patient in tribulation" – a struggle against the common enemies of man: tyranny, poverty, disease and war itself.

[24] Can we forge against these enemies a grand and global alliance, North and South, East and West, that can assure a more fruitful life for all mankind? Will you join in that historic effort?

[25] In the long history of the world, only a few generations have been granted the role of defending freedom in its hour of maximum danger. I do not shrink from this responsibility – I welcome it. I do not believe that any of us would exchange places with any other people or any other generation. The energy, the faith, the devotion which we bring to this endeavor will light our country and all who serve it – and the glow from that fire can truly light the world.

ASK NOT WHAT YOUR COUNTRY CAN DO FOR YOU –
ASK WHAT YOU CAN DO FOR YOUR COUNTRY

[26] And so, my fellow Americans: ask not what your country can do for you – ask what you can do for your country.

[27] My fellow citizens of the world: ask not what America will do for you, but what together we can do for the freedom of man.

sacrifice *Opfer*

[28] Finally, whether you are citizens of America or citizens of the world, ask of us here the same high standards of strength and sacrifice which we ask of you. With a good conscience our only sure reward, with history the final judge of our deeds, let us go forth to lead the land we love, asking His blessing and His help, but knowing that here on earth God's work must truly be our own.

Transcript from: *Voices of Democracy* and *The White House*
http://voicesofdemocracy.umd.edu/kennedy-inaugural-address-speech-text/

ASSIGNMENTS

A) Listening and Reading Comprehension

interactive classroom: think-pair-share / reading and listening for gist and detail / sharing ideas / peer support and feedback / mind mapping / writing a summary

1. Watch the video of John F. Kennedy's Inaugural Address: https://www.jfklibrary.org/Asset-Viewer/BqXIEM9F4024ntFl7SVAjA
2. Read the speech transcript and highlight the most important statements.
3. What are the main topics John F. Kennedy talks about?
4. How does Kennedy define the role of the United States?
5. How does Kennedy define the main elements of democracy? Draw a mind map.
6. Point out Kennedy's main arguments.

B) Analysis

▶ *think – pair – share / peer support and feedback / poster / using a tablet or laptop / presentation*

1. To whom does JFK address his speech?
2. List the most frequently used keywords, create a word cloud and analyse the significance.
3. Identify the rhetorical devices JFK uses in his Inaugural Address and point out their intended effects.

C) Evaluation, Comment, Creative Writing, Creative Activities

▶ *writing an article or a comment / peer support and feedback / research / WebQuest / debate / role play / discussion / speech / collaboration with Social Sciences classes / cross-curricular connections*

1. Kennedy says that "the torch has been passed to a new generation of Americans". What was expected of the younger generation in 1962? What is expected of the younger generation today? Write an article for a broadsheet newspaper in which you explain your own point of view.
2. "Ask not what your country can do for you – ask what you can do for your country." Write an article or start a debate in which you point out the significance of Kennedy's statement for the world today.
3. "A struggle against the common enemies of man: tyranny, poverty, disease and war itself." How can human rights, prosperity, the right to healthcare and medical treatment, and a fair and more peaceful world be achieved? Organise a debate with different roles and viewpoints represented.

E) For Thought and Discussion: Debating Society

▶ *mind mapping / warm-up / idea tower / research / WebQuest / share results / presentation: classroom stations / role play / discussion / debate / cooperation with Social Sciences classes / hot seat interviews / 60-second elevator pitch / evaluation / students teach each other / peer review*

1. Should democracy be imposed on other countries? Why do foreign countries or world organisations get involved in the affairs of other countries? Organise a debate with different roles and viewpoints represented.
2. Who decides whether military action in other countries is justified? Organise a debate with different roles and viewpoints represented.
3. Imagine that politicians from many different countries are taking part in a Peace Conference in the near future. They discuss recent, and future, political, social, environmental, educational, and cultural developments across the world. Organise a discussion and make sure that roles from different political systems are represented.
4. Inaugural Addresses of American Presidents.
   Your task: The class is divided into six groups. Each group researches and summarises the main points in one of the following American Presidents' Inaugural Addresses:
   Ronald Reagan, Jimmy Carter, George W. Bush, Bill Clinton, Barack Obama, or Donald Trump.
   Each group then presents their findings to the class, and the other pupils take notes on that speech. Finally, each group decides which speech they prefer, taking into account the arguments presented by their classmates; then a class vote is held to find the class's favourite speech.
5. Is democracy the best form of government? Explain the fundamental principles of democracy and give examples to prove your arguments. Prepare and give a three-minute speech.
6. "Only through discourse, debate, research and nuances do we get closer to finding solutions – together." Speech by Federal President Frank-Walter Steinmeier at re:publica 2019, in Berlin on May 6, 2019. Write a short comment.

“Let Us Create Together a New National Spirit of Unity and Trust.”

President Jimmy Carter’s Inaugural Address on January 20, 1977

RELATED TOPICS

THE AMERICAN DREAM · THE CONSTITUTION · THE DECLARATION OF INDEPENDENCE · DEMOCRACY · DIGNITY · EQUALITY · THE FOUNDING CREED · FREEDOM · GOD · THE GOVERNMENT · HISTORY · HUMAN RIGHTS · INJUSTICE · JUSTICE · LIBERTY · NATIONHOOD · POVERTY · RACE RELATIONS · SEGREGATION · SOCIAL SECURITY · TRUST · UNALIENABLE RIGHTS

Jimmy Carter: On January 20, 1977, the world witnessed President Jimmy Carter’s inauguration as he was sworn in on the East Portico of the Capitol Building.

Carter’s election at the end of 1976 suggested a period of great political and cultural upheaval, in particular to what the role of the ‘Leader of the Free World’ represented. As a deeply religious member of the Baptist Church, and hailing from the South, Carter was an underdog in the presidential race. He promised to restore the public’s confidence in the presidential office, an oath which he asserted in his Inauguration Speech: ‘A New Spirit, A New Commitment, A New America’.

The 39th President of the United States (1977-1981) was born in Plains, Georgia on October 1, 1924. His time in office coincided with a difficult period of domestic and international issues.

In fact, it is probably his subsequent humanitarian work following the four years as President for which he will be better remembered. Notably, the former President Carter has supported the work of Habitat for Humanity and established the Carter Presidential Center. The latter organisation strives to uphold human rights and to alleviate those who are struggling around the world.

Namely, Carter’s efforts have had a positive impact on the development of community-based healthcare systems in Africa, the upholding of free elections in Latin America, and the safeguarding of peace in the Middle East. The culmination of Carter’s commitment to humanitarian issues was the Nobel Peace Prize which he received in 2002.

As he made his Inaugural Address in January 1976, the newly-appointed President Jimmy Carter asserted the need for a strong United States domestically in order to exert its influence abroad. He emphasised his support for civil liberties and human rights across the globe and vowed to restore confidence in both the US Government and the accessibility of the American Dream.

THE PRESIDENT Jimmy Carter:

For myself and for our Nation, I want to thank my predecessor for all he has done to heal our land.

In this outward and physical ceremony, we attest once again to the inner and spiritual strength of our Nation. As my high school teacher, Miss Julia Coleman, used to say: "We must adjust to changing times and still hold to unchanging principles."

Here before me is the Bible used in the inauguration of our first President, in 1789, and I have just taken the oath of office on the Bible my mother gave me just a few years ago, opened to a timeless admonition from the ancient prophet Micah: "He hath showed thee, O man, what is good; and what doth the Lord require of thee, but to do justly, and to love mercy, and to walk humbly with thy God."

This inauguration ceremony marks a new beginning, a new dedication within our Government, and a new spirit among us all. A President may sense and proclaim that new spirit, but only a people can provide it.

Two centuries ago, our Nation's birth was a milestone in the long quest for freedom. But the bold and brilliant dream which excited the founders of this Nation still awaits its consummation. I have no new dream to set forth today, but rather urge a fresh faith in the old dream.

Ours was the first society openly to define itself, in terms of both spirituality, and human liberty. It is that unique self-definition which has given us an exceptional appeal, but it also imposes on us a special obligation to take on those moral duties which, when assumed, seem invariably to be in our own best interests.

LET US CREATE TOGETHER A NEW NATIONAL SPIRIT OF UNITY AND TRUST

You have given me a great responsibility – to stay close to you, to be worthy of you, and to exemplify what you are. Let us create together a new national spirit of unity and trust. Your strength can compensate for my weakness, and your wisdom can help to minimize my mistakes.

Let us learn together and laugh together and work together and pray together, confident that, in the end, we will triumph together in the right.

predecessor President Gerald R. Ford was the 38th president of the United States; *Amtsvorgänger*
to heal our land to reconcile the nation, to bring about reconciliation between Americans (after the Vietnam War and the Watergate Affair divided the nation)

our first President George Washington
oath of office *Amtseid als Präsident*
admonition piece of advice; *Ermahnung*
Micah was a prophet who lived in Judah from 737 to 696 BC, and wrote the Book of Micah in the Bible
he hath showed thee (*old use:*) he has shown you; **thee** you
what doth (*old use:*) what does
to require (*here:*) to demand
to do justly to behave/act fairly
humbly modestly; *bescheiden*
thy (*old use:*) your
to proclaim to declare, to announce
to provide (*here:*) to embody; *verkörpern*
milestone landmark, breakthrough
quest search
to await to wait for
consummation achievement, completion
to urge (*here:*) to encourage, to promote; *ermahnen, auffordern*
faith belief, trust; *Glaube, Vertrauen*
spirituality *Geistlichkeit*
obligation duty, responsibility
to assume (*here:*) to take on
invariably constantly, always

to be worthy of you *euch würdig sein*
to exemplify to embody, to represent
to compensate for to make up for; *ausgleichen*
wisdom knowledge, insight; *Weisheit*
to minimize (*AmE*), to minimise (*BrE*), to reduce

THE AMERICAN DREAM ENDURES

The American dream endures. We must once again have full faith in our country – and in one another. I believe America can be better. We can be even stronger than before.

Let our recent mistakes bring a resurgent commitment to the basic principles of our Nation, for we know that if we despise our own government, we have no future. We recall in special times when we have stood briefly, but magnificently, united. In those times, no prize was beyond our grasp.

But we cannot dwell upon remembered glory. We cannot afford to drift. We reject the prospect of failure or mediocrity or an inferior quality of life for any person. Our Government must at the same time be both competent and compassionate.

OUR COMMITMENT TO HUMAN RIGHTS MUST BE ABSOLUTE

We have already found a high degree of personal liberty, and we are now struggling to enhance equality of opportunity. Our commitment to human rights must be absolute, our laws fair, our national beauty preserved; the powerful must not persecute the weak, and human dignity must be enhanced.

We have learned that more is not necessarily better, that even our great Nation has its recognized limits, and that we can neither answer all questions nor solve all problems. We cannot afford to do everything, nor can we afford to lack boldness as we meet the future. So, together, in a spirit of individual sacrifice for the common good, we must simply do our best.

Our Nation can be strong abroad only if it is strong at home. And we know that the best way to enhance freedom in other lands is to demonstrate here that our democratic system is worthy of emulation.

To be true to ourselves, we must be true to others. We will not behave in foreign places so as to violate our rules and standards here at home, for we know that the trust which our Nation earns is essential to our strength.

The world itself is now dominated by a new spirit. Peoples more numerous and more politically aware are craving, and now demanding, their place in the sun – not just for the benefit of their own physical condition, but for basic human rights.

resurgent renewed
commitment dedication
to despise to hate, to feel contempt for; *verachten*
to recall to remember
no prize was beyond our grasp *kein Ziel war unerreichbar*
to dwell upon to linger over, to focus on; *verweilen*
remembered glory glorious days in the past; *glorreiche Vergangenheit, vergangene Erfolge*
the prospect the possibility of
failure *Misserfolg, Versagen*
mediocrity *Mittelmäßigkeit*
an inferior quality of life a poorer quality of life
compassionate concerned about its citizens, empathetic; *anteilnehmend, mitfühlend*
to enhance (*here:*) to achieve, to improve, to increase
commitment obligation, promise, engagement
to preserve (*here:*) to protect
to persecute to oppress, to mistreat
boldness courage, determination; *Mut, Unerschrockenheit*
emulation copying; *Nachahmung*
to crave to yearn for, to desire; *sich sehnen nach*
to demand to request, to ask for

HELP SHAPE A JUST AND PEACEFUL WORLD THAT IS TRULY HUMANE

The passion for freedom is on the rise. Tapping this new spirit, there can be no nobler nor more ambitious task for America to undertake on this day of a new beginning than to help shape a just and peaceful world that is truly humane.

We are a strong nation, and we will maintain strength so sufficient that it need not be proven in combat – a quiet strength based not merely on the size of an arsenal but on the nobility of ideas.

We will be ever vigilant and never vulnerable, and we will fight our wars against poverty, ignorance, and injustice, for those are the enemies against which our forces can be honorably marshaled.

We are a proudly idealistic nation, but let no one confuse our idealism with weakness.

WE CAN NEVER BE INDIFFERENT TO THE FATE OF FREEDOM ELSEWHERE

Because we are free, we can never be indifferent to the fate of freedom elsewhere. Our moral sense dictates a clear-cut preference for those societies which share with us an abiding respect for individual human rights. We do not seek to intimidate, but it is clear that a world which others can dominate with impunity would be inhospitable to decency and a threat to the well-being of all people.

OUR ULTIMATE GOAL – THE ELIMINATION OF ALL NUCLEAR WEAPONS FROM THIS EARTH

The world is still engaged in a massive armaments race designed to ensure continuing equivalent strength among potential adversaries. We pledge perseverance and wisdom in our efforts to limit the world's armaments to those necessary for each nation's own domestic safety. And we will move this year a step toward our ultimate goal – the elimination of all nuclear weapons from this Earth. We urge all other people to join us, for success can mean life instead of death.

Within us, the people of the United States, there is evident a serious and purposeful rekindling of confidence.

And I join in the hope that when my time as your President has ended, people might say this about our Nation:

- that we had remembered the words of Micah and renewed our search for humility, mercy, and justice;

tapping making use of

to maintain to uphold

arsenal collection of weapons

the nobility of ideas the quality of ideas

vigilant alert; *wachsam*

to marshal *aufstellen*

abiding enduring; *beständig*

to seek (*here:*) to want to, to search

to intimidate to frighten, to threaten, *einschüchtern*

with impunity *ungestraft*

inhospitable *unwirtlich, unvereinbar*

would be inhospitable to decency would reject our moral values

threat danger; *Bedrohung*

armaments race *Rüstungswettlauf*

to ensure to guarantee; *sicherstellen*

equivalent equal

adversaries opponents, enemies

to pledge to promise; *zusagen*

perseverance; *Beharrlichkeit*

elimination ban; *Abschaffung*

to urge *dringend bitten, jdn. auffordern etw. zu tun*

rekindling renewal; *Wiederaufleben*

humility modesty; *Bescheidenheit*

mercy kindness, compassion

mistrust distrust; *Misstrauen*
to enable *ermöglichen*
lasting permanent, enduring
precious dearly-held; *wertvoll*
accomplishment achievement
affirmation confirmation, declaration; *Bestätigung, Bekräftigung*
undiminished *unvermindert, ungeschmälert*

- that we had torn down the barriers that separated those of different race and region and religion, and where there had been mistrust, built unity, with a respect for diversity;
- that we had found productive work for those able to perform it;
- that we had strengthened the American family, which is the basis of our society;
- that we had ensured respect for the law and equal treatment under the law, for the weak and the powerful, for the rich and the poor; and
- that we had enabled our people to be proud of their own Government once again.

I would hope that the nations of the world might say that we had built a lasting peace, based not on weapons of war but on international policies which reflect our own most precious values.

These are not just my goals – and they will not be my accomplishments – but the affirmation of our Nation's continuing moral strength and our belief in an undiminished, ever-expanding American dream.

Thank you very much.

Jimmy Carter: "Inaugural Address," January 20, 1977
From: *The American Presidency Project*
https://www.presidency.ucsb.edu/documents/inaugural-address-0

ASSIGNMENTS

A) Pre-Reading Activity: The American Dream

interactive classroom / word cloud / mind mapping / work in pairs, then in groups, share your ideas

1. Take a look at the word cloud. What do you think are the main topics explored in Jimmy Carter's Inaugural Address?
2. Give a two-minute speech on the American Dream using ten words from the word cloud.

B) Comprehension

cooperative learning / think-pair-share / writing a summary, an analysis, a comment / peer support and feedback / poster / presentation / students teach each other / evaluation / peer review

1. Watch the video of President Jimmy Carter's Inaugural Address:
   https://www.cbsnews.com/video/jimmy-carter-inaugural-address-jan-20-1977/
2. Highlight the important keywords and significant statements on your speech transcript.
3. What advice does Carter give, and what appeal does he make to the American people?
4. Outline Jimmy Carter's main arguments in about ten sentences.

C) Analysis

1. Analyse the structure of Jimmy Carter's speech.
2. Work with a partner and take it in turns to analyse Jimmy Carter's understanding of the *American Dream*.
3. Jimmy Carter uses a number of rhetorical devices to make himself appear trustworthy and honest; he wants the audience to trust him. Analyse some examples.
4. Analyse some more rhetorical devices which Carter uses to get his message across.
5. Analyse Carter's final appeal to the audience.

D) Evaluation and Comment

1. Write a response to one of the following statements:
   a) "Let us create together a new national spirit of unity and trust."
   b) "The American dream endures."
   c) "Our commitment to human rights must be absolute."
   d) "We can never be indifferent to the fate of freedom elsewhere."
   e) "Our ultimate goal – the elimination of all nuclear weapons from this Earth."
2. According to Jimmy Carter, the most precious values are: "our Nation's continuing moral strength and our belief in an undiminished, ever-expanding American dream." Why is the American Dream so attractive? Or is the American Dream just a cliché? Write an article for a Social Sciences journal and/or for a school newspaper.
3. Compare Jimmy Carter and Barack Obama's Inaugural Addresses and evaluate their similarities and differences.

E) Creative Activity

idea lab / group work / idea tower / writing a speech / cue-cards / speech / discussion / evaluation

Writing your speech: Jimmy Carter asked his audience to "help shape a just and peaceful world that is truly humane." How can people, and how can you, help to shape a just and peaceful world?

a) Organise your ideas and make a plan. b) Write a first draft. c) In small groups read your drafts aloud and discuss them. d) Prepare a revised version of your speech. e) Use your manuscript – or use cue-cards with brief notes only – and give a short speech to your group, then to your class.

F) Further Information:

1. What is the American Dream?

James Truslow Adams, in his book *The Epic of America*, which was written in 1931, stated that the American dream is "that dream of a land in which life should be better and richer and fuller for everyone, with opportunity for each according to ability or achievement. [...] It is not a dream of motor cars and high wages merely, but a dream of social order in which each man and each woman shall be able to attain to the fullest stature of which they are innately capable, and be recognized by others for what they are, regardless of the fortuitous circumstances of birth or position." (pp. 214-215)

From: *Library of Congress* http://www.loc.gov/teachers/classroommaterials/lessons/american-dream/students/thedream.html (accessed Febr. 27, 2019)

2. The Transformation of the American Dream

By ROBERT J. SHILLER / *The New York Times*, August 4, 2017

https://www.nytimes.com/2017/08/04/upshot/the-transformation-of-the-american-dream.html

[...] the phrase, the American Dream, has changed radically through the years.

Mr. Trump and Ben Carson, the Secretary of Housing and Urban Development, have suggested it involves owning a beautiful home and a roaring business, but it wasn't always so. Instead, in the 1930s, it meant freedom, mutual respect and equality of opportunity. It had more to do with morality than material success. [...]

Robert J. Shiller is Sterling Professor of Economics at Yale University. "Sterling Professor" is the highest academic rank at Yale University.

G) The Transformation of the American Dream

▶ *WebQuest / mind map / tablet or laptop presentation / writing an editorial or an essay / discussion / cross-curricular connections / cooperation with History and Social Sciences classes / speech*

Tasks:

a) How did the US historian James Truslow Adams define the American Dream?
b) Evaluate Robert J. Shiller's point of view.
c) What does the American Dream mean today, according to Donald Trump and Ben Carson?
d) Is the USA still an attractive country for immigrants today who hope to follow the American Dream? Prepare and give a speech.
e) "The American Dream vs. the European Union's Dream": Prepare and give a short speech on this topic.
f) "Everyone's 'American Dream' is different." Organise a creative Poetry Slam Competition.

H) Is Basketball the Sport of the American Dream?

The incredible story of Dallas Maverick's NBA Superstar Dirk Nowitzki reminds us what it used to mean for an immigrant to 'Make It in America'. Dirk Nowitzki announced his retirement from the NBA on April 9, 2019. Watch his speech here: https://www.youtube.com/watch?v=2EFOQ6V_u6M. The NBA Legends paid tribute to Dirk Nowitzki after his final home game with the Dallas Mavericks: https://www.youtube.com/watch?v=M5g4BbA8jNI "You played the game the right way, man. You inspired me."

"America First."

President Donald J. Trump: The Inaugural Address on Friday, January 20, 2017 in Washington, D.C.

Donald Trump took the oath of office and officially became the 45th President of the United States of America.

RELATED TOPICS

AMERICA FIRST · AMERICAN CARNAGE · THE AMERICAN DREAM · THE CONSTITUTION · THE DECLARATION OF INDEPENDENCE · DEMOCRACY · ECONOMY · EDUCATION · THE FOUNDING CREED · THE ESTABLISHMENT · FREEDOM · GOD · THE GOVERNMENT · HISTORY · IMMIGRATION · INEQUALITY · INJUSTICE · JUSTICE · LIBERTY · THE MILITARY · NATIONHOOD · PATRIOTISM · PROTECTION · POWER

Donald J. Trump: On January 20, 2017, Donald J. Trump was sworn in as the 45th president of the United States by the Chief Justice of the United States, John Roberts. Trump took the oath of office by placing his hand on the same Bible that was used at Abraham Lincoln's inauguration, and then on his own family Bible, which was presented to him by his mother in 1955 when he graduated from Sunday school at his family's Presbyterian church.

In his Inaugural Address on January 20, Donald Trump said that he would put the American people above politics. "What truly matters is not which party controls our government, but whether our government is controlled by the people," he said. "January 20, 2017, will be remembered as the day the people became the rulers of this nation again."

He went on to paint a bleak picture of an America that had failed many of its citizens, describing families trapped in poverty, an ineffective education system, and the devastating impact of crime, drugs, and gangs. "This American carnage stops right here and stops right now," he said.

The day after Trump's inauguration, millions of protesters took part in demonstrations across the United States and around the world. The Women's March on Washington drew over half a million people to protest President Trump's stance on a variety of issues, ranging from immigration to climate change.

In the early days of his presidency, President Trump issued a number of back-to-back executive orders to make good on some of his campaign promises, as well as several orders aimed at rolling back policies and regulations that were put in place by the Obama administration.

From: *Biography* https://www.biography.com/people/donald-trump-9511238

THE PRESIDENT Donald J. Trump:

Chief Justice Roberts, President Carter, President Clinton, President Bush, President Obama, fellow Americans, and people of the world: thank you.

We, the citizens of America, are now joined in a great national effort to rebuild our country, and to restore its promise for all of our people.

Together, we will determine the course of America and the world for years to come.

We will face challenges. We will confront hardships. But we will get the job done.

Every four years, we gather on these steps to carry out the orderly and peaceful transfer of power, and we are grateful to President Obama and First Lady Michelle Obama for their gracious aid throughout this transition. They have been magnificent.

WE ARE TRANSFERRING POWER FROM WASHINGTON, D.C. AND GIVING IT BACK TO YOU, THE AMERICAN PEOPLE

Today's ceremony, however, has a very special meaning. Because today we are not merely transferring power from one Administration to another, or from one party to another – but we are transferring power from Washington, D.C. and giving it back to you, the American People.

For too long, a small group in our nation's Capital has reaped the rewards of government while the people have borne the cost.

Washington flourished – but the people did not share in its wealth.

Politicians prospered – but the jobs left, and the factories closed. The establishment protected itself, but not the citizens of our country.

Their victories have not been your victories; their triumphs have not been your triumphs; and while they celebrated in our nation's Capital, there was little to celebrate for struggling families all across our land.

That all changes – starting right here, and right now, because this moment is your moment: it belongs to you.
It belongs to everyone gathered here today and everyone watching all across America.

This is your day. This is your celebration.

to determine the course to set the course, to decide; *wir werden die Weichen stellen*

to confront hardships to face difficulties; *auf Schwierigkeiten stoßen*
we will get the job done we will succeed

gracious aid kind, friendly, considerate help; *liebenswürdige Hilfe*
transition *Zeit des Übergangs*
magnificent wonderful

transferring power Trump describes his presidency as a transfer of power from the political establishment to "the American People"

a small group in our nation's Capital has reaped the rewards of government *eine kleine Gruppe in der Hauptstadt unserer Nation hat die Früchte der Regierungsarbeit geerntet*
while the people have borne the cost *während das Volk die Kosten tragen musste*
flourished prospered, boomed
the people did not share in its wealth *die Leute hatten keinen Anteil am Reichtum*
politicians prospered politicians did well (for themselves), politicians became wealthy
the establishment the elite
struggling families poor families, families on the brink of/in danger of poverty
that all changes *das alles ändert sich*

And this, the United States of America, is your country.
What truly matters is not which party controls our government, but whether our government is controlled by the people.
January 20, 2017, will be remembered as the day the people became the rulers of this nation again.

THE FORGOTTEN MEN AND WOMEN OF OUR COUNTRY WILL BE FORGOTTEN NO LONGER

The forgotten men and women of our country will be forgotten no longer. Everyone is listening to you now.
You came by the tens of millions to become part of a historic movement the likes of which the world has never seen before.
At the center of this movement is a crucial conviction, that a nation exists to serve its citizens.
Americans want great schools for their children, safe neighborhoods for their families, and good jobs for themselves.
These are the just and reasonable demands of a righteous public.

But for too many of our citizens, a different reality exists: Mothers and children trapped in poverty in our inner cities; rusted-out factories scattered like tombstones across the landscape of our nation; an education system flush with cash, but which leaves our young and beautiful students deprived of knowledge; and the crime and gangs and drugs that have stolen too many lives and robbed our country of so much unrealized potential.

THIS AMERICAN CARNAGE STOPS RIGHT HERE AND STOPS RIGHT NOW

This American carnage stops right here and stops right now.

We are one nation – and their pain is our pain. Their dreams are our dreams; and their success will be our success. We share one heart, one home, and one glorious destiny.

The oath of office I take today is an oath of allegiance to all Americans.

For many decades, we've enriched foreign industry at the expense of American industry.

Subsidized the armies of other countries while allowing for the very sad depletion of our military.

We've defended other nation's borders while refusing to defend our own.

what truly matters is not *wirklich wichtig ist nicht*
the rulers of this nation the political leaders of this nation
a historic movement the likes of which the world has never seen before *eine historische Bewegung, wie sie die Welt noch nie gesehen hat*
crucial conviction fundamental belief
just and reasonable demands *richtige und vernünftige Forderungen*
righteous public honest, law-abiding public
trapped in poverty unable to escape poverty
rusted-out factories *verrostete Fabriken*
scattered like tombstones *liegen verstreut wie Grabsteine*
education system flush with cash *überteuertes Bildungssystem*
flush with a lot of money/funding
deprived of knowledge *denen Wissen vorenthalten wird*
unrealized potential *nicht erkanntes/nicht verwirklichtes Potenzial*
carnage violence, crime and chaos; *Gemetzel*
destiny future
oath of office *Amtseid*
oath of allegiance *Treueeid*
enriched (*here:*) made richer
at the expense of *auf Kosten von*
to subsidize (*AmE*), to subsidise (*BrE*), to fund, to finance
while allowing for *während wir es zuließen*
depletion (*here:*) decline (in size and quality)

trillions *Billionen*
disrepair *baufällig*
to fall into disrepair *baufällig werden*
decay ruin; *Verfall*

And spent trillions of dollars overseas while America's infrastructure has fallen into disrepair and decay.

We've made other countries rich while the wealth, strength, and confidence of our country has disappeared over the horizon.
One by one, the factories shuttered and left our shores, with not even a thought about the millions upon millions of American workers left behind.

to shutter (*here:*) to close, to shut down
left our shores left our country
left behind (*here:*) left behind without jobs

The wealth of our middle class has been ripped from their homes and then redistributed across the entire world.

ripped from taken away from
redistributed given away to others, *neu verteilt*

But that is the past. And now we are looking only to the future.
We assembled here today, are issuing a new decree to be heard in every city, in every foreign capital, and in every hall of power.

to issue a new decree *eine neue Verfügung erlassen*

FROM THIS MOMENT ON, IT'S GOING TO BE AMERICA FIRST

From this day forward, a new vision will govern our land.

From this moment on, it's going to be America First.

Every decision on trade, on taxes, on immigration, on foreign affairs, will be made to benefit American workers and American families.

to benefit to help

We must protect our borders from the ravages of other countries making our products, stealing our companies, and destroying our jobs. Protection will lead to great prosperity and strength.

we must protect our borders *wir müssen unsere Grenzen schützen*
ravages ruinous damages; (*here:*) *Angriffe durch Produktpiraterie*
protection (*here:*) Einfuhrzölle
prosperity wealth, affluence

I will fight for you with every breath in my body – and I will never, ever let you down.

America will start winning again, winning like never before.

We will bring back our jobs. We will bring back our borders. We will bring back our wealth. And we will bring back our dreams.

We will build new roads, and highways, and bridges, and airports, and tunnels, and railways all across our wonderful nation.

We will get our people off of welfare and back to work – rebuilding our country with American hands and American labor.

welfare (*here:*) *Sozialhilfe*
with American hands and American labor *mit amerikanischer Arbeitskraft*

BUY AMERICAN AND HIRE AMERICAN

We will follow two simple rules: Buy American and Hire American.

hire American *stelle amerikanische Arbeitskräfte/U.S. Bürger ein*

We will seek friendship and goodwill with the nations of the world – but we do so with the understanding that it is the right of all nations to put their own interests first.

with the understanding that *mit dem Verständnis/mit der Überzeugung, dass*

We do not seek to impose our way of life on anyone, but rather to let it shine as an example for everyone to follow.

to impose our way of life on to force our way of life on

We will reinforce old alliances and form new ones – and unite the civilized world against Radical Islamic Terrorism, which we will eradicate completely from the face of the Earth.

to reinforce to strengthen
alliance partnership; *Bündnis*
to eradicate to eliminate, to get rid of, to destroy; vom Angesicht der Erde hinwegfegen/tilgen

At the bedrock of our politics will be a total allegiance to the United States of America, and through our loyalty to our country, we will rediscover our loyalty to each other. When you open your heart to patriotism, there is no room for prejudice.

at the bedrock of the basis of
allegiance loyalty, commitment
prejudice *Vorurteil*

The Bible tells us, "how good and pleasant it is when God's people live together in unity." We must speak our minds openly, debate our disagreements honestly, but always pursue solidarity.

to pursue solidarity to practise unity

When America is united, America is totally unstoppable. There should be no fear – we are protected, and we will always be protected.

WE ARE PROTECTED BY GOD

We will be protected by the great men and women of our military and law enforcement and, most importantly, we are protected by God.

Finally, we must think big and dream even bigger. In America, we understand that a nation is only living as long as it is striving.

striving determined; *entschlossen*

We will no longer accept politicians who are all talk and no action – constantly complaining but never doing anything about it.

THE TIME FOR EMPTY TALK IS OVER.
NOW ARRIVES THE HOUR OF ACTION.

The time for empty talk is over. Now arrives the hour of action. Do not let anyone tell you it cannot be done. No challenge can match the heart and fight and spirit of America.

no challenge can match the heart and fight and spirit of America *keine Herausforderung ist für das Herz und den Kampfgeist Amerikas zu groß*

We will not fail. Our country will thrive and prosper again.

to thrive to flourish, to boom; *blühen*
to prosper to become well-off; *Wohlstand erleben*

We stand at the birth of a new millennium, ready to unlock the mysteries of space, to free the Earth from the miseries of disease, and to harness the energies, industries and technologies of tomorrow.

the birth of a new millennium *die Geburt (der Beginn) eines neuen Jahrtausends*
to harness to make use of

national pride love of one's country; *Nationalstolz*
to stir our souls to motivate us
to lift our sights (*here:*) to raise our ambitions
to heal our divisions *unsere Meinungsverschiedenheiten beilegen*
old wisdom *alte (und kluge) Weisheit*

A new national pride will stir our souls, lift our sights, and heal our divisions.

WE WILL MAKE AMERICA GREAT AGAIN

It is time to remember that old wisdom our soldiers will never forget: that whether we are black or brown or white, we all bleed the same red blood of patriots, we all enjoy the same glorious freedoms, and we all salute the same great American Flag.

urban sprawl *städtischer Ballungsraum*
windswept plains *windgepeitschte Ebenen*
infused with filled with

And whether a child is born in the urban sprawl of Detroit or the windswept plains of Nebraska, they look up at the same night sky, they fill their heart with the same dreams, and they are infused with the breath of life by the same almighty Creator.

So to all Americans, in every city near and far, small and large, from mountain to mountain, and from ocean to ocean, hear these words:

You will never be ignored again. Your voice, your hopes, and your dreams, will define our American destiny. And your courage and goodness and love will forever guide us along the way. Together, We Will Make America Strong Again.

We Will Make America Wealthy Again.

We Will Make America Proud Again.

We Will Make America Safe Again.

And, Yes, Together, We Will Make America Great Again.

Thank you, God Bless You, And God Bless America.

Source: The White House
https://www.whitehouse.gov/briefings-statements/the-inaugural-address/

ASSIGNMENTS

A) Listening and Reading Comprehension

agile work / listening for gist and for detail / paired work / peer support and feedback / mind map / writing a summary / presenting and sharing results / speaking skills training / evaluation

1. Watch President Donald Trump's Inaugural Address:
   The White House: https://www.whitehouse.gov/inaugural-address
2. Listening for detail:
   Listen to the speech again and complete the following sentences given below. The recording will be paused after each relevant section so that you can take notes and complete the following sentences:
   a) According to President Donald Trump, the citizens of America are now joined in a great national effort to rebuild our country and to restore its promise for all of our people.

b) Firstly, the president points out that American citizens will face many challenges, and that they ________________
c) Then Donald Trump emphasises that this inauguration ceremony has a special significance, because ________________
d) Furthermore, Trump criticises former U.S. governments by saying that Washington, D.C. flourished, while ________________
e) Trump states that the day he was inaugurated, January 20, 2017, will be remembered ________________
f) He also claims that, at the center of this movement, there is a crucial conviction, that ________________
g) Moreover, he emphasises that Americans want great schools for their children, ________________
h) In addition, Trump claims that a different reality exists: ________________
i) Furthermore, he proclaims that "we are one nation and we share ________________"
j) Finally, he states that from this day forward, ________________
k) The President promises that American citizens will never be ignored again and that ________________
l) At the end of his speech, he gives his audience three guarantees: ________________

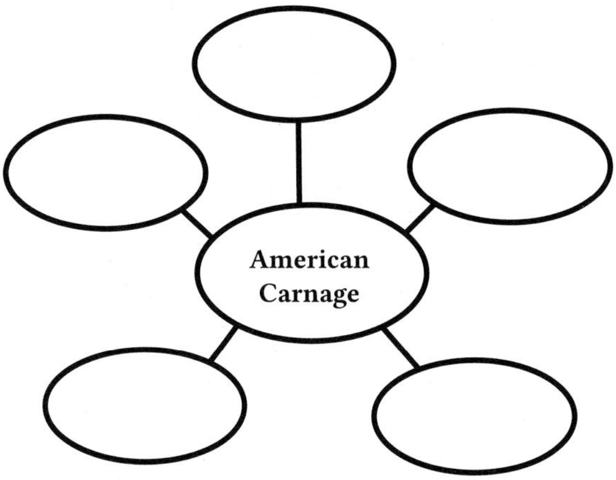

3. Read the transcript, highlight any important keywords or phrases.
4. *"American Carnage":* Point out some examples which, according to Donald Trump, prove the theory of "American Carnage". Use a mind map to illustrate Trump's ideas.
5. What topics does Trump *not* mention in his Inaugural Address?
6. Donald Trump emphasises: "America First: We Will Make America Great Again." Explain the significance of this statement, and how Trump wants to achieve this goal.
7. Point out President Donald Trump's main arguments.

B) Fact Checking

▶ *WebQuest / research / laptop / jigsaw / presentation / share ideas / discussion / evaluation*

Many journalists responded to Trump's Inaugural Address. Read the articles written in response to the statements in the table, and make notes on whether or not Trump's statements are correct/true.

Donald Trump's Statements	The Articles and Facts
1. "Washington flourished – but the people did not share in its wealth."	**Wealth and Poverty** Read the speech analysis written by *Alan Yuhas* and *Lois Beckett* in *The Guardian*, on January 20, 2017.
2. "Politicians prospered – but the jobs left, and the factories closed. [...] The establishment protected itself, but not the citizens of our country."	**The American Economy** Read the speech analysis written by *Julie Hirschfeld Davis,* in *The New York Times,* on January 20, 2017.
3. "This American carnage stops right here and stops right now."	**American Carnage** Read various articles in different newspapers and magazines.
4. "For many decades, we've enriched foreign industry at the expense of American industry".	**Globalisation and American Industry** Read the speech analysis written by *Binyamin Appelbaum,* in The *New York Times,* on January 20, 2017.

5. We must protect our borders from the ravages of other countries making our products, stealing our companies, and destroying our jobs. Protection will lead to great prosperity and strength."	**Outsourcing, Destroying Jobs and the Protection of Borders** *Read the analysis written by Glenn Kessler* and *Michelle Ye Hee Lee,* in *The Washington Post,* on January 20, 2017.
6. "We Will Make America Wealthy Again."	**The Distribution of Wealth** *Read the analysis written by Binyamin Appelbaum,* in *The New York Times,* on January 20, 2017.
7. "We've defended other nations' borders while refusing to defend our own".	**Immigration** *Read the analysis written by Oliver Laughland,* in *The Guardian,* on January 20, 2017.

C) Analysis

independent learning / think – pair – share / group work / peer support and feedback / sharing ideas / presenting results / gallery walk / stations learning / discussion / evaluation / tweet summary

1. Analyse: a) the structure, b) the language and c) the tone of Donald Trump's speech and point out the intended effects on the audience.
2. Watch a video of the speech and analyse: a) Donald Trump's body language, b) his appearance and c) his tone of voice.
3. American Carnage: Donald Trump paints a rather depressing portrait of what he calls "American Carnage". Analyse the examples which, according to Trump, prove the existence of "American Carnage".
4. Analyse the rhetorical devices Trump uses to get his message across to the audience. Here are some quotations to start off with:
   a) "Together, we will determine the course of America and the world for years to come. We will face challenges. We will confront hardships. But we will get the job done."
   b) "For too long, a small group in our nation's Capital has reaped the rewards of government while the people have borne the cost. Washington flourished – but the people did not share in its wealth. Politicians prospered – but the jobs left, and the factories closed."
   c) "The forgotten men and women of our country will be forgotten no longer. Everyone is listening to you now."
   d) "I will fight for you with every breath in my body – and I will never, ever let you down."
   e) "We will bring back our jobs. We will bring back our borders. We will bring back our wealth. And we will bring back our dreams. We will build new roads, and highways, and bridges, and airports, and tunnels, and railways all across our wonderful nation."
   f) "We will be protected by the great men and women of our military and law enforcement and, most importantly, we are protected by God."
5. Analyse Trump's final appeal to the audience and its intended effect.

D) Evaluation, Comment, Creative Writing

interactive classroom / research / WebQuest / interview / discussion / speech / tweet summary / writing an article, a comment / prepare and give a speech / Speakers' Corner / evaluation

1. "America First": Discuss and evaluate the significance of the following statement in the wider context of Trump's speech, and evaluate its significance today: "America First: We Will Make America Great Again."
2. In his speech, Trump says: "...today we are not merely transferring power from one Administration to another, or from one party to another – but we are transferring power from Washington, D.C. and giving it back to you, the American People." Discuss and evaluate the significance of this statement in the wider context of Trump's speech.

3. The journalist and political commentator Michael C. Bender wrote in *The Wall Street Journal* on January 20, 2017 that "Donald Trump delivered what historians and speechwriters said was one of the most ominous inaugural addresses ever, reinforcing campaign themes of American decline while positioning himself as the protector of the country's 'forgotten men and women.'"
   What do you think of this statement?
4. Donald Trump states: "A new national pride will stir our souls, lift our sights, and heal our divisions." Julie Hirschfeld Davis, a reporter for *The New York Times* wrote on January 20, 2017: "One of the biggest questions of his presidency will be whether it will heal or intensify the nation's divisions." What do you think? Write an email to Julie Hirschfeld Davis stating your opinion.
5. President Trump delivered an Inaugural Address that depicted the United States as a land of abandoned factories, economic fear, rising crime and dystopian carnage. He promised a new era in American politics. Is this an accurate and fair description of the current situation in the U.S.A.?
6. Write an article for your school newspaper, explaining your reaction to President Donald Trump's Inaugural Address.

E) Creative Activities

▶ *role play / hot seat / podcast / press conference / video recording / discussion / speech / SOLO taxonomy*

1. Imagine you are a journalist attending a press conference with the president. What kind of questions would you like to ask President Trump?
2. In groups, devise/write a press conference between President Trump and a group of journalists, then act out and record the press conference.
3. In his Inaugural Address, Trump did not mention the global problem of climate change. Prepare and give a speech explaining, why, in your opinion, he should have included this problem in his speech.

F) Mediation: (German = > English) **„Donald Trump macht die USA zur Provinz"**
Von Annette Ludwig, Westdeutsche Zeitung, 20.1. 2017
http://www.wz.de/home/leitartikel/donald-trump-macht-die-usa-zur-provinz-1.2359060

„Der Gedanke, dass es noch einen anderen Donald Trump gibt als den Wahlkämpfer, den wird kaum einer mehr haben nach dieser Antrittsrede. Es gibt nur den einen Donald Trump. Den, der auf der Klaviatur der Gefühle spielt. Den, der seinen Wählern genau das erzählt, was sie hören wollen. Den, der sich eindimensional auf sein Land konzentriert. Den, der die Mauern hochziehen und die USA abschotten wird. Es gibt ihn nicht, den Präsidenten Donald Trump, der Reife und Würde hat für dieses Amt. Der sein Land versöhnen wird und der eine Vision für die Welt da draußen hat.

Die Antrittsrede hat sämtliche Befürchtungen bestätigt. Aus Wahlkampfgetöse wird Politik. Keine ausgestreckte Hand für seine Kritiker oder Feinde, keine Worte der Versöhnung. Stattdessen eine schallende Ohrfeige für Barack Obama. Eine wütende, polemische Abrechnung mit der Politik der vergangenen acht Jahre, ein Rundumschlag gegen das Establishment. Amerika habe seinen Wohlstand verschleudert, andere reich gemacht, während viele Bürger im Land verarmt sind, sagt Trump. Damit soll Schluss sein. Ab sofort gilt: „America first". [...]"

Tasks:

1. Imagine you have a friend in the U.S.A. who cannot speak German but wants to know how Annette Ludwig responded to Trump's Inaugural Address. Explain Ludwig's main arguments in English in an email to your friend.
2. America first? Prepare and give a short speech about German-American relations.
3. Revisiting Donald Trump's Inauguration Speech: Look at the goals he promised and examine the current political situation.
4. "Keep America Great": President Donald Trump launched his re-election campaign in Orlando, Florida, on June 19, 2019. Watch, analyse and evaluate his speech: https://www.youtube.com/watch?v=KBGisI6n1tI

G) **Donald Trump's Tweets:** https://twitter.com/realDonaldTrump/status/954097213608570880 [January 18, 2018]

Donald J. Trump ✓
@realDonaldTrump

Follow

AMERICA will once again be a NATION that thinks big, dreams bigger, and always reaches for the stars. YOU are the ones who will shape America's destiny. YOU are the ones who will restore our prosperity. And YOU are the ones who are MAKING AMERICA GREAT AGAIN !
#MAGA

3:31 PM - Feb 22, 2018

Donald J. Trump ✓
@realDonaldTrump

Follow

A very big part of the Anger we see today in our society is caused by the purposely false and inaccurate reporting of the Mainstream Media that I refer to as Fake News. It has gotten so bad and hateful that it is beyond decription. Mainstream Media must clean up its act, FAST!

4:18 PM - Oct 25, 2018

President Donald Trump's tweets are presented in a slightly different layout in this textbook; they are based on his original tweets and are complete and unabridged.

Tasks:

1. Explain what Donald Trump's tweets mean.
2. Analyse the tone, language and stylistic devices Trump uses in these tweets.
3. Go online and find some more tweets which Donald Trump uses to declare his view on current issues. Point out the context of each tweet, analyse the language and the stylistic devices and evaluate the intended effects.
4. Write a response to President Trump's tweets.
5. *For Thought and Discussion:* Jennifer Sclafani, a linguist at Georgetown University, studies the way Donald Trump speaks. She says President Trump is a "unique" politician, because he doesn't speak like one. Watch her linguistic analysis here: https://www.youtube.com/watch?v=cpxCl8ylJgE
6. President Trump frequently sums up his policy with two words "America first." What does he mean? Is this slogan a responsible concept for the future role of the United States of America in our world today? Explain your opinion.
7. *Hot Seat:* Write an interview with President Donald Trump.
8. *Comedy Time:* President Donald Trump isn't pleased with Alec Baldwin's impression of him on *Saturday Night Live* (SNL). He doesn't like Alec Baldwin's latest comment that impersonating the president is "agony". Donald Trump tweeted: "Alec, it was agony for those who were forced to watch." Create an enjoyable scene for SNL featuring Alec Baldwin pretending to be Donald Trump.
9. **Go online and read some extracts from** *The Mueller Report On The Investigation Into Russian Interference In The 2016 Presidential Election*: "The Russian government interfered in the 2016 presidential election in sweeping and systematic fashion. Evidence of Russian government operation began to surface in mid-2016." Report by Special Counsel Robert S. Mueller, Washington, D.C., March 2019, page 9 https://www.justice.gov/storage/report.pdf

Civil Rights and Human Dignity – Achieved and Respected?

B

"What to the Slave Is the Fourth of July?"

Frederick Douglass, "The Hypocrisy of American Slavery."
An Address delivered in Rochester, New York State, on July 5, 1852.

RELATED TOPICS

THE AMERICAN DREAM · THE DECLARATION OF INDEPENDENCE · DEMOCRACY · DIGNITY · EDUCATION · THE FOUNDING CREED · FREEDOM · FUTURE GENERATIONS · HISTORY · HUMAN RIGHTS · IMMIGRATION · INEQUALITY · INJUSTICE · JUSTICE · LIBERTY · NATIONHOOD · RACE RELATIONS · SEGREGATION · SLAVERY · THE ANTI-SLAVERY MOVEMENT · SOCIAL SECURITY · UNALIENABLE RIGHTS

Frederick Douglass (1817-1895) was the best known and most influential African American leader of the 1800s. He was born a slave in Maryland but managed to escape to the North in 1838. He travelled to Massachusetts, a free state, and settled in New Bedford, where he worked as a labourer to support himself. In 1841, he attended a convention held by the Massachusetts Anti-Slavery Society and quickly came to the attention of its members, eventually becoming a leading figure in the New England abolitionist/anti-slavery movement.

In 1845, Douglass published his autobiography *The Narrative of the Life of Frederick Douglass: an American Slave.* Having revealed that he was an escaped slave, Douglass became fearful of possible re-enslavement and fled to Great Britain, where he stayed for two years, giving lectures in support of the anti-slavery movement in America. With the assistance of English Quakers, Douglass raised enough money to buy his freedom, and in 1847, he returned to America as a free man.

He settled in Rochester, New York State, where he published *The North Star*, an abolitionist newspaper. He directed the local Underground Railroad which smuggled escaped slaves into Canada, and also worked to end racial segregation in Rochester's public schools.

In 1852, the leading citizens of Rochester asked Douglass to give a speech as part of their Fourth of July celebrations. Douglass accepted their invitation. In his speech, however, Douglass delivered a scathing [*critical*] attack on the hypocrisy of a nation celebrating freedom and independence with speeches, parades and platitudes, while, within its borders, nearly four million humans were being kept as slaves.

Based on: *History Place* http://www.historyplace.com/speeches/douglass.htm

Frederick Douglass:

Mr. President, friends and fellow citizens: [...]

This, for the purpose of this celebration, is the Fourth of July. It is the birthday of your National Independence, and of your political freedom. [...]

Fellow citizens, pardon me, and allow me to ask, why am I called upon to speak here today? What have I or those I represent to do with your national independence? Are the great principles of political freedom and of natural justice, embodied in that Declaration of Independence, extended to us? And am I, therefore, called upon to bring our humble offering to the national altar, and to confess the benefits, and express devout gratitude for the blessings resulting from your independence to us?

Would to God, both for your sakes and ours, that an affirmative answer could be truthfully returned to these questions. Then would my task be light, and my burden easy and delightful. For who is there so cold that a nation's sympathy could not warm him? Who so obdurate and dead to the claims of gratitude, that would not thankfully acknowledge such priceless benefits? Who so stolid and selfish that would not give his voice to swell the hallelujahs of a nation's jubilee, when the chains of servitude had been torn from his limbs? I am not that man. In a case like that, the dumb might eloquently speak, and the "lame man leap as an hart."

THIS FOURTH OF JULY IS YOURS, NOT MINE

But such is not the state of the case. I say it with a sad sense of disparity between us. I am not included within the pale of this glorious anniversary! Your high independence only reveals the immeasurable distance between us. The blessings in which you this day rejoice are not enjoyed in common.

The rich inheritance of justice, liberty, prosperity, and independence bequeathed by your fathers is shared by you, not by me. The sunlight that brought life and healing to you has brought stripes and death to me. This Fourth of July is yours, not mine. You may rejoice, I must mourn.

To drag a man in fetters into the grand illuminated temple of liberty, and call upon him to join you in joyous anthems, were inhuman mockery and sacrilegious irony. Do you mean, citizens, to mock me, by asking me to speak today? [...]

FOURTH of JULY 1776 *see* ADDITIONAL NOTES

embodied (*here:*) included in

devout gratitude *ergebene Dankbarkeit*

Would to God I would like to thank God [a subjunctive verb form is used here to express a wish that has not been fulfilled yet]

affirmative answer *Bejahung*

truthfully honestly; *wahrheitsgemäß*

then would my task be light then my task would be easy

obdurate stubborn; *starrsinnig*

the lame man leap as an hart "the lame man will leap like a deer, and the tongue of the mute will sing; for waters will break out in the wilderness, and streams in the desert"; from: The Bible, Isaiah 35:6

within the pale of within the boundaries of

to be included within the pale of allowed to be part of

immeasurable distance a distance so long it can't be measured

to rejoice to celebrate

inheritance *Erbe*

bequeathed passed on

stripes (*here:*) *Peitschenhiebe*

to mourn *trauern*

fetters (*old use:*) chains; *Ketten*

mockery farce, joke

sacrilegious blasphemous; *frevlerisch*

My subject, then, fellow citizens, is "American Slavery." I shall see this day and its popular characteristics from the slave's point of view. Standing here, identified with the American bondman, making his wrongs mine, I do not hesitate to declare, with all my soul, that the character and conduct of this nation never looked blacker to me than on this Fourth of July.

bondman (*old use:*) slave
conduct behaviour

SLAVERY – THE GREAT SIN AND SHAME OF AMERICA!

Whether we turn to the declarations of the past, or to the professions of the present, the conduct of the nation seems equally hideous and revolting. America is false to the past, false to the present, and solemnly binds herself to be false to the future. Standing with God and the crushed and bleeding slave on this occasion, I will, in the name of humanity, which is outraged, in the name of liberty, which is fettered, in the name of the Constitution and the Bible, which are disregarded and trampled upon, dare to call in question and to denounce, with all the emphasis I can command, everything that serves to perpetuate slavery – the great sin and shame of America! [...]

hideous dreadful; *abscheulich, scheußlich*
revolting disgusting
fettered chained; *angekettet, gefesselt*
to perpetuate to continue, to carry on

MUST I PROVE THAT THE SLAVE IS A MAN?

What point in the anti-slavery creed would you have me argue? On what branch of the subject do the people of this country need light? Must I undertake to prove that the slave is a man? That point is conceded already. Nobody doubts it. The slave-holders themselves acknowledge it in the enactment of laws for their government. They acknowledge it when they punish disobedience on the part of the slave. There are seventy-two crimes in the State of Virginia, which, if committed by a black man (no matter how ignorant he be), subject him to the punishment of death; while only two of these same crimes will subject a white man to like punishment. [...]

disobedience *Ungehorsam*
subject him to the punishment of death a black man is given the death penalty

For the present, it is enough to affirm the equal manhood of the Negro race. Is it not astonishing that, while we are plowing, planting, and reaping, using all kinds of mechanical tools, erecting houses, constructing bridges, building ships, working in metals of brass, iron, copper, silver, and gold; that while we are reading, writing, and ciphering, acting as clerks, merchants, and secretaries, having among us lawyers, doctors, ministers, poets, authors, editors, orators, and teachers; that we are engaged in all the enterprises common to other men – digging gold in California, capturing the whale in the Pacific, feeding sheep and cattle on the hillside, living, moving, acting, thinking, planning, living in families as husbands, wives, and children, and above all, confessing and worshipping the Christian God, and looking hopefully for life and immortality beyond the grave – we are called upon to prove that we are men?

to affirm to confirm
plowing ploughing; *pflügen*
immortality *Unsterblichkeit*

MUST I ARGUE THE WRONGFULNESS OF SLAVERY?

Would you have me argue that man is entitled to liberty? That he is the rightful owner of his own body? You have already declared it. Must I argue the wrongfulness of slavery? Is that a question for republicans? Is it to be settled by the rules of logic and argumentation, as a matter beset with great difficulty, involving a doubtful application of the principle of justice, hard to understand?

How should I look today in the presence of Americans, dividing and subdividing a discourse, to show that men have a natural right to freedom, speaking of it relatively and positively, negatively and affirmatively? To do so would be to make myself ridiculous, and to offer an insult to your understanding. There is not a man beneath the canopy of heaven who does not know that slavery is wrong for him.

the canopy of heaven *das Himmelsgewölbe*

What! Am I to argue that it is wrong to make men brutes, to rob them of their liberty, to work them without wages, to keep them ignorant of their relations to their fellow men, to beat them with sticks, to flay their flesh with the lash, to load their limbs with irons, to hunt them with dogs, to sell them at auction, to sunder their families, to knock out their teeth, to burn their flesh, to starve them into obedience and submission to their masters? Must I argue that a system thus marked with blood and stained with pollution is wrong? No – I will not. I have better employment for my time and strength than such arguments would imply.

to flay to whip

to sunder to separate

obedience *Gehorsam*

submission *Unterwürfigkeit*

THAT WHICH IS INHUMAN CANNOT BE DIVINE

What, then, remains to be argued? Is it that slavery is not divine; that God did not establish it; that our doctors of divinity are mistaken? There is blasphemy in the thought. That which is inhuman cannot be divine. Who can reason on such a proposition? They that can, may – I cannot. The time for such argument is past.

doctors of divinity preachers, ministers

blasphemy *Gotteslästerung*

proposition proposal, idea

At a time like this, scorching irony, not convincing argument, is needed. Oh! had I the ability, and could I reach the nation's ear, I would today pour out a fiery stream of biting ridicule, blasting reproach, withering sarcasm, and stern rebuke. For it is not light that is needed, but fire; it is not the gentle shower, but thunder. We need the storm, the whirlwind, and the earthquake. The feeling of the nation must be quickened; the conscience of the nation must be roused; the propriety of the nation must be startled; the hypocrisy of the nation must be exposed; and its crimes against God and man must be proclaimed and denounced.

scorching irony *scharfe Ironie*

biting ridicule sarcastic remarks; *beißender Spott*

withering scornful; *vernichtend*

stern rebuke harsh criticism; *scharfe Zurechtweisung*

hypocrisy dishonesty, insincerity; *Heuchelei*

denounced condemned

What to the American slave is your Fourth of July? I answer, a day that reveals to him more than all other days of the year, the gross injustice and cruelty to which he is the constant victim.

To him your celebration is a sham; your boasted liberty an unholy license; your national greatness, swelling vanity; your sounds of rejoicing are empty and heartless; your shouts of liberty and equality, hollow mock; your prayers and hymns, your sermons and thanksgivings, with all your religious parade and solemnity, are to him mere bombast, fraud, deception, impiety, and hypocrisy – a thin veil to cover up crimes which would disgrace a nation of savages. There is not a nation of the earth guilty of practices more shocking and bloody than are the people of these United States at this very hour.

sham fake
vanity *Eitelkeit*
fraud *Betrug*
impiety godlessness; *Pietätlosigkeit*
to disgrace to bring shame on
savages uncivilised people, barbarians

Go search where you will, roam through all the monarchies and despotisms of the Old World, travel through South America, search out every abuse and when you have found the last, lay your facts by the side of the everyday practices of this nation, and you will say with me that, for revolting barbarity and shameless hypocrisy, America reigns without a rival.

abuse cruelty; *Missbrauch*
lay your facts by the side of compare your results with

THE AMERICAN SLAVE-TRADE IS PROSPEROUS

Take the American slave-trade, which, we are told by the papers, is especially prosperous just now. Ex-Senator Benton tells us that the price of men was never higher than now. He mentions the fact to show that slavery is in no danger. This trade is one of the peculiarities of American institutions. It is carried on in all the large towns and cities in one-half of this confederacy; and millions are pocketed every year, by dealers in this horrid traffic. In several states, this trade is a chief source of wealth. It is called (in contradistinction to the foreign slave-trade) "the internal slave-trade."

prosperous flourishing, booming
peculiarities *Besonderheiten*
traffic human trafficking; *Menschenhandel*
in contradistinction to in contrast to

Behold the practical operation of this internal slave-trade, the American slave-trade, sustained by American politics and American religion. Here you will see men and women reared like swine for the market. You know what a swine-drover is? I will show you a man-drover. They inhabit all our Southern States. They perambulate the country, and crowd the highways of the nation, with droves of human stock. You will see one of these human flesh-jobbers, armed with pistol, whip and bowie-knife, driving a company of a hundred men, women, and children, from the Potomac to the slave market at New Orleans. These wretched people are to be sold singly, or in lots, to suit purchasers. They are food for the cotton-field, and the deadly sugar-mill. Mark the sad procession, as it moves wearily along, and the inhuman wretch who drives them.

reared bred, brought up
swine-drover swineherd; *Schweinehirt*
to perambulate to walk around
jobbers sellers
wretched people pitiful, hopeless slaves
wretch (*here:*) scoundrel; *Schuft*
to drive (*here:*) *antreiben*

affrighted (*old use:*) frightened, terrified
captives prisoners, (*here also:*) slaves
locks hair
scorching hot, burning
briny salty

drove group
tardily slowly

Hear his savage yells and his blood-chilling oaths, as he hurries on his affrighted captives! There, see the old man, with locks thinned and gray. Cast one glance, if you please, upon that young mother, whose shoulders are bare to the scorching sun, her briny tears falling on the brow of the babe in her arms. See, too, that girl of thirteen, weeping, yes! Weeping, as she thinks of the mother from whom she has been torn! The drove moves tardily. Heat and sorrow have nearly consumed their strength; suddenly you hear a quick snap, like the discharge of a rifle; the fetters clank, and the chain rattles simultaneously; your ears are saluted with a scream, that seems to have torn its way to the center of your soul!

THE SOUND OF THE SLAVE-WHIP

gash cut, wound

forms bodies

fiendish brutal, cruel

The crack you heard, was the sound of the slave-whip; the scream you heard, was from the woman you saw with the babe. Her speed had faltered under the weight of her child and her chains! That gash on her shoulder tells her to move on. Follow the drove to New Orleans. Attend the auction; see men examined like horses; see the forms of women rudely and brutally exposed to the shocking gaze of American slave-buyers. See this drove sold and separated forever; and never forget the deep, sad sobs that arose from that scattered multitude. Tell me citizens, WHERE, under the sun, you can witness a spectacle more fiendish and shocking. Yet this is but a glance at the American slave-trade, as it exists, at this moment, in the ruling part of the United States.

wharves docks

waft blow
slave mart slave market

captivating charming

I was born amid such sights and scenes. To me, the American slave-trade is a terrible reality. When a child, my soul was often pierced with a sense of its horrors. I lived on Philpot Street, Fell's Point, Baltimore, and have watched from the wharves, the slave ships in the Basin, anchored from the shore, with their cargoes of human flesh, waiting for favorable winds to waft them down the Chesapeake. There was, at that time, a grand slave mart kept at the head of Pratt Street, by Austin Woldfolk. His agents were sent into every town and county in Maryland, announcing their arrival, through the papers, and on flaming "hand-bills," headed CASH FOR NEGROES. These men were generally well-dressed men, and very captivating in their manners. Ever ready to drink, to treat, and to gamble.

bargains deals

The fate of many a slave has depended upon the turn of a single card; and many a child has been snatched from the arms of its mother by bargains arranged in a state of brutal drunkenness. [...]

piteous sad, pitiful
chained gangs groups of slaves
anguish suffering, pain, distress

heart-rending heart-breaking

In the deep, still darkness of midnight, I have been often aroused by the dead heavy footsteps, and the piteous cries of the chained gangs that passed our door. The anguish of my boyish heart was intense; and I was often consoled, when speaking to my mistress in the morning, to hear her say that the custom was very wicked; that she hated to hear the rattle of the chains, and the heart-rending cries. I was glad to find one who sympathized with me in my horror. [...]

A SYSTEM BEGUN IN AVARICE, SUPPORTED IN PRIDE, AND PERPETUATED IN CRUELTY

Americans! Your republican politics, not less than your republican religion, are flagrantly inconsistent. You boast of your love of liberty, your superior civilization, and your pure Christianity, while the whole political power of the nation (as embodied in the two great political parties), is solemnly pledged to support and perpetuate the enslavement of three millions of your countrymen. You hurl your anathemas at the crowned headed tyrants of Russia and Austria, and pride yourselves on your Democratic institutions, while you yourselves consent to be the mere tools and bodyguards of the tyrants of Virginia and Carolina.

flagrantly (*here:*) *vollkommen*
inconsistent *unbeständig und widersprüchlich*
to perpetuate to continue
enslavement slavery; *Versklavung*
to hurl your anathemas at to criticize, to disapprove of

You invite to your shores fugitives of oppression from abroad, honor them with banquets, greet them with ovations, cheer them, toast them, salute them, protect them, and pour out your money to them like water; but the fugitives from your own land you advertise, hunt, arrest, shoot and kill. You glory in your refinement and your universal education yet you maintain a system as barbarous and dreadful as ever stained the character of a nation – a system begun in avarice, supported in pride, and perpetuated in cruelty. […]

fugitives of oppression refugees
refinement sophistication; *Vornehmheit, Kultiviertheit*
avarice greed; *Habgier*

I DO NOT DESPAIR OF THIS COUNTRY

Allow me to say, in conclusion, notwithstanding the dark picture I have this day presented of the state of the nation, I do not despair of this country. There are forces in operation, which must inevitably work the downfall of slavery. "The arm of the Lord is not shortened," and the doom of slavery is certain.

I, therefore, leave off where I began, with hope. While drawing encouragement from the Declaration of Independence, the great principles it contains, and the genius of American Institutions, my spirit is also cheered by the obvious tendencies of the age. Nations do not now stand in the same relation to each other that they did ages ago. No nation can now shut itself up from the surrounding world, and trot round in the same old path of its fathers without interference. The time was when such could be done. Long established customs of hurtful character could formerly fence themselves in, and do their evil work with social impunity. Knowledge was then confined and enjoyed by the privileged few, and the multitude walked on in mental darkness.

But a change has now come over the affairs of mankind. Walled cities and empires have become unfashionable. The arm of commerce has borne away the gates of the strong city. Intelligence is penetrating the darkest corners of the globe. It makes its pathway over and under the sea, as well as on the earth. Wind, steam, and lightning are its chartered agents. Oceans no longer divide, but link nations together. From

notwithstanding despite; *trotz (des düsteren Bildes)*
The arm of the Lord is not shortened a reference to the Bible: Isaiah 59:1: "Surely the arm of the LORD is not too short to save, nor his ear too dull to hear."
impunity *Straflosigkeit*
confined limited to
borne away carried away

annihilated *aufgehoben*
fiat (*old use:*) *Gebot*
Let there be Light a reference to the Bible: Genesis 1:3: "And God said, "Let there be light," and there was light."
abuse mistreatment, exploitation
William Lloyd Garrison (1805 – 1879) was an American journalist and social reformer. He was one of the founders of the American Anti-Slavery Society.
galling chains maddening, humiliating; *entwürdigende Ketten*
yoke (*here:*) burden, chain; *Joch*
clime climate
feuds conflicts
foe enemy
to cower to tremble
the thrall (*here:*) the slaves
to rend to break
gyve chain
to deprive to take away
Whate'er what ever
peril risk, danger

Boston to London is now a holiday excursion. Space is comparatively annihilated. Thoughts expressed on one side of the Atlantic are distinctly heard on the other. The far-off and almost fabulous Pacific rolls in grandeur at our feet. The Celestial Empire, the mystery of ages, is being solved. The fiat of the Almighty, "Let there be Light," has not yet spent its force. No abuse, no outrage whether in taste, sport or avarice, can now hide itself from the all-pervading light. [...] In the fervent aspirations of William Lloyd Garrison, I say, and let every heart join in saying it:

God speed the year of jubilee
  The wide world o'er!
When from their galling chains set free,
Th' oppressed shall vilely bend the knee,
And wear the yoke of tyranny
  Like brutes, no more:
That year will come, and Freedom's reign,
To man his plundered rights again
  Restore.
God speed the day when human blood
  Shall cease to flow!
In every clime be understood,
The claims of human brotherhood,
And each return for evil, good
  Not blow for blow:
That day will come, all feuds to end,
And change into a faithful friend
  Each foe.
God speed the hour, the glorious hour,
  When none on earth
Shall exercise a lordly power,
Nor in a tyrant's presence cower;
But all to Manhood's stature tower,
  By equal birth!
That hour will come, to each, to all,
And from his prison-house the thrall
  Go forth.
Until that year, day, hour arrive,
With head and heart and hand I'll strive,
To break the rod, and rend the gyve,
The spoiler of his prey deprive,
  So witness Heaven!
And never from my chosen post,
Whate'er the peril or the cost,
  Be driven.

Source: *National Humanities Center*
http://americainclass.org/wp-content/uploads/2011/04/Douglass-FullText.pdf

ASSIGNMENTS

A) Pre-Reading Activity

interactive classroom / four corners activity or walking and talking / inside-outside circle / discussion / collaboration with History and Social Sciences classes / cross-curricular connections

Discuss the following statements with different partners. Use the inside-outside circle technique.
1. "Slavery is a disgraceful aspect of history."
2. "Slavery did not end when it was abolished in the 19th century."
3. "Slavery continues to this day."
4. "Slavery affects people in every country in the world."

B) Comprehension

SQ3R reading method / think-pair-share / peer support and feedback / poster / gallery walk

1. What does Frederick Douglass try to do in his introduction? Cite evidence from the text to support your answer.
2. Why would it be "out of the common way" for Douglass to deliver a typical "Fourth of July" speech?
3. What arguments does Frederick Douglass use to persuade a northern, white audience to oppose slavery, and to support its abolition?
4. What conclusion does Frederick Douglass come to at the end of his speech?

C) Analysis

cooperative learning / paired work / group work / jigsaw / students teach each other / peer support and feedback / laptop or tablet / multimedia presentation / 60-second pitch / evaluation

1. Analyse the structure of the speech, paying particular attention to the introduction and the narrative style, as well as the use of facts, the use of arguments and counter-arguments, and the conclusion.
2. Analyse the rhetorical devices that Frederick Douglass uses to persuade his audience to abolish slavery.
3. Name some rhetorical devices that Frederick Douglass uses in the speech to help convince his listeners to accept his point of view.
4. Why does Douglass say he feels hopeful about America's future at the end of his speech? Cite evidence from the text to support your answer.
5. Analyse the significance of Douglass choosing to recite William Lloyd Garrison's poem at the end of the speech, and point out the function of the poem in the wider context of the speech.

D) Evaluation, Comment, Creative Writing

writing conference / peer support and feedback / tablet or laptop /multimedia presentation / speech

1. "I do not despair of this country." Explain Douglass's statement in the wider context of his speech.
2. Write an article for your school newspaper in which you evaluate the significance of Douglass's speech in the wider context of American society at the time.
3. Compare the social problems Frederick Douglass criticises in his speech to contemporary social issues in the United States. How are they similar? In what ways do they differ? Give a three-minute speech.

E) The "Fourth of July": A Cartoon by Dave Granlund

Tasks:
1. Take a closer look: What is shown in the cartoon?
   Describe all of the cartoon's elements/features in detail, and point out the relationship between them. You have already noticed what the Statue of Liberty is holding in her left hand. What is it?
2. Analyse the cartoon's message and the cartoonist's intentions. Explain what the artist wants to express by examining the relationship between the cartoon's characters, objects, and colours.
3. Evaluating the cartoon: After having described and analysed the cartoon, use your background knowledge of American history, and refer to Frederick Douglass's speech, to give your own opinion of the cartoon's historical significance.

Dave Granlund is a very famous American cartoonist. His cartoons are published in both daily and weekly newspapers.

F) Research Project: The Amistad Case

flipped classroom / independent learning / research / WebQuest / tablet or laptop / multimedia presentation / cross-curricular connections / creative writing / feedback / talk show

"Each of them are natives of Africa and were born free, and ever since have been, and still, of right, are, and ought to be free and not slaves." S. Staples, R. Baldwin, and T. Sedgewick, Proctors for the Amistad Africans, January 7, 1840, *National Archives* https://www.archives.gov/education/lessons/amistad/

Tasks:
1. Find out some more information about the *Amistad* Case.
2. Write an article for an 1841 newspaper describing the Supreme Court's decision in the *Amistad* Case.
3. Write a review of Steven Spielberg's film *Amistad*. Compare the film version to the historical events.

4. Lead a class discussion about the value of preserving the historical integrity of the story, and the value of changing that story for a screenplay.
5. Write and stage a one-act play about the events and personalities involved in the case. The play might focus on the formation of the *Amistad* Committee by abolitionists Lewis Tappan, Joshua Levitt, and Symeon Jocelyn; or on the decision by John Quincy Adams to represent the Africans.
6. Cross-curricular connections: Share these ideas with your History, Social Sciences, Art, and Drama classes.

G) Further Research and Projects

1. **Read Rebecca Caesar's essay**: *Frederick Douglass's Relationship with Abraham Lincoln. University of Rochester*: http://rbscp.lib.rochester.edu/4071. Present the main ideas to your English class.
2. **The film *12 Years a Slave*** (2013) is based on the true story of one man's fight for survival and freedom. In the pre-Civil War United States, Solomon Northup, a free black man from upstate New York, is kidnapped and sold into slavery. Facing the cruelty of slave owners, Solomon Northup struggles to stay alive, and to retain his dignity. You could present, analyse and discuss some selected scenes from the film in your English class.

H) "Modern Slavery": A WebQuest

▶ *agile work / WebQuest / internet research / evaluating website content / interview / tablet or laptop presentation / discussion / cooperation with Social Sciences and History classes / cross-curricular connections / feedback / podcast / video clip production / stations learning / SOLO taxonomy*

Slavery has been a disgraceful aspect of human society for most of human history. Slavery did not end with its abolition in the 19th century. Slavery continues to this day and harms people in every country in the world. Although this kind of exploitation is not often called slavery today, but rather "human trafficking", the conditions are very much the same. People are sold like objects, forced to work for little or no pay and are at the mercy of their "employers". According to the International Labour Organisation (ILO), around 21 million men, women and children around the world are trapped in a form of slavery today.

Tasks:

1. Imagine that you and your group are part of a team of reporters. Find out more about this modern form of slavery, called "human trafficking", and report your findings to your English class.
2. Modern Slavery – a Hidden Problem: Download the full PDF of the annual *Global Slavery Index* here: https://www.globalslaveryindex.org/resources/downloads/
3. **More than 40 Million Forced into Modern Slavery**: "Globally, more than 40 million people are subject to modern forms of slavery - 71 per cent of them women and girls." *United Nations* on October 26, 2018. Further information: https://www.un.org/press/en/2018/gashc4244.doc.htm [accessed January 5, 2019]
4. In your groups, produce a Sunday magazine supplement for a newspaper about the problem of modern slavery. Present your magazine supplement to your class.

I) Further Project: Songs and Books about Slavery

1. Many powerful and inspirational songs have been written about slavery. Terrible times are often revisited in songs, and slavery has been a popular topic for musicians for decades. There are modern songs about slavery, and songs about slavery that were written by civil rights activists. Visual material, such as historical paintings and graphic novels, can also be examined. Making cross-curricular connections with your Music, Art, History and Drama classes is recommended.
2. **"We're still living with slavery."** From prize-winners Esi Edugyan and Marlon James to debut novelists such as Sara Collins, a new generation of novelists is exploring a painful past. Colin Grant in: *The Guardian*, March 23, 2019 https://www.theguardian.com/books/2019/mar/23/colin-grant-slavery-novels

"This Nation Will Not Be Free Until All Its Citizens Are Free."

President John F. Kennedy's Civil Rights Address
on June 11, 1963, at the White House, in Washington, D.C.

RELATED TOPICS

THE AMERICAN DREAM · CIVIL RIGHTS · THE CONSTITUTION · THE DECLARATION OF INDEPENDENCE · DEMOCRACY · DIGNITY · EDUCATION · EQUALITY · THE FOUNDING CREED · FREEDOM · FUTURE GENERATIONS · GOD · THE GOVERNMENT · HISTORY · HUMAN RIGHTS · INEQUALITY · INJUSTICE · JUSTICE · LIBERTY · NATIONHOOD · PEACE · RACE RELATIONS · SCHOOL · SEGREGATION · SLAVERY · SOCIAL SECURITY · THE SUPREME COURT · UNALIENABLE RIGHTS · VIOLENCE

John F. Kennedy

When John F. Kennedy was elected president in 1960, the lives of African Americans across the United States were extremely tough. In the South, they were denied civil liberties, such as the right to vote, access to public facilities and fair representation in the courts. There were also still problems in the North, with African Americans being unfairly treated in relation to housing, employment and education amongst other sectors. However, President Kennedy's inauguration in 1961 offered African Americans hope that they could build on the progress made by the Civil Rights Movement.

Nonetheless, JFK's election victory was slim and this resulted in a cautious attitude towards introducing new civil rights legislation. Instead of risking the loss of southern support, he appointed a number of African Americans to high-level governmental roles and strengthened the Civil Rights Commission. He remained a vocal supporter of the Civil Rights Movement, called out discrimination and praised integration. Vice President Lyndon B. Johnson was given responsibility of the President's Committee on Equal Employment Opportunity.

Soon though, Kennedy could no longer ignore the plight of African Americans as his administration was forced to show its hand. The commitment of newly-elected Alabama Governor George Wallace to "segregation now, segregation tomorrow, and segregation forever" led to him preventing two black students from matriculating at the University of Alabama. President Kennedy made Wallace stand down and ensured that the students were protected from racists by the National Guard.

In short, Kennedy's support for civil rights was not merely political, or legal, it was based on his moral values. He announced major civil rights legislation to guarantee access to public spaces and facilities, to remove segregation at educational institutions and to assure that people would receive the necessary protection so they could vote.

Before completing his presidential term, Kennedy was assassinated on November 22, 1963. The following July, the Civil Rights Act was passed. This implemented an important demand of the Civil Rights Movement: equality in the eyes of the law.

THE PRESIDENT John F. Kennedy:

Good evening, my fellow citizens:

This afternoon, following a series of threats and defiant statements, the presence of Alabama National Guardsmen was required at the University of Alabama to carry out the final and unequivocal order of the United States District Court of the Northern District of Alabama. That order called for the admission of two clearly qualified young Alabama residents who happened to have been born Negro. That they were admitted peacefully on the campus is due in good measure to the conduct of the students of the University of Alabama, who met their responsibilities in a constructive way.

defiant (*here:*) aggressive, resistant; *trotzig, herausfordernd*

unequivocal definite, clear; *klar und deutlich*

THE RIGHTS OF EVERY MAN ARE DIMINISHED WHEN THE RIGHTS OF ONE MAN ARE THREATENED

I hope that every American, regardless of where he lives, will stop and examine his conscience about this and other related incidents. This Nation was founded by men of many nations and backgrounds. It was founded on the principle that all men are created equal, and that the rights of every man are diminished when the rights of one man are threatened.

diminished reduced

Today, we are committed to a worldwide struggle to promote and protect the rights of all who wish to be free. And when Americans are sent to Vietnam or West Berlin, we do not ask for whites only. It ought to be possible, therefore, for American students of any color to attend any public institution they select without having to be backed up by troops. It ought to be possible for American consumers of any color to receive equal service in places of public accommodation, such as hotels and restaurants and theaters and retail stores, without being forced to resort to demonstrations in the street, and it ought to be possible for American citizens of any color to register and to vote in a free election without interference or fear of reprisal.

reprisal *Vergeltungsmaßnahme*

It ought to be possible, in short, for every American to enjoy the privileges of being American without regard to his race or his color. In short, every American ought to have the right to be treated as he would wish to be treated, as one would wish [for] his children to be treated. But this is not the case.

The Negro baby born in America today, regardless of the section of the State in which he is born, has about one-half as much chance of completing high school as a white baby born in the same place on the same day, one-third as much chance of completing college, one-third as much chance of becoming a professional man, twice as much chance of becoming unemployed, about one-seventh as much chance

about one-half as much chance *die Chancen stehen bei etwa der Hälfte*
one-third as much chance *die Chancen stehen bei einem Drittel*
twice as much chance *doppelt so hoch*
one-seventh as much chance *mit einer Wahrscheinlichkeit von einem Siebtel*

of earning $10,000 a year, and a life expectancy which is seven years shorter, with the prospect of earning only half as much.

WE ARE CONFRONTED WITH A MORAL ISSUE

this is not a sectional issue *es handelt sich hier nicht um ein Problem, das sich auf bestimmte Teile der Nation beschränkt*
segregation *Rassentrennung*
a rising tide of discontent *eine wachsende Welle des Unmuts*
a partisan issue a problem only one party is concerned about; *parteigebunden*
bipartisan *parteiübergreifend*

the Scriptures the Bible

This is not a sectional issue. Difficulties over segregation and discrimination exist in every city, in every State of the Union, producing in many cities a rising tide of discontent that threatens public safety. Nor is this a partisan issue. In a time of domestic crisis, men of good will and generosity should be able to unite, regardless of party or politics. This is not even a legal or legislative issue alone. It is better to settle these matters in the courts than on the streets, and new laws are needed at every level, but law alone cannot make men see right. We are confronted primarily with a moral issue. It is as old as the Scriptures and is as clear as the American Constitution.

The heart of the question is whether all Americans are to be afforded equal rights and equal opportunities, whether we are going to treat our fellow Americans as we want to be treated. If an American, because his skin is dark, cannot eat lunch in a restaurant open to the public, if he cannot send his children to the best public school available, if he cannot vote for the public officials who will represent him, if, in short, he cannot enjoy the full and free life which all of us want, then who among us would be content to have the color of his skin changed and stand in his place? Who among us would then be content with the counsels of patience and delay?

who among us would then be content with the counsels of patience and delay? *Wer von uns wäre zufrieden, wenn man ihm dazu raten würde, geduldig zu sein und Verzögerungen in Kauf zu nehmen?*

THIS NATION WILL NOT BE FULLY FREE UNTIL ALL ITS CITIZENS ARE FREE

heirs *Erben*
bonds (*here:*) chains

boasts pride; *Stolz, Angabe, Prahlerei*

One hundred years of delay have passed since President Lincoln freed the slaves, yet their heirs, their grandsons, are not fully free. They are not yet freed from the bonds of injustice. They are not yet freed from social and economic oppression. And this Nation, for all its hopes and all its boasts, will not be fully free until all its citizens are free.

We preach freedom around the world, and we mean it, and we cherish our freedom here at home, but are we to say to the world, and much more importantly, to each other, that this is the land of the free except for the Negroes; that we have no second-class citizens except Negroes; that we have no class or caste system, no ghettoes, no master race except with respect to Negroes?

Birmingham the largest city in Alabama; in the 1960s it became a focal point for the civil rights movement

legal remedies legal solutions

Now the time has come for this Nation to fulfil its promise. The events in Birmingham and elsewhere have so increased the cries for equality that no city or State or legislative body can prudently choose to ignore them. The fires of frustration and discord are burning in every city, North and South, where legal remedies are not at hand.

Redress is sought in the streets, in demonstrations, parades, and protests which create tensions and threaten violence and threaten lives.

We face, therefore, a moral crisis as a country and a people. It cannot be met by repressive police action. It cannot be left to increased demonstrations in the streets. It cannot be quieted by token moves or talk. It is a time to act in the Congress, in your State and local legislative body and, above all, in all of our daily lives.

It is not enough to pin the blame on others, to say this is a problem of one section of the country or another, or deplore the facts that we face. A great change is at hand, and our task, our obligation, is to make that revolution, that change, peaceful and constructive for all. Those who do nothing are inviting shame, as well as violence. Those who act boldly are recognizing right, as well as reality.

RACE HAS NO PLACE IN AMERICAN LIFE OR LAW

Next week, I shall ask the Congress of the United States to act, to make a commitment it has not fully made in this century to the proposition that race has no place in American life or law. The Federal judiciary has upheld that proposition in a series of forthright cases. The Executive Branch has adopted that proposition in the conduct of its affairs, including the employment of Federal personnel, the use of Federal facilities, and the sale of federally financed housing.

But there are other necessary measures which only the Congress can provide, and they must be provided at this session. The old code of equity law under which we live commands for every wrong a remedy, but in too many communities, in too many parts of the country, wrongs are inflicted on Negro citizens and there are no remedies in the law. Unless the Congress acts, their only remedy is the street.

I am, therefore, asking the Congress to enact legislation giving all Americans the right to be served in facilities which are open to the public – hotels, restaurants, theaters, retail stores, and similar establishments. This seems to me to be an elementary right. Its denial is an arbitrary indignity that no American in 1963 should have to endure, but many do.

I have recently met with scores of business leaders urging them to take voluntary action to end this discrimination, and I have been encouraged by their response, and in the last two weeks, over 75 cities have seen progress made in desegregating these kinds of facilities.

But many are unwilling to act alone, and for this reason, nationwide legislation is needed if we are to move this problem from the streets to the courts.

redress *Wiedergutmachung*
to seek, sought, sought to look for, to try to get

it cannot be quieted by token moves or talk *durch symbolische Handlungen oder Worte lässt sich [die Stimmung] nicht beruhigen*

shame *Scham*

proposition proposal; *Gesetzesvorhaben*
race (*here:*) racism
the Federal judiciary *Bundesgerichte*
forthright straightforward, clear

wrongs are inflicted on Negro citizens *an Schwarzen wird Unrecht begangen*
unless the Congress acts, their only remedy is the street *sollte der Kongress nicht handeln, bleibt nur noch die Option, auf der Straße zu demonstrieren.*

its denial is an arbitrary indignity *die Verweigerung dieses Rechts ist eine willkürliche Demütigung*

progress made in desegregating these kinds of facilities *bei der Aufhebung der Rassentrennung werden in diesen Einrichtungen Erfolge verzeichnet*

END SEGREGATION IN PUBLIC EDUCATION

I'm also asking the Congress to authorize the Federal Government to participate more fully in lawsuits designed to end segregation in public education. We have succeeded in persuading many districts to desegregate voluntarily. Dozens have admitted Negroes without violence. Today, a Negro is attending a state-supported institution in every one of our 50 states, but the pace is very slow.

to desegregate to integrate; *die Rassentrennung aufheben*

THE LACK OF AN ADEQUATE EDUCATION DENIES THE NEGRO A CHANCE TO GET A DECENT JOB

Too many Negro children entering segregated grade schools at the time of the Supreme Court's decision nine years ago will enter segregated high schools this fall, having suffered a loss which can never be restored. The lack of an adequate education denies the Negro a chance to get a decent job.

The orderly implementation of the Supreme Court decision, therefore, cannot be left solely to those who may not have the economic resources to carry the legal action or who may be subject to harassment.

the orderly implementation of the Supreme Court decision *die ordnungsgemäße Umsetzung des Beschlusses des Obersten Bundesgerichts*
who may not have the economic resources to carry the legal action *die für das Gerichtsverfahren nicht genug Geld haben*
subject to harassment *Opfer von Schikanierung*
I wanna pay I want to pay; 'wanna' is a colloquial short form of 'want to'

Other features will be also requested, including greater protection for the right to vote. But legislation, I repeat, cannot solve this problem alone. It must be solved in the homes of every American in every community across our country. In this respect, I wanna pay tribute to those citizens North and South who've been working in their communities to make life better for all. They are acting not out of sense of legal duty but out of a sense of human decency. Like our soldiers and sailors in all parts of the world, they are meeting freedom's challenge on the firing line, and I salute them for their honor and their courage.

a sense of human decency a sense of social responsibility; *Gefühl des menschlichen Anstands*
on the firing line *im Brennpunkt*

My fellow Americans, this is a problem which faces us all – in every city of the North as well as the South. Today, there are Negroes unemployed, two or three times as many compared to whites, inadequate education, moving into the large cities, unable to find work, young people particularly out of work without hope:

- denied equal rights,
- denied the opportunity to eat at a restaurant or a lunch counter or to go to a movie theatre,
- denied the right to a decent education,
- denied, almost today, the right to attend a state university even though qualified.

denied equal rights *denen gleiche Rechte verwehrt werden*

It seems to me that these are matters which concern us all, not merely Presidents or Congressmen or Governors, but every citizen of the United States.

matters which concern us all *Angelegenheiten, die uns alle angehen*

This is one country. It has become one country because all of us and all the people who came here [before us] had an equal chance to develop their talents. We cannot say to ten percent of the population that you can't have that right; that your children cannot have the chance to develop whatever talents they have; that the only way that they are going to get their rights is to go in the street and demonstrate. I think we owe them and we owe ourselves a better country than that.

we owe them we have an obligation to them; *wir sind ihnen (etwas) schuldig*

GIVE A CHANCE FOR EVERY CHILD TO BE EDUCATED TO THE LIMIT OF HIS TALENTS

Therefore, I'm asking for your help in making it easier for us to move ahead and to provide the kind of equality of treatment which we would want ourselves; to give a chance for every child to be educated to the limit of his talents.

As I've said before, not every child has an equal talent or an equal ability or an equal motivation, but they should have the equal right to develop their talent and their ability and their motivation, to make something of themselves.

We have a right to expect that the Negro community will be responsible, will uphold the law, but they have a right to expect that the law will be fair, that the Constitution will be color blind, as Justice Harlan said at the turn of the century.

Justice John Marshall Harlan civil rights activist, Supreme Court justice and lawyer (1833–1911)

This is what we're talking about and this is a matter which concerns this country and what it stands for, and in meeting it I ask the support of all our citizens. Thank you very much.

Speech transcript taken from: *American Rhetoric*
http://www.americanrhetoric.com/speeches/jfkcivilrights.htm

ASSIGNMENTS

A) Pre-Listening and Pre-Reading Activity

▶ *cooperative learning / communicative classroom: four corners activity or inside-outside circle or idea lab or milling around / share ideas / idea tower / speed debating / evaluation*

Discuss the following statements with different partners:

1. "Racism has no place in society."
2. "The rights of every man are diminished when the rights of one man are threatened."
3. "The lack of an adequate education denies people a chance to get a decent job."

B) Listening and Reading Comprehension

SQ3R method / group work / peer support / students teach each other / presentation / discussion

1. Listen to John F. Kennedy's Civil Rights speech and highlight any significant keywords in your speech transcript.
2. Divide the speech into nine sections and summarise JFK's main points in each section.
3. Make a list of the problems and conflicts Kennedy mentions.
4. Why is it, according to Kennedy, especially important to end segregation in public education?
5. What are Kennedy's "remedies" and suggestions?
6. Now, write a summary of Kennedy's main arguments.

C) Analysis

1. Analyse the structure of the speech.
2. Analyse the text as a persuasive speech and identify the rhetorical devices and arguments Kennedy uses to try to convince the nation that all Americans deserve equal treatment, regardless of race.
3. President Kennedy believed in the power of words to set goals, to change minds, to move nations. He took care to choose the right words and phrases that would send the right message.

D) Evaluation, Response, Creative Writing

self-immersion / group work / preparing a speech / multimedia presentation / feedback / discussion

1. Evaluate the significance of Kennedy's speech in the wider context of the social and political problems in the United States at that time.
2. How does JFK show leadership through ideas, words, and deeds? What tools does he use to try to persuade the public to agree with him on a controversial issue?
3. Compare John F. Kennedy and Martin Luther King's speeches on Civil Rights. Evaluate their similarities and differences.
3. Write a speech about how to solve the current problems of racial conflict, integration and segregation, and the discrimination of minorities across the world today.
4. John F. Kennedy: "We have a moral crisis": Create a multimedia presentation about the Civil Rights Movement based on what you have already learnt about the topic. Think of an interesting way to present the topic.

E) Further Reading For Thought and Discussion

George Wallace: "Segregation Now, Segregation Tomorrow, Segregation Forever"

From: *Radio Diaries* January 10, 2013
http://www.radiodiaries.org/segregation-now-segregation-forever-the-speech-that-changed-american-politics/

"It was just a single line in an inauguration speech given 50 years ago, but Alabama Governor George Wallace's 'Segregation Now, Segregation Tomorrow, Segregation Forever' is remembered as one of the most vehement rallying cries against racial equality in American history.
The year was 1963. Civil rights activists were fighting for equal access to schools and to the voting booth, and the federal government was preparing to intervene in many southern states. In Montgomery, Alabama, newly elected governor George Wallace stepped up to a podium to deliver his inaugural address. In his later years, George Wallace embarked on an apology tour, making amends with civil rights activists and appearing in black churches to ask for forgiveness. In his last election as governor of Alabama, in 1982, he won with more than ninety percent of the black vote."

F) Mediation (German = > English)

Please translate the main ideas of the following report into English, then send your summary via email to a class at your English-speaking partner school.

Für ein gerechteres Amerika: JFK und die Bürgerrechte

Von Martin Ganslmeier *SÜDWESTRUNDFUNK, SWR 1* am 15.11.2013

„*Das Amerika der 50er:* John F. Kennedy und die Bürgerrechtsbewegung – das war keine Liebe auf den ersten Blick. Der irisch-katholische Millionärssohn aus Massachusetts kannte lange Zeit das Leben der Afroamerikaner nur vom Hörensagen. Auch als Präsidentschaftskandidat hielt Kennedy Distanz zur Bürgerrechtsbewegung, um seine Wahlchancen in den Südstaaten nicht zu gefährden. Im Süden regierten damals Gouverneure wie George Wallace aus Alabama. Der hatte bei seinem Amtsantritt geschworen: "Rassentrennung jetzt, Rassentrennung morgen und Rassentrennung für immer." [...]
Kampf gegen die Rassentrennung: Zunächst tat der neue Präsident *John F. Kennedy* wenig für die Gleichberechtigung der Afroamerikaner. Erst die brutalen Fernsehbilder von Polizeihunden, die auf schwarze Schulkinder gehetzt wurden, führten bei Kennedy zu einem Umdenken. Ab sofort setzte er die Nationalgarde ein, um die schwarze Bevölkerung vor rassistischen Übergriffen zu schützen. Und im Juni 1963 kündigte Kennedy in einer Fernsehansprache Bürgerrechtsgesetze und ein Verbot der Rassentrennung an. Seinen weißen Mitbürgern hielt Kennedy einen Spiegel vor: „Dies ist das Land der Freien, außer für Schwarze. Wir haben keine Bürger zweiter Klasse, außer den Schwarzen. Wir haben keine Kasten und keine Ghettos, außer für Schwarze."
Der lange Marsch: Im August 1963 marschierten 200.000 Demonstranten nach Washington. Kennedy befürchtete zunächst gewaltsame Auseinandersetzungen. Die berühmte Abschlussrede von Martin Luther King ("I have a dream") schaute er sich im Fernsehen an. Von Kings Rede war Kennedy dann so beeindruckt, dass er die Anführer der Bürgerrechtsbewegung spontan ins Weiße Haus einlud. Wenig später brachte er die Bürgerrechtsgesetze im Kongress ein.
Ein teurer Sieg: Das Inkrafttreten dieser „Jahrhundertgesetze" hat John F. Kennedy nicht mehr erlebt. Die emotionale Erschütterung nach seiner Ermordung sorgte jedoch dafür, dass der Kongress endlich zustimmte. Dass die Gleichberechtigung nicht bloß auf dem Papier stand, sondern verwirklicht wurde, dafür engagierten sich besonders Kennedys Bruder Robert und Martin Luther King – bis auch sie wenige Jahre später ermordet wurden.

G) For Thought and Discussion: Inspirational Quotations by *John F. Kennedy*

a) **"Mankind must put an end to war or war will put an end to mankind."** Address Before The United Nations General Assembly, 25 September 1961.

b) **"And if we cannot end now our differences, at least we can help make the world safe for diversity. For, in the final analysis, our most basic common link is that we all inhabit this small planet. We all breathe the same air. We all cherish our children's future. And we are all mortal."** Commencement Address at American University, Washington, D.C., June 10, 1963.

c) **"Children are the world's most valuable resource and its best hope for the future."** United States Committee for UNICEF, July 25, 1963.

d) **"Change is the law of life. And those who look only to the past or the present are certain to miss the future."** Address in the Assembly Hall at the Paulskirche in Frankfurt, June 25, 1963.

e) **"Without debate, without criticism no administration and no country can succeed and no republic can survive."** President John F. Kennedy's Address before the American Newspaper Publishers Association, Waldorf-Astoria Hotel, New York City, April 27, 1961.

f) **"Let us accept our own responsibility for the future."** Remarks of Senator John F. Kennedy at the Loyola College Annual Alumni Banquet, Baltimore, Maryland, February 18, 1958.

Source: *John F. Kennedy Library* https://www.jfklibrary.org/archives

Tasks:

1. Explain, discuss and evaluate one of these quotations.
2. You might want to prepare and give a two-minute speech to present your ideas.
3. Give a short speech on the significance of Civil Rights and Human Rights in the world today.

H) Recommended Film:

Director Peter Farrelly's **Green Book**, about a black piano player (played by Mahershala Ali) touring the segregated South with a white chauffeur (Viggo Mortensen), won the Oscar 2019 for best picture. The film also won for supporting actor (Ali) and original screenplay.

"I Have a Dream."

Martin Luther King Jr.'s speech, delivered on August 28, 1963, at the Lincoln Memorial, in Washington D.C.

RELATED TOPICS

THE AMERICAN DREAM · THE CIVIL RIGHTS MOVEMENT · THE CONSTITUTION · THE DECLARATION OF INDEPENDENCE · DEMOCRACY · DIGNITY · THE FOUNDING CREED · FREEDOM · FUTURE GENERATIONS · GOD · THE GOVERNMENT · HISTORY · HUMAN RIGHTS · INEQUALITY · INJUSTICE · JUSTICE · LIBERTY · NATIONHOOD · NON-VIOLENCE · PEACE · RACE RELATIONS · SEGREGATION · SLAVERY · SOCIAL SECURITY · UNALIENABLE RIGHTS · VIOLENCE

Martin Luther King Jr., born on January 15, 1929, was a prominent Baptist figure and a leader of the Civil Rights Movement in the United States. A combination of his religious beliefs and his admiration for Indian activist Mahatma Gandhi influenced King's strong view that change would only be achieved through a non-violent approach.

At the famous March on Washington on August 28, 1963, Martin Luther King Jr. delivered his iconic "I Have a Dream" speech from the steps of the Lincoln Memorial. An estimated 250,000-strong crowd listened and cheered as he outlined his vision for the country's future as a nation without discrimination and segregation.

The speech is recognised as one of the best ever. Including poignant historical and biblical references, it inspired considerable progress in the pursuit of civil rights.

At its core, the speech initially aimed to celebrate President Abraham Lincoln who had overseen the freeing of all slaves. This Emancipation Proclamation was decreed on January 1, 1863 and Martin Luther King Jr.'s speech was intended to coincide with the hundred-year anniversary of this monumental occasion.

The 1964 Civil Rights Act, which was subsequently passed, is regarded as a particularly significant victory for the Civil Rights Movement. The legislation of that bill legally ended segregation in public spaces and outlawed discrimination in the work place.

Martin Luther King Jr. was assassinated on April 4, 1968.

Martin Luther King Jr.:

I am happy to join with you today in what will go down in history as the greatest demonstration for freedom in the history of our nation. Five score years ago, a great American, in whose symbolic shadow we stand today, signed the Emancipation Proclamation.

This momentous decree came as a great beacon light of hope to millions of Negro slaves who had been seared in the flames of withering injustice.

It came as a joyous daybreak to end the long night of their captivity.

BUT ONE HUNDRED YEARS LATER, THE NEGRO STILL IS NOT FREE

But one hundred years later, the Negro still is not free. One hundred years later, the life of the Negro is still sadly crippled by the manacles of segregation and the chains of discrimination.

One hundred years later, the Negro lives on a lonely island of poverty in the midst of a vast ocean of material prosperity.

One hundred years later, the Negro is still languished in the corners of American society and finds himself an exile in his own land.

And so we've come here today to dramatize a shameful condition.

In a sense we've come to our nation's capital to cash a check. When the architects of our republic wrote the magnificent words of the Constitution and the Declaration of Independence, they were signing a promissory note to which every American was to fall heir.

This note was a promise that all men, yes, black men as well as white men, would be guaranteed the "unalienable Rights" of "Life, Liberty and the pursuit of Happiness."

five score years ago 5x20 = 100 years ago; score is an old English word for "twenty"; King is referring to the Gettysburg Address given by President Abraham Lincoln
Emancipation Proclamation see ADDITIONAL NOTES
momentous decree *bedeutsamer Erlass*
beacon light of hope (*metaphorical:*) *Leuchtfeuer der Hoffnung*
seared burnt
withering (*here:*) devastating
joyous daybreak *freudiger Tagesanbruch*
captivity imprisonment; *Gefangenschaft*

crippled impaired, hindered
the manacles of segregation *die Handfesseln der Rassentrennung*
chains *Ketten*

material prosperity wealth, riches, affluence; *materieller Wohlstand*

to languish to suffer; *leiden*

to dramatize (*AmE*), to dramatise (*BrE*), (*here:*) to draw attention to

to cash a check (*here metaphorical:*) *einen Scheck einlösen; eine Zusage / ein Versprechen einlösen*

a promissory note to which every American was to fall heir (*metaphorical*) *jeder Amerikaner sollte Erbe dieses Versprechens sein*
this note the Declaration of Independence, July 4, 1776
unalienable rights rights that cannot be taken away; *unveräußerliche Rechte*
Life, Liberty and the pursuit of Happiness *The Declaration of Independence, July 4, 1776: "We hold these truths to be self-evident, that all men are created equal, that they are endowed by their Creator with certain unalienable Rights, that among these are Life, Liberty and the pursuit of Happiness."*
the pursuit of Happiness *das Streben nach Glück*

It is obvious today that America has defaulted on this promissory note, insofar as her citizens of color are concerned.

Instead of honoring this sacred obligation, America has given the Negro people a bad check, a check which has come back marked "insufficient funds."

WE REFUSE TO BELIEVE THAT
THE BANK OF JUSTICE IS BANKRUPT

But we refuse to believe that the bank of justice is bankrupt. We refuse to believe that there are insufficient funds in the great vaults of opportunity of this nation.

And so, we've come to cash this check, a check that will give us upon demand the riches of freedom and the security of justice.

We have also come to this hallowed spot to remind America of the fierce urgency of Now.

This is no time to engage in the luxury of cooling off or to take the tranquilizing drug of gradualism.

NOW IS THE TIME TO MAKE JUSTICE
A REALITY FOR ALL OF GOD'S CHILDREN

Now is the time to make real the promises of democracy.

Now is the time to rise from the dark and desolate valley of segregation to the sunlit path of racial justice.

America has defaulted on this promissory note *(metaphorical:) das Versprechen der Emancipation Proclamation ist noch nicht eingelöst*
citizens of color non-white people
obligation duty; *Verpflichtung*

insufficient funds *fehlende Kontodeckung; (metaphorical:)* the promise is not fulfilled; *die garantierten Versprechen sind nicht eingehalten*
vaults of opportunity (*metaphorical:*) America, the richest and most powerful nation in the world, has huge resources; *Tresorräume, Reichtümer der Möglichkeiten*
upon demand *auf Verlangen*
hallowed spot sacred place; *heiliger Ort*
the fierce urgency of Now (*metaphorical:*) the passionate and urgent demands of today
to cool off to relax, to sit back, to take it easy
tranquilizing drug *Beruhigungsmittel*
gradualism (*here:*) *Verzögerung, Politik der kleinen Schritte*

desolate *trostlos*
the valley of segregation *(metaphorical:) das Tal der Rassentrennung*
the sunlit path of racial justice (*metaphorical:*) *der sonnenbeschienene Pfad der Rassengerechtigkeit*

Cartoon by
Dave Granlund

Now is the time to lift our nation from the quick sands of racial injustice to the solid rock of brotherhood.

Now is the time to make justice a reality for all of God's children.

It would be fatal for the nation to overlook the urgency of the moment.

This sweltering summer of the Negro's legitimate discontent will not pass until there is an invigorating autumn of freedom and equality.

Nineteen sixty-three is not an end, but a beginning. And those who hope that the Negro needed to blow off steam and will now be content will have a rude awakening if the nation returns to business as usual.

And there will be neither rest nor tranquility in America until the Negro is granted his citizenship rights.

The whirlwinds of revolt will continue to shake the foundations of our nation until the bright day of justice emerges.

LET US NOT SEEK TO SATISFY OUR THIRST FOR FREEDOM BY DRINKING FROM THE CUP OF BITTERNESS AND HATRED

But there is something that I must say to my people, who stand on the warm threshold which leads into the palace of justice: In the process of gaining our rightful place, we must not be guilty of wrongful deeds.

Let us not seek to satisfy our thirst for freedom by drinking from the cup of bitterness and hatred.

We must forever conduct our struggle on the high plane of dignity and discipline.

We must not allow our creative protest to degenerate into physical violence. Again and again, we must rise to the majestic heights of meeting physical force with soul force.

The marvelous new militancy which has engulfed the Negro community must not lead us to a distrust of all white people, for many of our white brothers, as evidenced by their presence here today, have come to realize that their destiny is tied up with our destiny. And they have come to realize that their freedom is inextricably bound to our freedom.

quick sands *Treibsand*
brotherhood community
to overlook to ignore; *außer Acht lassen*
urgency importance, *Dringlichkeit*
sweltering very hot, boiling
discontent dissatisfaction; *Unzufriedenheit*
invigorating energizing; *stärkend*
to blow off steam *Dampf ablassen*
a rude awakening *ein böses Erwachen*
tranquility peace
citizenship rights *Bürgerrechte*
to emerge (*here:*) to happen
threshold *Schwelle*
to gain to get
wrongful deeds (*here:*) violent acts; *ungerechte Taten*
to degenerate (*here:*) to lead to; *ausarten*
rise to the majestic heights *zu majestätischen Höhen erheben*
to meet physical force with soul force to react to physical violence with non-violent action; *physischer Gewalt mit der Kraft der Seele begegnen*
militancy *Kampfgeist*
to engulf to overwhelm; *umgeben*
distrust *Misstrauen*
evidenced shown
destiny fate; *Schicksal*
tied up *verbunden*
inextricably bound inseparably linked; *eng verknüpft, untrennbar verbunden*

We cannot walk alone.

pledge promise

And as we walk, we must make the pledge that we shall always march ahead.

We cannot turn back.

devotee follower, supporter; *Anhänger*

There are those who are asking the devotees of civil rights, "When will you be satisfied?"

WE CAN NEVER BE SATISFIED
AS LONG AS THE NEGRO IS THE VICTIM

We can never be satisfied as long as the Negro is the victim of the unspeakable horrors of police brutality.

fatigue exhaustion

We can never be satisfied as long as our bodies, heavy with the fatigue of travel, cannot gain lodging in the motels of the highways and the hotels of the cities.

We cannot be satisfied as long as the Negro's basic mobility is from a smaller ghetto to a larger one.

stripped of their self-hood and robbed of their dignity *ihre Individualität genommen und ihrer Würde beraubt*
self-hood individuality, identity

We can never be satisfied as long as our children are stripped of their self-hood and robbed of their dignity by signs stating: "For Whites Only."

Cartoon by
Dave Granlund

... UNTIL JUSTICE ROLLS DOWN LIKE WATERS, AND RIGHTEOUSNESS LIKE A MIGHTY STREAM

We cannot be satisfied as long as a Negro in Mississippi cannot vote and a Negro in New York believes he has nothing for which to vote. No, no, we are not satisfied, and we will not be satisfied until "justice rolls down like waters, and righteousness like a mighty stream."

I am not unmindful that some of you have come here out of great trials and tribulations. Some of you have come fresh from narrow jail cells. And some of you have come from areas where your quest – quest for freedom – left you battered by the storms of persecution and staggered by the winds of police brutality. You have been the veterans of creative suffering. Continue to work with the faith that unearned suffering is redemptive.

Go back to Mississippi, go back to Alabama, go back to South Carolina, go back to Georgia, go back to Louisiana, go back to the slums and ghettos of our northern cities, knowing that somehow this situation can and will be changed.

Let us not wallow in the valley of despair, I say to you today, my friends.

I HAVE A DREAM ...

And so even though we face the difficulties of today and tomorrow, I still have a dream. It is a dream deeply rooted in the American dream. I have a dream that one day this nation will rise up and live out the true meaning of its creed: "We hold these truths to be self-evident, that all men are created equal."

I have a dream that one day on the red hills of Georgia, the sons of former slaves and the sons of former slave owners will be able to sit down together at the table of brotherhood.

I have a dream that one day even the state of Mississippi, a state sweltering with the heat of injustice, sweltering with the heat of oppression, will be transformed into an oasis of freedom and justice.

I have a dream that my four little children will one day live in a nation where they will not be judged by the color of their skin but by the content of their character.

I have a *dream* today!

righteousness justice, fairness, goodness

justice rolls down like waters, and righteousness like a mighty stream allusion to the Bible; Amos 5:24; *bis die Gerechtigkeit wie ein Gewässer und Rechtschaffenheit wie ein mächtiger Strom herunterquellen*

I am not unmindful I am not unaware

trials and tribulations *Irrungen und Wirrungen*

quest search; *Suche*

to batter to beat, to hit

persecution oppression; *Verfolgung*

staggered shocked

the winds of the effects of

suffering (*here:*) hardship, misery

faith belief

redemptive saving; *erlösend, befreiend*

Let us not wallow in the valley of despair (*here:*) let us not give up hope; *lasst uns nicht im Tal der Verzweiflung verharren*

to face the difficulties *sich den Schwierigkeiten stellen*

a dream deeply rooted in the American dream *ein Traum, der seine Wurzel tief im amerikanischen Traum hat*

creed belief; a reference to The Declaration of Independence

brotherhood *Gemeinschaft aller Menschen*

sweltering suffocating, burning; *umkommen*

sweltering with the heat of injustice ... [and] **oppression** (metaphorical:) *in der Hitze der Ungerechtigkeit und Unterdrückung umkommen*

LITTLE BLACK BOYS AND BLACK GIRLS WILL BE ABLE TO JOIN HANDS WITH LITTLE WHITE BOYS AND WHITE GIRLS AS SISTERS AND BROTHERS

vicious cruel, brutal
Governor a reference to George C. Wallace (1919 –1998), former Governor of Alabama, who is remembered for his pro-segregation position at the time
interposition *Einsprüche gegen die Aufhebung der Rassentrennung*
nullification *Nichtigkeitserklärung, Annulierung*

I have a dream that one day, down in Alabama, with its vicious racists, with its governor having his lips dripping with the words of "interposition" and "nullification" – one day right there in Alabama little black boys and black girls will be able to join hands with little white boys and white girls as sisters and brothers.

I have a *dream* today!

exalted *erhöht*
Isaiah 40:4-5:
"Every valley shall be raised up, every mountain and hill made low …"

I have a dream that one day every valley shall be exalted, and every hill and mountain shall be made low, the rough places will be made plain, and the crooked places will be made straight; "and the glory of the Lord shall be revealed and all flesh shall see it together."

This is our hope, and this is the faith that I go back to the South with.

STAND UP FOR FREEDOM TOGETHER, KNOWING THAT WE WILL BE FREE ONE DAY

to hew out to carve out; *herausmeißeln*
jangling discords *schrille Zwietracht*

With this faith, we will be able to hew out of the mountain of despair a stone of hope. With this faith, we will be able to transform the jangling discords of our nation into a beautiful symphony of brotherhood. With this faith, we will be able to work together, to pray together, to struggle together, to go to jail together, to stand up for freedom together, knowing that we will be free one day.

And this will be the day – this will be the day when all of God's children will be able to sing with new meaning:

"My Country, 'Tis of Thee" a famous, patriotic American song

My country 'tis of thee, sweet land of liberty, of thee I sing.
Land where my fathers died, land of the Pilgrim's pride,
From every mountainside, let freedom ring!

LET FREEDOM RING!

prodigious (*here:*) vast; *gewaltig*
curvaceous round

And if America is to be a great nation, this must become true.
And so let freedom ring from the prodigious hilltops of New Hampshire.
Let freedom ring from the mighty mountains of New York.
Let freedom ring from the heightening Alleghenies of Pennsylvania.
Let freedom ring from the snow-capped Rockies of Colorado.
Let freedom ring from the curvaceous slopes of California
But not only that:
Let freedom ring from Stone Mountain of Georgia.
Let freedom ring from Lookout Mountain of Tennessee.

Let freedom ring from every hill and molehill of Mississippi.
From every mountainside, let freedom ring.

And when this happens, and when we allow freedom to ring, when we let it ring from every village and every hamlet, from every state and every city, we will be able to speed up that day when *all* of God's children, black men and white men, Jews and Gentiles, Protestants and Catholics, will be able to join hands and sing in the words of the old Negro spiritual:

hamlet a small village

Gentiles non-Jewish people

Free at last! Free at last!

Thank God Almighty, we are free at last!

Audio Source: Linked directly to: http://www.archive.org/details/MLKDream
External Link: *The King Center* http://www.thekingcenter.org/
American Rhetoric:
http://www.americanrhetoric.com/speeches/mlkihaveadream.htm

ASSIGNMENTS

A) Pre-Listening and Pre-Reading Activity

▶ *warm-up speech training: "I have a dream" / market place or inside-outside circle / feedback*

Before you start listening to and reading Martin Luther King Jr.'s "I Have a Dream" speech, please prepare and give a short speech to your partner about:

1. your own personal dreams for the future (*one minute*),
2. your dreams for the future of the world (*one minute*),
3. what you already know about Martin Luther King Jr. (*one minute*).

Then give each other some feedback (*one minute*).

B) Comprehension

▶ *SQ3R / interactive classroom using laptops or tablets / peer support and feedback / presentation*

1. Watch Martin Luther King Jr.'s speech and highlight important keywords and phrases in your speech transcript: https://www.youtube.com/watch?v=I47Y6VHc3Ms
2. Outline his main thoughts about the application of the American Dream to black people in the USA in the 1960s.
3. What is Martin Luther King Jr.'s suggestion of how best to resist police violence? How does he suggest that black people should react to injustice and violence?
4. "The marvelous new militancy which has engulfed the Negro community must not lead us to a distrust of all white people, for many of our white brothers, as evidenced by their presence here today, have come to realize that their destiny is tied up with our destiny. And they have come to realize that their freedom is inextricably bound to our freedom." What does Martin Luther King Jr. point out here?
5. Summarise the key message of the speech.

C) Analysis

▶ *paired work / group work / share ideas / using laptops / presenting results / evaluation*

1. Divide the speech into two sections and give a suitable heading to each section.
2. Analyse the structure of Martin Luther King Jr.'s speech in detail.
3. Watch the video and analyse Martin Luther King Jr.'s body language and tone of voice.
4. Analyse the rhetorical devices he uses. Make a list of rhetorical devices, note down some examples of them, then point out their intended effects. You may start with a detailed analysis of the introductory paragraphs of Martin Luther King's speech. Here are some ideas to start off with:

Rhetorical Devices	Examples	Intended Effects
superlative	*"the greatest demonstration for freedom"*	to emphasise the significance of this event (the 1963 March on Washington)
repetition	*"One hundred years later" (used four times in the third paragraph)*	even after such a long period of time, the discrimination and segregation of black people have not stopped and are still going on
metaphors	*"a great American, in whose symbolic shadow we stand today"* *"a great beacon light of hope"* *"crippled by the manacles of segregation"* *"the chains of discrimination"*	a reference to Abraham Lincoln, who tried to abolish slavery and to stop racism, discrimination and segregation / this metaphor emphasises confidence, hope, optimism for a better future and a fairer society / these metaphors emphasise that black people are still treated like criminals; they describe the cruel treatment and oppression black people experienced at that time
contrast	*"a lonely island of poverty in the midst of a vast ocean of material prosperity"*	the contrast (poverty vs. prosperity) signifies social injustice

5. Do not forget to analyse the following rhetorical devices: repetition / alliteration / the use of contrast / metaphor (such as the pay-check metaphor) / religious allusions / strong appeals etc.
6. Analyse Martin Luther King's assessment of the social and political situation in 1960s America.
   a) First of all, decide on and write down any relevant quotations in the middle column.
   b) Then list the rhetorical devices in each quotation in the left-hand column.
   c) Analyse the rhetorical devices' intended effects in the right-hand column.
7. "Let us not wallow in the valley of despair, I say to you today, my friends."
   At this point, Martin Luther King Jr. may have intended to end his speech. But gospel singer Mahalia Jackson, who was on stage with Martin Luther King Jr., called out: "Tell them about the dream, Martin. Tell them about the dream." Encouraged by shouts from the audience, he pushed his notes aside and improvised the most memorable section of the speech. From: *https://www.history.com/this-day-in-history/mahalia-jackson-the-queen-of-gospel-puts-her-stamp-on-the-march-on-washington (accessed: April 30, 2019)*
8. Analyse the final section of Martin Luther King Jr.'s speech and the inspiring impact of his personal message.

D) Evaluation, Comment and Creative Writing

▶ *flipped classroom / cooperative learning / paired work / group work / mind map / using laptops / multimedia presentation / whiteboard or smartboard / discussion / evaluation / speech training*

1. Evaluate the **significance of** Martin Luther King Jr.'s role in the civil rights movement.
2. Evaluate the enduring significance/impact of Martin Luther King Jr.'s speech in the context of the **current** political and social situation in the USA.

3. Choose one of the most significant statements from Martin Luther King's speech.
   a) Firstly, evaluate and discuss it. Then explain why you have chosen it.
   b) Give a three-minute speech on the significance of this statement today.
4. How can we make Martin Luther King Jr.'s dream a reality across the world today?
5. **Senator Bernie Sanders: "Our diversity is one of our greatest strengths."**
   The following statements are taken from a speech delivered by Senator Bernie Sanders on the first night of the 2016 Democratic National Convention in Philadelphia, Pennsylvania:
   "Our diversity is one of our greatest strengths. Yes, we become stronger when black and white, Latino, Asian American and Native American people stand together, when all of us stand together. Yes, we become stronger when men and women, young and old, gay and straight, native-born and immigrant, fight together to create the kind of country we all know we can become." Write an email to Bernie Sanders in response to his speech.
   From: *The Washington Post*, July 26, 2016
   https://www.washingtonpost.com/news/post-politics/wp/2016/07/26/transcript-bernie-sanderss-full-speech-at-the-2016-dnc/?utm_term=.92863773c876
6. **Martin Luther King Day** is a federal holiday in the USA, held on the third Monday in January each year. It celebrates the life and achievements of Martin Luther King Jr., the American civil rights leader. Imagine that you have been invited to give a speech at a partner school in the USA on the next Martin Luther King Day. Prepare a speech in which you evaluate Martin Luther King's social and political ideas and their enduring significance for the world today. Practise your five-minute speech in class.
7. Go online and study the Nobel Prize lesson "Martin Luther King Jr. and the civil rights movement".
   https://www.nobelprize.org/nobel-prize-lessons-theme-martin-luther-king-jr-and-the-civil-rights-movement/

E) Martin Luther King Jr. – Cartoons by Dave Granlund

Tasks:

1. Take a closer look at the three cartoons on pages 58, 60 and 65: What do they depict? Describe all the elements of the cartoons in detail and suggest how the three cartoons might be connected.
2. Analyse the cartoons' messages and the cartoonist's intentions. Explain what the cartoonist wants to express through this series of cartoons by examining the relationship between the three cartoons, as well as their historical and political context.
3. Now link the cartoons to Martin Luther King's "I Have a Dream" speech.

F) Mediation *(German = > English)*

Please summarise the most important arguments from the following article in English, then send your summary to a class at your English-speaking partner school.
Erinnerung an einen Traum «I Have a Dream» – die Rede, die ganz anders geplant war
Von Franz Kaspersk, Schweizer Radio und Fernsehen (SRF), Dienstag, 4. April 2017
https://www.srf.ch/kultur/im-fokus/der-archivar/i-have-a-dream-die-rede-die-ganz-anders-geplant-war

G) Further Project: Mahatma Gandhi and Martin Luther King Jr.

Mahatma Gandhi (1869 – 1948) was the leader of India's non-violent independence movement, which forced the British to grant India its independence. Martin Luther King Jr. was a great admirer of Mahatma Gandhi, and of his belief in non-violent protest as a means of bringing about social change. He implemented many of Gandhi's non-violent tactics into the fight for civil rights in the USA. Martin Luther King Jr. said the following about the impact of Gandhi's teachings on the American civil rights movement: "This principle became the guiding light of our movement. Christ furnished the spirit and motivation while Gandhi furnished the method."
Martin Luther King: Pilgrimage to Nonviolence, April 13, 1960, page 423
http://okra.stanford.edu/transcription/document_images/Vol05Scans/13Apr1960_PilgrimagetoNonviolence.pdf

Task: Evaluate the impact of Gandhi's teachings on Martin Luther King Jr., and on the American civil rights movement.

H) The song "One Day" by Bakermat: https://www.youtube.com/watch?v=40Cc0Yu1weY

1. Which core aspects of Martin Luther King Jr.'s original speech does the DJ cover in his song?
2. Which features make the song successful?
3. Do you think this song would make young people more interested in studying Martin Luther King Jr. and the American civil rights movement?
4. Write and perform a new song inspired by Martin Luther King Jr.'s speech. Making cross-curricular connections with your Music and Drama classes is recommended.
5. Create a short story / a play / an audio or a video clip / a multimedia presentation about the worldwide significance of Civil Rights and Human Rights today.

I) Further Research: For Thought and Discussion

1. **"How Martin Luther King Jr.'s Civil Rights Movement still affects us today"** by Peniel E. Joseph, The Washington Post, January 15, 2018 https://www.washingtonpost.com/news/post-nation/wp/2018/01/15/kings-assassination-shaped-americas-identity-50-years-ago-and-continues-to-shape-it-today/?utm_term=.33a03e6237d7 (July 16, 2018)
2. **"Dr. King Today: Dr. King's Importance to the 21st Century"** Source: *The King Center* http://thekingcenter.org (July 16, 2018)
3. **The day Martin Luther King Jr. died:** Listen to *The Washington Post* "Cape Up" podcast series by Jonathan Capehart, April 4, 2019 https://www.washingtonpost.com/opinions/2019/04/04/day-martin-luther-king-jr-died-voices-movement-episode/?utm_term=.a391d3ddd44c
4. **"UNANTASTBAR – Der Kampf für Menschenrechte":** An excellent documentary about Human Rights produced by Angela Andersen and Claus Kleber. Watch the video here: https://www.zdf.de/dokumentation/zdfzeit/unantastbar-menschenrechte-100.html (December 20, 2018)

"Martin Luther King Was Shot and Killed Tonight."

Senator Robert F. Kennedy: Statement on the Assassination of Martin Luther King Jr., in Indianapolis, Indiana, on April 4, 1968

RELATED TOPICS

THE AMERICAN DREAM · THE CIVIL RIGHTS MOVEMENT · DECLARATION OF INDEPENDENCE · DIGNITY · THE FOUNDING CREED · FREEDOM · FUTURE GENERATIONS · HISTORY · HUMAN RIGHTS · INEQUALITY · INJUSTICE · LIBERTY · NON-VIOLENCE · RACE RELATIONS · SEGREGATION · SOCIAL SECURITY · UNALIENABLE RIGHTS

Robert F. 'Bobby' Kennedy was the brother of former U.S. President John F. Kennedy, and the leading Democratic candidate in the 1968 election. He was scheduled to make a routine tour stop in Indianapolis on April 4 when he heard about Martin Luther King Jr.'s death. Martin Luther King Jr., the figurehead of the civil rights movement, was shot and killed on April 4, 1968 in Memphis, Tennessee.

Journalist Will Higgins gives the following account of what happened: "Every April 4, several hundred residents of Indianapolis gather at 17th and Broadway Streets to remember what happened there in 1968.

It was the day Robert F. Kennedy likely saved Indianapolis, a story told less often. He was popular among the black community, and in an effort to get more black people to register to vote, he wanted to speak in the heart of Indianapolis's inner-city. Shortly before his speech, as Kennedy's plane landed in Indianapolis, the senator from New York learned that Martin Luther King Jr. had been assassinated. Indianapolis's Mayor Richard Lugar, fearing a race riot, told Kennedy's staff that his city's police officers could not guarantee Kennedy's safety at 17th and Broadway. Lugar urged Kennedy to cancel his speech. But Kennedy insisted that he and his team carried on alone, without a police escort. The audience in Indianapolis was estimated to be only around 2,500 people, but they were influencers, members of young, somewhat radical black groups like the College Room, the Watoto Wa Simba, the Black Panthers and the Black Radical Action Project.

Kennedy arrived at around 9 pm. He knew more than his audience knew – he knew Dr. King was dead. He stood on a flat bed truck, faced the crowd and told them the news. The crowd gasped in shock. With practically no time to prepare – he had come straight from the airport – and speaking off the cuff, Kennedy broke the news with such compassion and empathy that when he had finished many people in the crowd departed saddened though not hateful and, in at least one notable case, with renewed resolve to make the world a better place. Kennedy talked for just five minutes, yet people who study speeches consider his to be among history's greatest speeches. When he had finished, the crowd surged towards him and tried to touch him, and when he drove off they left feeling mournful, not vengeful. Some were changed forever. Robert Kennedy went on to win the Indiana Democratic primary. He was assassinated two months later in California."

By Will Higgins, Indy Star, Part of the USA Today Network, Indiana. Published March 30, 2018
http://www.indystar.com/story/life/2015/04/02/april-rfk-saved-indianapolis/70817218/

Robert F. Kennedy:

I have bad news for you, for all of our fellow citizens, and people who love peace all over the world, and that is that Martin Luther King was shot and killed tonight.

Martin Luther King dedicated his life to love and to justice for his fellow human beings, and he died because of that effort.

In this difficult day, in this difficult time for the United States, it is perhaps well to ask what kind of a nation we are and what direction we want to move in. For those of you who are black – considering the evidence that white people were responsible – you can be filled with bitterness, with hatred, and a desire for revenge. We can move in that direction as a country, in great polarization – black people amongst black, white people amongst white, filled with hatred toward one another.

evidence proof
revenge vengeance; *Rache*
polarization (*AmE*), polarisation (*BrE*); *Polarisierung*

Or we can make an effort, as Martin Luther King did, to understand and to comprehend, and to replace that violence, that stain of bloodshed that has spread across our land, with an effort to understand with compassion and love.

stain of bloodshed (*metaphorical:*) *Makel des Blutvergießens*

For those of you who are black and are tempted to be filled with hatred and distrust at the injustice of such an act, against all white people, I can only say that I feel in my own heart the same kind of feeling. I had a member of my family killed, but he was killed by a white man. But we have to make an effort in the United States, we have to make an effort to understand, to go beyond these rather difficult times.

My favorite poet was Aeschylus. He wrote:

I had a member of my family killed a reference to his brother, John F. Kennedy, the former U.S. President, who was assassinated on November 22, 1963 in Dallas, Texas
Aeschylus an Ancient Greek playwright (525 – 455 BC) who is often considered to be the father of tragedy

"In our sleep, pain which cannot forget

falls drop by drop upon the heart

until, in our own despair,

against our will,

comes wisdom

through the awful grace of God."

What we need in the United States is not division; what we need in the United States is not hatred; what we need in the United States is not violence or lawlessness; but love and wisdom, and compassion toward one another, and a feeling of justice toward those who still suffer within our country, whether they be white or they be black.

So I shall ask you tonight to return home, to say a prayer for the family of Martin Luther King, that's true, but more importantly to say a prayer for our own country, which all of us love – a prayer for understanding and that compassion of which I spoke.

compassion empathy, kindness; *Mitgefühl*

We can do well in this country. We will have difficult times; we've had difficult times in the past; we will have difficult times in the future. It is not the end of violence; it is not the end of lawlessness; it is not the end of disorder.

lawlessness *Gesetzlosigkeit*

But the vast majority of white people and the vast majority of black people in this country want to live together, want to improve the quality of our life, and want justice for all human beings who abide in our land.

to abide to live

Let us dedicate ourselves to what the Greeks wrote so many years ago: to tame the savageness of man and make gentle the life of this world.

to tame *bändigen*
savageness inhumanity, viciousness; *Barbarei*

Let us dedicate ourselves to that, and say a prayer for our country and for our people.

to dedicate ourselves to to commit ourselves to; *sich zur Aufgabe machen*

The speech transcript is taken from: *John F. Kennedy, Presidential Library and Museum* https://www.jfklibrary.org/learn/about-jfk/the-kennedy-family/robert-f-kennedy-speeches/statement-on-assassination-of-martin-luther-king-jr-indianapolis-indiana-april-4-1968

ASSIGNMENTS

A) Reading and Listening Comprehension

▶ *reading and listening for gist and for detail / kwl reading method / group work / peer feedback / presentation / writing a summary / collaboration with History class / cross-curricular connections*

1. Listen to Robert F. Kennedy's speech, and read along using your speech transcript. https://www.jfklibrary.org/Research/Research-Aids/Ready-Reference/RFK-Speeches/Statement-on-the-Assassination-of-Martin-Luther-King.aspx
2. Watch the video: https://www.youtube.com/watch?v=zuv0TR79Fhc and listen to the audio: https://www.jfklibrary.org/asset-viewer/statement-on-the-death-of-martin-luther-king-jr-april4-1968
3. When Kennedy informs the people of the devastating news of Martin Luther King Jr.'s assassination, how do they react?
4. April 4, 1968: "How RFK saved Indianapolis" by Will Higgins.
   Read the background information on page 67. How did Kennedy manage to prevent the situation from getting completely out of control in Indianapolis?
5. Highlight the keywords in your speech transcript.

6. Kennedy talks about how Martin Luther King Jr. dedicated his life to promoting love, peace, and justice among his fellow human beings. Summarise what he considers to have been Martin Luther King Jr.'s achievements.
7. Sum up what Kennedy believes to be the USA's basic values, and what problems American society was confronted with when he made his speech.

B) Analysis

independent learning / interactive classroom / group work / peer support and feedback / writing conference / laptop, tablet presentation / discussion / speaking and writing skills training / podcast

1. Analyse the structure of Robert F. Kennedy's speech.
2. How does Kennedy start his speech?
3. Despite the fact that Kennedy had very little time to prepare his speech, he still uses some rhetorical devices to get his message across. Give some examples and explain why he uses them.
4. How does Kennedy try to prevent hatred, revenge and racial conflict, and how does he manage to achieve a more peaceful and thoughtful reaction from his audience, as well as encouraging them to embrace empathy, wisdom and compassion?
5. How does Kennedy appeal to the audience's emotions?
6. Which events does he encourage them to remember, and why?
7. Kennedy recognises that his audience members might turn to violence because they could be "filled with hatred and distrust" because of Martin Luther King Jr.'s death. How does he caution them against this response?
8. Analyse the significance of the poem by Ancient Greek playwright Aeschylus in the wider context of the speech.
9. Why does Kennedy refer to his brother John F. Kennedy's assassination in his speech?
10. Analyse Kennedy's final appeal to the audience.

C) Evaluation, Comment, Creative Activity

individual work / group work / creative writing / peer support and feedback / speech / discussion

1. Evaluate the significance of Robert F. Kennedy's speech.
2. Kennedy emphasises the following question: "What kind of a nation are we and what direction do we want to move in?"
   a) Write an article for an American newspaper about the current political situation in the USA.
   b) Prepare and give a four-minute speech in response to Kennedy's question. Bear in mind the current social and political problems in the USA, in Germany, and in the European Union.

D) Further Projects for Thought and Discussion

1. The late South African president, Nelson Mandela, said: "No one is born hating another person because of the color of his skin or his background or his religion."
   Respond to this statement by writing an article or giving a short speech.
2. Former Vice President Joe Biden says America has to "turn off this hate machine" after authorities intercepted two mail bombs addressed to him. "We gotta turn off this hate machine. We gotta come together. The American public, all over the nation, people want us to be more civil. People want us to choose hope over hate. People understand that words matter. And our children are listening."
   From: *The Buffalo News*, October 26, 2018
   https://buffalonews.com/2018/10/25/joe-biden-campaigns-nathan-mcmurray-lancaster-restaurant/

“Yes We Can!”

Barack Obama’s Victory Speech delivered in Chicago, Illinois on November 5, 2008

RELATED TOPICS

THE AMERICAN DREAM · CHALLENGES · CHANGE · THE CONSTITUTION · CREED · THE DECLARATION OF INDEPENDENCE · DEMOCRACY · DIGNITY · THE EARTH IN DANGER · FAMILY · THE FOUNDING CREED · FREEDOM · FRIENDS · FUTURE GENERATIONS · GOD · THE GOVERNMENT · HISTORY · HOPE · HUMAN RIGHTS · IDEALS · INEQUALITY · INJUSTICE · JUSTICE · LEADERSHIP · LIBERTY · NATIONHOOD · OPPORTUNITY · PATRIOTISM · PEACE · RACE RELATIONS · THE RIGHT TO VOTE · SEGREGATION · SOCIAL SECURITY · UNALIENABLE RIGHTS · VALUES

Barack Obama:
In November 2008, Barack Obama was elected President of the United States.
He was the 44th President of the United States and the first African American to hold the position.
He was born on August 4, 1961, in Honolulu, Hawaii.
Obama previously served as Senator of Illinois.
He is a member of the Democratic Party.
He gave his famous victory speech at Grant Park in his home city of Chicago, Illinois on November 5, 2008.

From: https://abcnews.go.com/Politics/Vote2008/story?id=6181477&page=1

Section 1: group 1 and group 4 / give this section an appropriate heading: ____________________________________

THE PRESIDENT Barack Obama:

Hello, Chicago.

If there is anyone out there who still doubts that America is a place where all things are possible; who still wonders if the dream of our founders is alive in our time; who still questions the power of our democracy, tonight is your answer.

It's the answer told by lines that stretched around schools and churches in numbers this nation has never seen; by people who waited three hours and four hours, many for the very first time in their lives, because they believed that this time must be different; that their voice could be that difference.

Native American *amerikanische/r Ureinwohner/in*
straight heterosexual
disabled *Behinderte*

It's the answer spoken by young and old, rich and poor, Democrat and Republican, black and white, Latino, Asian, and Native American, gay and straight, disabled and non-disabled – Americans who sent a message to the world that we have never been a collection of Red States and Blue States: we are, and always will be, the United States of America.

cynical scornful; *zynisch*
to bend the arc of history *den Verlauf der Geschichte ändern*

It's the answer that led those who have been told for so long by so many to be cynical, and fearful, and doubtful of what we can achieve to put their hands on the arc of history and bend it once more toward the hope of a better day.

It's been a long time coming, but tonight, because of what we did on this day, in this election, at this defining moment, change has come to America.

Senator John McCain the Republican candidate in the 2008 U.S. presidential election; he died on August 25, 2018
he has endured sacrifices er hat *Opfer gebracht*
to render a service *einen Dienst leisten*
selfless *selbstlos*
Governor Sarah Palin the Republican candidate for the role of Vice President of the United States in the 2008 election

I just received a very gracious call from Senator McCain. He fought long and hard in this campaign, and he's fought even longer and harder for the country he loves. He has endured sacrifices for America that most of us cannot begin to imagine, and we are better off for the service rendered by this brave and selfless leader. I congratulate him and Governor Palin for all they have achieved, and I look forward to working with them to renew this nation's promise in the months ahead.

I want to thank my partner in this journey, a man who campaigned from his heart and spoke for the men and women he grew up with on the streets of Scranton and rode with on that train home to Delaware, the Vice President-elect of the United States, Joe Biden.

unyielding support *unablässige Unterstützung*

I know that my debt to them is beyond measure *ich weiß, dass ich ihnen unermesslich viel verdanke*

I would not be standing here tonight without the unyielding support of my best friend for the last sixteen years, the rock of our family and the love of my life, our nation's next First Lady, Michelle Obama. Sasha and Malia, I love you both so much, and you have earned the new puppy that's coming with us to the White House. And while she's no longer with us, I know my grandmother is watching, along with the family that made me who I am. I miss them tonight, and know that my debt to them is beyond measure.

To my campaign manager David Plouffe, my chief strategist David Axelrod, and the best campaign team ever assembled in the history of politics – you made this happen, and I am forever grateful for what you've sacrificed to get it done.

But above all, I will never forget who this victory truly belongs to – it belongs to you.

I was never the likeliest candidate for this office. We didn't start with much money or many endorsements. Our campaign was not hatched in the halls of Washington – it began in the backyards of Des Moines, and the living rooms of Concord, and the front porches of Charleston.

It was built by working men and women who dug into what little savings they had to give five dollars, and ten dollars, and twenty dollars to this cause. It grew strength from the young people who rejected the myth of their generation's apathy; who left their homes and their families for jobs that offered little pay and less sleep; from the not-so-young people who braved the bitter cold and scorching heat to knock on the doors of perfect strangers; from the millions of Americans who volunteered, and organized, and proved that more than two centuries later, a government of the people, by the people and for the people has not perished from this Earth. This is your victory.

I was never the likeliest candidate for this office *es war äußerst unwahrscheinlich, dass jemand wie ich ein solches Amt erreichen könnte*
many endorsements much backing, support
hatched started
backyards *Hinterhöfe*
front porches *Veranden*
who dug into what little savings they had *die auf ihre kleinen Ersparnisse zurückgriffen*
young people who rejected the myth of their generation's apathy *junge Menschen, die den Mythos der Apathie ihrer Generation ablehnten*
who braved the bitter cold and scorching heat *die der eisigen Kälte und sengenden Hitze trotzten*
to perish to disappear

Section 2: group 2 and group 5 / give this section an appropriate heading: ________________________________

I know you didn't do this just to win an election and I know you didn't do it for me. You did it because you understand the enormity of the task that lies ahead. For even as we celebrate tonight, we know the challenges that tomorrow will bring are the greatest of our lifetime – two wars, a planet in peril, the worst financial crisis in a century. Even as we stand here tonight, we know there are brave Americans waking up in the deserts of Iraq and the mountains of Afghanistan to risk their lives for us. There are mothers and fathers who will lie awake after their children fall asleep and wonder how they'll make the mortgage, or pay their doctor's bills, or save enough for college. There is new energy to harness and new jobs to be created; new schools to build and threats to meet and alliances to repair.

in peril in danger
mortgage home-owners' loan; *Hypothek*
to harness to make use of; *nutzbar machen*
threats to meet and alliances to repair *Bedrohungen müssen angegangen und Bündnisse wiederhergestellt werden*

The road ahead will be long. Our climb will be steep. We may not get there in one year or even one term, but America – I have never been more hopeful than I am tonight that we will get there. I promise you – we as a people will get there.

There will be setbacks and false starts. There are many who won't agree with every decision or policy I make as President, and we know that government can't solve every problem. But I will always be hon-

challenges problems; *Herausforderungen*

brick by brick, calloused hand by calloused hand *Stein um Stein, Handgriff um Handgriff*
calloused hand *schwielige Hand*

to summon to call for
to resolve to to decide to
to pitch in to contribute; *sich beteiligen*
thriving booming
Wall Street the financial district in Lower Manhattan, New York
Main Street suffers see ADDITIONAL NOTES

temptation *Versuchung*
partisanship one-sidedness; *Parteilichkeit*
pettiness *Kleinlichkeit*
immaturity childishness; *Unreife*

self-reliance independence; *Eigenständigkeit*
humility modesty; *Bescheidenheit*
determination *Entschlossenheit*
to heal the divides *das Trennende überwinden*
though passion may have strained them, it must not break our bonds of affection *obwohl Auseinandersetzungen unser Band der Wertschätzung strapaziert haben, dürfen sie es nicht zerreißen*

a new dawn of American leadership is at hand a new beginning for American leadership is about to start

beacon light; *Leuchtfeuer*

enduring lasting
unyielding hope unwavering hope; *unbeirrbare Hoffnung*

est with you about the challenges we face. I will listen to you, especially when we disagree.

And above all, I will ask you join in the work of remaking this nation the only way it's been done in America for two-hundred and twenty-one years – block by block, brick by brick, calloused hand by calloused hand.

What began twenty-one months ago in the depths of winter must not end on this autumn night. This victory alone is not the change we seek – it is only the chance for us to make that change. And that cannot happen if we go back to the way things were. It cannot happen without you.

So let us summon a new spirit of patriotism; of service and responsibility where each of us resolves to pitch in and work harder and look after not only ourselves, but each other. Let us remember that if this financial crisis taught us anything, it's that we cannot have a thriving Wall Street while Main Street suffers – in this country, we rise or fall as one nation; as one people.

Let us resist the temptation to fall back on the same partisanship and pettiness and immaturity that has poisoned our politics for so long. Let us remember that it was a man from this state who first carried the banner of the Republican Party to the White House – a party founded on the values of self-reliance, individual liberty, and national unity. Those are values we all share, and while the Democratic Party has won a great victory tonight, we do so with a measure of humility and determination to heal the divides that have held back our progress. As Lincoln said to a nation far more divided than ours: "We are not enemies, but friends ... though passion may have strained them, it must not break our bonds of affection." And to those Americans whose support I have yet to earn – I may not have won your vote, but I hear your voices, I need your help, and I will be your President too.

And to all those watching tonight from beyond our shores, from parliaments and palaces to those who are huddled around radios in the forgotten corners of our world – our stories are singular, but our destiny is shared, and a new dawn of American leadership is at hand. To those who would tear this world down – we will defeat you. To those who seek peace and security – we support you. And to all those who have wondered if America's beacon still burns as bright – tonight we proved once more that the true strength of our nation comes not from the might of our arms or the scale of our wealth, but from the enduring power of our ideals: democracy, liberty, opportunity, and unyielding hope.

For that is the true genius of America – that America can change. Our union can be perfected. And what we have already achieved gives us hope for what we can and must achieve tomorrow.

Section 3: group 3 and group 6 / give this section an appropriate heading: ____________________________

This election had many firsts and many stories that will be told for generations. But one that's on my mind tonight is about a woman who cast her ballot in Atlanta. She's a lot like the millions of others who stood in line to make their voice heard in this election except for one thing – Ann Nixon Cooper is 106 years old.

She was born just a generation past slavery; a time when there were no cars on the road or planes in the sky; when someone like her couldn't vote for two reasons – because she was a woman and because of the color of her skin.

And tonight, I think about all that she's seen throughout her century in America – the heartache and the hope; the struggle and the progress; the times we were told that we can't, and the people who pressed on with that American creed:

Yes, we can!

At a time when women's voices were silenced and their hopes dismissed, she lived to see them stand up and speak out and reach for the ballot.

Yes, we can!

When there was despair in the dust bowl and depression across the land, she saw a nation conquer fear itself with a New Deal, new jobs and a new sense of common purpose.

Yes, we can!

When the bombs fell on our harbor and tyranny threatened the world, she was there to witness a generation rise to greatness and a democracy was saved.

Yes, we can!

She was there for the buses in Montgomery, the hoses in Birmingham, a bridge in Selma, and a preacher from Atlanta who told a people that "We Shall Overcome".

many firsts *viele Premieren*

she cast her ballot she voted

creed belief

women's voices ... reach for the ballot in 1920, under the *Nineteenth Amendment to the Constitution of the United States*, women obtained the right to vote

The New Deal the domestic program of the administration of U.S. President Franklin D. Roosevelt between 1933 and 1939; *see Additional Notes*

The Pearl Harbor attack the surprise aerial attack on the U.S. naval base at Pearl Harbor by Japanese forces during the Second World War; *see Additional Notes*

tyranny threatened the world a reference to multiple dictatorships which threatened the world, such as Nazi Germany and Soviet Russia

to witness to see for oneself; *Zeitzeuge sein*

the Montgomery bus boycott a mass protest against the segregated bus system in Montgomery, Alabama, by civil rights activists; *see Additional Notes*

hoses (*here:*) *Wasserwerfer*

hoses in Birmingham during the 1960s, Birmingham was the location of violent protests over racial segregation; *see Additional Notes*

a bridge in Selma Selma was the location of the "Bloody Sunday"-conflict on March 7, 1965; *see Additional Notes*

a preacher from Atlanta a reference to Martin Luther King Jr.

Yes, we can!

a man touched down on the moon *see* ADDITIONAL NOTES

to reclaim to regain, to get back

cynicism disbelief; *Zweifel, Zynismus*

A man touched down on the moon, a wall came down in Berlin, a world was connected by our own science and imagination. And this year, in this election, she touched her finger to a screen, and cast her vote, because after 106 years in America, through the best of times and the darkest of hours, she knows how America can change.

Yes, we can!

America, we have come so far. We have seen so much. But there is so much more to do. So tonight, let us ask ourselves – if our children should live to see the next century; if my daughters should be so lucky to live as long as Ann Nixon Cooper, what change will they see? What progress will we have made?

This is our chance to answer that call. This is our moment. This is our time – to put our people back to work and open doors of opportunity for our kids; to restore prosperity and promote the cause of peace; to reclaim the American Dream and reaffirm that fundamental truth – that out of many, we are one; that while we breathe, we hope, and where we are met with cynicism, and doubt, and those who tell us that we can't, we will respond with that timeless creed that sums up the spirit of a people:

Yes, we can! Thank you, God bless you, and may God Bless the United States of America.

ASSIGNMENTS

A) Pre-Listening and Pre-Reading Activities

interactive classroom / inspiration cards or placemats: "Yes, I can!" & "Yes, we can!" / brainstorming / inside – outside circle / paired work / mind mapping / chain technique: comment chain / speech competition / poetry slam

1. 1. "Yes, I can!" Write down some things that you have already achieved successfully, or that you can achieve in the future. You may use a set of inspiration cards. Each idea should be noted on a separate card. Share ideas with your partner.
2. What do you associate with Barack Obama's slogan: "Yes, we can!"? Share your ideas with other members of your English class. Make sure every group member's ideas are included in a mind map or placemat.
3. Present your mind map or placemat to the class and a) start a discussion on important ideas and concepts, or b) start a one-minute "Yes, We Can" speech competition.

B) Reading and Listening Comprehension

jigsaw activity / Divide the class into groups. Give each group a section of the speech to analyse. Each group must then present their section to the rest of the class, and must teach each other to get a complete overview of the whole speech. / writing a news report

1. Watch Barack Obama's speech and highlight what he says about the following aspects in your speech transcript: a) the United States and the power of democracy, b) his electoral victory, c) the challenges the nation has to confront, d) the power of the ideals guiding American society, e) the historical achievements Ann Nixon Cooper witnessed and f) any other significant ideas.
2. Imagine you are a journalist for a British newspaper. Write a news report about Obama's speech.

C) Analysis

1. Analyse the structure of the speech.
2. Analyse some of the rhetorical devices used as well as their intended effects and message. List your results in a table and present it to the class. You can find some examples of rhetorical devices on pages 297–301 of this textbook.

Quotation	Rhetorical Device	Intended Effects and Message
[...]	[...]	[...]

D) For Thought and Discussion: Evaluation, Comment, Creative Activities

WebQuest / research / tablet / writing conference / presentation / interview / discussion / speech

1. Compare Barack Obama's victory speech to Donald Trump's Inaugural Address.
2. In his Gettysburg Address, Abraham Lincoln said that: "that government of the people, by the people, for the people, *shall not perish* from the earth." In his victory speech, Barack Obama emphasised that: "a government of the people, by the people and for the people *has not perished* from this Earth." Discuss and evaluate the significance of Barack Obama's reference to Abraham Lincoln's words.
3. Write an essay or give a speech in which you compare Martin Luther King Jr.'s "I Have a Dream" speech to Barack Obama's "Yes, We Can!" victory speech.
4. Imagine that you have been given the opportunity to interview Barack Obama. Based on your knowledge of his two terms in office, ask him about his achievements as president, his goals now he is no longer president, and his hopes for the future.
5. "Yes, we can!": Prepare and give a three-minute speech to encourage your classmates to take part in an important project of your choice.
6. Barack Obama: "I see Americans of every party, every background, every faith who believe that we are stronger together: black, white, Latino, Asian, Native American; young, old; gay, straight; men, women, folks with disabilities, all pledging allegiance under the same proud flag to this big, bold country that we love. That's what I see. That's the America I know!"
   From: *President Obama's Speech At The Democratic Convention, July 28, 2016* – Source: *Obama White House Archives* https://obamawhitehouse.archives.gov/the-press-office/2016/07/28/remarks-president-democratic-national-convention
7. Produce a "Yes, We Can" or "Yes, I Can" video clip or a podcast that illustrates a significant moment of your personal experience.
8. Research one of the following topics: Barack Obama's upbringing, his education, his work before becoming president, his work as president, or his current goals, now he is no longer president. Present your findings to the class.

C War and Peace

"The Gettysburg Address."

President Abraham Lincoln: The Gettysburg Address, on November 19, 1863

RELATED TOPICS

THE AMERICAN DREAM · AMERICAN CIVIL WAR · THE DECLARATION OF INDEPENDENCE · DEMOCRACY · THE FOUNDING CREED · FREEDOM · FUTURE GENERATIONS · THE GOVERNMENT · HISTORY · HUMAN RIGHTS · JUSTICE · LIBERTY · NATIONHOOD · RACE RELATIONS · SLAVERY · UNALIENABLE RIGHTS

Abraham Lincoln (February 12, 1809 – April 15, 1865) served as the 16th President of the United States from March 1861 until April 1865 when his term was prematurely ended with his assassination. During his time as a politician, Lincoln strengthened the Union and its federal government. However, his greatest legacy is undoubtedly bringing an end to slavery in the United States through his Emancipation Proclamation on January 1, 1863. This policy finally came into law on December 6, 1865, eight months after his assassination. It was the Thirteenth Amendment to the US Constitution.

Lincoln's presidency coincided with the American Civil War which raged between 1861 and 1865. Twenty-five States, known as 'the Union' and made up of mostly Northern and Border States, fought against twelve Southern states who had unilaterally declared their independence from the United States of America. 'The Union' was led by Lincoln, whereas the Southern States were under the command of Jefferson Davis. The conflict's conclusion would lead to the abolition of slavery.

One of the biggest battles took place near Gettysburg, Pennsylvania between July 1 and July 3, 1863. Around 25,000 soldiers would die fighting in the battle and it ultimately decided the outcome of the war. The Confederates suffered defeat in what was one of the bloodiest battles of the conflict.

It was on the old battlegrounds at the newly-assembled Soldiers' National Cemetery where Lincoln delivered his Gettysburg Address on November 19, 1863. The main orator Edward Everett warmed up the crowd at the dedication ceremony with a two-hour speech. In comparison, Lincoln spoke for just over two minutes when it was his turn – the conciseness of his words initially disappointing. However, this conclusion failed to really hone in on the substance of Lincoln's speech. His closing remarks outlining a 'government of the People, by the People, for the People' have come to define democracy as we know it. Lincoln also reiterated the significance of the notion of human equality as indicated by the Declaration of Independence, related the war's losses to a yearning for 'a new birth of freedom' and emphasised the importance of maintaining the Union of 1776 and its notion of self-government. Lincoln paid homage to the lives that had been lost at Gettysburg and reasoned that their cost would not be in vain as they had fought to protect democracy, end slavery and enlarge the range of people's individual freedoms.

THE PRESIDENT Abraham Lincoln:

ALL MEN ARE CREATED EQUAL

Four score and seven years ago

our fathers brought forth on this continent,

a new nation, conceived in liberty,

and dedicated to the proposition

that all men are created equal.

Now we are engaged in a great civil war,

testing whether that nation, or any nation so conceived and so dedicated,

can long endure.

We are met on a great battlefield of that war.

We have come to dedicate a portion of that field,

as a final resting place for those

who here gave their lives

that that nation might live.

It is altogether fitting and proper

that we should do this.

But in a larger sense,

– we cannot dedicate

– we cannot consecrate

– we cannot hallow this ground.

The brave men,

living and dead,

who struggled here,

Four score and seven years ago (4x20) +7 = 87 years ago; score is an old English word for "twenty"
brought forth *gründeten*

conceived in liberty created free and independent

dedicated to the proposition that committed to the idea that; *dem Grundsatz verpflichtet*
all men are created equal all people are born equal (and have the same rights); Lincoln is citing the Declaration of Independence (1776)
civil war (*here:*) *der Sezessionskrieg, der Amerikanische Bürgerkrieg*

can long endure can last a long time

we are met we are meeting

to dedicate *widmen*

as a final resting place for those who here gave their lives as a cemetery for the soldiers who died here

fitting and proper right, appropriate

in a larger sense *in einem höheren Sinne*

to dedicate *widmen*

to consecrate *segnen*

to hallow to bless; *heiligen, weihen*

the brave men, living and dead *die mutigen Männer, die Lebenden und die Toten*

struggled (*here:*) fought

have consecrated it (*here:*) *haben (den Boden) geweiht*

far above our poor power to add or detract *weit über das hinaus, was unsere schwachen Kräfte hinzufügen oder hinweg nehmen könnten*

the world will little note, nor long remember few people will be aware of or remember for a long time

it can never forget what they did here no one can ever forget what those soldiers did here

it is for us the living, rather, to be dedicated here to the unfinished work which they who fought here have thus far so nobly advanced *es liegt vielmehr an uns, den Lebenden, uns dem noch nicht vollendeten Werk zu widmen, das diejenigen, die hier kämpften, so weit und so edelmütig begonnen haben*

dedicated to the great task remaining before us we are dedicated to solving the other great problems that still lie ahead of us

honored (*AmE*), **honoured** (*BrE*) *geehrt*

devotion committment, faithfulness; *Hingabe, Aufopferung*

that cause for which they gave the last full measure of devotion that cause they died for

highly resolve firmly promise; *schwören*

in vain for no reason; *vergeblich, sinnlos*

under God guided by God's rules

to perish to disappear

have consecrated it,

far above our poor power to add or detract.

The world will little note, nor long remember,

what we say here, but it can never forget what they did here.

It is for us the living, rather,

to be dedicated here to the unfinished work

which they who fought here have thus far so nobly advanced.

GOVERNMENT OF THE PEOPLE,
BY THE PEOPLE, FOR THE PEOPLE

It is rather for us to be here dedicated to the great task remaining

before us –

that from these honored dead

we take increased devotion

to that cause for which they gave the last full measure of devotion –

that we here highly resolve.

that these dead shall not have died in vain –

that this nation, under God, shall have a new birth of freedom

and that government of the people, by the people,

for the people, shall not perish from the earth.

Transcript from: https://millercenter.org/the-presidency/presidential-speeches/november-19-1863-gettysburg-address

ASSIGNMENTS

A) Pre-Listening and Pre-Reading Activity

quiz / research competition / individual work / group work / using smartphones, laptops or tablets / feedback / presentation / elevator pitches: 60 seconds / podcast

Read the introduction on page 78 and go online, then answer the following questions:
1. When was Abraham Lincoln born?
2. On what date did the American Civil War begin?
3. Gettysburg was the site of a very cruel and bloody battle during the American Civil war. In what state is it located?
4. What is the title of President Lincoln's best-known speech?
5. On what date did President Lincoln give his famous Gettysburg Address?
6. How long was Abraham Lincoln's Gettysburg Address?
7. On what date was Abraham Lincoln assassinated?
8. Who was John Wilkes Booth?
9. What was the Emancipation Proclamation?
10. When was the Thirteenth Amendment to the United States Constitution ratified?

B) Reading and Listening Comprehension

paired work / group work / dramatisation / word cloud / using tablets or laptops / peer support and feedback / idea tower / share ideas / writing a summary

1. Read the text in groups of four students. Write a dramatisation of the speech. Rehearse and perform your dramatisation in front of your English class.
2. Watch this video of Jeff Daniels reading the speech: https://www.youtube.com/watch?v=9TCMHVmNc5w
3. Create a word cloud of the speech's keywords.
4. What are the most important aspects of democracy, according to Abraham Lincoln?
5. Sum up Abraham Lincoln's main arguments.

C) Analysis
1. Analyse the significance of the keywords Lincoln uses.
2. Analyse the structure of the speech.
3. Analyse the rhetorical devices Lincoln uses and explain their intended effects.

D) Evaluation, Comment and Creative Activities

independent learning / flipped classroom / paired work / group work / students teach each other / presentation / using tablet or laptops / speech training / evaluation / SOLO taxonomy

1. Work in pairs, then in groups: go online, watch one of the following videos, analyse it, then present it to your class.
2. Point out the similarities and differences between the following videos:
   a) *John Mansfield:* Abraham Lincoln, Gettysburg Address
   b) *Abraham Lincoln:* Gettysburg Address from the movie *Saving Lincoln*
   c) *Barack Obama:* Lincoln's Gettysburg Address
   d) *Johnny Cash:* The Gettysburg Address
3. Nick Morgan said the following of the speech on April 15, 2009: "At just under 250 words, Lincoln's 'Gettysburg Address' packs more greatness in two minutes than any other speech. Why is it so power-

ful?" http://www.publicwords.com/2009/04/15/the-greatest-250word-speech-ever-written/ Do you agree or disagree with Nick Morgan's opinion? How would you answer Nick Morgan's question?
4. "Government of the people, by the people, for the people." Is Lincoln's statement still relevant today? Prepare and give a three-minute speech giving your own opinion.

E) Ideas for Further Projects
1. Read the German Translation of Lincoln's speech by Erich Heller:
http://www.zeit.de/reden/die_historische_rede/200110_gettysburg/komplettansicht
2. Read the Modern English Version of Lincoln's speech:
http://www.flawlesswalrus.com/2011/02/gettysburg-address-modern-translation/
3. Abraham Lincoln's Gettysburg Address is considered a masterpiece today, but it wasn't viewed that way at the time. A journalist for *The Chicago Times,* accused Lincoln of showing "ignorant rudeness," "boorishness" and "vulgarity" in his Gettysburg speech in an article published on November 23, 1863. The writer was especially upset by Lincoln's statement that "all men are created equal".
From: Tom Kacich: "Lincoln's speech sparked criticism from some papers." In: The News-Gazette, Nov. 19, 2013
http://www.news-gazette.com/news/local/2013-11-19/tom-kacich-lincolns-speech-sparked-criticism-some-papers.html

F) Research Project: The American Civil War

flipped classroom / mind mapping / internet research / paired work / group work / peer support and feedback / WebQuest / presentation / tablet, laptop / debate / speech / comment chain

1. A New Birth of Peace and Freedom? Watch the official trailer of *Lincoln* (2012), directed by Steven Spielberg: https://www.youtube.com/watch?v=VWpMt2-Z-fc
2. Was the American Civil War worth it? Explain why or why not.
3. Do some research on the American Civil War, then present your findings to the class.
4. Read and analyse "An Occurrence at Owl Creek Bridge", a famous short story by Ambrose Bierce.

G) Inspirational Quotations by Abraham Lincoln – For Thought, Discussion and Speech Training.
1. "If slavery is not wrong, nothing is wrong."
2. "Be sure you put your feet in the right place, then stand firm."
3. "America will never be destroyed from the outside. If we falter and lose our freedoms, it will be because we destroyed ourselves."
4. "You cannot escape the responsibility of tomorrow by evading it today."
5. "Leave nothing for tomorrow which can be done today."
6. "If you want to test a man's character, give him power."
7. "Books serve to show a man that those original thoughts of his aren't very new at all."
8. "The best way to predict your future is to create it."
9. "Government of the people, by the people, for the people, shall not perish from the Earth."

H) Salvador Dali's Lincoln in Dalivision
1. Many artists have been inspired to create some sort of homage to Abraham Lincoln. Most of these show Lincoln in a grand and resolute pose. The Spanish painter *Salvador Dalí* (1904-1989) created a lithograph known as *Lincoln in Dalivision.* Start a cross-curricular project with your Art class and analyse and evaluate the picture.
2. Go online and choose your favourite Abraham Lincoln Pop Art style portrait and your favourite Lincoln cartoon.

„Ich bin ein Berliner."

President John F. Kennedy in Berlin on June 26, 1963

RELATED TOPICS

THE AMERICAN DREAM · THE BERLIN WALL · THE COLD WAR · COMMUNISM · CONFLICT · THE DECLARATION OF INDEPENDENCE · DEMOCRACY · DIGNITY · EUROPE · FREEDOM · FUTURE GENERATIONS · THE GOVERNMENT · HISTORY · HUMAN RIGHTS · JUSTICE · LIBERTY · NATIONHOOD · PEACE · UNALIENABLE RIGHTS

The summer of 1963 saw **President John F. Kennedy** embark on a European tour in order to strengthen the United States' international ties with the respective nations. The first country on the list was Germany with whom the U.S. had been engaged in a bloody conflict some 20 years previously. The days of Adolf Hitler's quest for global domination were long gone and following her ultimate defeat, Germany had been divided. The Soviet Union assumed control of what became East Germany, whereas the Western allies – Great Britain, France and the USA – took on responsibility for West Germany until it once again regained its status as a sovereign nation. The border between East and West Germany became a microcosm for much larger tensions between the United States and the Soviet Union. Nowhere was this clearer as in Berlin, which found itself in East Germany but was actually divided up between all four of the allied powers. Consequently, the city's administration was controlled by the Soviets in the East, and Great Britain, France and the United States shared responsibility for West Berlin.

Tensions famously came to a head in 1948 when the Soviets attempted to block access to West Berlin's infrastructure including its railways, roads and waterways. Faced with this crisis, Britain and the U.S. had to resort to radical methods to keep the people under their jurisdiction supplied. For eleven months, they airlifted nearly two million tonnes of items, such as: food, coal and industrial supplies. The Berlin Airlift eventually came to a conclusion; however the tensions between East and West did not disappear. In 1961, the East Berlin authorities began construction of a 12-foot-high wall in an effort to prevent the masses from leaving for the West. It stretched about 100 miles around West Berlin and nearly 200 people would lose their lives attempting to conquer the wall.

Kennedy's arrival in West Berlin on June 26, 1963 followed massive speeches in the West German cities: Bonn, Cologne and Frankfurt. Similarly, a great crowd congregated at Rudolph Wilde Platz within the setting of the Berlin Wall to listen to what the President had to say. The subsequent words from Kennedy have transcended the generations, with the famous line 'Ich bin ein Berliner' particularly living long in the memory. In fact, the street was even renamed John F. Kennedy Platz to honour the speech that day. On November 22 later that year, the President was assassinated in Dallas, Texas.

THE PRESIDENT John F. Kennedy:

distinguished Mayor *verehrter regierender Bürgermeister;* Willy Brandt was the Governing Mayor of Berlin from 1957 to 1966; he was West Germany's Chancellor from 1969 until 1974
fighting spirit (*here:*) *Widerstandskraft*
Konrad Adenauer was the Chancellor of West Germany from 1949 until 1963
General Lucius Dubignon Clay (April 23, 1898 – April 16, 1978) was an American army officer, known for his administration of occupied Germany after World War II. Clay organized the Berlin Airlift (1948–1949) when the USSR blockaded West Berlin from June 24, 1948, until May 12, 1949, when the Soviets lifted the ban.
the proudest boast *der stolzeste Satz*
civis Romanus sum *Ich bin ein Bürger Roms*
translating my German (*here:*) translating this sentence into German

I am proud to come to this city as the guest of your distinguished Mayor, who has symbolized throughout the world the fighting spirit of West Berlin. And I am proud to visit the Federal Republic with your distinguished Chancellor who for so many years has committed Germany to democracy and freedom and progress, and to come here in the company of my fellow American, General Clay, who has been in this city during its great moments of crisis and will come again if ever needed.

ICH BIN EIN BERLINER

Two thousand years ago, the proudest boast was "civis Romanus sum." Today, in the world of freedom, the proudest boast is "Ich bin ein Berliner."

I appreciate my interpreter translating my German!

LET THEM COME TO BERLIN

what is the great issue between the free world and the Communist world *worum es heute in der Auseinandersetzung zwischen der freien Welt und dem Kommunismus geht*
Communism is the wave of the future *dem Kommunismus gehört die Zukunft*

There are many people in the world who really don't understand, or say they don't, what is the great issue between the free world and the Communist world. Let them come to Berlin. There are some who say that communism is the wave of the future. Let them come to Berlin. And there are some who say in Europe and elsewhere we can work with the Communists. Let them come to Berlin. And there are even a few who say that it's true that Communism is an evil system, but it permits us to make economic progress. Lasst sie nach Berlin kommen. Let them come to Berlin.

FREEDOM HAS MANY DIFFICULTIES AND DEMOCRACY IS NOT PERFECT

the Berlin Wall see Additional Notes
besieged *belagert*

Freedom has many difficulties and democracy is not perfect, but we have never had to put a wall up to keep our people in, to prevent them from leaving us. I want to say, on behalf of my countrymen, who live many miles away on the other side of the Atlantic, who are far distant from you, that they take the greatest pride that they have been able to share with you, even from a distance, the story of the last 18 years. I know of no town, no city, that has been besieged for 18 years that still lives with the vitality and the force, and the hope and the determination of the city of West Berlin.

offense (*AmE*), **offence** (*BrE*) attack; *Angriff*

While the wall is the most obvious and vivid demonstration of the failures of the Communist system, for all the world to see, we take no satisfaction in it, for it is, as your Mayor has said, an offense not only against history but an offense against humanity, separating families, dividing husbands and wives and brothers and sisters, and dividing a people who wish to be joined together.

What is true of this city is true of Germany – real, lasting peace in Europe can never be assured as long as one German out of four is denied the elementary right of free men, and that is to make a free choice. In 18 years of peace and good faith, this generation of Germans has earned the right to be free, including the right to unite their families and their nation in lasting peace, with good will to all people.

as long as one German out of four is denied the elementary right to make a free choice *solange jedem vierten Deutschen das Grundrecht einer freien Wahl vorenthalten wird*
good faith *Gutwilligkeit, nach Treu und Glauben handeln*

You live in a defended island of freedom, but your life is part of the main. So let me ask you as I close, to lift your eyes beyond the dangers of today, to the hopes of tomorrow, beyond the freedom merely of this city of Berlin, or your country of Germany, to the advance of freedom everywhere, beyond the wall, to the day of peace with justice, beyond yourselves and ourselves, to all mankind.

your life is part of the main *Ihr Leben ist mit dem des Festlandes /Heimatlandes verbunden*
beyond the dangers of today *über die Gefahren der Gegenwart hinweg*
beyond the wall *über die Mauer hinweg*

WHEN ONE MAN IS ENSLAVED, ALL ARE NOT FREE

Freedom is indivisible, and when one man is enslaved, all are not free. When all are free, then we can look forward to that day when this city will be joined as one, and this country and this great continent of Europe [will be joined] in a peaceful and hopeful globe. When that day finally comes, as it will, the people of West Berlin can take sober satisfaction in the fact that they were in the front lines for almost two decades.

indivisible inseparable
sober satisfaction (*here:*) *ernsthafte und nüchterne Zufriedenheit/Feststellung*

"ICH BIN EIN BERLINER"

All free men, wherever they may live, are citizens of Berlin, and, therefore, as a free man, I take pride in the words "Ich bin ein Berliner."

Transcript from: *History Place*
http://www.historyplace.com/speeches/jfk-berliner.htm
and from: *BBC News* http://news.bbc.co.uk/2/hi/europe/3022166.stm

---

ASSIGNMENTS

A) Reading and Listening Comprehension

think – pair – share / peer support and feedback / designing a poster / writing a summary

1. Watch Kennedy's speech and write down your first impression of its tone and content:
   https://www.youtube.com/watch?v=56V6r2dpYH8
   History Place: http://www.historyplace.com/speeches/jfk-berliner.htm
2. While listening to the speech, read the transcript and highlight in different colours:
   a) the main arguments and b) important keywords.
3. Summarise Kennedy's main arguments.

B) Analysis

work with a partner / share ideas with classmates / peer support and feedback / tablet / presentation

1. In your speech transcript, highlight in different colours:
   a) rhetorical devices and b) historical and political references.
2. Analyse how John F. Kennedy:
   a) addresses the audience directly, b) praises the audience's courage and resilience, c) refers to both past and future developments, d) outlines the possibility of world peace, e) empathises with the audience, f) encourages the audience.

C) Evaluation, Comment, Creative Activities

think – pair – share / writing conference / peer support and feedback / tablet or laptop presentation / panel discussion / press conference / interview / speech / evaluation

1. John F. Kennedy states: "Freedom has many difficulties and democracy is not perfect, but we have never had to put a wall up to keep our people in, to prevent them from leaving us." Evaluate the significance of Kennedy's statement in the context of the world today.
2. Kennedy emphasises: "Freedom is indivisible, and when one man is enslaved, all are not free." Comment on the importance of freedom today.
3. Kennedy says: "When all are free, then we can look forward to that day when this city will be joined as one, and this country and this great continent of Europe [will be joined] in a peaceful and hopeful globe." Imagine that JFK could give a speech today on the current political and social situation in the European Union. What would he say? Write and give a short speech, considering both the positive and the negative aspects of the European Union today.
4. Evaluate the relationship between Germany and the USA today.
5. Kennedy is still seen as a charismatic leader who served during a period of immense change in the USA. How would Kennedy describe the USA's current political and social situation?

D) Ideas for Further Research: The Cold War and the Berlin Wall

research / WebQuest / presentation / poster / gallery walk / collaboration with History class

1. Der Kalte Krieg: *Bundeszentrale für Politische Bildung:* Kalter Krieg: 1945 – 1989 / Ursachen des Kalten Krieges / Das geteilte Berlin
2. The Cold War and the Berlin Wall : *History / Encyclopaedia Britannica / John F. Kennedy: Presidential Library*
3. **„Hoffnungsträger einer neuen Zeit: John F. Kennedy"**
   Von Andreas Etges, *Bundeszentrale für Politische Bildung*, 11.10.2008 (22.6.2018)
   http://www.bpb.de/internationales/amerika/usa/10610/john-f-kennedy

Tasks:

1. Go online and read the articles listed above.
2. Work in small groups. Each group should summarise a different paragraph of one of the articles in English, then present their summary in poster-format to the class.
3. Find out some more information about JFK that you could also use in your History classes.
4. A New Cold War? Are the world powers about to enter a new Cold War? Prepare and give a three-minute speech.
5. „Break Down The Walls": Watch Chancellor Angela Merkel's Commencement Speech at Harvard University on May 30, 2019: https://www.youtube.com/watch?v=UOuFYsbBRqw

"Our Mission Is to Report These Horrors of War."

Speech given by Marie Catherine Colvin at St Bride's Church, Fleet Street, London, on November 10, 2010.

RELATED TOPICS

COURAGE · DIGNITY · FAKE NEWS · FREEDOM · FUTURE GENERATIONS · THE GOVERNMENT · HISTORY · THE HORRORS OF WAR · HUMAN RIGHTS · INEQUALITY · INJUSTICE · JOURNALISM · THE MEDIA · OPPRESSION · PEACE · THE PRESS · PROPAGANDA · REPORTERS WITHOUT BORDERS · RESPONSIBILITY · TERROR · WAR · WAR REPORTING

Born on January 12, 1956, **Marie Colvin** was an American journalist and war correspondent who reported the effects of war on the people often affected the most: the general public.

Colvin continuously risked her own health and well-being to report on the tragedies and effects of conflict on the people involved, directly or indirectly.

She served as The Sunday Times' Middle East correspondent for nearly ten years between 1986 and 1995. Subsequently, she worked as the Foreign Affairs correspondent until she died in 2012. Her pursuit of the stories that matter even led to her losing her left eye. This occurred during an attack in Sri Lanka while reporting on a skirmish between government troops and Tamil rebel forces.

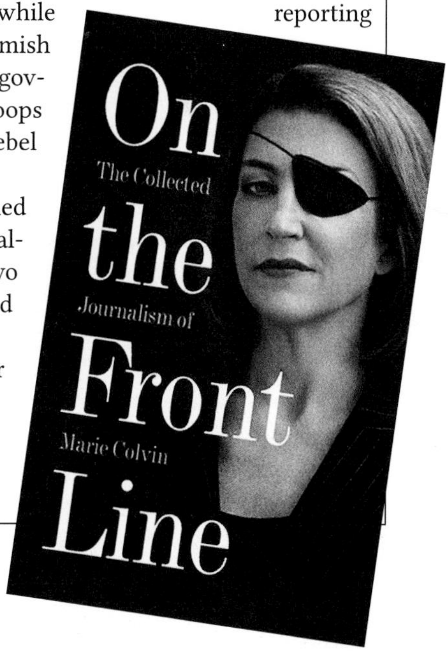

Her work led to a number of journalistic prizes. In 2000, Colvin was named Journalist of the Year by the Foreign Press Association. She also received two British Press Awards for her coverage of foreign affairs in 2001 and 2010, respectively.

Three days preceding her death, Colvin released her final article for The Sunday Times. The journalist was killed as she covered fighting in Homs, Syria when a bomb struck the house where she was lodging. Hours earlier, she had broadcast from a building in which Syrian civilians were taking cover from government forces.

Marie Colvin:

I am honoured and humbled *ich bin geehrt und voller Demut*
support staff people, such as translators, drivers, proofreaders, and cameramen, who help journalists to do their jobs, but don't work as journalists themselves
hard calling dangerous job, dangerous vocation
frontline reporting not only refers to reporting from warzones specifically, but also to up-to-date, advanced reporting in general
compelling urgent
torn by chaos *vom Chaos zerrissen*
to bear witness (*here:*) to record events; *als Augenzeuge berichten*

to sanitize to clean, to sterilize, (*here:*) to leave out unpleasant details to make something more palatable [acceptable] to the public; *etwas abschwächen*
smart bombs bombs guided by computers and lasers so that they hit their targets accurately
pinpoint strikes bombing carried out with great accuracy
mutilated *verstümmelt*

bravery courage; *Mut, Tapferkeit*
bravado foolhardiness, showing off; *Wagemut, Draufgängertum*
covering combat reporting from war zones
to shoulder great responsibilities to bear [have] great responsibilities
they pay the ultimate price they are killed
to honour *Ehre erweisen*
to our shores to our country
maimed *verstümmelt*
held hostage *als Geiseln gefangen*
prime target *vorrangiges Ziel*
in an ambush trap, surprise attack; *Überfall im Hinterhalt*
unreported not reported, unpublicised
to launch (*here:*) to shoot, to throw
shrapnel *Granatsplitter*
to slice to cut
Joao Silva an award-winning war photographer, who was severely wounded in southern Afghanistan after stepping on a mine while on patrol with US soldiers
to contain to control, to hold back

Your Royal Highness, ladies and gentlemen, I am honoured and humbled to be speaking to you at this service tonight to remember the journalists, and their support staff, who gave their lives to report from the war zones of the 21st century. I have been a war correspondent for most of my professional life. It has always been a hard calling. But the need for frontline, objective reporting has never been more compelling.

Covering a war means going to places torn by chaos, destruction and death, and trying to bear witness. It means trying to find the truth in a sandstorm of propaganda when armies, tribes or terrorists clash. And yes, it means taking risks, not just for yourself but often for the people who work closely with you.

Despite all the videos you see from the Ministry of Defence or the Pentagon, and all the sanitized language describing smart bombs and pinpoint strikes, the scene on the ground has remained remarkably the same for hundreds of years. Craters. Burned houses. Mutilated bodies. Women weeping for children and husbands. Men for their wives, mothers children.

OUR MISSION IS TO REPORT THESE HORRORS OF WAR WITH ACCURACY AND WITHOUT PREJUDICE

Our mission is to report these horrors of war with accuracy and without prejudice. We always have to ask ourselves whether the level of risk is worth the story. What is bravery, and what is bravado?

Journalists covering combat shoulder great responsibilities and face difficult choices. Sometimes they pay the ultimate price. Tonight we honour the 49 journalists and support staff who were killed bringing the news to our shores. We also remember journalists around the world who have been wounded, maimed or kidnapped and held hostage for months. It has never been more dangerous to be a war correspondent, because the journalist in the combat zone has become a prime target.

I lost my eye in an ambush in the Sri Lankan civil war. I had gone to the northern Tamil area from which journalists were banned and found an unreported humanitarian disaster. As I was smuggled back across the internal border, a soldier launched a grenade at me and the shrapnel sliced into my face and chest. He knew what he was doing.

Just last week, I had a coffee in Afghanistan with a photographer friend, Joao Silva. We talked about the terror one feels and must contain when patrolling on an embed with the armed forces through fields and villages in Afghanistan ... putting one foot in front of the other, steeling yourself with each step for the blast. The expectation of that blast is the stuff of nightmares. Two days after our meeting, Joao stepped on a mine and lost both legs at the knee.

steeling yourself bracing yourself [getting ready] for something difficult or unpleasant
the blast the explosion

IS IT WORTH THE COST IN LIVES, HEARTBREAK, LOSS?

Many of you here must have asked yourselves, or be asking yourselves now, is it worth the cost in lives, heartbreak, loss? Can we really make a difference?

I faced that question when I was injured. In fact one paper ran a headline saying, has Marie Colvin gone too far this time? My answer then, and now, was that it is worth it.

Today in this church are friends, colleagues and families who know exactly what I am talking about, and bear the cost of those experiences, as do their families and loved ones.

this church St Bride's Church is known worldwide as the Journalists' Church, offering a spiritual home to all those who work in the media.
bear the cost *die Konsequenzen erleiden*

Today we must also remember how important it is that news organisations continue to invest in sending us out at great cost, both financial and emotional, to cover stories.

to cover stories to report on stories, to write stories

WE SEND HOME THAT FIRST ROUGH DRAFT OF HISTORY

We go to remote war zones to report what is happening. The public have a right to know what our government, and our armed forces, are doing in our name. Our mission is to speak the truth to power. We send home that first rough draft of history. We can and do make a difference in exposing the horrors of war and especially the atrocities that befall civilians.

remote far away, distant
rough draft *grober Entwurf*
atrocities *Gräueltaten*
befall *widerfahren*
civilians *Zivilpersonen*

The history of our profession is one to be proud of. The first war correspondent in the modern era was William Howard Russell of the *Times*, who was sent to cover the Crimean conflict when a British-led coalition fought an invading Russian army.

William Howard Russell (1821-1907) a famous war correspondent

Billy Russell, as the troops called him, created a firestorm of public indignation back home by revealing inadequate equipment, scandalous treatment of the wounded, especially when they were repatriated – does this sound familiar? – and an incompetent high command that led to the folly of the Charge of the Light Brigade.

indignation outrage
to reveal to uncover, (*here:*) to make public; *aufdecken*
repatriated sent home
high command leadership
folly stupidity
Charge of the Light Brigade a charge of British light cavalry led by Lord Cardigan against Russian forces during the Battle of Balaclava on October 25, 1854 in the Crimean War; the assault ended with very high British casualties and no gains

It was a breakthrough in war reporting. Until then, wars were reported by junior officers who sent back dispatches to newspapers. Billy Russell went to war with an open mind, a telescope, a notebook and a bottle of brandy. I first went to war with a typewriter, and learned to tap out a telex tape. It could take days to get from the front to a telephone or telex machine.

flak jacket *Splitterschutzweste*

24/7 rolling news Nachrichten *rund um die Uhr, 7 Tage die Woche, 24 Stunden am Tag*

War reporting has changed greatly in just the last few years. Now we go to war with a satellite phone, laptop, video camera and a flak jacket. I point my satellite phone to south southwest in Afghanistan, press a button and I have filed.
In an age of 24/7 rolling news, blogs and Twitter, we are on constant call wherever we are. But war reporting is still essentially the same – someone has to go there and see what is happening.

faith (*here:*) confidence, trust
humanity die Menschheit
file report

You can't get that information without going to places where people are being shot at, and where others are shooting at you. The real difficulty is having enough faith in humanity to believe that enough people, be they government, military or the man on the street, will care when your file reaches the printed page, the website or the TV screen.

fixers proofreaders
appalling (*here:*) unacceptably high
pursuit search, quest

We do have that faith because we believe we do make a difference.
And we could not make that difference – or begin to do our job – without the fixers, drivers and translators, who face the same risks and die in appalling numbers. Today we honour them as much as the front line journalists who have died in pursuit of the truth. They have kept the faith as we who remain must continue to do.

The speech transcript is taken from:
http://www.stbrides.com/news/2010/11/truth-at-all-costs.html

ASSIGNMENTS

A) Reading Comprehension

▶ *think - pair - share / question and comment chain technique / idea tower / writing a summary / peer support and feedback / evaluation*

1. Describe some of Marie Colvin's experiences as a war reporter.
2. What are the dangers war correspondents are confronted with?
3. According to Colvin, what decisions do journalists reporting from war zones have to make?
4. "You can't get that information without going to places where people are being shot at, and where others are shooting at you. The real difficulty is having enough faith in humanity to believe that enough people [...] will care when your file reaches the printed page, the website or the TV screen." Explain what Marie Colvin means by this statement.
5. Outline Marie Colvin's main arguments.

B) Analysis

▶ *reading for detail / group work / peer support and feedback / posters / presentation*

1. Analyse the rhetorical devices Marie Colvin uses.
2. Examine Marie Colvin's image of a tightrope walk between "bravery and bravado" and what it means.

C) Evaluation, Comment, Creative Activities

creative writing / self-immersion / peer support and feedback / research / WebQuest / debate / role play / radio talk / speech / one-act play / collaboration with Social Sciences and History classes

1. Should editors of media agencies still send journalists to war zones? Discuss the pros and cons.
2. "War reporting is still essentially the same – someone has to go there and see what is happening. There can be no freedom of thought without knowledge of reality." Discuss and explain your opinion.
3. Describe the difficulty of deciding whether or not to take the risk of entering a war zone. For example, you could analyse the risks of reporting on chemical weapon attacks on innocent people.
4. "We send home that first rough draft of history." Explain why you agree or disagree with this statement.
5. Write an article about the role of the media across the world today.
6. "Our mission is to report these horrors of war with accuracy and without prejudice." Prepare and give a three-minute speech to your group, then to your class in response to this statement.
7. In a group, write a one-act play in which you act out/dramatise the personal situation of a young journalist who has the chance to go to a war zone.

D) Further Projects: The Defense of Media Freedom

1. Reporters Without Borders (RSF) is the world's largest NGO (non-governmental organisation) specializing in the defence of media freedom.
   In 1948, the United Nations said in article 19 of the Universal Declaration of Human Rights that "freedom of opinion and expression" is the right to "seek, receive and impart information and ideas through any medium, regardless of frontiers." At the turn of the 21st century, nearly half of the world's population still lacks access to unbiased information. In 2018, 80 journalists were killed, 348 are in prison, 60 are being held hostage, according to the annual report released by *Reporters Without Borders*: https://rsf.org/en (December 18, 2018)
2. **The famous German photojournalist Anja Niedringhaus** dedicated her life to telling humanity's most troubling stories at the front lines of conflict and war. She was born on October 12, 1965 in Hoxter, Germany. She was killed on April 4, 2014 in Khost, Afghanistan. She won the Pulitzer Prize 2005.

E) For Thought and Discussion

In authoritarian states and dictatorships, free-thinking journalists are often regarded as enemies of the state. These journalists are often accused of treason and charged under anti-terror laws, which are also used to convict human rights activists. Human rights activists campaign against the oppression people face in authoritarian states, while free-thinking journalists report on these acts of oppression to make the whole world aware of them. This is why authoritarian states and dictatorships see free-thinking journalists and human rights activists as troublemakers - and terrorists.

F) Mediation (German = > English)

Die Frau, die nicht wegsah: Marie Colvin, die Kriegsreporterin der "Sunday Times", starb im Bürgerkrieg in Syrien. Von Jörg Burger, *DIE Zeit* vom 28. Februar 2013

1. Go online, read the article and summarise the main arguments in English.
2. Find out more information about Reporters Without Borders and present your findings to your class.

G) Mediation (German = > English)

Rüstungsindustrie und Militärausgaben

WDR 5 Radio: Kosten des Krieges: Sterben tun immer die anderen. Wer verdient am Waffenhandel? WDR 5 „Tiefenblick", Sonntag, 15.4.2018, 8.05 - 8.35 Uhr

Die weltweiten Militärausgaben beliefen sich 2016 nach Berechnungen des schwedischen Friedensforschungsinstituts SIPRI auf 1,686 Billionen US-Dollar. [...] Die USA führen mit 611 Milliarden US-Dollar, auf Platz zwei steht China mit 215 Milliarden Dollar. Die Europäische Union gibt, zusammengerechnet, eine ähnliche Summe aus. Es folgen: Russland, Saudi-Arabien und Indien. In den 1990er hoffte die Welt auf Frieden und rüstete ab. Heute feiert der Waffenhandel sein Comeback. [...] 2016 verkauften die 100 größten Waffenfirmen der Welt Rüstungsgüter im Wert von 374,8 Milliarden Dollar. Deutsche Firmen waren – mit einer Steigerungsrate von 6,6 Prozent – nach Südkorea die größten Gewinner. [...] Die Giganten der Rüstungsindustrie verschmelzen zu immer größeren Einheiten. [...]

From: *WDR 5* https://www1.wdr.de/radio/wdr5/index.html

H) Trends in International Arms Transfers, SIPRI Fact Sheet, 2019, Key Facts

https://www.sipri.org/publications/2019/sipri-fact-sheets/trends-international-arms-transfers-2018 (accessed: April 2, 2019)

1. Go online and analyse the diagram: The 25 largest exporters of major arms and their clients.
2. What countries are the five largest arms exporters?
3. What countries were the five largest arms importers?
4. Consider the five largest arms importing countries, and discuss what events in these countries might be the driving factors for them to be top arms importers.
5. After the killing of Washington Post columnist Jamal Khashoggi and in a move that could put further pressure on President Trump to stop arms sales to Saudi Arabia, German Chancellor Angela Merkel announced that her government would not approve new arms exports to the kingdom until further notice.
   „Der Konzern Rheinmetall droht der Bundesregierung wegen des Lieferstopps für Rüstungsgüter nach Saudi-Arabien offenbar mit einer Schadenersatz-Klage." *Rheinische Post* vom 21.1.2019
   „Kurz nach der Lockerung des Rüstungsexportstopps für Saudi-Arabien hat der Bundessicherheitsrat wieder eine erste Lieferung für das am Jemen-Krieg beteiligte Königreich genehmigt." *Süddeutsche Zeitung* vom 13.4.2019, S. 6.

I) Cartoon by Gerhard Mester. Give this cartoon a catchy title that reflects the message.

Gerhard Mester is a very famous German cartoonist.

Tasks:

1. State your first impression of the cartoon. What is the cartoon about?
2. Analyse the cartoon. How does Mester get his message across?
3. Evaluate the cartoon using your background knowledge of this topic. Evaluate how the cartoon relates to current, global problems.
4. Evaluate the combined impact of Marie Colvin's speech, the Reporters without Borders Initiative, the Sipri Fact Sheet on International Arms Transfers, and Gerhard Mester's cartoon.

Violence and Terror: Threats to Civil Society

D

"Enemies of Freedom Committed an Act of War."

George W. Bush: State of the Union Address on Friday, September 21, 2001

RELATED TOPICS

AMERICAN RESOLVE · CHAOS · COURAGE · DESTRUCTION · DIGNITY · ENEMIES OF FREEDOM · EXTREMISM · FEAR · THE FOUNDATION OF AMERICA · FREEDOM · HOPE · INTERNATIONAL TERRORISM · JUSTICE · LIBERTY · MASS MURDER · PEACE · PERSECUTION · SOLIDARITY · TERRORISM · TERRORIST ATTACKS · VIOLENCE · WAR ON TERROR · WEAPONS OF MASS DESTRUCTION

In 2001, **George W. Bush** became America's 43rd President, a position he would hold for two terms until the end of 2009. The terrorist attacks on the World Trade Center, the Pentagon and attempts on the White House and the Capitol Building took place on September 11. As a consequence, Bush quickly found himself in the role of a wartime president. The 9/11 attacks ended the lives of nearly 3,000 people, and naturally, the vast majority were Americans. Bush's need to respond forced him to delay many of the hopes and plans he had previously had for his presidency. His father, George H.W. Bush, the 41st President, went as far as asserting that the challenge before his son was the 'greatest' since Abraham Lincoln.

In a direct response to the terrorist attack, the President created the new Department of Homeland Security. Bush sent the U.S. Armed Forces abroad to Afghanistan in an effort to defeat the Taliban, an organisation with significant links to Osama bin Laden who had orchestrated the attacks in America. The campaign managed to reduce the Taliban's power in Afghanistan but the United States were unable to apprehend the terrorist leader throughout the entirety of President Bush's time in office. This was despite a number of reforms made to the nation's intelligence gathering and analysis services, as well as countless military reforms to prepare America for this modern enemy.

Controversially, Bush ordered the invasion of Iraq to depose President Saddam Hussein who he believed posed a very credible threat – in terms of weapons of mass destruction – to the United States. The offensive resulted in the capture of the Iraqi leader but, as time progressed, the disruption of Iraq and the losses of American soldiers and Iraqi civilians became harder and harder for the Bush administration to justify.

As part of his State of the Union Address in 2005, the President pledged his support to form a functioning democratic government in Iraq, claiming that a stable country – one which drew hope rather than fear – would provide the U.S. with another ally in the war on terror.

THE PRESIDENT George W. Bush:

Mr Speaker, members of Congress, and fellow Americans:

In the normal course of events, Presidents come to this chamber to report on the state of the Union. Tonight, no such report is needed. It has already been delivered by the American people.

THE STATE OF THE UNION:
THE COURAGE OF THE AMERICAN PEOPLE

We have seen it in the courage of passengers, who rushed past terrorists to save others on the ground – passengers like an exceptional man named Todd Beamer. And would you please help me to welcome his wife, Lisa Beamer, here tonight.

endurance perseverance; *Durchhaltevermögen*
working past exhaustion *bis zur Erschöpfung arbeiten*
grief sorrow; *Trauer*

We have seen the state of our Union in the endurance of rescuers, working past exhaustion. We have seen the unfurling of flags, the lighting of candles, the giving of blood, the saying of prayers – in English, Hebrew, and Arabic. We have seen the decency of a loving and giving people who have made the grief of strangers their own.

My fellow citizens, for the last nine days, the entire world has seen for itself the state of our Union – and it is strong.

resolution determination; *Entschlossenheit*

Tonight we are a country awakened to danger and called to defend freedom. Our grief has turned to anger, and anger to resolution. Whether we bring our enemies to justice, or bring justice to our enemies, justice will be done.

needs *Bedürfnisse, Anforderungen*

I thank the Congress for its leadership at such an important time. All of America was touched on the evening of the tragedy to see Republicans and Democrats joined together on the steps of this Capitol, singing "God Bless America." And you did more than sing; you acted, by delivering $40 billion to rebuild our communities and meet the needs of our military. [...]

SUPPORT AND PRAYERS OF SYMPATHY

on behalf of the American people *im Namen des amerikanischen Volkes*
an outpouring of support *Welle der Unterstützung*

And on behalf of the American people, I thank the world for its outpouring of support.

America will never forget the sounds of our National Anthem playing at Buckingham Palace, in the streets of Paris, and at Berlin's Brandenburg Gate.

mosque *Moschee*

We will not forget South Korean children gathering to pray outside our embassy in Seoul, or the prayers of sympathy offered at a mosque in Cairo. We will not forget moments of silence and days of mourning in Australia and Africa and Latin America.

REMEMBER THE VICTIMS

Nor will we forget the citizens of 80 other nations who died with our own: dozens of Pakistanis; more than 130 Israelis; more than 250 citizens of India; men and women from El Salvador, Iran, Mexico and Japan; and hundreds of British citizens.

America has no truer friend than Great Britain. Once again, we are joined together in a great cause – so honored that the British Prime Minister has crossed an ocean to show his unity of purpose with America. Thank you for coming, friend.

ENEMIES OF FREEDOM COMMITTED AN ACT OF WAR

On September the 11th, enemies of freedom committed an act of war against our country. Americans have known wars – but for the past 136 years, they have been wars on foreign soil, except for one Sunday in 1941.

Americans have known the casualties of war – but not at the center of a great city on a peaceful morning. Americans have known surprise attacks – but never before on thousands of civilians. All of this was brought upon us in a single day – and night fell on a different world, a world where freedom itself is under attack.

WHO ATTACKED OUR COUNTRY?

Americans have many questions tonight. Americans are asking: Who attacked our country? The evidence we have gathered all points to a collection of loosely affiliated terrorist organizations known as al-Qaeda. They are the same murderers indicted for bombing American embassies in Tanzania and Kenya, and responsible for bombing the USS Cole.

Al-Qaeda is to terror what the mafia is to crime. But its goal is not making money; its goal is remaking the world – and imposing its radical beliefs on people everywhere.

The terrorists practise a fringe form of Islamic extremism that has been rejected by Muslim scholars and the vast majority of Muslim clerics – a fringe movement that perverts the peaceful teachings of Islam. The terrorists' directive commands them to kill Christians and Jews, to kill all Americans, and make no distinction among military and civilians, including women and children.

days of mourning *Tage der Trauer*

to show his unity of purpose *seine Verbundenheit zeigen*

on foreign soil in foreign countries
one Sunday in 1941 a reference to the **Pearl Harbor attack** (December 7, 1941), which was a surprise aerial attack on the U.S. naval base at Pearl Harbor on Oahu Island, Hawaii, by the Japanese that brought the United States into World War II. The strike was the culmination of a decade of worsening relations between the United States and Japan.
casualties wounded and dead people; *Opfer*
civilians *Zivilisten*
evidence *Anzeichen*
affiliated associated; *angegliedert*
bombing the USS Cole Bush is referring to an attack by Muslim militants associated with the organisation al-Qaeda against a U.S. naval destroyer, the USS Cole, on October 12, 2000. Suicide bombers in a small boat steered their boat into the side of the USS Cole, which was preparing to refuel in the harbour of the Yemeni port of Aden; the blast ripped a 1,600-square-foot (150-square-metre) hole in its hull and left 17 sailors dead and a further 39 wounded.
a fringe form (*here:*) *eine extreme Randerscheinung*
scholar *Gelehrter*
clerics *Kleriker*
to pervert to corrupt; *ins Gegenteil verdrehen*
the terrorists' directive commands them the terrorists are commanded to
distinction *Unterschied*

This group and its leader – a person named Osama bin Laden – are linked to many other organizations in different countries, including the Egyptian Islamic Jihad and the Islamic Movement of Uzbekistan. There are thousands of these terrorists in more than 60 countries. They are recruited from their own nations and neighborhoods and brought to camps in places like Afghanistan, where they are trained in the tactics of terror. They are sent back to their homes or sent to hide in countries around the world to plot evil and destruction.

to plot to plan

The leadership of al-Qaeda has great influence in Afghanistan and supports the Taliban regime in controlling most of that country. In Afghanistan, we see al-Qaeda's vision for the world. Afghanistan's people have been brutalized – many are starving and many have fled. Women are not allowed to attend school. You can be jailed for owning a television. Religion can be practised only as their leaders dictate. A man can be jailed in Afghanistan if his beard is not long enough.

brutalized abused; *brutal behandelt*

The United States respects the people of Afghanistan – after all, we are currently its largest source of humanitarian aid – but we condemn the Taliban regime. It is not only repressing its own people, it is threatening people everywhere by sponsoring and sheltering and supplying terrorists. By aiding and abetting murder, the Taliban regime is committing murder.

humanitarian aid *humanitäre Hilfe*

to aid and abet to help someone to commit a crime; *Beihilfe leisten*

DEMANDS ON THE TALIBAN

And tonight, the United States of America makes the following demands on the Taliban: Deliver to the United States authorities all the leaders of al-Qaeda who are hiding in your land. Release all the foreign nationals, including American citizens, who you have unjustly imprisoned. Protect foreign journalists, diplomats and aid workers in your country.

Close immediately and permanently every terrorist training camp in Afghanistan, and hand over every terrorist, and every person in their support structure, to the appropriate authorities. Give the United States full access to terrorist training camps, so we can make sure they are no longer operating.

full access right of entry

These demands are not open to negotiation or discussion. The Taliban must act, and act immediately. They will hand over the terrorists, or they will share in their fate.

these demands are not open to negotiation *diese Forderungen sind nicht verhandelbar*

THE MUSLIM FAITH: ITS TEACHINGS ARE GOOD AND PEACEFUL

I also want to speak tonight directly to Muslims throughout the world. We respect your faith. It's practiced freely by many millions of

Americans, and by millions more in countries that America counts as friends. Its teachings are good and peaceful, and those who commit evil in the name of Allah blaspheme the name of Allah. The terrorists are traitors to their own faith, trying, in effect, to hijack Islam itself. The enemy of America is not our many Muslim friends; it is not our many Arab friends. Our enemy is a radical network of terrorists, and every government that supports them.

OUR WAR ON TERROR BEGINS

Our War on Terror begins with al-Qaeda, but it does not end there. It will not end until every terrorist group of global reach has been found, stopped and defeated.

Americans are asking, why do they hate us? They hate what we see right here in this chamber – a democratically elected government. Their leaders are self-appointed. They hate our freedoms – our freedom of religion, our freedom of speech, our freedom to vote and assemble and disagree with each other.

They want to overthrow existing governments in many Muslim countries, such as Egypt, Saudi Arabia, and Jordan. They want to drive Israel out of the Middle East. They want to drive Christians and Jews out of vast regions of Asia and Africa.

These terrorists kill not merely to end lives, but to disrupt and end a way of life.

With every atrocity, they hope that America grows fearful, retreating from the world and forsaking our friends. They stand against us, because we stand in their way.

We are not deceived by their pretences to piety. We have seen their kind before. They are the heirs of all the murderous ideologies of the 20th century. By sacrificing human life to serve their radical visions – by abandoning every value except the will to power – they follow in the path of fascism, and Nazism, and totalitarianism. And they will follow that path all the way, to where it ends: in history's unmarked grave of discarded lies.

HOW WILL WE FIGHT AND WIN THIS WAR?

Americans are asking: How will we fight and win this war? We will direct every resource at our command – every means of diplomacy, every tool of intelligence, every instrument of law enforcement, every financial influence, and every necessary weapon of war – to the disruption and to the defeat of the global terror network.

to blaspheme to use offensive words that show no respect for God or for religion; *Gotteslästerung betreiben*

traitor *Verräter*

to hijack Islam (*here:*) to use Islam for their own purposes; *entführen (here:) den Islam verfälschen und missbrauchen*

of global reach *mit globalem Einflussbereich*

self-appointed not elected; *selbst ernannt*

to disrupt to break up; *zerstören*

atrocity *Gräueltat*

to forsake to abandon ; (*here:*) *im Stich lassen*

we are not deceived *wir lassen uns nicht täuschen*

pretences to piety façade of devout religious belief; *vorgetäuschte Frömmigkeit*

heir descendant; *Erbe*

unmarked grave *anonymes Grab*

discarded lies (*here:*) *Lügengebäude*

disruption *Auflösung*

This war will not be like the war against Iraq a decade ago, with a decisive liberation of territory and a swift conclusion. It will not look like the air war above Kosovo two years ago, where no ground troops were used and not a single American was lost in combat.

combat battle

WE WILL PURSUE NATIONS THAT PROVIDE AID OR SAFE HAVEN TO TERRORISM

Our response involves far more than instant retaliation and isolated strikes. Americans should not expect one battle, but a lengthy campaign, unlike any other we have ever seen. It may include dramatic strikes, visible on TV, and covert operations, secret even in success. We will starve terrorists of funding, turn them against one another, drive them from place to place, until there is no refuge and no rest. And we will pursue nations that provide aid or safe haven to terrorism.

retaliation revenge; *Rache, Vergeltung*

refuge shelter, place of safety; *Schutzort, Zufluchtsort*

to pursue to go after

Every nation, in every region, now has a decision to make. Either you are with us, or you are with the terrorists. From this day forward, any nation that continues to harbor or support terrorism will be regarded by the United States as a hostile regime. [...]

hostile *feindlich*

THIS IS THE WORLD'S FIGHT. THIS IS CIVILIZATION'S FIGHT

This is not, however, just America's fight. And what is at stake is not just America's freedom. This is the world's fight. This is civilization's fight. This is the fight of all who believe in progress and pluralism, tolerance and freedom.

at stake at risk; *auf dem Spiel stehen, in Gefahr sein*

We ask every nation to join us. We will ask, and we will need, the help of police forces, intelligence services, and banking systems around the world. The United States is grateful that many nations and many international organizations have already responded – with sympathy and with support. Nations from Latin America, to Asia, to Africa, to Europe, to the Islamic world. Perhaps the NATO Charter reflects best the attitude of the world: An attack on one is an attack on all.

The civilized world is rallying to America's side. They understand that if this terror goes unpunished, their own cities, their own citizens may be next. Terror, unanswered, can not only bring down buildings, it can threaten the stability of legitimate governments. And you know what – we're not going to allow it.

to rally to assemble; *sich versammeln*

WHAT IS EXPECTED OF US?

Americans are asking: What is expected of us? I ask you to live your lives, and hug your children. I know many citizens have fears tonight, and I ask you to be calm and resolute, even in the face of a continuing threat.

I ask you to uphold the values of America, and remember why so many have come here. We are in a fight for our principles, and our first responsibility is to live by them. No one should be singled out for unfair treatment or unkind words because of their ethnic background or religious faith. [...]

to uphold to support, to defend

I ask for your patience, with the delays and inconveniences that may accompany tighter security; and for your patience in what will be a long struggle.

delay *Verzögerung*
inconvenience *Unannehmlichkeit*

I ask your continued participation and confidence in the American economy. Terrorists attacked a symbol of American prosperity. They did not touch its source.

America is successful because of the hard work, and creativity, and enterprise of our people. These were the true strengths of our economy before September 11th, and they are our strengths today.

And, finally, please continue praying for the victims of terror and their families, for those in uniform, and for our great country. Prayer has comforted us in sorrow, and will help strengthen us for the journey ahead.

Tonight I thank my fellow Americans for what you have already done and for what you will do. And ladies and gentlemen of the Congress, I thank you, their representatives, for what you have already done and for what we will do together.

Tonight, we face new and sudden national challenges. We will come together to improve air safety, to dramatically expand the number of air marshals on domestic flights, and to take new measures to prevent hijacking. We will come together to promote stability and keep our airlines flying, with direct assistance during this emergency.

challenges *Herausforderungen*

hijacking (*here:*) unlawfully and criminally taking control of an aircraft; *Flugzeugentführung*

We will come together to give law enforcement the additional tools it needs to track down terror here at home. We will come together to strengthen our intelligence capabilities to know the plans of terrorists before they act, and to find them before they strike.

law enforcement *Strafverfolgungsbehörden*

We will come together to take active steps that strengthen America's economy, and put our people back to work. [...]

THIS WILL NOT BE AN AGE OF TERROR.
THIS WILL BE AN AGE OF LIBERTY

After all that has just passed – all the lives taken, and all the possibilities and hopes that died with them – it is natural to wonder if America's future is one of fear. Some speak of an age of terror. I know there are struggles ahead, and dangers to face. But this country will define our times, not be defined by them. As long as the United States of America is determined and strong, this will not be an age of terror; this will be an age of liberty, here and across the world.

harm *Schaden, Verletzung*
great losses *große Verluste*

Great harm has been done to us. We have suffered great losses. And in our grief and anger we have found our mission and our moment. Freedom and fear are at war. The advance of human freedom – the great achievement of our time, and the great hope of every time – now depends on us.
Our nation – this generation – will lift a dark threat of violence from our people and our future. We will rally the world to this cause by our efforts, by our courage. We will not tire, we will not falter, and we will not fail.

to tire to get tired; *müde werden*
to falter to hesitate; *zögern*
to fail to be unsuccessful; *versagen*

It is my hope that in the months and years ahead, life will return almost to normal. We'll go back to our lives and routines, and that is good. Even grief recedes with time and grace. But our resolve must not pass. Each of us will remember what happened that day, and to whom it happened. We'll remember the moment the news came – where we were and what we were doing. Some will remember an image of a fire, or a story of rescue. Some will carry memories of a face and a voice gone forever.

grief recedes the pain of mourning fades/lessens; *Trauer nimmt ab*
grace benevolence (of God); *Gnade (Gottes)*
resolve determination; *Entschlossenheit*

And I will carry this: It is the police shield of a man named George Howard, who died at the World Trade Center trying to save others. It was given to me by his mom, Arlene, as a proud memorial to her son. This is my reminder of lives that ended, and a task that does not end. I will not forget this wound to our country or those who inflicted it. I will not yield; I will not rest; I will not relent in waging this struggle for freedom and security for the American people.

to inflict to perpetrate; *zufügen*
to relent to give up
to wage this struggle to carry out this fight; *diesen Kampf führen*

The course of this conflict is not known, yet its outcome is certain. Freedom and fear, justice and cruelty, have always been at war, and we know that God is not neutral between them. Fellow citizens, we'll meet violence with patient justice – assured of the rightness of our cause, and confident of the victories to come. In all that lies before us, may God grant us wisdom, and may He watch over the United States of America. Thank you.

Source: http://edition.cnn.com/2001/US/09/20/gen.bush.transcript/

ASSIGNMENTS

A) Comprehension

SQ3R reading method / think-pair-share / peer support and feedback / summary writing

1. Read the speech transcript and highlight President George W. Bush's main arguments.
2. Write eight questions which can be answered by your classmates; work in pairs or in groups.
3. Write a comprehensive summary of President Bush's speech.

B) Analysis

think - pair - share / peer support and feedback / group work / using tablets or laptops / presentation

1. Analyse the structure of the speech.
2. President Bush claims that Americans are not intimidated by these terror attacks; instead, they show strength, endurance and a sense of unity. Analyse the key terms he uses to prove his point.
3. Work in groups and analyse some of the rhetorical devices which support Bush's message.

C) Evaluation, Comment, Creative Activities

research / WebQuest / using tablets or laptops / smartboard / collaboration with History or Social Sciences classes / cross-curricular connections / speech / evaluating website content / discussion

1. In his speech, George W. Bush encourages American citizens to stay strong after the terrorist attacks and aims to convince the audience of the anti-terror policy he wants to adopt. Has he achieved these aims? Write an article, or prepare and give a speech, in response to this question.
2. It is important to note President Bush's distinction between:
   a) Muslim scholars, the vast majority of Muslim clerics, and the peaceful teachings of Islam, and
   b) the terrorists who practise a fringe form of Islamist extremism.
   Discuss the significance of this distinction.
3. "Fellow citizens, we'll meet violence with patient justice – assured of the rightness of our cause, and confident of the victories to come." Discuss this statement in pairs or in groups.
4. "Whether we bring our enemies to justice, or bring justice to our enemies, justice will be done." Discuss George W. Bush's statement in the context of his political decisions.

D) Ideas for Research and Mediation (English = > German), For Thought and Discussion:

"German Leader Says No to Iraq War"

By John Hooper, a journalist based in Hanover, for *The Guardian* on Tuesday, August 6, 2002

German chancellor Gerhard Schröder and his Social Democratic party yesterday broke ranks with America's other European allies by declaring at the start of their election campaign that Germany would refuse to provide troops or money for an invasion of Iraq.

The SPD's top official indicated that Germany was prepared to stay out of the conflict, even if the UN gave its blessing to a war. Germany's rebuff to Washington came as Iraq further tried to split western opinion by inviting the US Congress to send a mission to Baghdad, offering free access to any site alleged to be developing weapons of mass destruction. The White House dismissed the invitation.

Mr Schröder declared: "We are ready to offer solidarity. But this country, under my leadership, is not available for adventure."

From: *The Guardian* https://www.theguardian.com/world/2002/aug/06/iraq.johnhooper

E) Further Research: For Thought and Discussion

1. What are George W. Bush's arguments for the invasion of Iraq?
2. Why did the German Chancellor Gerhard Schröder say "No" to Germany taking part in the Iraq war?
3. Find out why the British Prime Minister Tony Blair supported the US invasion of Iraq.
4. Did US troops find any weapons of mass destruction in Iraq?
   The following websites may give you some background information:
   The Guardian, October 7, 2004: https://www.theguardian.com
   The Telegraph, March 18, 2013: http://www.telegraph.co.uk
   The Washington Post, August 12, 2004: http://www.washingtonpost.com
   Süddeutsche Zeitung vom 17. Mai 2010: http://www.sueddeutsche.de
   DER SPIEGEL vom 6. Juli 2016: http://www.spiegel.de
5. Prepare and give a three-minute speech or a multimedia presentation about your findings.

F) For Thought and Discussion: President Barack Obama's Address on September 10, 2016

"Fifteen years ago, a September day that began like any other became one of the darkest in our nation's history. The Twin Towers were reduced to rubble. The Pentagon was in flames. A Pennsylvania field burned with the wreckage of an airplane. And nearly 3,000 innocent lives were lost. Sons and daughters, husbands and wives, neighbors and colleagues and friends. They were from all walks of life, all races and religions, all colors and creeds, from across America and around the world.

This weekend, we honor their memory once more. We stand with the survivors who still bear the scars of that day. We thank the first responders who risked everything to save others. And we salute a generation of Americans – our men and women in uniform, diplomats and our intelligence, homeland security and law enforcement professionals – who serve, and have given their lives, to help keep us safe.

A lot has changed over these past 15 years. We've delivered devastating blows to the al Qaeda leaders that attacked us on 9/11. We delivered justice to Osama bin Laden. We've strengthened our homeland security. We've prevented attacks. We've saved lives.

At the same time, the terrorist threat has evolved, as we've seen so tragically from Boston to Chattanooga, from San Bernardino to Orlando. So in Afghanistan, Iraq, Syria and beyond, we'll stay relentless against terrorists like al Qaeda and ISIL. We will destroy them. And we'll keep doing everything in our power to protect our homeland.

As we reflect on these past 15 years, it's also important to remember what has not changed – the core values that define us as Americans. The resilience that sustains us. After all, terrorists will never be able to defeat the United States. Their only hope is to terrorize us into changing who we are or our way of life. That's why we Americans will never give in to fear. And it's why this weekend we remember the true spirit of 9/11. We're still the America of heroes who ran into harm's way; of ordinary folks who took down the hijackers; of families who turned their pain into hope. We are still the America that looks out for one another, bound by our shared belief that I am my brother's keeper, I am my sister's keeper.

In the face of terrorism, how we respond matters. We cannot give in to those who would divide us. We cannot react in ways that erode the fabric of our society. Because it's our diversity, our welcoming of all talent, our treating of everybody fairly – no matter their race, gender, ethnicity, or faith – that's part of what makes our country great. It's what makes us resilient. And if we stay true to those values, we'll uphold the legacy of those we've lost, and keep our nation strong and free. God bless you, and God bless the United States of America."

Source: *Obama White House Archives* https://obamawhitehouse.archives.gov/the-press-office/2016/09/10/weekly-address-upholding-legacy-those-we-lost-september-11th

"Keeping the American People Safe."

President Barack Obama's Weekly Address from Sunday, December 6, 2015

RELATED TOPICS

AMERICAN RESOLVE / COURAGE / DESTRUCTION / DIGNITY / FREEDOM / EXTREMISM / FEAR / FREEDOM / HOPE / IDEOLOGY / INTERNATIONAL TERRORISM / JUSTICE / LIBERTY / MASS MURDER / PEACE / PERSECUTION / SOLIDARITY / TERRORISM / TERRORIST ATTACKS / TRAGEDY / VIOLENCE / WAR ON TERROR

In terms of governance, one of the main responsibilities which falls to an administration is the protection of its people. Speaking from the Oval Office on December 6, 2015, **Barack Obama** addressed this issue.
The speech was delivered within a higher state of alarm after a married couple had carried out a calculated attack in San Bernardino, California. Obama identified the incident as an act of terrorism and suggested it was inspired by – though not directly connected with – the group known as the Islamic State in Iraq and Syria (ISIS). In order to counter this threat, Obama pledged more aerial bombardments to negate the threats posed by ISIS, otherwise referred to as ISIL.
While the President's speech did not offer a widely-new strategy to take out the threat posed by terrorist acts, his words reaffirmed his administration's efforts to wipe out Islamic State. Equally as important was his message to the general public. He told the American people that they should not lose hope and be scared or direct anger at the countless law-abiding, peaceful Muslims or their places of worship.

THE PRESIDENT Barack Obama:

Good evening.

On Wednesday, 14 Americans were killed as they came together to celebrate the holidays. They were taken from their family and friends who loved them deeply. They were white and black; Latino and Asian; immigrants and American-born; moms and dads; daughters and sons. Each of them served their fellow citizens and all of them were part of our American family.

THE THREAT OF TERRORISM,
DESIGNED TO KILL INNOCENT PEOPLE

Tonight, I want to talk with you about this tragedy, the broader threat of terrorism, and how we can keep our country safe.

The FBI is still gathering the facts about what happened in San Bernardino, but here is what we know. The victims were brutally murdered and injured by one of their co-workers and his wife. So far, we have no evidence that the killers were directed by a terrorist organization overseas, or that they were part of a broader conspiracy here at home. But it is clear that the two of them had gone down the dark path of radicalization, embracing a perverted interpretation of Islam that calls for war against America and the West. They had stockpiled assault weapons, ammunition, and pipe bombs. So this was an act of terrorism, designed to kill innocent people.

embracing agreeing with
to stockpile to pile up, to collect; *anhäufen*
assault weapons *Angriffswaffen*
ammunition *Munition*
pipe bombs bombs hidden in pipes; *Rohrbomben*

AT WAR WITH TERRORISTS

Our nation has been at war with terrorists since al-Qaeda killed nearly 3,000 Americans on 9/11. In the process, we've hardened our defenses – from airports to financial centers, to other critical infrastructure. Intelligence and law enforcement agencies have disrupted countless plots here and overseas, and worked around the clock to keep us safe.

Our military and counterterrorism professionals have relentlessly pursued terrorist networks overseas – disrupting safe havens in several different countries, killing Osama bin Laden, and decimating al-Qaeda's leadership.

Over the last few years, however, the terrorist threat has evolved into a new phase. As we've become better at preventing complex, multifaceted attacks like 9/11, terrorists turned to less complicated acts of violence like the mass shootings that are all too common in our society. It is this type of attack that we saw at Fort Hood in 2009; in Chattanooga earlier this year; and now in San Bernardino. And as groups like ISIL grew stronger amidst the chaos of war in Iraq and then Syria, and as the Internet erases the distance between countries, we see growing efforts by terrorists to poison the minds of people like the Boston Marathon bombers and the San Bernardino killers.

defenses security measures; *Verteidigungsmaßnahmen*
intelligence agencies *Geheimdienste*
law enforcement agencies *Strafverfolgungsbehörden*
to disrupt countless plots (*here:*) *unzählige geplante Terroranschläge vereiteln*
relentlessly *unnachgiebig*
to pursue to track down
to disrupt *unterbrechen, vereiteln*
to decimate to destroy; *dezimieren*
to evolve into (*here:*) to enter, to develop
multifaceted complex; *facettenreich*

ISIL Islamic State of Iraq and the Levant; a terrorist organisation
to erase to wipe out

WE SEE OUR KIDS IN THE FACES OF THE YOUNG PEOPLE KILLED IN PARIS

For seven years, I've confronted this evolving threat each morning in my intelligence briefing. And since the day I took this office, I've authorized U.S. forces to take out terrorists abroad precisely because I know how real the danger is. As Commander-in-Chief, I have no greater responsibility than the security of the American people. As a father to two young daughters who are the most precious part of my life, I know that we see ourselves with friends and co-workers at a holiday party like the one in San Bernardino. I know we see our kids in the faces of the young people killed in Paris. And I know that after so much war, many Americans are asking whether we are confronted by a cancer that has no immediate cure.

Well, here's what I want you to know: The threat from terrorism is real, but we will overcome it. We will destroy ISIL and any other organization that tries to harm us. Our success won't depend on tough talk, or abandoning our values, or giving into fear. That's what groups like ISIL are hoping for. Instead, we will prevail by being strong and smart, resilient and relentless, and by drawing upon every aspect of American power. Here's how. [...]

giving into fear becoming resigned to anxiety; *der Angst nachgeben*
to prevail to succeed
resilient tough; *widerstandsfähig*
by drawing upon by using

WE CANNOT TURN AGAINST ONE ANOTHER BY LETTING THIS FIGHT BE DEFINED AS A WAR BETWEEN AMERICA AND ISLAM

Here's what we cannot do. We cannot turn against one another by letting this fight be defined as a war between America and Islam. That, too, is what groups like ISIL want. ISIL does not speak for Islam. They are thugs and killers, part of a cult of death, and they account for a tiny fraction of more than a billion Muslims around the world – including millions of patriotic Muslim Americans who reject their hateful ideology. Moreover, the vast majority of terrorists' victims around the world are Muslims. If we're to succeed in defeating terrorism we must enlist Muslim communities as some of our strongest allies, rather than push them away through suspicion and hate.

That does not mean denying the fact that an extremist ideology has spread within some Muslim communities. This is a real problem that Muslims must confront, without making excuses. Muslim leaders here and around the globe have to continue working with us to decisively and unequivocally reject the hateful ideology that groups like ISIL and al-Qaeda promote; to speak out against not just acts of violence, but also those interpretations of Islam that are incompatible with the values of religious tolerance, mutual respect, and human dignity.

But just as it is the responsibility of Muslims around the world to root out misguided ideas that lead to radicalization, it is the responsibility of all Americans – of every faith – to reject discrimination. It is our responsibility to reject religious tests on who we admit into this country. It's our responsibility to reject proposals that Muslim Americans should somehow be treated differently. Because when we travel down that road, we lose. That kind of divisiveness, that betrayal of our values plays into the hands of groups like ISIL. Muslim Americans are our friends and our neighbors, our co-workers, our sports heroes – and, yes, they are our men and women in uniform who are willing to die in defense of our country. We have to remember that.

thug violent criminal
to enlist to sign people up, (*here:*) to win support of the Muslim communities
suspicion mistrust
when we travel down that road *wenn wir uns für diesen Weg entscheiden*
divisiveness *Uneinigkeit, Gespaltenheit*
betrayal (*here:*) rejection; *Verrat*, (*here:*) *Preisgabe*
neighbor (*AmE*), neighbour (*BrE*)
in defense of (*AmE*), defence (*BrE*); *zur Verteidigung, zum Schutz*

WE WERE FOUNDED UPON A BELIEF IN HUMAN DIGNITY

My fellow Americans, I am confident we will succeed in this mission because we are on the right side of history.

We were founded upon a belief in human dignity – that no matter who you are, or where you come from, or what you look like, or what

to practice (*AmE*), to practise (*BrE*); *ausüben*

to prevail to succeed

religion you practice, you are equal in the eyes of God and equal in the eyes of the law. Even in this political season, even as we properly debate what steps I and future Presidents must take to keep our country safe, let's make sure we never forget what makes us exceptional. Let's not forget that freedom is more powerful than fear; that we have always met challenges – whether war or depression, natural disasters or terrorist attacks – by coming together around our common ideals as one nation, as one people. So long as we stay true to that tradition, I have no doubt America will prevail. Thank you.
God bless you, and may God bless the United States of America.

The speech transcript is taken from: *The Obama White House Archives*
Watch the full video and read the President's speech:
https://medium.com/@ObamaWhiteHouse/president-obama-addresses-the-nation-on-keeping-the-american-people-safe-b4cfa8a0f143

ASSIGNMENTS

A) Reading and Listening Comprehension

▶ *SQ3R reading method / think – pair – share / idea tower / mind map / presentation*

1. Watch the video and highlight Barack Obama's main arguments in your speech transcript.
2. Explain Barack Obama's main arguments and take into consideration:
   a) the terrorist attacks he refers to
   b) how the US can overcome the threat of terrorism
   c) what the US should not do in the fight against terrorism
   d) what kind of advice the President gives to the nation.
3. Present your findings in the form of an idea tower.

B) Analysis

▶ *group work / mind map / peer support and feedback / designing posters / gallery walk*

1. Analyse the structure of Barack Obama's speech.
2. Analyse some of the rhetorical devices Obama uses to get his message across to the audience.
3. Analyse Obama's final appeal to the audience.

C) Evaluation, Comment, Creative Activities

▶ *paired work / creative writing / interview / role play / discussion / speech / feedback / evaluation*

1. Obama emphasises that: "Our success won't depend on tough talk, or abandoning our values, or giving into fear." Analyse this statement and explain your opinion of it.
2. "We cannot turn against one another by letting this fight be defined as a war between America and Islam." Discuss in pairs what Obama means when he says this.
3. "Our fight to defeat ISIL is not a war with Islam." Evaluate the significance of this statement.
4. Write an interview with former President Barack Obama.
5. Prepare and give a three-minute speech in response to Obama's speech.

"In the Face of Terror, We Stand as One."

Vice-President Joe Biden's Weekly Address from November 21, 2015

RELATED TOPICS

AMERICAN RESOLVE · AMERICAN VALUES · COURAGE · DIGNITY · FREEDOM · EXTREMISM · FEAR · FOUNDATION OF AMERICA · FREEDOM · HOPE · IDEOLOGY · INTERNATIONAL TERRORISM · JUSTICE · LIBERTY · MASS MURDER · OPENNESS · PEACE · PERSECUTION · SOLIDARITY · TERRORISM · TERRORIST ATTACKS · VIOLENCE · WAR ON TERROR

In this address, former **Vice-President Joe Biden** spoke out about his and President Obama's commitment to protecting America from terrorists, while also providing refuge for some of the world's most vulnerable people.
He emphasized that he and the President consider the safety of the American people to be their first priority but that slamming the door in the face of refugees fleeing precisely the type of senseless violence that occurred in Paris in November 2015 would be a betrayal of American values.
The vast majority of Syrian refugees are women and children, many of whom are orphans, survivors of torture, and people desperately in need of medical attention.
And all refugees undergo the highest level of security checks of any category of traveller to the United States. The Vice-President reminded his audience that ISIL wants us to turn our backs on Muslims victimized by terrorism. Biden argues that we will win the War on Terror by prioritizing security while refusing to compromise the fundamental American values of freedom, openness, and tolerance.

From: *The Obama White House Archives*
https://obamawhitehouse.archives.gov/the-press-office/2015/11/21/weekly-address-face-terror-we-stand-one

Joe Biden:

Group 1: ______________________ *(give this section a suitable heading)*

Good morning everyone. This past week we've seen the best and the worst of humanity. The heinous terrorist attacks in Paris and Beirut, in Iraq and Nigeria. They showed us once again the depths of the terrorist's depravity.
And at the same time we saw the world come together in solidarity. Parisians opening their doors to anyone trapped in the street, taxi drivers turning off their meters to get people home safely, people lining up to donate blood. These simple human acts are a powerful reminder that we cannot be broken and that in the face of terror, we stand as one. In the wake of these terrible events, I understand the anxiety that many Americans feel. I really do. I don't dismiss the fear of a terrorist bomb going off. There's nothing President Obama and I take more seriously though, than keeping the American people safe.

Group 2: ______________________ *(give this section a suitable heading)*

In the past few weeks though, we've heard an awful lot of people suggest that the best way to keep America safe is to prevent any Syrian refugee from gaining asylum in the United States.
So let's set the record straight on how a refugee gets asylum. Refugees face the most rigorous screening of anyone who comes to the United States. First, they are finger printed, then they undergo a thorough background check, then they are interviewed by the Department of Homeland Security. And after that, the FBI, the National Counterterrorism Center, the Department of Defense and the Department of State, all have to sign off on giving them access to the USA.

Group 3: ______________________ *(give this section a suitable heading)*

And to address the specific terrorism concerns we are talking about now, we've instituted another layer of checks just for Syrian refugees. There is no possibility of being overwhelmed by a flood of refugees landing on our doorstep tomorrow. Right now, refugees wait 18 to 24 months while the screening process is completed. And unlike in Europe, refugees don't set foot in the United States until they are thoroughly vetted.
Let's also remember who the vast majority of these refugees are: women, children, orphans, survivors of torture, people desperately in need of medical help.

Group 4: ______________________ *(give this section a suitable heading)*

To turn them away and say there is no way you can ever get here would play right into the terrorists' hands. We know what ISIL – we know what they hope to accomplish. They flat-out told us.
Earlier this year, the top ISIL leader al-Baghdadi revealed the true goal of their attacks. Here's what he said: "Compel the crusaders to actively destroy the gray zone themselves. Muslims in the West will quickly find themselves between one and two choices. Either apostatize or emigrate to the Islamic State and thereby escape persecution." So it's clear. It's clear what ISIL wants. They want to manufacture a clash between civilizations. They want frightened people to think in terms of "us versus them."

Group 5: ______________________ *(give this section a suitable heading)*

They want us to turn our backs on Muslims victimized by terrorism. But this gang of thugs peddling a warped ideology, they will never prevail. The world is united in our resolve to end their evil. And the only thing ISIL can do is spread terror in the hopes that we will, in turn, turn on each other.
We will betray our ideals and take actions, actions motivated by fear that will drive more recruits into the arms of ISIL. That's how they win. We win by prioritizing our security as we have been doing. Refusing to compromise our fundamental American values: freedom, openness, tolerance. That's who we are. That's how we win.
May God continue to bless the United States of America and God bless our troops.

ASSIGNMENTS

A) Group Work

▶ *group work / idea tower / mind map / peer support and feedback / presentation*

a) The speech is divided into five sections so divide the class into five groups.

b) Each group should analyse a different section of the speech.
c) Please translate your assigned section of the speech into German.
d) Each group should give their assigned section of the speech a suitable heading.
e) Follow the reading comprehension and analysis tasks below.
f) Each group should then present their section, and their answers to B) and C), to the class.

B) Reading Comprehension

1. Look up any words you don't know that you need in order to understand the speech.
2. Then highlight Joe Biden's main arguments on your speech transcript.
3. Summarise Joe Biden's main arguments.

C) Analysis

1. How does Joe Biden structure his speech? Analyse the structure of the speech briefly and explain the significance of your section in the context of the whole speech.
2. How does Biden try to convince the audience of his arguments? Analyse the rhetorical devices Biden uses in your assigned section of the speech.

D) Evaluation, Comment and Creative Activities

▶ *interview / hot seat / debate / discussion / creative writing / TV talk show / speech competition*

1. "In the past few weeks though, we've heard an awful lot of people suggest that the best way to keep America safe is to prevent any Syrian refugee from gaining asylum in the United States." Explain your own opinion of this statement. You may organize a debate or speech competition in class.
2. "We win by prioritizing our security as we have been doing. Refusing to compromise our fundamental American values: freedom, openness, tolerance. That's who we are. That's how we win." Analyse this appeal to the audience and explain your own opinion of it in a three-minute speech.
3. Imagine you are a journalist who has been given the opportunity to interview Joe Biden. What questions would you like to ask him? What possible answers might he give you? Prepare your interview questions and act them out with a partner who should respond as if they were Joe Biden.
4. **"We expected the war on terror to unite us. What went wrong?"**
   By Charles Lane, *The Washington Post*, September 10, 2018
   https://www.washingtonpost.com/opinions/we-expected-the-war-on-terror-to-unite-us-what-went-wrong/2018/09/10/5fb58c38-b4ff-11e8-a7b5-adaaa5b2a57f_story.html?noredirect=on&utm_term=.9e7eef1b7c62
   Throughout our history, external threats have forced the American people to put aside their differences for the sake of the common defense. Obviously, it has not worked out that way. Gone, long gone, are the singing, flag-waving and bipartisanship of the 9/11 aftermath. In their place, we have a polarized, hate-filled political climate often, and not inaccurately, described as a "cold civil war." [...] What went wrong?"
5. **Terror attack on mosques in New Zealand** on March 15, 2019: At least 50 people were killed and 50 wounded, in a hate-filled terror attack targeting two mosques in the New Zealand city of Christchurch. New Zealand's Prime Minister Jacinda Ardern described the terror attack as "one of New Zealand's darkest days." She says that "we represent diversity, kindness, compassion, a home for those who share our values, refuge for those who need it. And those values, I can assure you, will not, and cannot, be shaken by this attack. We are a proud nation of more than 200 ethnicities, 160 languages. And amongst that diversity we share common values. And the one that we place the currency on right now – and tonight – is our compassion and support for the community of those directly affected by this tragedy."
   Go online and listen to her speech:
   https://edition.cnn.com/2019/03/15/asia/new-zealand-jacinda-ardern-full-statement-intl/index.html

E The Earth in Danger: Climate Change

"Must, Can, Will We Change?"

Al Gore: Speech at the Ashden Awards Ceremony 2017, at the Royal Geographical Society in London, on June 15, 2017

RELATED TOPICS

THE ABOLITIONIST MOVEMENT · THE AMERICAN DREAM · THE CIVIL RIGHTS MOVEMENT · CLIMATE CHANGE · DIGNITY · EDUCATION · ENERGY · THE ENVIRONMENT · FREEDOM · FUTURE GENERATIONS · GLOBAL WARMING · THE GOVERNMENT · HUMAN RIGHTS · JUSTICE · LIBERTY · NATIONHOOD · THE PARIS AGREEMENT · POLLUTION · RENEWABLE ENERGY · SUSTAINABILITY

Al Gore was responsible for a rousing speech on the climate emergency and how the U.N. aimed to counteract the threat with its Sustainable Development Goals. The former US Vice-President addressed the Ashden Awards Ceremony with a sense of optimism about what could be achieved. This was all in spite of the USA's controversial withdrawal from the Paris Agreement. He asserted, 'No one person can stop the climate movement or the sustainability revolution – we are going to win no matter what President Donald Trump tries to do.'

The significance of award-winning projects which aim to reverse the effects of the global environmental crisis forms the opening of Gore's speech. As he progresses, three questions come to the fore: Must, can and will we change our behaviour to find a solution for the climate emergency?

In essence, the Ashden Awards Ceremony is a yearly event which encompasses the latest developments in the green energy sector. The awards themselves are received by those who are making significant contributions to the field of sustainable energy production. The recipients hail from the UK, around Europe and also parts of the developing world. They all share a common mission: to live in a world of low-carbon emissions. On top of the prize money they are awarded, the Award also enables the winners to take their place amongst the leading figures of the sustainable energy movement.

This is an excerpt of Al Gore's keynote speech at the 2017 Ashden Awards Ceremony in London: http://www.inspiring-sustainability.com/blog/al-gore-at-2017-ashden-awards-ceremony

Al Gore:

[...] There are really only three questions remaining where the climate crisis is concerned.

The first, for some still, is do we really have to change? Must we change?

The second question is can we change?

And the third question, perhaps the most important, is will we change?

MOTHER NATURE IS TELLING US WE MUST CHANGE

First of all, we must change not only because the global scientific community has been virtually unanimous in telling us that the science is crystal clear, but also because there is a new advocate, more persuasive than all the scientists put together. Mother Nature is telling us we must change.

unanimous in agreement; *übereinstimmend, einhellig*

A year ago in December, the United Kingdom had the heaviest rainfalls in recorded history with flooding that caused a great deal of suffering. In some of the developing countries that have been represented on this stage tonight, we've already heard about the changes in the timing of rain falls, the periodicity of rain falls. For generations running back 'til the memory of man cannot track it further, generations have been able to rely on a rainy season, dry season pattern to decide when to plant and when to harvest. But all of those well-known patterns are being disrupted because more precipitation falls in one time large downpours at odd times of the year, out of season. And then during the periods between the rainfalls, the extra heat in the atmosphere pulls the soil's moisture more quickly out of the ground, makes droughts appear more readily, last longer and have a deeper impact.

the periodicity *die Häufigkeit des Auftretens in einem bestimmten Zeitraum*

to rely on *sich verlassen auf*

disrupted disturbed

precipitation (*here:*) rain

the soil's moisture how wet the soil is; die *Feuchtigkeit des Bodens*

drought lack of rain, water shortage; *Dürre*

The entire water cycle of the earth is being disrupted because we put 110 million tons of man-made global warming pollution into the atmosphere every day and the accumulated amount that now is up there traps as much extra heat energy in the earth's system each day than would be released by 400,000 Hiroshima class atomic bombs exploding every 24 hours. It's a big planet but that is an enormous amount of energy.

Air temperatures are going up. You know full well that 16 of the 17 hotitures ever measured have occurred since 2001. You know the ice is melting, and in places like Bangladesh, the Maldives, and Miami Beach, Florida, there are now fish from the ocean swimming in

hotitures hottest periods

high tide *Tide-Hochwasser*
disease *Krankheit*
latitude *Breitengrad (here:) Gegend*
to be familiar with something *mit etwas vertraut sein*
validated confirmed
sustainability *Nachhaltigkeit*
magnitude great impact
to jump start *auf Touren bringen*
inflection point turning point; *Wendepunkt*

streets at high tide that are not intended for fishing. Ninety per cent of that heat is going into the oceans and that is what is disrupting the water cycle. We're seeing the spread of diseases to latitudes where people are not familiar with them. We're seeing storms get stronger.

So the answer to the first question – must we change – is increasingly clear and obvious. Yes, we must change. And by the way, the scientists, many of them here in the UK, who predicted these consequences long ago, have already been proven right. So because their record has been validated, we should listen very carefully to what they tell us would happen if we did not make these changes to prevent the most catastrophic outcomes that would occur if we did not change. So, yes, we must change.

YES, WE CAN CHANGE

The answer to the second question – can we change? – was visible on this stage this evening. Yes, we can change. There is now in our world a sustainability revolution and it is best understood in my view by placing it in the context of other great global transformations – the agricultural revolution, the industrial revolution, and the digital revolution. This sustainability revolution has the breadth and magnitude of the industrial revolution, but it has the speed of the digital revolution. And instead of beginning in a corner of the United Kingdom in a world of 1.5 billion people and then slowly spreading to Western Europe and North America, the sustainability revolution is being jump started in rich and poor countries alike, in every corner of this world of 7.4 billion people. [...]

This sustainability revolution is growing in speed and magnitude, but it is not yet growing as fast as it must because we have not yet reached the point where emissions of global warming pollution are starting to come down. We have, over the last three years, seen for the first time in the absence of a depression or great recession, a stabilising of global warming pollution worldwide and the first hint that it is beginning to decline. Looks like an inflection point. [...]

So this is an exciting time and I want to respond since you mentioned the Paris Agreement. I had worried when the President of my country, [*coughs*] [...] What did I mean? I meant another country. I meant no disrespect, but when the President of my country was preparing to make his announcement about the Paris Agreement and we did not know what it would be, I was very worried that if he pulled the US out of the agreement then other countries, perhaps those not entirely enthusiastic about the Paris Agreement, would use it as an excuse to pull out themselves.

NO ONE PERSON CAN STOP THE CLIMATE MOVEMENT OR THE SUSTAINABILITY REVOLUTION

I can tell you that in the aftermath of that decision there has been no such cascade of other countries following the decision announced by President Trump. To the contrary, what I have seen and heard is an expression of solidarity not only in all of the other countries of the world, but also on the part of governors of states and mayors of cities and leaders of businesses in the United States of America. No one person can stop the climate movement or the sustainability revolution. We are going to win no matter what President Donald Trump tries to do.

in the aftermath of (*here:*) as a consequence of, after
cascade (*here:*) rush

The Paris Agreement, I believe, is actually stronger today. I say that with all sincerity and conviction. Since the Paris Agreement was reached, many hundreds of coal-plants have been cancelled in China and India and in quite a few other places. We saw just two days ago the announcement that the sales of coal fell in the year just measured by a larger amount than ever before in history. We have seen the beginning of construction of large utility scale solar farms and wind farms and the introduction of many other new sustainable technologies. India just announced a major switch from its plans for a lot more coal fired plants to a stunning increase in solar farms, and announced just three weeks ago that within 13 years, 100 per cent of the vehicles in India must be electric vehicles. That is a dramatic and inspiring announcement.

conviction *Überzeugung*
cancelled (*here:*) shut down
stunning (*here:*) enormous

WILL WE CHANGE?

We can change, we must change and we can change. So what about that final question – will we change? Just as the sustainability revolution should be understood in the context of the technological revolutions that came before it, the climate movement should be seen in the context of the great moral causes that have transformed and improved the outlook for humanity.

In every one of the great moral movements, there has been discouragement. There has been despair. There have been advocates who have asked: "How long will this take? Is it ever going to succeed?"

discouragement pessimism; *Entmutigung*

The Abolition Movement, which began more than 200 years ago here in this country, met with such ferocious opposition, that many felt it a lost cause. But it prevailed. The Women's Suffrage Movement in this country and my country and around the world was met with no, no, no after no, but it prevailed. The Civil Rights Movement in my country, the Anti-Apartheid Movement in South Africa, and more recently the Gay Rights Movement in so many parts of the world, what all of these transformative movements have had in common is that

The Abolition Movement a historical movement that campaigned to end the slave trade and to set slaves free
ferocious fierce, hateful, violent
to prevail to succeed
The Women's Suffrage Movement *see* Additional Notes
The Civil Rights Movement *see* Additional Notes

they were met with the same kind of ferocious resistance that led to despair on the part of many advocates. The late Nelson Mandela once said – "It's always impossible until it's done."

We have seen people continue in spite of their concern that it might be impossible. During some of the bleakest days of the Civil Rights Movement in my country, Dr. Martin Luther King Jr. was asked by one of his fellow advocates: "How long is this going to take?" And he famously answered: "How long? Not long, because no lie can live forever." How long? Not long because "the arc of the moral universe is long, but it bends toward justice." And in every single case, when the obfuscations and the side issues and the distractions were cleared away, what was left was a very simple and clear choice, a binary choice, between what is right and what is wrong.

bleak (*here:*) most difficult

"the arc of the moral universe is long, but it bends toward justice" from: Martin Luther King Jr.'s sermon [*Predigt*] at Temple Israel of Hollywood on February 26, 1965

obfuscation confusion

binary choice a choice between two things

IT IS WRONG TO USE THE SKY AS AN OPEN SEWER

It was wrong to allow slavery to continue. It was wrong to deny women the right to vote. It was wrong to discriminate on the basis of skin colour or who you fell in love with. It was wrong to allow apartheid to continue and when the central issue was thus framed in stark relief because of who we are as human beings, the outcome became fore ordained. We chose what was right and now, in this case, it is clearly wrong to destroy the prospects of living prosperously and sustainably on a clean earth when we bequeath it to our children. It is wrong to use the sky as an open sewer.

fore ordained predestined, inevitable

to bequeath *vererben*

sewer *Abwasserkanal, Kanalisation*

It is wrong to condemn future generations to a life time haunted by continual declines in their standard of living and to give them a world with political disruption and all the chaos that scientists have warned us about.

haunted oppressed, tormented; *heimgesucht*

It is right to give them hope. It is right to give them a clean future and a sustainable and prosperous future, and for those who say: "We may not have the will to change," always remember that the will to change is in itself a renewable resource.
Thank you.

ASSIGNMENTS

A) Pre-Listening and Pre-Reading Activity

communicative activities / speaking skills training / market place / inside-outside circle / cooperative learning / exchange some first ideas / idea tower / comment chain technique / discussion

1. Watch the trailer for Al Gore's film *An Inconvenient Sequel: Truth To Power* (2017)
2. Discuss your first impression of the trailer with your classmates.

B) Reading and Listening Comprehension

▶ *communicative activities / paired work / idea tower / mind map / writing a summary or a news report*

1. Watch Al Gore's speech, read the transcript, and highlight any significant statements: https://www.youtube.com/watch?v=iAIXqcHQTD0
2. What are the three questions about the climate crisis that Al Gore asks the audience?
3. Make a list of the answers Al Gore gives to each question.
4. "This sustainability revolution has the breadth and magnitude of the industrial revolution, but it has the speed of the digital revolution." Explain what Al Gore means when he says this.
5. Summarise Al Gore's main arguments.

C) Analysis

▶ *paired work / presentation / writing an analysis / peer support and feedback / sharing ideas*

1. Analyse the structure of Al Gore's speech.
2. Analyse some of the rhetorical devices Al Gore uses to emphasise his message.
3. Have a closer look at the conclusion of Al Gore's speech. What does he say about the responsibility we have to future generations?
4. Write a comprehensive analysis of Al Gore's speech.

D) Evaluation, Comment, Creative Activities

▶ *cooperative learning / classroom stations technique / role play / press conference / discussion / hot seat / creative writing / speech / feedback / evaluation / SOLO taxonomy*

1. Former US Vice-President Al Gore argues that "the sustainability revolution" is similar to the transformative advances made during the agricultural, industrial and digital revolutions. What do you think of this argument?
2. Al Gore compares the fight against climate change to historic events such as the abolition of the slave trade, the campaign for universal suffrage, the anti-apartheid movement, and the fight for civil and gay rights. Write an interview with Al Gore, in which you explain your own opinion as to whether or not this comparison is appropriate.
3. The annual Ashden Awards recognise sustainable, ecological, and environmental projects. Al Gore says that he is "extremely inspired" by the winners, and that they "can inspire policy makers, governmental officials and community leaders". Come up with an ecological project that could inspire your school community or the community leaders in your city to recognise our responsibility to protect the environment.
4. Climate change campaigners, like Al Gore, argue that the carbon dioxide (CO_2) concentration in our atmosphere can only be reduced if we are willing to accept a drastic change in our lifestyle. What do you think of this argument?
5. Imagine you and your classmates have been chosen to take part in a conference for young people about climage change in New York:
   Work in groups of four and discuss what you want to tell the politicians at the conference about climate change. You might want to talk about energy-saving concepts, alternative energy forms, the role of developing and of rich countries in the fight against climate change, and some outstanding regional, national or international climate change projects you know about. Take notes and present your ideas to your class. Your presentation to the class could be in the form of a short speech.

E) Further Projects for Thought and Discussion

research / interview / hot seat / creative writing / audio or video recording / presentation / speech

1. **The 2017 Ashden Award Winners** https://www.ashden.org/winners/awards-winners/p2
   Take a look at the list of Ashden Award winners to find out more about the projects.
2. ***An Inconvenient Truth* (2006)**
   The documentary *An Inconvenient Truth* emphasises that global warming is real, man-made, and that its effects will be disastrous if we don't act now. Al Gore presents a wide variety of facts and arguments.
3. ***An Inconvenient Sequel: Truth To Power* (2017)**
   Al Gore continues his campaign to combat climate change in his sequel to *An Inconvenient Truth* by travelling around the world to influence international climate change policy. He argues that the perils of climate change can be overcome if we all take action against it. From: https://www.algore.com/library/
   a) Watch *An Inconvenient Sequel: Truth to Power* and write a film review of it.
   b) Prepare, write and act out an inspiring interview with Al Gore.

F) Greta Thunberg: "Our House is on Fire"

Greta Thunberg, 16, the Swedish "Fridays for Climate" activist, gave a speech at the *World Economic Forum* in Davos, Switzerland, on January 25, 2019. Read her speech here:

"Our house is on fire. I am here to say, our house is on fire. [...] We are facing a disaster of unspoken sufferings for enormous amounts of people. And now is not the time for speaking politely or focusing on what we can or cannot say. Now is the time to speak clearly.

Solving the climate crisis is the greatest and most complex challenge that Homo sapiens have ever faced. The main solution, however, is so simple that even a small child can understand it. We have to stop our emissions of greenhouse gases. Either we do that or we don't.

You say nothing in life is black or white. But that is a lie. A very dangerous lie. Either we prevent 1.5 C of warming or we don't. Either we avoid setting off that irreversible chain reaction beyond human control or we don't. Either we choose to go on as a civilisation or we don't. That is as black or white as it gets. There are no grey areas when it comes to survival. We all have a choice. We can create transformational action that will safeguard the living conditions for future generations. Or we can continue with our business as usual and fail.

That is up to you and me. [...]

We must change almost everything in our current societies. The bigger your carbon footprint, the bigger your moral duty. The bigger your platform, the bigger your responsibility. Adults keep saying: "We owe it to the young people to give them hope." But I don't want your hope. I don't want you to be hopeful. I want you to panic. I want you to feel the fear I feel every day. And then I want you to act. I want you to act as you would in a crisis. I want you to act as if our house is on fire. Because it is."

From: https://www.fridaysforfuture.org/greta-speeches#greta_speech_jan25_2019

"Meeting the Global Threat of Climate Change."

Former President Barack Obama's Weekly Address from August 29, 2015

RELATED TOPICS

THE ARCTIC CIRCLE · CLIMATE CHANGE · CLIMATE NEGOTIATIONS · CLIMATE TARGETS · EDUCATION · ENERGY SOURCES · THE ENVIRONMENT · FOSSIL FUELS · FUTURE GENERATIONS · GLACIERS · GLOBAL WARMING · THE GOVERNMENT · HEALTH · HUMAN RIGHTS · NATIONHOOD · RENEWABLE ENERGY SOURCES · RESPONSIBILITY · RISING SEA LEVELS · RISING TEMPERATURES · THE THREAT OF CLIMATE CHANGE · A WAKE-UP CALL

In this weekly address from August 2015, **President Barack Obama** talks about an upcoming trip to Alaska, during which he expects to see the effects of climate change for himself. In his address, the President emphasises the importance of the transition from fossil fuels to more renewable energy sources, like wind and solar power.

Speech transcript taken from: *The Obama White House Archives*
https://obamawhitehouse.archives.gov/blog/2015/08/29/weekly-address-meeting-global-threat-climate-change

THE PRESIDENT Barack Obama:

Hi, everybody. This Monday, I'm heading to Alaska for a three-day tour of the state.

I've been looking forward to this for a long time. Not only because Alaska is one of the most beautiful places in a country that's full of beautiful places – but because I'll have several opportunities to meet with everyday Alaskans about what's going on in their lives. I'll travel all over the state, meeting with Alaskans who live above the Arctic Circle, with Alaska natives, and with folks who earn their livelihoods through fishing and tourism. And I expect to learn a lot.

livelihoods *Lebensunterhalt*

One thing I've learned so far is that a lot of these conversations begin with climate change. And that's because Alaskans are already living with its effects. More frequent and extensive wildfires. Bigger storm

storm surge coastal tsunami-like flood

shoreline erosion *Küstenerosion*

to threaten (*here:*) to affect; *beeinträchtigen, bedrohen*

imminent danger danger that is about to happen
relocated moved to another place
to swallow (*here:*) to drown; *verschlingen*

to convene to call together

ambitious *ehrgeizig*
target goal, aim
emitter *Verursacher von Treibhausgasen*

negotiation (*here:*) conference; *Versammlung, Konferenz*

to accelerate to speed up; *beschleunigen*
transition change; *Übergang*
to rely on to depend on; *abhängen von*

application request
to drill a well *eine Bohrung nach Öl vornehmen*
lease (*here:*) *Nutzungsrecht*
to purchase to buy
offshore drilling *küstennahe Ölbohrungen*
the BP spill in the Gulf of Mexico the largest marine oil spill in history, caused by an explosion (on April 20, 2010) on the Deepwater Horizon oil rig, in the Gulf of Mexico; the oil rig sank on April 22, 2010.

surges as sea ice melts faster. Some of the swiftest shoreline erosion in the world – in some places, more than three feet a year.

Alaska's glaciers are melting faster too, threatening tourism and adding to rising seas. And if we do nothing, Alaskan temperatures are projected to rise between six and twelve degrees by the end of the century, changing all sorts of industries forever.

This is all real. This is happening to our fellow Americans right now. In fact, Alaska's governor recently told me that four villages are in "imminent danger" and have to be relocated. Already, rising sea levels are beginning to swallow one island community.

Think about that. If another country threatened to wipe out an American town, we'd do everything in our power to protect ourselves. Climate change poses the same threat, right now.

That's why one of the things I'll do while I'm in Alaska is to convene other nations to meet this threat. Several Arctic nations have already committed to action. Since the United States and China worked together to set ambitious climate targets last year, leading by example, many of the world's biggest emitters have come forward with new climate plans of their own. And that's a good sign as we approach this December's global climate negotiations in Paris.

DIRTY ENERGY SOURCES THREATEN OUR HEALTH AND OUR ENVIRONMENT

Now, one of the ways America is leading is by transitioning away from dirty energy sources that threaten our health and our environment, and by going all-in on clean, renewable energy sources like wind and solar power. And Alaska has the natural resources to be a global leader in this effort.

Now even as we accelerate this transition, our economy still has to rely on oil and gas. As long as that's the case, I believe we should rely more on domestic production than on foreign imports, and we should demand the highest safety standards in the industry – our own. Still, I know there are Americans who are concerned about oil companies drilling in environmentally sensitive waters.

Some are also concerned with my administration's decision to approve Shell's application to drill a well off the Alaskan coast, using leases they purchased before I took office. I share people's concerns about offshore drilling. I remember the BP spill in the Gulf of Mexico all too well.

That's precisely why my administration has worked to make sure that our oil exploration conducted under these leases is done at the highest standards possible, with requirements specifically tailored to the risks of drilling off Alaska.

to conduct (*here:*) to carry out
tailored to *zugeschnitten auf*

We don't rubber-stamp permits. We made it clear that Shell has to meet our high standards in how they conduct their operations – and it's a testament to how rigorously we've applied those standards that Shell has delayed and limited its exploration off Alaska while trying to meet them. Safety has always been and will continue to be my administration's top priority when it comes to oil and gas exploration off America's precious coasts – even as we push our economy and the world to ultimately transition off of fossil fuels.

we don't rubber-stamp permits *wir vergeben nicht leichtfertig eine Bohrerlaubnis*
a testament to proof, confirmation of
rigorously strictly; *streng*

AMERICA WILL LEAD THE WORLD TO MEET THE THREAT OF CLIMATE CHANGE BEFORE IT'S TOO LATE

So I'm looking forward to talking to Alaskans about how we can work together to make America the global leader of climate change around the globe. And we're going to offer unique and engaging ways for you to join me on this trip all week online at WhiteHouse.gov/Alaska. Because what's happening in Alaska is happening to us. It's our wake-up call. And as long as I'm President, America will lead the world to meet the threat of climate change before it's too late.

wake-up call something that alerts people to a dangerous situation and makes them commit to changing it; *Weckruf*

Thanks, and have a great weekend.

ASSIGNMENTS

A) Reading and Listening Comprehension

1. Watch the video of Barack Obama's speech here:
   https://obamawhitehouse.archives.gov/blog/2015/08/29/weekly-address-meeting-global-threat-climate-change or on You Tube: https://www.youtube.com/watch?v=sFLTjqVS7AE
2. Read the transcript of Barack Obama's speech and highlight any important statements.
3. Outline the consequences of climate change that Barack Obama refers to in his address.

B) Rearranging the Text / Mediation (English → German)

▶ *paired work / peer support and feedback / sharing ideas / evaluation*

Put the following sentences into the correct order. Then translate the main ideas into German.

a) Then Barack Obama emphasises the fact that Alaskans are already living with the impact of climate change: glaciers are melting faster than ever before, and temperatures are projected to rise between 6°C and 12°C by the end of the century.
b) Finally, the President says he is looking forward to his upcoming trip, and promises that, while he is in office, America will lead the world's efforts to meet the threat of climate change before it's too late.

c) Furthermore, the President suggests ways of dealing with these challenges, including transitioning away from fossil fuels to more renewable energy sources, like wind and solar power, which is an effort in which America is leading the field.
d) At the beginning of this week's address, the President talks about his upcoming trip to Alaska, during which he expects to witness the effects of climate change for himself.
e) In addition, Obama stresses that, even though the American economy will still have to rely on oil and gas during the transition period, the American government should rely more on domestic production than importing fossil fuels from foreign countries because these countries do not have the same environmental or safety standards as the United States.

C) Analysis

think – pair – share / posters / presentation / writing an analysis / feedback / discussion

1. Analyse the structure of Barack Obama's speech.
2. Analyse the significance of the two introductory paragraphs.
3. Analyse some rhetorical devices Obama uses and point out their intended effects.
4. Write a comprehensive analysis of Barack Obama's speech.

D) Evaluation, Comment, Creative Activities

inspiration cards / WebQuest / research / collaboration with Social Sciences classes / cross-curricular connections / panel discussion / speech / radio talk / creative writing

1. "We are the first generation to feel the impact of climate change, and the last generation that can do something about it." Prepare and give a three-minute speech to your group, then to your class, in response to this statement.
2. "Strong economic growth and a safer environment no longer have to conflict with one another." Do you agree with Barack Obama? How can strong economic growth and a safer environment be achieved?
3. "And as long as I'm President, America will lead the world to meet the threat of climate change before it's too late." How has American climate change policy changed since Obama left office?

E) For Thought and Discussion

The amount of carbon dioxide in the atmosphere just hit its highest level in 800,000 years, and scientists predict deadly consequences.
By Kevin Loria, *Business Insider*, June 12, 2018
From: https://www.businessinsider.de/carbon-dioxide-record-human-health-effects-2018-5?r=US&IR=T

- The average concentration of carbon dioxide in Earth's atmosphere topped 411 parts per million in May 2018.
- In April 2018 the concentration hit 410 ppm for the first time in recorded history.
- These are the highest CO_2 levels in the 800,000 years for which we have good data.
- In our 800,000-year record, it took about 1,000 years for CO_2 levels to increase by 35 ppm. We're currently averaging an increase of more than 2 ppm a year, meaning we could hit an average of 500 ppm within the next 45 years.
- This is expected to have a catastrophic effect on human health and the planet.
- The record is not a coincidence – humans have rapidly transformed the air we breathe by pumping CO_2 into it over the past two centuries.
- Carbon dioxide also contributes to warming that causes sea-level rise, searing heat waves, and superstorms.
- The potential effects of higher average temperatures include tens of thousands of deaths from heat waves, more extreme weather events, and the spread of diseases.
- We are continuing full speed ahead with an unprecedented experiment with our planet, the only home we have.

Tasks:

1. Is global warming really happening?
2. Make a "Top 10" list of the ten largest emitters of CO_2.
3. Is global warming a natural cycle of changing temperature and/or a man-made phenomenon?
4. Create a climate change poster and prepare and give a powerful three-minute speech.

F) "A Dependent Relationship": Cartoon by Gerhard Mester

group work / brainstorming / inspiration cards / research / debate / discussion / creative writing

Cartoon by Gerhard Mester, a famous German cartoonist.

Tasks:

1. Describe and analyse the cartoon.
2. Evaluate how the cartoon relates to current global problems.
3. Prepare and act out a discussion between Barack Obama and Donald Trump about climate change.
4. Write an article for your school magazine explaining how the Earth can be saved from the threat of climate change.
5. Write a poem or a short story, a one-act play or the first chapter of a science-fiction novel or a scene of a storyboard for a new film which illustrates the problems of climate change.
6. Germany's federal government confirmed that the country will not be introducing a 130 kph (80 mph) speed limit on its autobahn road network. Do you think speed limits on German motorways are necessary? Start a heated debate in the car-loving country.
7. **For Thought and Discussion**: „Der Anteil der Flugreisen an allen Urlaubsreisen der Deutschen ist seit der Jahrtausendwende von 30 auf 41 Prozent gestiegen; der Anteil der Bahn hingegen verharrt bei fünf Prozent. Wer mit dem Zug von München nach Paris fährt, setzt 3,3 Kilogramm Kohlendioxid frei, wer fliegt, kommt auf 125,9 Kilogramm. Kann das so weitergehen?" Detlef Esslinger: „Preis der Zukunft". *Süddeutsche Zeitung* vom 20.4.2019, S.1.

"The Next Generation Is Watching What We Do."

Keynote Speech made by President Barack Obama at the First Session of COP21, in Paris, France on November 30, 2015

RELATED TOPICS

CARBON EMISSIONS · OUR CHILDREN'S FATE · CLIMATE CHANGE · CLIMATE NEGOTIATIONS · CLIMATE TARGETS · CONFLICT · COOPERATION · ECOLOGY · THE ECONOMY · EDUCATION · ENERGY EFFICIENCY · ENERGY SOURCES · THE ENVIRONMENT · FOSSIL FUELS · FUTURE GENERATIONS · GLOBAL WARMING · HEALTH · IMMIGRATION · POWER PLANTS · REFUGEES · RENEWABLE ENERGY SOURCES · RESPONSIBILITY · RISING SEA LEVELS · RISING TEMPERATURES · SAVE OUR PLANET· SEEKING ASYLUM · SOLAR POWER · SUFFERING · THE THREAT OF CLIMATE CHANGE · A WAKE-UP CALL · WIND POWER

President Barack Obama delivered a keynote speech and addressed world leaders at the opening session of the Global Climate Change Conference, in Paris (21st Conference of the Parties: COP21) on November 30, 2015.

The United Nations Framework Convention on Climate Change (UNFCCC) took place from November 30 to December 11, 2015, in Paris.

The participating nations worked on achieving a new international agreement on carbon emissions aimed at keeping global temperature increases below 2°C by 2050.

Barack Obama emphasized: "Let that be the common purpose here in Paris. A world that is worthy of our children. A world that is marked not by conflict, but by cooperation; and not by human suffering, but by human progress."

Speech transcript taken from: *The Obama White House Archives*
https://obamawhitehouse.archives.gov/the-press-office/2015/11/30/remarks-president-obama-first-session-cop21
Watch the video here: YouTube https://www.youtube.com/watch?v=vCWKy9zN90A

THE PRESIDENT Barack OBAMA:

THE GROWING THREAT OF CLIMATE CHANGE

Nearly 200 nations have assembled here this week – a declaration that for all the challenges we face, the growing threat of climate change could define the contours of this century more dramatically than any other. What should give us hope that this is a turning point, that this is the moment we finally determined we would save our

to define the contours of this century to characterize this century planet, is the fact that our nations share a sense of urgency about this challenge and a growing realization that it is within our power to do something about it.

urgency *Dringlichkeit*

Fourteen of the fifteen warmest years on record have occurred since the year 2000 – and 2015 is on pace to be the warmest year of all. No nation – large or small, wealthy or poor – is immune to what this means.

is on pace is set to be; *auf dem besten Weg sein*

A GLIMPSE OF OUR CHILDREN'S FATE

This summer, I saw the effects of climate change firsthand in our northernmost state, Alaska, where the sea is already swallowing villages and eroding shorelines; where permafrost thaws and the tundra burns; where glaciers are melting at a pace unprecedented in modern times. And it was a preview of one possible future – a glimpse of our children's fate if the climate keeps changing faster than our efforts to address it. Submerged countries. Abandoned cities. Fields that no longer grow. Political disruptions that trigger new conflict, and even more floods of desperate people seeking the sanctuary of nations not their own.

to thaw to warm up and then melt
unprecedented unparalleled
glimpse brief look; *Blick*
to address it to deal with it
submerged flooded
abandoned deserted
disruption *Zerwürfnis*
to trigger to cause
sanctuary asylum, shelter, safe haven

WE ARE THE FIRST GENERATION TO FEEL THE IMPACT OF CLIMATE CHANGE, AND THE LAST GENERATION THAT CAN DO SOMETHING ABOUT IT

That future is not one of strong economies, nor is it one where fragile states can find their footing. That future is one that we have the power to change. Right here. Right now. But only if we rise to this moment. As one of America's governors has said: "We are the first generation to feel the impact of climate change, and the last generation that can do something about it." […]

as one of America's governors has said a reference to Jay Inslee, the Governor of Washington State, who made this point on the series *Years of Living Dangerously*

I've come here personally, as the leader of the world's largest economy and the second-largest emitter, to say that the United States of America not only recognizes our role in creating this problem, we embrace our responsibility to do something about it.

to embrace (*here:*) to accept

Over the last seven years, we've made ambitious investments in clean energy, and ambitious reductions in our carbon emissions. We've multiplied wind power threefold, and solar power more than twentyfold, helping create parts of America where these clean power sources are finally cheaper than dirtier, conventional power sources. We've invested in energy efficiency in every way imaginable. We've said no to infrastructure that would pull high-carbon fossil fuels from the ground, and we've said yes to the first-ever set of national standards limiting the amount of carbon pollution our power plants can release into the sky.

ambitious (*here:*) large
multiplied wind power threefold *Windkraft verdreifacht*
twentyfold *zwanzigfach*
energy efficiency *Energieeffizienz*
first-ever set *erstmalige Festsetzung*
carbon pollution *Kohlenstoffbelastung*

The advances we've made have helped drive our economic output to all-time highs, and drive our carbon pollution to its lowest level in nearly two decades.

STRONG ECONOMIC GROWTH AND A SAFER ENVIRONMENT NO LONGER HAVE TO CONFLICT WITH ONE ANOTHER

But the good news is this is not an American trend alone. Last year, the global economy grew while global carbon emissions from burning fossil fuels stayed flat. And what this means can't be overstated. We have broken the old arguments for inaction. We have proved that strong economic growth and a safer environment no longer have to conflict with one another; they can work in concert with one another.

carbon emissions *CO_2 Ausstoß, Kohlenstoffdioxid-Emissionen*

to conflict (*here:*) to compete with
in concert with one another together

And that should give us hope. One of the enemies that we'll be fighting at this conference is cynicism, the notion that we can't do anything about climate change. Our progress should give us hope during these two weeks – hope that is rooted in collective action. [...]

cynicism pessimism, doubt, sarcasm; *Zweifel, Zynismus*

So our task here in Paris is to turn these achievements into an enduring framework for human progress – not a stopgap solution, but a long-term strategy that gives the world confidence in a low-carbon future.

stopgap temporary
confidence faith, assurance; *Vertrauen, Zuversicht*

Here, in Paris, let's secure an agreement that builds in ambition, where progress paves the way for regularly updated targets – targets that are not set for each of us but by each of us, taking into account the differences that each nation is facing.

differences (*here:*) different challenges

Here in Paris, let's agree to a strong system of transparency that gives each of us the confidence that all of us are meeting our commitments. And let's make sure that the countries who don't yet have the full capacity to report on their targets receive the support that they need. [...]

to meet a commitment *eine Verpflichtung eingehen*

That's what we seek in these next two weeks. Not simply an agreement to roll back the pollution we put into our skies, but an agreement that helps us lift people from poverty without condemning the next generation to a planet that's beyond its capacity to repair. Here, in Paris, we can show the world what is possible when we come together, united in common effort and by a common purpose.

common (*here:*) *gemeinsam*

THE NEXT GENERATION IS WATCHING WHAT WE DO

And let there be no doubt, the next generation is watching what we do. Just over a week ago, I was in Malaysia, where I met with young people in a town hall, and the first question I received was from a young Indonesian woman. And it wasn't about terrorism, it wasn't about the economy, it wasn't about human rights. It was about climate change. And she asked whether I was optimistic about what we can achieve here in Paris, and what young people like her could do to help.

I want our actions to show her that we're listening. I want our actions to be big enough to draw on the talents of all our people – men and women, rich and poor – I want to show her passionate, idealistic young generation that we care about their future.

to draw on *auf etwas zurückgreifen*

For I believe, in the words of Dr. Martin Luther King Jr., that there is such a thing as being too late. And when it comes to climate change, that hour is almost upon us. But if we act here, if we act now, if we place our own short-term interests behind the air that our young people will breathe, and the food that they will eat, and the water that they will drink, and the hopes and dreams that sustain their lives, then we won't be too late for them.

that hour is almost upon us it is almost too late
if we place our own short-term interests behind *wenn wir unsere kurzfristigen Interessen zurückstellen*

And, my fellow leaders, accepting this challenge will not reward us with moments of victory that are clear or quick. Our progress will be measured differently – in the suffering that is averted, and a planet that's preserved. And that's what's always made this so hard.

suffering pain, misery; *Leid*
averted prevented; *verhindert*

Our generation may not even live to see the full realization of what we do here. But the knowledge that the next generation will be better off for what we do here – can we imagine a more worthy reward than that? By passing that on to our children and our grandchildren, so that when they look back and they see what we did here in Paris, they can take pride in our achievement.

worthy *lohnend*

Let that be the common purpose here in Paris. A world that is worthy of our children. A world that is marked not by conflict, but by cooperation; and not by human suffering, but by human progress. A world that's safer, and more prosperous, and more secure, and more free than the one that we inherited.

inherited *geerbt*

Let's get to work. Thank you very much. (*Applause.*)

ASSIGNMENTS

A) Pre-Listening and Pre-Reading Activity: Global Warming – Climate Change

interactive classroom / word cloud / group work / sharing your ideas with your classmates / speech

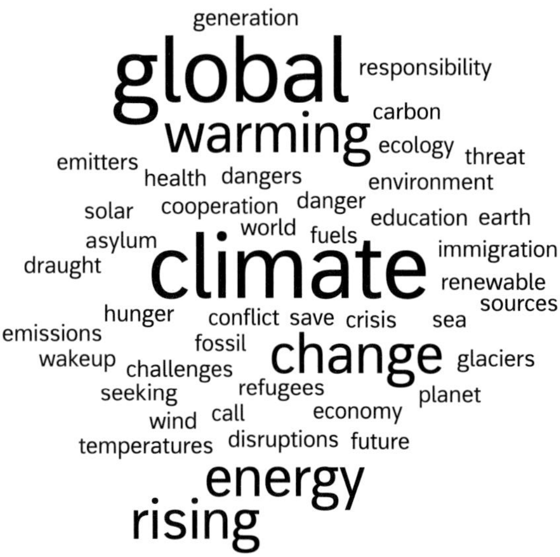

Look at the word cloud. Prepare and give a speech using words from the word cloud.
Think: What do you think the speech might be about? Note down your ideas.
Pair: Talk to a partner about your ideas, then prepare a two-minute-speech about your ideas using at least 20 words from the word cloud.
Share: Share your ideas with another pair, then give your speech to the class.

B) Reading and Listening Comprehension

think – pair – share / reading with confidence / peer support and feedback / writing a summary

1. You can watch the video of Barack Obama's speech here: https://www.youtube.com/watch?v=vCWKy9zN90A
2. Read the transcript of Barack Obama's speech and highlight his main arguments.
3. Summarise his main arguments.

C) Mediation (English = > German) / (German = > English)

1. Translate the following excerpt from Obama's speech into German:

And, my fellow leaders, accepting this challenge will not reward us with moments of victory that are clear or quick. Our progress will be measured differently – in the suffering that is averted, and a planet that's preserved. And that's what's always made this so hard. Our generation may not even live to see the full realization of what we do here. But the knowledge that the next generation will be better off for what we do here – can we imagine a more worthy reward than that? By passing that on to our children and our grandchildren, so that when they look back and they see what we did here in Paris, they can take pride in our achievement.

2. Mediation: Translate the following extract from an article in *Der Spiegel* into English:

"Obama beim Klimagipfel: Noch kurz vor Schluss die Welt retten:

Für Barack Obama wird die Zukunft des Planeten auch auf dem Weltgipfel in Paris entschieden. Schon ganz zu Beginn seiner Rede spricht der US-Präsident von seiner Reise nach Alaska in diesem Sommer. Wo das Meer Dörfer zu verschlucken droht und an der Küstenlinie knabbert. Wo der Permafrost taut und die Tundra brennt. Wo Gletscher in ungekanntem Tempo schmelzen. "Es war ein Blick in eine mögliche Zukunft", sagt Obama. "Wir haben die Macht, diese Zukunft zu ändern. Genau hier. Genau jetzt", ruft er den Delegierten anschließend zu. Einer der größten Feinde einer erfolgreichen Klimakonferenz sei der Zynismus – die Haltung, dass man ja doch nichts tun könne gegen die weitere Erwärmung der Erdatmosphäre. Doch er, das macht Obama klar, will nicht zynisch sein – sondern visionär. [...]."
SPIEGEL ONLINE, Christoph Seidler und Veit Medick, 30.11.2015, http://www.spiegel.de/politik/ausland/klimagipfel-in-paris-so-lief-obamas-auftritt-a-1065330.html

D) "Mind the Gap": Vocabulary Training. Fill in the missing words.

Part A:

Nearly 200 nations have ____________ here this week – a ____________ that for all the ____________ we face, the growing ____________ of climate ____________ could define the contours of this ____________ more dramatically than any other. What should give us hope that this is a ____________, that this is the moment we finally ____________ we would ____________ our planet, is the fact that our nations ____________ a sense of ____________ about this ____________ and a ____________ realization that it is within our ____________ to do something about it.

Part B:

Over the last seven years, we've made ____________ investments in ____________ energy, and ambitious ____________ in our carbon ____________. We've ____________ wind ____________ threefold, and ____________ power more than twentyfold, helping ____________ parts of America where these clean power ____________ are finally cheaper than dirtier, ____________ power sources. We've ____________ in energy ____________ in every way ____________. We've said no to ____________ that would pull high-carbon ____________ ____________ from the ground, and we've said yes to the first-ever set of national standards ____________ the amount of carbon ____________ our power plants can ____________ into the sky.

Part C:

And, my fellow leaders, ____________ this challenge will not ____________ us with moments of ____________ that are clear or quick. Our ____________ will be measured differently – in the ____________ that is ____________, and a planet that's preserved. And that's what's always made this so hard. Our ____________ may not even live to see the full ____________ of what we do here. But the ____________ that the next generation will be better off for what we do here – can we ____________ a more ____________ reward than that? By passing that on to our children and our grandchildren, so that when they look back and they see what we did here in Paris, they can take ____________ in our ____________.

E) Analysis

▶ *think - pair - share / peer support and feedback / writing an analysis / presentation*

1. Analyse the structure of the speech.
2. Analyse the rhetorical devices Obama uses in the speech and why he uses them.
3. Write a comprehensive analysis of the speech.

F) Evaluation, Comment, Creative Activities

▶ *group work / posters / creative writing / presentation / panel discussion / speech / evaluation*

1. "We are the first generation to feel the impact of climate change, and the last generation that can do something about it." Discuss and evaluate the significance of this statement.
2. "Strong economic growth and a safer environment no longer have to conflict with one another." Prepare a panel discussion in class in which some students agree with this statement and other students argue against it.
3. "The next generation is watching what we do."
   a) Write an article addressing this statement for your school magazine.
   b) Prepare and give a three-minute speech in which you illustrate your point of view regarding this statement.
4. "Let that be the common purpose here in Paris. [...] A world that is marked not by conflict, but by co-operation; and not by human suffering, but by human progress." Is this a utopian aim or is there indeed a chance that it might happen? How can this aim be achieved worldwide? Prepare and give a presentation to convince your class of your argument.
5. Write an email to Barack Obama explaining how you think we could combat climate change.

G) Further Projects

▶ *research / WebQuest / enquiry-based learning / evaluating website content / using tablets or laptops / presentation / discussion / feedback / speech / SOLO taxonomy / producing a video*

Choose one of the following projects to research. Present your findings to the class in the form of a digital presentation or a speech or an article for a newspaper.

Project 1: Climate Refugees

"Under a changing climate, the likelihood of extreme weather events will increase, affecting people's lives all around the globe. Some areas will likely become uninhabitable or insufficient to support livelihoods, meaning many may choose to or be forced to leave their homes and move elsewhere."
In "Rising Tides", John Wennersten and Denise Robbins focus on these so-called "climate refugees", millions of whom they predict "will wander the world within the next few decades." The scenarios described in "Rising Tides" are thoroughly bleak, projecting that hundreds of millions of people will be displaced due to climate change by 2050.
From: *Science* July 7, 2017: Vol. 357, Issue 6346, p. 41 http://science.sciencemag.org

Project 2: Deaths Caused by Air Pollution

"But the problem is now pressing, as new research is revealing the extent of the damage being done routinely to our health, particularly to the majority of the world's population who live in cities. About 7% of deaths are caused or contributed to by air pollution, according to the World Health Organisation, and the effect on people's quality of life is even greater. Long a silent killer, air pollution is now being recognised for its devastating effects, particularly on small children and elderly people. The question those breathing the pollution will be asking is whether governments are prepared to act." From: Fiona Harvey, Environment correspondent for *The Guardian,* April 21, 2016
https://www.theguardian.com/environment/2016/apr/21/what-is-behind-the-diesel-cars-emissions-scandal

Project 3: Diesel Engines

"Diesel engines produce much higher levels of air pollutants than petrol-driven engines, although they produce less carbon dioxide. This has led EU member states to encourage drivers to buy diesel cars, reducing the impact of driving on climate change but vastly increasing the problem of air pollution. The UK is one of the few EU countries that taxes diesel at the same rate as petrol, as most countries skew their taxation levels in favour of diesel (although tax parity still favours diesel, because diesel-powered vehicles do more miles per gallon). It is ironic that the push for lower carbon dioxide emissions to combat climate change has led to higher air pollution. And the European Commission has been slow to get to grips with the problem." From: *The Guardian,* April 21, 2016 https://www.theguardian.com/environment

Project 4: Famine and Hunger Crisis

"Millions of people are on the brink of starvation. Millions of people are facing starvation across East Africa, South Sudan and Yemen. This is the largest hunger emergency in the world. If these crises are left unresolved, malnutrition and deaths will increase exponentially in a catastrophic deterioration. Oxfam is on the ground providing food, clean water and sanitation." From: *Oxfam* October 20, 2018 https://www.oxfam.org/en/emergencies/famine-and-hunger-crisis

Project 5: The Effects Of Climate Change

We're facing the biggest environmental challenge our generation has ever seen. Over the past 150 years, we've changed the balance of our planet by living beyond our means. We've burnt huge amounts of fossil fuels (such as coal, oil, gas), bred huge amounts of methane-producing livestock and cut down vast swathes of forests, which would naturally absorb carbon dioxide from the air. From: *WWF* https://www.wwf.org.uk/effectsofclimatechange [accessed October 26, 2018]

Project 6: World Water Development Report 2019: "Leaving no one behind"

Access to water and sanitation is internationally recognized human right. Yet more than two billion people lack even the most basic of services. The latest *United Nations World Water Development Report, Leaving No One Behind*, explores the symptoms of exclusion and investigates ways to overcome inequalities. [...] On a global scale, half of the people who drink water from unsafe sources live in Africa. In Sub-Saharan Africa, only 24% of the population have access to safe drinking water. Go online and read the UN Report:
http://www.unwater.org/world-water-development-report-2019-leaving-no-one-behind/

"In Damaging Our Climate We Become the Architects of Our Own Destruction."

Keynote speech given by His Royal Highness Charles, Prince of Wales, at the COP21 Opening Session, Paris, France, on November 30, 2015

RELATED TOPICS

CARBON EMISSIONS · CLIMATE CHANGE · DEFORESTATION · DESTRUCTION · ECOLOGY · THE ECONOMY · THE ENVIRONMENT · EXPLOITATION · FOSSIL FUELS · FUTURE GENERATIONS · GLOBAL WARMING · HEALTH · HUMANITARIAN DISASTERS · IMMIGRATION · REFUGEES · RENEWABLE ENERGY SOURCES · RESPONSIBILITY · RISING TEMPERATURES · SAVE OUR PLANET· SUSTAINABILITY

His Royal Highness Charles, Prince of Wales, delivered a keynote speech at the opening session of the COP21 global climate change conference in Paris.
He points out that global warming is the greatest threat that humanity faces: "On an increasingly crowded planet, humanity faces many threats, but none is greater than climate change. It magnifies every hazard and tension of our existence."
Prince Charles emphasises: "We must act now. Already we are being overtaken by other events and crises that can be seen as greater and more immediate threats. But, in reality, many are already, and will increasingly be, related to the growing effects of climate change."
The twenty-first session of the Conference of the Parties (COP) and the eleventh session of the Conference of the Parties – serving as the meeting of the Parties to the Kyoto Protocol (CMP) – took place from November 30, to December 11, 2015, in Paris.
The Prince of Wales continues to help address the challenge of climate change through the work of his various initiatives and projects, often in partnership with governments, the private sector, and non-governmental organisations.

Speech transcript from: *The Prince of Wales*
https://www.princeofwales.gov.uk/media/speeches/speech-hrh-the-prince-of-wales-the-cop21-opening-session-paris
Watch the video on YouTube: https://www.youtube.com/watch?v=nFMS3xjjCLk

deliberations debates, discussions
fate destiny; *Schicksal*
hope is the rarest of sensations *Hoffnung ist die seltenste der Empfindungen*
distant prospect *ferne Aussicht*
"for our today they should give up their tomorrow" Prince Charles is referring to the following famous epitaph: "For your Tomorrow, we gave our Today," written by John Maxwell Edmonds (1875-1958), an English poet and dramatist.
threats dangers
to magnify to multiply; *vergrößern*
hazard danger, risk
tension pressure
to avert to prevent
humanitarian disaster *humanitäre Katastrophe*
scorching burning
carbon emissions *CO_2 Ausstoß, Kohlenstoffdioxid-Emissionen*
the right low carbon path *auf dem richtigen Weg der CO_2-Beschränkung*
subsidy *Subvention*
sustainable renewable; *nachhaltig*
deforestation *Rodung, Abholzen (tropischer Regenwälder)*
exploitation *Ausbeutung*
premium (*here:*) price
long-term insurance policy *langfristige Versicherungspolice*

His Royal Highness Charles, Prince of Wales:

Ladies and Gentlemen, as the Executive Secretary has just said, rarely in human history have so many people around the world placed their trust in so few [people]. Your deliberations over the next two weeks will decide the fate, not only of those alive today, but also of generations yet unborn.

So I can only urge you to think of your grandchildren, as I think of mine, and of those billions of people without a voice; those for whom hope is the rarest of sensations; those for whom a secure life is a distant prospect.

Most of all, I urge you to consider the needs of the youngest generation, because none of us has the right to assume that "for our today they should give up their tomorrow."

On an increasingly crowded planet, humanity faces many threats – but none is greater than climate change. It magnifies every hazard and tension of our existence. It threatens our ability to feed ourselves; to remain healthy and safe from extreme weather; to manage the natural resources that support our economies, and to avert the humanitarian disaster of mass migration and increasing conflict.

IN DAMAGING OUR CLIMATE, WE BECOME THE ARCHITECTS OF OUR OWN DESTRUCTION

In damaging our climate, we become the architects of our own destruction. While the planet can survive the scorching of the earth and the rising of the waters, the human race cannot. The absurd thing is that we know exactly what needs to be done; we know we cannot adapt sufficiently to go on as we are, nor can we build ourselves a new atmosphere. To avoid catastrophe we must restrict climate change to less than two degrees, which requires a dramatic reduction in carbon emissions.

This can be done. We have the knowledge, the tools and the money – only 1.7% per cent of global annual consumption would be required to put us on the right low carbon path for 2030. We lack only the will and the framework to use them wisely, consistently and on the required global scale. Governments collectively spend more than a trillion dollars every year on subsidies to energy, agriculture and fisheries.

Just imagine what could be done if those vast sums supported sustainable energy, farming and fishing, rather than fossil fuels, deforestation and over-exploitation of the seas. It is the premium we need to pay for our collective, long-term insurance policy. We are always hearing nowadays that all our actions must be based on "good science". We have that science. Why, then, when it comes to climate change is this apparently no longer applicable?

We have also seen how fast innovation and investment can drive low carbon energy technologies and we are learning how to develop circular economies, in which everything we previously regarded as waste becomes the feedstock for future growth.

feedstock *Rohstoff*

So I pray that in pursuing national interest you will not lose sight of international necessity. Back in 2009, just before COP15, in Copenhagen, I remember trying to point out that the best scientific projections gave us less than a hundred months to alter our behaviour before we risk the tipping point of catastrophic climate change, beyond which there is no recovery. Have we really reached such a collective inertia that ignores so clear a warning? Eighty of those hundred months have now passed, so we must act now. Already we are being overtaken by other events and crises that can be seen as greater and more immediate threats. But in reality many are already and will increasingly be related to the rapidly growing effects of climate change.

inertia lack of energy and/or interest; *Trägheit, Interessenlosigkeit*

THE WHOLE OF NATURE CRIES OUT AT OUR MISTREATMENT OF HER

The whole of Nature cries out at our mistreatment of Her. If the planet were a patient, we would have treated her long ago. You, Ladies and Gentlemen, have the power to put her on life support, and you must surely start the emergency procedures without further procrastination!

mistreatment exploitation, abuse

procrastination delay; *Verzögerung, Aufschieben*

So today, after far too long an interval, you are all here to set us on the road to a saner future. If, at last, the moment has arrived to take those long-awaited steps towards rescuing our planet and our fellow man from impending catastrophe, then let us pursue that vital goal in a spirit of enlightened and humane collaboration.

long-awaited steps *lang erwartete Maßnahmen*
to pursue (*here:*) to reach, to achieve
humane humanitarian, civilized
collaboration teamwork

Ladies and Gentlemen, I wish you well in your endeavours and I shall pray for your success.

ASSIGNMENTS

A) Reading and Listening Comprehension

reading and listening comprehension / group work / peer support and feedback / writing a summary

1. Watch the video of Prince Charles's speech here: https://www.youtube.com/watch?v=nFMS3xjjCLk
2. Read the speech transcript.
3. Summarise Prince Charles's main arguments.

B) **Mediation** (English = > German) / (German = > English)

1. *Translate the following extract from Prince Charles's speech into German:*
   "We have the knowledge, the tools and the money – only 1.7% per cent of global annual consumption would be required to put us on the right low carbon path for 2030. We lack only the will and the framework to use them wisely, consistently and at the required global scale. Governments collectively spend more than a trillion dollars every year on subsidies to energy, agriculture and fisheries. Just imagine what could be done if those vast sums supported sustainable energy, farming and fishing, rather than fossil fuels, deforestation and over-exploitation of the seas. It is the premium we need to pay for our collective, long-term insurance policy. We are always hearing nowadays that all our actions must be based on "good science". We have that science. Why, then, when it comes to climate change is this apparently no longer applicable?"

2. *Translate the following text into English:*
   Prinz Charles mahnt konkrete Ergebnisse an
   Prinz Charles hat konkrete und rasche Ergebnisse bei der Klimakonferenz der Vereinten Nationen in Paris angemahnt. „Wir wissen genau, was zu tun ist", sagte der 67-Jährige am Montag, dem 30 November 2015, zur Eröffnung der Pariser Gespräche, „wir haben das Wissen, die Möglichkeiten und das Geld." Es fehle nur der Willen und der Rahmen für eine Vereinbarung. „Wir müssen jetzt handeln", forderte der Prinz von Wales. Die Zukunft der jungen Generation dürfe nicht aufgegeben werden. Keine Herausforderung sei größer als der Klimawechsel. Er warnte davor, die Menschheit werde ohne eine Vereinbarung zum „Architekt des eigenen Untergangs". In Paris wollen Vertreter aus 195 Staaten knapp zwei Wochen lang über Treibhausgase und Erderwärmung verhandeln.
   (wgr/© dpa, 30.11.2015)

C) Analysis

think - pair - share / peer support and feedback / writing an analysis / presentation / evaluation

1. Analyse the structure of the speech.
2. Analyse the rhetorical devices Prince Charles uses to get his message across.
3. Why does Prince Charles use the personal pronoun ("She / Her") to describe nature in this context?
4. Explain why Prince Charles refers to a famous epitaph by John Maxwell Edmonds in the following line of his speech: "Most of all, I urge you to consider the needs of the youngest generation, because none of us has the right to assume that 'for our today they should give up their tomorrow.'"
5. Write a comprehensive analysis of Prince Charles's speech.

D) Evaluation, Comment, Creative Activities

creative writing / email / article / using tablets or laptops / smartboard / interview / role play

1. "In damaging our climate, we become the architects of our own destruction." Explain your own opinion of this statement.
2. "The whole of Nature cries out at our mistreatment of Her. If the planet were a patient, we would have treated her long ago." Give some examples of the ways in which we have mistreated the planet and what we should do to treat it in a more responsible and sustainable way.

3. Write an email to Prince Charles and explain your own opinion of how the earth can be saved from the threat of climate change.
4. Work in pairs to write an interview with Prince Charles about his campaigns to combat climate change. Then act out your interview in front of the class. One of you should play the role of Prince Charles and the other one should play the role of the journalist interviewing him.

E) Further Projects

internet research / enquiry-based learning / evaluating website content / using tablets or laptops / smartboard / presenting your findings / discussion / speech / collaboration with Social Sciences classes / stations learning / students teach each other / feedback / evaluation / SOLO taxonomy

Divide the class into eight groups. Each group should research one of the following environmental issues:

1) CO_2 emissions and air pollution
2) destruction of biodiversity
3) the overuse of pesticides and artificial fertilisers in the agricultural industry
4) lasting damage to the environment through atomic power
5) the problem of deforestation
6) the problem of waste and plastic disposal (*photo*)
7) the growing shortage of clean drinking water.

Each group should gather information from encyclopaedias and the internet, and must then create a multimedia presentation or prepare and give speeches about the environmental issue they have researched.

Plastic Ocean Pollution - plastic bag and rubbish floating in ocean. Copyright Credit: © Shutterstock / Rich Carey / WWF

F) Postcards from the Future

inspiration cards / internet research / presentation of postcards / cross-curricular project / discussion

U.K.-based artists Robert Graves and Didier Madoc-Jones researched the issue of global warming and created a set of "Postcards from the Future" that portray a future London transformed by floods, harsher winters, and fiercer storms. You can view the "Postcards" here: https://www.telegraph.co.uk/news/earth/earthpicturegalleries/8044199/Postcards-from-the-future-illustrators-imagine-how-London-could-be-affected-by-climate-change.html

Tasks:

1. Choose one of the "Postcards from the Future".
2. Describe, analyse and evaluate the postcard you have chosen and present it to your group.
3. Start a cross-curricular project with your Art class and create a work of art about the effects of climate change.
4. Create your own "Postcard from the Future" that depicts your hometown in the year 2030.
5. Write a poem, a short story, a one-act play, or the first chapter of a science fiction novel about climate change.
6. Produce a video clip entitled "Greetings from the Future."
7. Contact an environmental scientist in your area and ask for an interview on climate change. Record this interview and present your interview in class and in your school.
8. Go online and find songs about plastic waste and pollution: *Gorillas: Little Pink Plastic Bags and Plastic Beach / The Cure: Plastic Passion / The Kinks: Plastic Man etc.*

"America First: The United States Will Withdraw from the Paris Climate Agreement."

Statement made by President Donald Trump about the Paris Climate Accord in the Rose Garden at The White House, on June 1, 2017

RELATED TOPICS

AMERICA FIRST · THE AMERICAN DREAM · CLIMATE CHANGE · THE ECONOMY · ECOLOGY · ENERGY · THE ENVIRONMENT · FUTURE GENERATIONS · THE GLOBAL ECONOMY · GLOBAL WARMING · THE GOVERNMENT · IMMIGRATION · NATIONHOOD · THE PARIS AGREEMENT · THE PARIS CLIMATE ACCORD · POLLUTION · RENEWABLE ENERGY · SUSTAINABILITY · TERRORISM

In what came as a massive setback for the fight against the climate emergency, President **Donald Trump** acted decisively and pulled the United States out of the Paris Climate Accord. Trump's decision was heavily influenced by the effect of the Paris Agreement on the American economy: isolationist advisors contended that the deal would seriously threaten the prosperity and sovereignty of the whole country.

In particular, the President asserted that the monumental accord, which was secured in 2015, would result in American businesses and workers having to adhere to damaging environmental standards. While the President of the United States has long been known as the 'Leader of the Free World', Trump stated that he was 'elected to represent the citizens of Pittsburgh, not Paris.' These words may have endeared him to the members of his Republican Party; however they were swiftly condemned en masse by political leaders, business leaders and environmentalists who felt that Trump was relieving himself of his obligations.

In this sense, the indignation of the various heads of state, environmentalists, industrialists, as well as some of his own staff was justifiable after their calls to reconsider were ignored by the President. 195 countries had originally signed the Paris Agreement and its purpose was to create a unified response to climate change and rising temperatures. Naturally, the rejection of these goals by the Earth's second-most polluting country limits the significance of what can be achieved.

THE PRESIDENT Donald Trump:

Section 1: Give this section a suitable heading:

____

Thank you very much. (*Applause.*) Thank you. I would like to begin by addressing the terrorist attack in Manila. We're closely monitoring the situation, and I will continue to give updates if anything happens during this period of time. But it is really very sad, what's going on throughout the world with terror. Our thoughts and our prayers are with all of those affected.

Before we discuss the Paris Accord, I'd like to begin with an update on our tremendous – absolutely tremendous – economic progress since Election Day on November 8th. The economy is starting to come back, and very, very rapidly. We've added $3.3 trillion in stock market value to our economy, and more than a million private sector jobs.

the Paris Climate Accord the Paris Agreement; see *Additional Notes*
tremendous fantastic

I have just returned from a trip overseas where we concluded nearly $350 billion of military and economic development for the United States, creating hundreds of thousands of jobs. It was a very, very successful trip, believe me. (*Applause.*) Thank you. Thank you.

In my meetings at the G7 summit, we took historic steps to demand fair and reciprocal trade that gives Americans a level playing field against other nations. We're also working very hard for peace in the Middle East, and perhaps even peace between the Israelis and the Palestinians. Our attacks on terrorism are greatly stepped up – and you see that, you see it all over – from the previous administration, including getting many other countries to make major contributions to the fight against terror. Big, big contributions are being made by countries that weren't doing so much in the form of contribution before.

reciprocal *gegenseitig*
a level playing field fair conditions for all parties; *gleiche Voraussetzungen/Rahmenbedingungen für alle*
contribution *Beitrag, Beitragsleistung*

Section 2: Give this section a suitable heading:

____

One by one, we are keeping the promises I made to the American people during my Presidential campaign – whether it's cutting job-killing regulations; appointing and confirming a tremendous Supreme Court justice; putting in place tough new ethics rules; achieving a record reduction in illegal immigration on our southern border; or bringing jobs, plants, and factories back into the United States at numbers which no one until this point thought even possible.

And believe me, we've only just begun. The fruits of our labor will be seen very shortly, even more so.

the fruits of our labor *die Früchte unserer Arbeit*

On these issues and so many more, we're following through on our commitments. And I don't want anything to get in our way. I am fighting every day for the great people of this country. Therefore, in order to fulfil my solemn duty to protect America and its citizens, the United States will withdraw from the Paris Climate Accord – (*Applause*) – thank you, thank you – but begin negotiations to reenter either the Paris Accord or a really entirely new transaction on terms that are fair to the United States, its businesses, its workers, its people, its taxpayers. So we're getting out. But we will start to negotiate, and we will see if we can make a deal that's fair. And if we can, that's great. And if we can't, that's fine. (*Applause.*)

solemn (*here:*) *feierlich*
to withdraw from to pull out of; *sich zurückziehen*
negotiations talks; *Verhandlung*
to negotiate to work out a deal; *verhandeln*

Section 3: Give this section a suitable heading:

____

As President, I can put no other consideration before the wellbeing of American citizens. The Paris Climate Accord is simply the latest example of Washington entering into an agreement that disadvantages the United States to the exclusive benefit of other countries, leaving American workers – who I love – and taxpayers to absorb the cost in terms of lost jobs, lower wages, shuttered factories, and vastly diminished economic production.

to disadvantage *benachteiligen*
to absorb the cost *die Kosten tragen*

Thus, as of today, the United States will cease all implementation of the non-binding Paris Accord and the draconian financial and economic burdens the agreement imposes on our country. This includes ending the implementation of the nationally determined contribution and, very importantly, the Green Climate Fund which is costing the United States a vast fortune.

draconian harsh, drastic, extreme, oppressive; *drakonisch*
The Green Climate Fund (GCF) *see* Additional Notes

Section 4: Give this section a suitable heading:

____

Compliance with the terms of the Paris Accord and the onerous energy restrictions it has placed on the United States could cost America as much as 2.7 million lost jobs by 2025 according to the National Economic Research Associates.

compliance agreement; *Übereinstimmung*
onerous excessive; *erdrückend*
The National Economic Research Associates strong opponents of the Paris Agreement, *see* Additional Notes

This includes 440,000 fewer manufacturing jobs – not what we need – believe me, this is not what we need – including automobile jobs, and the further decimation of vital American industries on which countless communities rely. They rely on them for so much, and we would be giving them so little.

decimation *Dezimierung, Schwächung*

According to this same study, by 2040, compliance with the commitments put into place by the previous administration would cut production for the following sectors: paper down 12 percent; cement down 23 percent; iron and steel down 38 percent; coal – and I happen to love the coal miners – down 86 percent; natural gas down 31 percent. The cost to the economy at this time would be close to $3 trillion in lost GDP and 6.5 million industrial jobs, while households would have $7,000 less income [on average] and, in many cases, much worse than that.

GDP (Gross Domestic Product) the total value of goods and services produced annually by a country; *Bruttoinlandsprodukt*

Section 5: Give this section a suitable heading:

____

Not only does this deal subject our citizens to harsh economic restrictions, it fails to live up to our environmental ideals. As someone who cares deeply about the environment, which I do, I cannot in good conscience support a deal that punishes the United States – which is what it does – the world's leader in environmental protection, while imposing no meaningful obligations on the world's leading polluters.

to subject our citizens to harsh economic restrictions *unsere Bürger strengen wirtschaftlichen Einschränkungen aussetzen*

For example, under the agreement, China will be able to increase these emissions by a staggering number of years – 13. They can do whatever they want for 13 years. Not us. India makes its participation contingent on receiving billions and billions and billions of dollars in foreign aid from developed countries. There are many other examples. But the bottom line is that the Paris Accord is very unfair, at the highest level, to the United States.

the bottom line is *unterm Strich bedeutet das*

Furthermore, while the current agreement effectively blocks the development of clean coal in America – which it does, and the mines are starting to open up. We're having a big opening in two weeks. In Pennsylvania, Ohio, West Virginia, so many places. A big opening of a brand-new mine. It's unheard of. For many, many years, that hasn't happened. They asked me if I'd go. I'm going to try.

China will be allowed to build hundreds of additional coal plants. So we can't build the plants, but they can, according to this agreement. India will be allowed to double its coal production by 2020. Think of it: India can double their coal production. We're supposed to get rid of ours. Even Europe is allowed to continue the construction of coal plants.

In short, the agreement doesn't eliminate coal jobs, it just transfers those jobs out of America and the United States, and ships them to foreign countries.

to eliminate to get rid of; *abschaffen*

Section 6: Give this section a suitable heading:

____

This agreement is less about the climate and more about other countries gaining a financial advantage over the United States. The rest of the world applauded when we signed the Paris Agreement – they went wild; they were so happy – for the simple reason that it put our country, the United States of America, which we all love, at a very, very big economic disadvantage. A cynic would say the obvious reason for economic competitors and their wish to see us remain in the agreement is so that we continue to suffer this self-inflicted major economic wound. We would find it very hard to compete with other countries from other parts of the world.

self-inflicted something that you have done to yourself; *selbst verschuldet*

We have among the most abundant energy reserves on the planet, sufficient to lift millions of America's poorest workers out of poverty. Yet, under this agreement, we are effectively putting these reserves under lock and key, taking away the great wealth of our nation – it's great wealth, it's phenomenal wealth; not so long ago, we had no idea we had such wealth – and leaving millions and millions of families trapped in poverty and joblessness.

the most abundant the largest

Section 7: Give this section a suitable heading:

____

The agreement is a massive redistribution of United States wealth to other countries. At 1 percent growth, renewable sources of energy can meet some of our domestic demand, but at 3 or 4 percent growth, which I expect, we need all forms of available American energy, or our country – (*Applause*) – will be at grave risk of brownouts and blackouts, our businesses will come to a halt in many cases, and the American family will suffer the consequences in the form of lost jobs and a very diminished quality of life.

redistribution *Neuverteilung*

brownout a drop in voltage in an electrical power supply system; *partieller Stromausfall, Spannungsabfall*

Even if the Paris Agreement were implemented in full, with total compliance from all nations, it is estimated it would only produce two-tenths of one degree – think of that; this much – Celsius reduction in global temperature by the year 2100. A tiny, tiny amount.

compliance agreement; *Zustimmung*

In fact, 14 days of carbon emissions from China alone would wipe out the gains from America – and this is an incredible statistic – would totally wipe out the gains from America's expected reductions in the year 2030, after we have had to spend billions and billions of dollars, lost jobs, closed factories, and suffered much higher energy costs for our businesses and for our homes.

As the *Wall Street Journal* wrote this morning: "The reality is that withdrawing is in America's economic interest and won't matter much to the climate." The United States, under the Trump administration, will continue to be the cleanest and most environmentally friendly country on Earth. We'll be the cleanest. We're going to have the cleanest air. We're going to have the cleanest water. We will be environmentally friendly, but we're not going to put our businesses out of work and we're not going to lose our jobs. We're going to grow; we're going to grow rapidly. (*Applause.*)

And I think you just read – it just came out minutes ago, the small business report – small businesses as of just now are booming, hiring people. One of the best reports they've seen in many years.

I'm willing to immediately work with Democratic leaders to either negotiate our way back into Paris, under the terms that are fair to the United States and its workers, or to negotiate a new deal that protects our country and its taxpayers. (*Applause.*)

Section 8: Give this section a suitable heading:

____

So if the obstructionists want to get together with me, let's make them non-obstructionists. We will all sit down, and we will get back into the deal. And we'll make it good, and we won't be closing up our factories, and we won't be losing our jobs. And we'll sit down with the Democrats and all of the people that represent either the Paris Accord or something that we can do that's much better than the Paris Accord. And I think the people of our country will be thrilled, and I think then the people of the world will be thrilled. But until we do that, we're out of the agreement.

obstructionist objector; *Quertreiber*

I will work to ensure that America remains the world's leader on environmental issues, but under a framework that is fair and where the burdens and responsibilities are equally shared among the many nations all around the world.

under a framework under a system of rules; *bei/unter den Rahmenbedingungen*

Section 9: Give this section a suitable heading:

____

No responsible leader can put the workers – and the people – of their country at this debilitating and tremendous disadvantage. The fact that the Paris deal hamstrings the United States, while empowering some of the world's top polluting countries, should dispel any doubt as to the real reason why foreign lobbyists wish to keep our magnificent country tied up and bound down by this agreement: It's to give their country an economic edge over the United States. That's not going to happen while I'm President. I'm sorry. (*Applause.*)

debilitating devastating

to hamstring *handlungsunfähig machen, lähmen*

economic edge (*here:*) economic advantage; *ökonomischer Vorteil*

My job as President is to do everything within my power to give America a level playing field and to create the economic, regulatory and tax structures that make America the most prosperous and productive country on Earth, and with the highest standard of living and the highest standard of environmental protection.

Our tax bill is moving along in Congress, and I believe it's doing very well. I think a lot of people will be very pleasantly surprised. The Republicans are working very, very hard. We'd love to have support from the Democrats, but we may have to go it alone. But it's going very well.

Section 10: Give this section a suitable heading:

____

at our country's expense to the financial detriment of our country; *auf Kosten unseres Landes*

The Paris Agreement handicaps the United States' economy in order to win praise from the very foreign capitals and global activists that have long sought to gain wealth at our country's expense. They don't put America first. I do, and I always will. (*Applause.*)

The same nations asking us to stay in the agreement are the countries that have collectively cost America trillions of dollars through tough trade practices and, in many cases, lax contributions to our critical military alliance. You see what's happening. It's pretty obvious to those that want to keep an open mind.

demeaned humiliated, degraded

At what point does America get demeaned? At what point do they start laughing at us as a country? We want fair treatment for our citizens, and we want fair treatment for our taxpayers. We don't want other leaders and other countries laughing at us anymore. And they won't be. They won't be.

Section 11: Give this section a suitable heading:

____

to renegotiate to negotiate again; *neu verhandeln*
renegotiation new talks; *Neuverhandlung*

I was elected to represent the citizens of Pittsburgh, not Paris. (*Applause.*) I promised I would exit or renegotiate any deal which fails to serve America's interests. Many trade deals will soon be under renegotiation. Very rarely do we have a deal that works for this country, but they'll soon be under renegotiation. The process has begun from day one. But now we're down to business.

one dime 10-cent coin

Beyond the severe energy restrictions inflicted by the Paris Accord, it includes yet another scheme to redistribute wealth out of the United States through the so-called Green Climate Fund – nice name – which calls for developed countries to send $100 billion to developing countries all on top of America's existing and massive foreign aid payments. So we're going to be paying billions and billions and billions of dollars, and we're already way ahead of anybody else. Many of the other countries haven't spent anything, and many of them will never pay one dime.

The Green Fund would likely obligate the United States to commit potentially tens of billions of dollars, of which the United States has already handed over $1 billion – nobody else is even close; most of them haven't even paid anything – including funds raided out of America's budget for the war against terrorism. That's where they came. Believe me, they didn't come from me. They came just before I came into office. Not good. And not good the way they took the money.

Section 12: Give this section a suitable heading:

In 2015, the United Nation's departing top climate officials reportedly described the $100 billion per year as "peanuts," and stated that "the $100 billion is the tail that wags the dog." In 2015, the Green Climate Fund's executive director reportedly stated that the estimated funding needed would increase to $450 billion per year after 2020. And nobody even knows where the money is going to. Nobody has been able to say, where is it going to?

Of course, the world's top polluters have no affirmative obligations under the Green Fund, which we terminated. America is $20 trillion in debt. Cash-strapped cities cannot hire enough police officers or fix vital infrastructure. Millions of our citizens are out of work. And yet, under the Paris Accord, billions of dollars that ought to be invested right here in America will be sent to the very countries that have taken our factories and our jobs away from us. So think of that.

cash-strapped cities cities which don't have much money and/or have debts; *Städte, die ein Haushaltsdefizit haben*

Section 13: Give this section a suitable heading:

There are serious legal and constitutional issues as well. Foreign leaders in Europe, Asia, and across the world should not have more to say with respect to the U.S. economy than our own citizens and their elected representatives. Thus, our withdrawal from the agreement represents a reassertion of America's sovereignty. (*Applause.*) Our Constitution is unique among all the nations of the world, and it is my highest obligation and greatest honor to protect it. And I will.

reassertion re-establishment; *Wiederherstellung*

Staying in the agreement could also pose serious obstacles for the United States as we begin the process of unlocking the restrictions on America's abundant energy reserves, which we have started very strongly. It would once have been unthinkable that an international agreement could prevent the United States from conducting its own domestic economic affairs, but this is the new reality we face if we do not leave the agreement or if we do not negotiate a far better deal.

The risks grow as historically these agreements only tend to become more and more ambitious over time. In other words, the Paris framework is a starting point – as bad as it is – not an end point. And exit-

intrusion interference; *Einmischung*
liability (*here:*) responsibility, *Verantwortung*

ing the agreement protects the United States from future intrusions on the United States' sovereignty and massive future legal liability. Believe me, we'd have massive legal liability if we stayed in.

Section 14: Give this section a suitable heading:

____

obligation duty, commitment, responsibility

As President, I have one obligation, and that obligation is to the American people. The Paris Accord would undermine our economy, hamstring our workers, weaken our sovereignty, impose unacceptable legal risks, and put us at a permanent disadvantage to the other countries of the world.

It is time to exit the Paris Accord – (*Applause*) – and time to pursue a new deal that protects the environment, our companies, our citizens, and our country.

It is time to put Youngstown, Ohio, Detroit, Michigan, and Pittsburgh, Pennsylvania – along with many, many other locations within our great country – before Paris, France.

It is time to make America great again. (*Applause.*)

Thank you. Thank you. Thank you very much.

Speech transcript taken from: *The White House*
https://www.whitehouse.gov/the-press-office/2017/06/01/statement-president-trump-paris-climate-accord

---

ASSIGNMENTS

A) Pre-Listening and Pre-Reading Activities

▶ *interactive classroom / inside-outside circle / market place / share ideas / discussion*

1. Donald Trump's most controversial tweets about climate change/global warming:

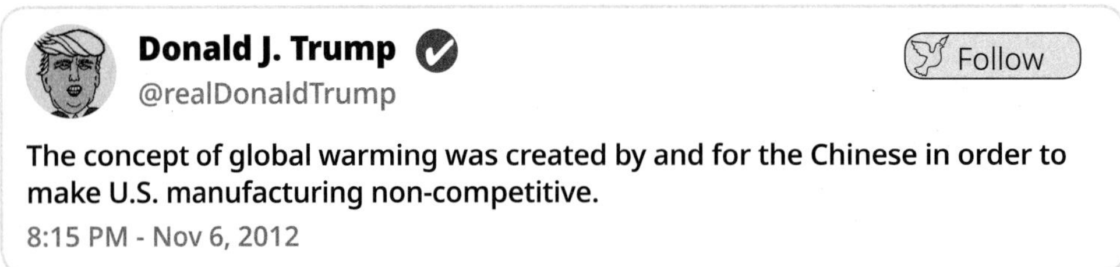

Donald J. Trump
@realDonaldTrump
Follow

Wow, 25 degrees below zero, record cold and snow spell. Global warming anyone?

3:37 PM - Feb 15, 2015

Task: Analyse the tweets in detail. Share your ideas with different partners.

2. **Global Warming: Cartoon by Dave Granlund**

The artist Dave Granlund is one of the most famous cartoonists in the USA. In response to Donald Trump's global warming tweets, Dave Granlund drew this cartoon:

Tasks:

Describe, analyse and evaluate the cartoon. Please take the following points into consideration:

1. *Cartoonist and Source*
   a) Go ahead, give us your funny caption.
   b) Have a guess: when and where was the cartoon published?

2. *Setting*
   a) Describe the setting in detail.
   b) What is taking place on the left/on the right/in the foreground/in the background?
   c) Which event or issue may have inspired the cartoonist Dave Granlund?
3. *Intention and Message*
   a) What topic or problem does the cartoon focus on?
   b) What kind of devices does Dave Granlund use to express his message clearly? You may consider humour, irony, wit, satire, exaggeration, understatement, parody, caricature, sarcasm, metaphor etc.
4. *Evaluation*
   a) Evaluate the significance and impact of this cartoon.
   b) Write a letter or an email to Dave Granlund to tell him what you think of the cartoon.
   c) Prepare and give a two-minute speech in response to Dave Granlund's cartoon.

B) Reading and Listening Comprehension

reading and listening comprehension / group work / writing a summary / peer support and feedback

1. Watch President Donald Trump's speech on YouTube.
2. Listen to President Trump's speech again and highlight the keywords in your speech transcript.
3. Imagine you are a speechwriter. Give each of the speech's fourteen sections a suitable heading.
4. Why does the President want to withdraw from the Paris Climate Accord? Highlight some of his most significant statements in your speech transcript.
5. Summarise Trump's speech in about 14 sentences.

C) Checking Facts

paired work / WebQuest / using tablets or laptops / smartboard / presentation / discussion

Compare President Trump's statements to the facts and responses written by journalists for *The New York Times, The Washington Post, The Guardian* and other newspapers.

Donald Trump's Statements	**Facts and Responses** Go online, read the facts and responses, then take notes:
[...]	[...]

D) Analysis

think – pair – share / writing an analysis / posters / gallery walk / discussion / feedback

1. Analyse the structure of President Donald Trump's speech.
2. According to Donald Trump, the Paris Agreement is an instrument that allows other countries to get rich at the expense of the United States. Analyse some significant rhetorical devices which he uses to get his point of view across to the audience.
3. Analyse Trump's appeal to the audience at the end of the speech.
4. Write a comprehensive analysis of Trump's speech.

E) Evaluation, Comment, Creative Writing, Creative Activities

▶ *group work / discussion / hot seat interview / role play / writing a comment / three-minute speech*

1. President Donald Trump emphasises: "The Paris Agreement handicaps the United States economy [...]. They don't put America first. I do, and I always will."
   a) Analyse this statement. b) Prepare and give a three-minute speech in response to this statement.
2. What does President Trump mean when he makes the following statements:
   a) "I was elected to represent the citizens of Pittsburgh, not Paris."
   b) "As President, I have one obligation, and that obligation is to the American people."
3. "Trump's withdrawal is a catastrophe for the climate. The U.S. is the second-largest emitter of greenhouse gases – behind China – and is now no longer part of global efforts to put a stop to climate change. It's America against the rest of the world, along with Syria and Nicaragua, the only other countries that haven't signed the Paris deal."
   From: "Paris Disagreement. Donald Trump's Triumph of Stupidity." *DER SPIEGEL*, June 2, 2017
   https://www.spiegel.de/international/world/trump-pulls-out-of-climate-deal-western-rift-deepens-a-1150486.html
   Write a hot seat interview with President Trump.
4. Scott Pruitt, the 14th Administrator of the Environmental Protection Agency (EPA) of the United States, congratulated the President for his speech and said: *"Thank you, Mr. President. Your decision today to exit the Paris Accord reflects your unflinching commitment to put America first. And by exiting, you're fulfilling yet one more campaign promise to the American people. Please know that I am thankful for your fortitude, your courage, and your steadfastness as you serve and lead our country. America finally has a leader who answers only to the people [...]. You're a champion for the hardworking citizens all across this land who just want a government that listens to them and represents their interests. [...] Thank you, Mr. President."*
   From: https://www.whitehouse.gov/the-press-office/2017/06/01/statement-president-trump-paris-climate-accord
   Scott Pruitt submitted his resignation letter to President Trump on July 5, 2018. Write an email to Scott Pruitt, or prepare and give a three-minute speech, in response to Pruitt's statement.
5. Some US newspapers praised President Trump's decision to withdraw America from the Paris Agreement. These responses were selected by Donald Trump's White House Press Office and published on the *White House* website.
   https://www.whitehouse.gov/the-press-office/2017/06/02/editorial-boards-praise-president-trumps-paris-decision.
   Analyse these articles and give your own opinion of Trump's withdrawal from the Paris Agreement. You could also do this by preparing and giving a speech, if you prefer.
6. *Role Play:* Imagine that German Chancellor Angela Merkel, French President Emmanuel Macron, US President Donald Trump, Canadian Prime Minister Justin Trudeau, and Xi Jinping, President of the People's Republic of China, are discussing climate change and the challenges it poses all over the world. Select a role and act out a lively and creative discussion between these world leaders with your classmates.

F) More Creative Activities

▶ *speech writer / interview / role play / hot seat / panel discussion / video recording / Speakers' Corner*

1. **The Earth in Danger: Panel Discussion**: Organise a panel discussion in class about whether our earth is in danger, and what we can do to combat climate change. A variety of different opinions should be expressed in the panel discussion.
2. Imagine you are a speech writer for an influential German politician who has to give a speech at the next International Conference about climate change. Write a speech about current and future problems caused by climate change and global warming. Give and record your speech in class.

“The Threat from Climate Change Is Real, Urgent, Serious.”

12-year-old Timoci Naulusala from Fiji gave a speech about the impact of climate change on him, his community, and his country at the UN Climate Change Conference (COP23) in Bonn on November 16, 2017

RELATED TOPICS

CLIMATE CHANGE · THE EARTH IN DANGER · EDUCATION · THE ENVIRONMENT · FUTURE GENERATIONS · GLOBAL WARMING · GOD · GREENHOUSE GASES · HUMANITY · LIBERTY · THE PARIS AGREEMENT · RESPONSIBILITY · SCHOOLS · SUSTAINABILITY

Timoci Naulusala was invited to Bonn after winning a nationwide speech competition held in Fiji. This is the first time that a small developing country has presided over a UN Climate Change Conference.

The Naivicula native received a standing ovation from the world leaders he shared the stage with, including UNFCC Executive Secretary Patricia Espinoza, German President Frank-Walter Steinmeier, United Nations Secretary-General António Guterres, and COP23 President, Prime Minister Josaia Voreqe ‘Frank’ Bainimarama.

The National Speech Competition in Fiji was organised by UNICEF, the Fijian Government, and the COP23 Presidency Secretariat.

Timoci Naulusala made a touching and passionate plea for listeners to take action to tackle climate change: “The sea is swallowing villages, eating away at shorelines, withering crops. Relocation of people ... cries over lost loved ones, dying of hunger and thirst. It’s catastrophic. It’s sad ... but it’s real. You may think it will only affect small nations ... you are wrong.”

Please read and watch Timoci Naulusala’s fascinating speech.

Based on the United Nations’ website: https://cop23.unfccc.int/news/calls-for-rapid-progress-at-cop23-as-ministers-and-heads-of-state-arrive-in-bonn

Acknowledgement: We would like to thank the Fijian Government, UNICEF and the COP23 Presidency Secretariat for the information in this foreword and for the speech transcript.

Timoci Naulusala:

In the beginning, God created the Universe.
It was spectacular in every way.
There were beautiful trees, plants, multi-colored birds, and animals filled the land with their cries and songs of delight.
In the sea, the colorful fishes and marine life illuminated the vast ocean bodies.

The world was indeed impeccable!
Then he decided that all these creatures needed a leader ...

Alas! The creation of mankind.
The dawn of a new era.

To the panel of judges, distinguished guests, fellow orators, teachers, ladies and gentlemen:
Ni sa bula vinaka, Namaste, As-Salaam-Alaikum, and good morning to you all.

Many of us here today recognize that the threat from climate change is real! Urgent! Serious and is growing overnight.

According to Former President of America, Mr. Barack Obama, he states that, and I quote:
"Climate change is no longer some far-off problem; it is happening here, it is happening now."

Yes! Ladies and gentlemen, this is real, it is not a mere dream.

Are you ready to face life without Earth?
Have you contemplated what will happen if we ignore this reality?
This nightmare?

That is the core reason of us being here.
It's time to take action: as our theme depicts: LEADERSHIP, ACTION AND COP23.
Again LEADERSHIP, ACTION AND COP23.

The question is
- WHAT TO DO?
- HOW TO DO IT?
- WHO TO DO IT?

Well my dear audience, it's about WHAT, HOW or WHO,
it's about what you can do as an individual:
- AS PARENTS ... WHAT CAN YOU DO?
- AS TEACHERS ... WHAT CAN YOU DO?

In the beginning a reference to the book of Genesis in the Bible

impeccable perfect

the dawn the beginning; (*here used metaphorically:*) *Morgendämmerung*

Ni sa bula vinaka, Namaste, As-Salaam-Alaikum greetings in different languages; the first is Fijian, the second is Hindi, and the last is Arabic

- AS STUDENTS ... WHAT CAN YOU DO? OR
- AS LEADERS ... WHAT CAN YOU DO?

It is time to rise and act now.
It is a terrible problem, and it needs to be solved,
it deserves to be a huge priority.

to deserve to be (*here:*) should be; *(eine hohe Priorität) verdienen*

Ladies and Gentlemen,
I sit at home watching and hearing the news where the sea is swallowing villages, eating away at shorelines, withering of crops, relocation of people, cries over lost loved ones, dying, hunger and thirst.

withering of crops *verdörrte Ernte*
relocation *Umsiedlung*
cries (*here:*) *Hilferufe*

It's catastrophic. It's sad, but it's real.

You may think it will only affect small nations; you are wrong.

No nation, not even a powerful and successful one is immune to climate change and especially not a small island nation like Fiji.

If we search Google today, you will get almost 65 million pages of results.

But are we doing enough?
Is it possible to reverse it?
Or are we contributing to it?

elsewhere (*he means:*) everywhere

My dear audience, all of this [is] happening elsewhere.
Let me tell you my story to bring you closer to home.

to hail from to come from

I hail from the beautiful province of Tailevu, in a small village in Wainibuka called Naivicula.

cyclone *Zyklon*

Earlier in 2016, we were hit by one of the strongest cyclones that ever struck Fiji, the strongest in the Southern Hemisphere.

My home ...
my school ...
our source of food, water, money was totally destroyed.

My life was in chaos.

I asked myself:

- Why is it happening?
- Why is the cyclone getting stronger?
- What am I going to do?
- Will I go back to school?

Then I thought to myself ... this is it ...
- My life
- My dream
- My ambition just zapped out of my eyes.

zapped destroyed

I walked along our plantation, searching for what to take home for dinner.
Fish in the river for fish or prawns.
Walked amongst once a dense forest.

dense thick

Only to be filled with despair and frustration.

despair hopelessness

My once beautiful village, I once called home, is now a barren and empty wasteland.

barren desolate, infertile

In the months that followed, summer temperatures continued rising, the reduction of soil moisture turning our land infertile.
- Trees not bearing fruit in its usual season.
- Water bodies getting drier each day.
- Fish, shrimps, prawns, eels dead in lakes and rivers.

soil moisture *Feuchtigkeit des Bodens*
infertile *unfruchtbar*

I feel the pain, the remorse. I feel my life being sucked out right in front of me.

remorse grief, regret, sorrow; *Gewissensbisse*

I don't feel like going to school.
I feel the anger ... the loss.
I feel the terror ... the insecurity.
I feel worthless and useless as I watch everything around me turning from green to yellow then brown ... a sure sign that we are dying.

I ask myself ...
- That's a category 5 cyclone. What's next?
- Will I be able to survive what's next?
- Will my village last?

Well ... only time can tell ...

Ladies and Gentlemen. It's time to unite to move forward;
we have to row together. Let's make a stand and fight.
We have HEARD.
We have SEEN.
We have WITNESSED.
We were VICTIMS.
Now ... IT'S TIME TO CONQUER.

we have to row together (*here:*) we must all take action
to witness to see for oneself; *bezeugen*
victim sufferer; *Opfer*
to conquer *siegen*

Desmond Tutu states that – and I quote – ...
"Twenty-five years ago, people could be excused for not knowing or doing much, about climate change.

Desmond Tutu Archbishop, civil rights activist, teacher, South African Anglican cleric and winner of the 1984 Nobel Peace Prize, known for opposing apartheid

Today, we have no excuses."
This is not going to happen if we pretend and wait for others.

Ladies and Gentlemen ... it's not too late to start now.
Please hear me out.
Hear my cry. Hear my plea. Let's save our home.
Thank you.

plea appeal, request

ASSIGNMENTS

A) Pre-Listening and Pre-Reading Activities

▶ *brainstorming / mind mapping / milling around / pair-share / placemat or idea tower / speech*

1. What do you know about Fiji?
2. What impression does the photo of Timoci Naulusala convey?
3. Discuss the title of the speech.
4. If you were invited to give a speech at the next international conference about climate change, what would you say to the audience?

B) Reading and Listening Comprehension

▶ *reading and listening comprehension / think-pair-share / dramatised reading / using tablets or laptops / whiteboard or smartboard / presentation / peer support and feedback / writing a summary*

1. Watch the video of Timoci Naulusala's speech on YouTube.
2. Highlight Timoci Naulusala's most important statements on your speech transcript.
3. Outline his main arguments.
4. Outline the consequences of global warming mentioned.
5. Analyse his final appeal to the audience.

C) Analysis

▶ *think-pair-share / peer support and feedback / writing conference / presentation / discussion*

1. Timoci Naulusala is a Naivicula native whose speech won a nationwide speech competition for children in Fiji. He received a standing ovation from the world leaders he shared the stage with at COP23. Analyse why his speech is so effective.
2. How does Timoci Naulusala start his speech?
3. How does he get across the contrasting emotions of despair and hope to the audience?

D) Evaluation, Comment, Creative Activities

▶ *self-immersion / sharing ideas with classmates / peer support and feedback / email / interview / skype interview / presentation / discussion / essay writing / speech competition*

1. Write a personal response to Timoci Naulusala's speech and email it to Ben Simonds, Deputy Director of Communications, and COP23 Presidency Secretariat to Fiji, and to Cate Heinrich of UNICEF, who supported the Fijian Government in holding this speech competition.
2. Prepare and give a four-minute speech on the current problem of climate change, and the environmental plans and projects aimed at tackling climate change in your local area.
3. Desmond Tutu stated in *The Guardian* on April 10, 2014: "Twenty-five years ago, people could be excused for not knowing or doing much about climate change. Today we have no excuses." What do you think of this statement?

E) Further Projects: For Thought and Discussion

Comment on the following quotations. Do you agree or disagree with them?

1. "Climate change is an issue that will determine our destiny as mankind – it will determine the well-being of all of us," Angela Merkel stated at the climate summit in Bonn on November 15, 2017.
2. "Climate change is undeniable. Climate action is unstoppable," says António Guterres, the UN Secretary-General.

   Address on Climate Action at New York University Stern School of Business, on May 30, 2017 / https://www.un.org/sg/en/content/sg/statement/2017-05-30/secretary-general-climate-action-delivered

F) Cartoon by Gerhard Mester. Give this cartoon a catchy title that reflects the message.

Gerhard Mester is a very famous German cartoonist.

Tasks:

1. Describe and analyse the cartoon in detail.
2. Evaluate how the cartoon relates to the issue of climate change, and to Timoci Naulusala's speech.
3. ESA astronaut Alexander Gerst recorded a message in German to his future grandchildren from the International Space Station's Cupola observatory during his Horizons mission in 2018. Watch the video and translate his powerful message into English and send it to your English-speaking partner school.

   ESA https://www.esa.int/spaceinvideos/Videos/2018/12/Letter_to_my_grandchildren

G) Training: Giving a Speech

1. Work in pairs and prepare a powerful speech about the effects of global warming and what can be done to save the earth.
2. Imagine that you are taking part in the next international conference about climate change. Prepare a speech for the event. Practise your speech until you feel comfortable with it. Record your speech, then listen back to it and evaluate it.

"Every Single Person on This Earth Has the Power to Change the World."

Shalvi Shakshi presented her speech at the "Youth and Future Generations Day" at the UN Climate Change Conference (COP23) in Bonn on November 9, 2017.

RELATED TOPICS

CLIMATE CHANGE · THE EARTH IN DANGER · EDUCATION · THE ENVIRONMENT · FUTURE GENERATIONS · GLOBAL WARMING · GOD · GREENHOUSE GASES · HUMANITY · LIBERTY · NATURE · THE PARIS AGREEMENT · RESPONSIBILITY · SCHOOLS · SUSTAINABILITY

The 11-year-old Shalvi Shakshi from Fiji is the runner-up [*Zweitplatzierte*] of the school Climate Change Speech Competition held in Fiji. She is the second eldest daughter in a family of four children. Her father's name is Surendra Kumar Raj and her mother's name is Ashwin Sangeeta Prasad. Shalvi Shakshi's father is a school teacher and her mother is a housewife. The family lives in Tua Tua, in Labasa, Fiji.
Shalvi Shakshi is 11 years old and she is in Year Five at Nasarawaqa Primary School. She has keen interests in dancing, singing, reading, acting, and making people aware of climate change. Shalvi emphasises: "Climate change is happening and it's my plea to everyone to save our planet." Her speech and the interactive discussion between young people from various parts of the world raised awareness of the need to take action against climate change.

Acknowledgement: We would like to thank the Fijian Government, UNICEF and the COP23 Presidency Secretariat for the speech transcript and for the information provided in this foreword.

Shalvi Shakshi:

A very good morning to you all.

The famous activist Emma Thompson once said and I quote: "Every single person on this Earth has the power to change the world" and I repeat: "Every single person on this Earth has the power to change the world."

To the honorable Prime Minister of our country, panel of judges, other distinguished guests, ladies and gentlemen. I am standing here to show my forceful support on the theme of climate change: leadership action and COP23.

Firstly, let me define what climate change is.

It is changing in the climate of the earth due to human activities, and, I repeat, due to human activities. It is not happening from a few years back, but human activities from many years back have contributed to it. Due to these activities, the temperature is rising and some natural disasters occur.

Why should we care? Does it affect us?

Yes surely, surely it does, it affects us and we should be more considerate of our actions which bring about these changes.

The issue of concern is the rise of sea level. The harmful gases such as carbon dioxide and carbon monoxide makes the ozone layer thin and thus the harmful rays from sun reach the earth and melts the polar regions which increases the sea level.

The Pacific Island countries are greatly affected from it as these are small islands.

Trees take in carbon dioxide but when people cut down trees or burn forests the carbon dioxide comes in abundance and goes to the atmosphere where the first stage of climate change starts. To avoid these we should pass the message to everyone of not burning forests but planting trees when one cuts it down.

Just imagine when we grow up and notice that the tide which used to reach about 100 meters from your home is now only 50 meters away.

What would you do?

Run away and make your house at a higher level or say that I'll do something when it comes closer. No, it will be too late and won't solve the problem. This is the time dear colleagues; this is the time to act and do something which slows down the rising of sea level.

The major concern is the unpredictable disasters such as hurricanes. On 21st February 2016, Fiji was badly struck and extensively affected by Cyclone Winston. I repeat Cyclone Winston. Cyclone Winston affected the lives of 40 percent of people in Fiji leaving 44 dead, 45,000 people displaced and 350,000 directly impacted. The disaster caused

the honorable Prime Minister of our country Voreqe 'Frank' Bainimarama is the Prime Minister of Fiji, and was the President of COP23 in Bonn
forceful strong
natural disasters *Naturkatastrophen*
to occur to happen, to take place
considerate mindful, responsible
carbon dioxide *Kohlenstoffdioxid oder Kohlendioxid ist eine chemische Verbindung aus Kohlenstoff und Sauerstoff mit der Summenformel* CO_2
carbon monoxide *Kohlenstoffmonoxid ist eine chemische Verbindung aus Kohlenstoff und Sauerstoff mit der Summenformel CO*
ozone layer *Ozonschicht*
rays from sun *Sonnenstrahlen*
to take in to absorb; *aufnehmen*
in abundance in large quantities
unpredictable unforeseeable; *unvorhersehbar*
struck hit
extensively hugely; *in weiten Teilen*
affected by *beeinträchtigt durch*
Cyclone Winston On February 20, 2016, a category 5 tropical cyclone hit Fiji. It was the second strongest cyclone in recorded history.
impacted (*here:*) affected, hit with force

damages worth 650 million dollars, just imagine ladies and gentlemen 650 million dollars.

homeless *obdachlos*

mourning grief; *Trauer*

My community Nasarawaqa, in Bua, Fiji, was also part of this crisis where many people were homeless. 127 people of my community were situated in the evacuation center without proper supplies of food and water. Their days passed by mourning and waiting for a favourable and a better day.

we need to pull our socks up now (*here:*) we have to take action now; *wir müssen uns jetzt am Riemen reißen*

After one week they were back at their home starting a fresh life once again. People have gone through many crises and in order to have a better Fiji we need to pull our socks up now.

Who has to stand up for this?

I repeat: Who has to stand up for this? Who is responsible for this? I ask you, ladies and gentlemen, who is responsible for this? Well, it is our action which brings about changes. Plant a tree, walk instead of taking your car to go for a short distance.

Finally, to control climate change our school has opted for an action plan which is to plant trees, have 3 r's, that is: reduce, reuse and recycle, use organic farm products, create awareness campaigns in communities and advocate to our young generations at large. Let us together hand in hand start our preparation in solving the problem caused by climate change and make our country a very beautiful place to live in.

About my dress, underneath is the ocean and above are beautiful trees and flowers. Thank you.

ASSIGNMENTS

A) Reading and Listening Comprehension

▶ *listening and reading comprehension / dramatised reading / self-immersion / think-pair-share / peer support / students teach each other / writing a summary and an analysis*

1. Watch the video of Shalvi Shakshi's speech on ViralVideo: http://www.viralvideo.win
2. Highlight some important statements in your speech transcript.
3. Outline Shalvi Shakshi's arguments.
4. Explain Shalvi Shakshi's school's action plan to control climate change.

B) Analysis

1. Watch the video and analyse Shalvi Shakshi's delivery of the speech.
2. Analyse the structure of the speech.
3. Analyse some rhetorical devices that Shakshi uses to get her message across to the audience.

4. Analyse Shalvi Shakshi's passionate final appeal to the audience to take action to tackle climate change.

C) Evaluation, Comment, Creative Activities

interactive classroom / self-immersion / role play / talk show / panel discussion / creative writing / WebQuest / research / audio or video recording / presentation / feedback / evaluation

1. "Who has to stand up for this? I repeat: Who has to stand up for this? Who is responsible for this?" Write a comprehensive answer to Shalvi Shakshi's questions.
2. Send an email to Shalvi Shakshi and express your opinion of her speech.
3. The interactive discussion between young people from around the world has introduced various innovative methods to raise awareness of, and to take action against, climate change. Prepare a role play, a panel discussion or a talk show about climate change, including representatives from various countries.
4. Shalvi Shakshi points out that, in order to combat climate change, her school has come up with an action plan. Prepare and give a three-minute-speech on the current problems in Germany caused by climate change, and the plans and projects designed to tackle it in your local area, and at your school.
5. **Creative Writing: Part 1**: "Just imagine when we grow up and notice that the tide which used to reach about 100 meters from your home is now only 50 meters away." Imagine that you live in Fiji. Your house is now only 50 meters away from the ocean. Write a short story which reveals the thoughts and fears, hopes and dreams of people experiencing the effects of climate change.
6. **Creative Writing: Part 2**: "Let us together hand in hand start our preparation in solving the problem caused by climate change and make our country a very beautiful place to live in." Write a poem or a song which reveals the thoughts and fears, hopes and dreams of people experiencing the effects of climate change.
7. **Creative Activity: Part 3**: Produce a four-minute video about climate change.

D) Further Projects for Thought and Discussion

group work / WebQuest / research / exchanging knowledge at stalls / discussion / feedback

1. Find out some more information about Fiji. Divide the class into groups:
   Group A: Prepare a presentation about the political and social situation in Fiji for your classmates.
   Group B: Prepare a presentation about the economic and ecological problems Fiji is confronted with.
2. Prepare and give a speech in response to one of the following quotations:
   a) "We want our children to live in an America that [...] isn't threatened by the destructive power of a warming planet," from Barack Obama's re-election speech on November 7, 2012.
   b) "Climate change does not respect borders; it does not respect who you are - rich and poor, small and big. Therefore, this is what we call 'global challenges,' which require global solidarity," from Ban Ki-moon's speech at the United Nations' Headquarters on December 6, 2011.
   https://www.un.org/sg/en/content/sg/speeches/2011-12-06/remarks-momentum-change-initiative
3. **Greta Thunberg**, a 15-year-old student from Sweden, captured the attention of the world, when she criticised climate change negotiators at the UN Climate Summit, COP24 in Katowice, Poland, on December 14, 2018. Watch her speech on CNN, December 17, 2018
   https://edition.cnn.com/2018/12/16/world/greta-thunberg-cop24/index.html
4. **Chancellor Angela Merkel backs *Friday for Future* climate protests**:
   Angela Merkel praised *Friday for Future* climate protests by school pupils urging more action on climate change: „Wir können unsere Klimaschutzziele nur dann erreichen, wenn wir auch Rückhalt in der Gesellschaft haben. Deshalb begrüße ich es sehr, dass junge Menschen, Schülerinnen und Schüler demonstrieren und uns mahnen, schnell etwas für den Klimaschutz zu tun. Ich glaube, dass das eine sehr gute Initiative ist." From: German Chancellor Angela Merkel: Video Podcast on March 2, 2019
   https://www.bundeskanzlerin.de/bkin-de/mediathek/die-kanzlerin-direkt

5. **„Die Schülerdemos sind richtig und wichtig!"** Go online and read Werner Kolhoff's editorial: *Westdeutsche Zeitung*, March 15, 2019
https://www.wz.de/meinung/fridays-for-future-die-schuelerdemos-sind-richtig-und-wichtig_aid-37465151
6. **Hot Seat with President Donald Trump:**

Donald J. Trump ✔ — Follow
@realDonaldTrump

This very expensive GLOBAL WARMING bullshit has got to stop. Our planet is freezing, record low temps and our GW scientists are stuck in ice.

4:39 PM - Jan 1, 2014

Choose one of the following tasks:

1. Write an interview with President Donald Trump about his global warming related tweets.
2. Write an article for your school newspaper about Trump's global warming related tweets.
3. Prepare and give a speech in response to Donald Trump's speech and his tweets.

E) **Further Projects for Thought and Discussion**

▶ *cooperative learning / paired work / WebQuest / presentation / speech evaluation / SOLO taxonomy*

1. Write and give a short speech in response to one of the following videos:
   a) Climate Change – It's Time for Action: https://cop23.com.fj/climate-change-time-action/
   b) Ambitious Action Achieved at COP23: https://cop23.com.fj/ambitious-action-achieved-cop23/
2. **Frank Bainimarama, the Prime Minister of Fiji and the President of COP23,** is one of the leading voices calling on the international community to commit to more ambitious targets to curb the carbon emissions that are increasing temperatures across the globe. He is committed to drawing global attention to the impact climate change is having on vulnerable communities, including Pacific Islanders, and on the residents of other Small Island Developing States (SIDS), and low-lying areas of the world. Under his leadership, Fiji was the first country to ratify the Paris Agreement. It has also offered to give permanent refuge to the people of Kiribati and Tuvalu, should their countries become uninhabitable due to rising sea levels.
   a) Read, analyse and evaluate Frank Bainimarama's speech at the 20th Conference of Commonwealth Education Ministers on February 20, 2018. You can read and download a transcript of the speech here: https://cop23.com.fj/we-must-do-everything-in-our-power-to-meet-the-challenge-posed-by-climate-change-cop-presidents-speech-for-20th-conference-of-commonwealth-education-ministers/
   b) Prepare and give a speech in response to the Fijian Prime Minister's speech.
3. „[...] Wir ziehen es vor zu glauben, das Klima werde vor allem den Leuten auf [...] Kiribati um die Ohren fliegen. [...] Selbst wenn die Erderwärmung nur um zwei Grad steigt, werden Städte wie Karatschi und Kalkutta nahezu unbewohnbar sein. [...]"
   Jakob Augstein: "Wir! Werden! Sterben!" in *Der Spiegel*, Nr. 47/Nov. 18, 2017, page 12
4. **Mehr Extremwetter durch die Störung gigantischer Luftströme in der Atmosphäre**
   Computersimulationen zeigen einen starken Anstieg von Ereignissen, bei denen die Wellenbewegungen des Jetstreams in der Atmosphäre aufhören sich weiter voran zu bewegen. Dadurch könnten Wetterextreme am Boden häufiger werden: Wenn die Westwinde aufhören, Wettersysteme voranzutreiben, halten diese länger an – aus ein paar sonnigen Tagen kann eine Hitzewelle werden, anhaltender Regen kann zu Überschwemmungen führen. Ein internationales Team von Wissenschaftlern führt das auf die vom Menschen verursachte Erwärmung speziell in der Arktis zurück.

   Quelle: *Potsdam-Institut für Klimafolgenforschung* v. 1.11.2018: https://www.pik-potsdam.de/aktuelles/pressemitteilungen/mehr-extremwetter-durch-die-stoerung-gigantischer-luftstroeme-in-der-atmosphaere?set_language=de

"I Believe New Immigrants Are Good for America."

President William Jefferson "Bill" Clinton delivers an address at Portland State University's Commencement Ceremony, on June 13, 1998

RELATED TOPICS

THE AMERICAN DREAM · CITIZENSHIP · CONSTITUTION · COMMUNITY · CULTURE · THE DECLARATION OF INDEPENDENCE · DIVERSITY · EDUCATION · ENRICHMENT · THE FOUNDATION OF AMERICA · FREEDOM · HERITAGE · HISTORY · HOPE · IMMIGRATION · LIBERTY · MIGRATION · NATIONHOOD · PEACE · PREJUDICE · RELIGION · RESCUE · RESPONSIBILITY · SCHOOL · SOLIDARITY · TOLERANCE

The 42nd President of the United States assumed office in 1993 and served two terms, lasting until 2001. His name was **William Jefferson 'Bill' Clinton**, born on August 19, 1946 in Hope, Arkansas.

The fact that Clinton ran and won a second term as President was highly significant: he was the first Democrat to do so since Franklin D. Roosevelt. During his time in office, he presided over the lowest unemployment and inflation rates of the modern era, increased the number of Americans owning their own homes, and reduced crime in a number of areas. This coincided with achieving the first balanced budget in decades and even a budget surplus. In conjunction with the millennium celebrations in 2000, Clinton called on the American people to move towards eradicating racial discrimination.

The former President is an alumnus of Georgetown University and also attended Oxford University. Moreover, he also holds a law degree from Yale University.

In 1976, Bill Clinton became the Attorney General of Arkansas and was elected Governor two years later. Although he failed to secure a consecutive second stint in office, he was once again elected after four years away from the governorship and remained in the position until he was elected President in 1992. Together, Bill Clinton and his prospective Vice President Albert Gore Jr. represented a fresh style of leadership.

At Portland State University's State Commencement, President Clinton honed in on an often controversial subject: immigration. Namely, he commended the strengths of immigrants coming to the United States. He asserted that, 'They are building our new economy. They are energizing our culture and broadening our vision of the world, renewing our most basic values.'

THE PRESIDENT Bill Clinton:

Section 1

Give this section a heading. ______________________________

Ladies and gentlemen, thank you for the wonderful, warm welcome. [...]

What I want to talk to all of you about, particularly the graduates, is the America of your future. We all know that at the edge of a new century and a new millennium, America is changing at breathtaking speed. We know that most of these changes have been good. We're grateful as a nation to have the lowest unemployment rate in 28 years, the lowest crime rate in 25 years, the lowest welfare rolls in 29 years – (*Applause*) – the first balanced budget and surplus in 29 years, and the highest home ownership in history. (*Applause.*) We feel gratitude. We know that none of us alone is responsible for these things, but all of us together have come to terms with the challenges of the modern world and its opportunities and we're moving America in a good direction.

But this spring I have attempted to go out across the country and address graduates about the challenges this new era poses – not only because, even when there is a lot of good news out there, we should never forget that there are challenges, but perhaps even more importantly, because when times are good, it imposes upon Americans a special responsibility to take our confidence and our prosperity and look to the long-term challenges of the country, to address them in a forthright, constructive way so that our country will continue to grow and prosper.

This spring I have talked about three things. At the Naval Academy I talked about defending our nation against the new security threats of the 21st century, including terrorism, biological and chemical weapons, and global environmental degradation. At MIT, not very long ago, I talked about the challenges of the information age and the importance of bringing those opportunities to all Americans, bringing the Internet into every classroom, ensuring that every young student is computer-literate. (*Applause.*) Maybe I should have given that speech here. (*Laughter.*)

Today, I want to talk to you about what may be the most important subject of all – how we can strengthen the bonds of our national community as we grow more racially and ethnically diverse. (*Applause.*)

It was just a year ago tomorrow that I launched a national initiative on race, asking Americans to address the persistent problems and the limitless possibilities of our diversity. This effort is especially important right now, because, as we grow more diverse, our ability to deal with the challenges will determine whether we can really bind ourselves together as one America. And even more importantly in the near-future, and over the next few years, perhaps, as well, is our ability to exercise world leadership for peace, for freedom, for prosperity in a world that is both smaller and more closely connected, and yet increasingly gripped with tense, often bloody conflicts rooted in racial, ethnic and religious divisions – our ability to lead that kind of world to a better place rests in no small measure on our ability to be a better place here in the United States that can serve as a model for the world. (*Applause.*)

Section 2

Give this section a heading. ______________________________

The driving force behind our increasing diversity is a new, large wave of immigration. It is changing the face of America. And while most of the changes are good, they do present challenges which demand more both from new immigrants and from our citizens. Citizens share a responsibility to welcome new immigrants, to ensure that they strengthen our nation, to give them their chance at the brass ring. (*Applause.*)

In turn, new immigrants have a responsibility to learn, to work, and to contribute to America. If both citizens and immigrants do their part, we will grow ever stronger in the new global information economy. More than any other nation on Earth, America has constantly drawn strength and spirit from wave after wave of immigrants. In each generation, they have proved to be the most restless, the most adventurous, the most innovative, and the most industrious of people. Bearing different memories, honoring different heritages, they have strengthened our economy, enriched our culture, and renewed our promise of freedom and opportunity for all.

Of course, the path has not always run smoothly. Some Americans have met each group of newcomers with suspicion and violence and discrimination. So great was the hatred of Irish immigrants 150 years ago that they were greeted with signs that read: "No Dogs or Irish." So profound was the fear of Chinese immigrants in the 1880s that they were barred from entering the country. So deep was the distrust of immigrants from Southern and Eastern Europe at the beginning of this century that they were forced to take literacy tests specifically designed to keep them out of America. Eventually, the guarantees of our Constitution and the better angels of our nature prevailed over ignorance and insecurity, over prejudice and fear.

But now we are being tested again – by a new wave of immigration larger than any in a century, far more diverse than any in our history. Each year, nearly a million people come legally to America. Today, nearly one in ten people in America was born in another country; one in five school children are from immigrant families. Today, largely because of immigration, there is no majority race in Hawaii or Houston or New York City. Within five years there will be no majority race in our most populous state, California. In a little more than 50 years there will be no majority race in the United States. (*Applause.*) No other nation in history has gone through demographic change of this magnitude in so short a time. What do the changes mean? They can either strengthen and unite us, or they can weaken and divide us. We must decide.

Section 3

Give this section a heading. ______________________________

Let me state my view unequivocally. I believe new immigrants are good for America. They are revitalizing our cities. They are building our new economy. They are strengthening our ties to the global economy, just as earlier waves of immigrants settled the new frontier and powered the Industrial Revolution. They are energizing our culture and broadening our vision of the world. They are renewing our most basic values and reminding us all of what it truly means to be an American.

It means working hard, like a teenager from Vietnam who does his homework as he watches the cash register at his family's grocery store. It means making a better life for your children, like a father from Russia who works two jobs and still finds time to take his daughter to the public library to practise her reading. It means dreaming big dreams, and passing them on to your children. You have a lot of stories like that here at Portland State. Just this morning I met one of your graduates – or two, to be specific. Mago Gilson, an immigrant from Mexico who came here without a high school education. Twelve years later she is receiving her Master's Degree in Education, on her way to realizing her dream of becoming a teacher. (*Applause.*)

She is joined in this graduating class by her son Eddi, who had dreams of his own and worked full-time for seven years to put himself through school. Today he receives a Bachelor's Degree in Business Administration. (*Applause.*) And soon – there's more. Soon her son, Oscar, whom I also met, will receive his own Master's Degree in Education. I'd like to ask the Gilsons and their family members who are here to rise and be recognized. There she is. Give them a hand. (*Applause.*) In the Gilson family and countless like them, we see the spirit that built America – the drive to succeed, the commitment to family, to education, to work, and the hope for a better life. In their stories we see a reflection of our own parents' and grandparents' journeys – a powerful reminder that our America is now so much a place as a promise; not a guarantee but a chance; not a particular race, but an embrace of our common humanity.

Now, some Americans don't see it that way. When they hear new accents or see new faces, they feel unsettled. They worry that new immigrants come not to work hard, but to live off our largesse. They're afraid the America they know and love is becoming a foreign land. This reaction may be understandable, but it's wrong. It's especially wrong when anxiety and fear give rise to policies and ballot propositions to exclude immigrants from our civic life. (*Applause.*) I believe it's wrong to deny law-abiding immigrants benefits available to everyone else; wrong to ignore them as people not worthy of being counted in the census. It's not only wrong, it's un-American. (*Applause.*)

Section 4

Give this section a heading. ______________________________

Let me be clear: I also think it's wrong to condone illegal immigration that flouts our laws, strains our tolerance, and taxes our resources. Even a nation of immigrants must have rules and conditions and limits, and when they are disregarded, public support for immigration erodes in ways that are destructive to those who are newly arrived and those who are still waiting patiently to come. (*Applause.*)

We must remember, however, that the vast majority of immigrants are here legally. In every measurable way, they give more to our society than they take. Consider this: on average, immigrants pay $1,800 more in taxes every year than they cost our system in benefits. Immigrants are paying into Social Security at record rates. Most of them are young, and they will help to balance the budget when we baby boomers retire and put strains on it. New immigrants also benefit the nation in ways not so easily measured, but still very important. We should be honored that America, whether it's called the City on a Hill, or the Old Gold Mountain, or El Norte, is still seen around the world as the Land of New Beginnings. We should all be proud that people living in isolated villages in far corners of the world actually recognize the Statue of Liberty. We should rejoice that children the world over study our Declaration of Independence and embrace its creed.

My fellow Americans, we descendants of those who passed through the portals of Ellis Island must not lock the door behind us. Americans whose parents were denied the rights of citizenship simply because of the color of their skin must not deny those rights to others because of the country of their birth or the nature of their faith. We should treat new immigrants as we would have wanted our own grandparents to be treated. We should share our country with them, not shun them or shut them out. But mark my words, unless we handle this well, immigration of this sweep and scope could threaten the bonds of our union.

Around the world we see what can happen when people who live on the same land put race and ethnicity before country and humanity. If America is to remain the world's most diverse democracy, if immigration is to strengthen America as it has throughout our history, then we must say to one another: whether your ancestors came here in slave ships or on the Mayflower, whether they landed on Ellis Island or at Los Angeles International Airport, or have been here for thousands of years, if you believe in the Declaration of Independence and the Constitution, if you accept the responsibilities as well as the rights embedded in them, then you are an American. (*Applause.*)

Section 5

Give this section a heading. ______________________________

Only that belief can keep us one America in the 21st century. So I say, as President, to all our immigrants, you are welcome here. But you must honor our laws, embrace our culture, learn our language, know our history; and when the time comes, you should become citizens. And I say to all Americans, we have responsibilities as well to welcome our newest immigrants, to vigorously enforce laws against discrimination. And I'm very proud that our nation's top civil rights enforcer is Bill Lam Lee, the son of Chinese immigrants who grew up in Harlem.

We must protect immigrants' rights and ensure their access to education, health care, and housing, and help them to become successful, productive citizens. When immigrants take responsibility to become citizens and have met all the requirements to do so, they should be promptly evaluated and accepted. The present delays in the citizenship process are unacceptable and indefensible. (*Applause.*)

And together, immigrants and citizens alike, let me say we must recommit ourselves to the general duties of citizenship. Not just immigrants, but every American should know what's in our Constitution and understand our shared history. Not just immigrants, but every American should participate in our democracy by voting, by volunteering and by running for office. Not just immigrants, but every American, on our campuses and in our communities, should serve – community service breeds good citizenship. (*Applause.*) And not just immigrants, but every American should reject identity politics that seeks to separate us, not bring us together.

Ethnic pride is a very good thing. America is one of the places which most reveres the distinctive ethnic, racial, religious heritage of our various peoples. The days when immigrants felt compelled to anglicize their last name or deny their heritage are, thankfully, gone. But pride in one's ethnic and racial heritage must never become an excuse to withdraw from the wider American community. That does not honor diversity; it breeds divisiveness. And that could weaken America. (*Applause.*) Not just immigrants, but every American should recognize that our public schools must be more than places where our children learn to read, they must also learn to be good citizens. They must all be able to make America's heroes, from Washington to Lincoln to Eleanor Roosevelt and Rosa Parks and Cesar Chavez, their own.

Today, too many Americans, and far too many immigrant children attend crowded, often crumbling inner city schools. Too many drop out of school altogether. And with more children from immigrant families entering our country and our schools than at any time since the turn of the century, we must renew our efforts to rebuild our schools and make them the best in the world. They must have better facilities; they must have smaller classes; they must have properly trained teachers; they must have access to technology; they must be the best in the world. (*Applause.*) All of us, immigrants and citizens alike, must ensure that our new group of children learns our language, and we should find a way to do this together instead of launching another round of divisive political fights. (*Applause.*)

Section 6

Give this section a heading. ______________________________

In the schools within the White House – in the schools within just a few miles of the White House, across the Potomac River, we have the most diverse school district in America, where there are children from 180 different racial and ethnic groups, speaking as native tongues over 100 languages. Now, it's all very well for someone to say, every one of them should learn English immediately. But we don't at this time necessarily have people who are trained to teach them English in all those languages. So I say to you, it is important for children to retain their native language (*Applause.*) But unless they also learn English, they will never reach their full potential in the United States. (*Applause.*)

Of course, people learn English at different rates, and, of course, children have individual needs. But that cannot be an excuse for making sure that when children come into our school system, we do whatever it takes with whatever resources are at hand to make sure they learn as quickly as they can the language that will be the dominant language of this country's commerce and citizenship in the future. We owe it to these children to do that. And we should not either delay behind excuses or look for ways to turn what is essentially a human issue of basic decency and citizenship and opportunity into a divisive political debate. We have a joint stake in getting together and moving forward on this. (*Applause.*)

Let me say, I applaud the students here at Portland State who are tutoring immigrant children to speak and read English. You are setting the kind of example I want our country to follow. One hundred and forty years ago, in the First Lady's hometown of Chicago, immigrants outnumbered native American citizens. Addressing a crowd there in 1858, Abraham Lincoln asked what connection those immigrants could possibly feel to people like George Washington and Thomas Jefferson and John Adams, who founded our nation. Here was his answer: If they, the immigrants, look back through this history to trace their connection to those days by blood, they will find they have none. But our founders proclaimed that we are all created equal in the eyes of God. And that, Lincoln said, is the electric cord in that Declaration that links the hearts of patriotic and liberty-loving people everywhere.

Well, that electric cord, the conviction that we are all created equal in the eyes of God, still links every graduate here with every new immigrant coming to our shores and every American who ever came before us. If you carry it with conscience and courage into the new century, it will light our way to America's greatest days – your days. So, members of the class of 1998, go out and build the future of your dreams. Do it together, for your children, for your grandchildren, for your country. Good luck, and God bless you. (*Applause.*)

From: *Clinton White House Archives*
https://clintonwhitehouse4.archives.gov/textonly/WH/new/html/19980615-12352.html

---

ASSIGNMENTS

A) Comprehension, Analysis, Evaluation

listening and reading for gist and for detail / jigsaw activity step 1: each student of a "home group" specializes in one section of the speech, and works on the following assignments:

1. Watch the video and listen to your section of Bill Clinton's speech.

2. Read the transcript and look up any words you don't know which you need to understand the speech. *(Comprehension)*
3. Highlight the significant statements on your speech transcript. *(Comprehension)*
4. Choose an appropriate heading for your section of the speech. *(Comprehension)*
5. Point out the main ideas and statements in your section of the speech. *(Comprehension)*
6. Highlight some of the rhetorical devices Clinton uses in your section to emphasize his message. *(Analysis)*
7. Evaluate your section of Clinton's speech. *(Evaluation)*

	Suggested Heading for this Section	Significant Statements	Rhetorical Devices	Messages	Evaluation
Section 1					
Section 2					
[...]	[...]	[...]	[...]	[...]	[...]

B) Understanding, Analysing and Evaluating the Whole Speech.

▶ *jigsaw activity step 2 – students work in "mixed groups", they help and teach each other, and "build" the complete jigsaw puzzle, the whole speech, together*

1. Work in "mixed groups": Share the information gathered by all the groups.
2. Help each other to understand the whole speech.

C) Discussion and Creative Writing

▶ *internet research / communicative activities / creative writing / writing a news article and a feature article / pros and cons debate / speed debate / speech training / evaluation*

1. Discuss Bill Clinton's message in your groups, then as a class.
2. More and more countries are building barriers to stop immigrants and refugees crossing their borders. What do you think of this?
3. Many countries are also discussing imposing a maximum limit on the number of refugees who are allowed to enter their country. What do you think of this proposal?
4. Can you imagine helping refugees in your school or working voluntarily in a refugee aid group in your town? Share your opinion with your partner, then with your group, and then with your class.
5. Write a news article or a feature article on one of these topics for a newspaper.

> A ***news article*** is about local, national, or international news stories or events; it informs readers what happened/is happening; it answers the standard "five w's (and h)": who, what, when, where, why, and how, and contains factual information.
> A ***feature article*** deals with a topic or an event in more depth than a news article and places emphasis on the complex background of a particular topic, often humanizing events and issues rather than just giving an account of facts.

6. Write an article for your school newspaper about the refugee situation. Include the following aspects: refugees in your school, your town/village/local area, and your opinion of the situation refugees face in Germany/in the USA/in the European Union/in the UK. Do some research and find out more information about the current situation.

"Between Despair and Hope."

Statement by the UN High Commissioner for Refugees, Filippo Grandi, on World Refugee Day, on June 20, 2018

RELATED TOPICS

ASYLUM SEEKERS · COMPASSION · CONFLICT · DESPAIR · DIGNITY · DISPLACEMENT · DIVERSITY · FEAR · FUTURE GENERATIONS · HOPE · HUMAN RIGHTS · INCLUSION · INTEGRATION · INTERNATIONAL PEACEMAKING · PERSECUTION · REFUGEES · RESPONSIBILITY · SOLIDARITY · SUPPORT · HUMAN TRAFFICKING · THE UNITED NATIONS · VIOLENCE · WAR

Filippo Grandi is the 11th United Nations High Commissioner for Refugees.
He was elected by the UN General Assembly on January 1, 2016 to serve a five-year term, until December 31, 2020.
Grandi was born in Milan, Italy, in 1957 and has been engaged in refugee and humanitarian work for over 30 years.
From 2010 to 2014, he served as the Commissioner-General of UNRWA, the UN Agency for Palestinian Refugees, having previously been its Deputy Commissioner-General from 2005 to 2010. He also served as the Deputy Special Representative of the UN Secretary-General in Afghanistan and has worked with NGOs and the UNHCR in Africa, Asia, the Middle East and at the UN's Geneva headquarters.
Grandi holds a Bachelor's degree in Modern History from the State University in Milan [Università degli Studi di Milano], a Bachelor's degree in Philosophy from the Gregorian University in Rome [Università Gregoriana di Roma], and an honorary Doctorate from the University of Coventry.
In his video message for World Refugee Day, marked annually on June 20, Filippo Grandi called on the international community to express support for and solidarity with refugees. In his speech, Grandi said that World Refugee Day is also an occasion which recognizes those communities and people around the world who help refugees and the internally displaced in their midst, offering them a safe haven, and welcoming them into their societies.

From: *UNHCR* http://www.unhcr.org/the-high-commissioner.html
Speech transcript taken from *UNHCR*: http://www.unhcr.org/news/press/2018/6/5b28bef94/statement-un-high-commissioner-refugees-filippo-grandi-world-refugee-day.html

Filippo Grandi:

68.5 MILLION PEOPLE ARE UPROOTED

Today, World Refugee Day, is a time for solidarity with refugees – and with the communities that welcome them. As conflicts emerge, recur, persist and deepen, 68.5 million people are uprooted around the world. Nine out of 10 are in their own countries or neighbouring countries, and the impact is massive – on refugees themselves, and on the communities that open their doors to them. Now, more than ever, taking care of refugees must be a global – and shared – responsibility. It's time to do things differently.

to emerge to start, to begin; *auftauchen*
to recur to happen again
to persist to continue, to go on
to deepen to expand, to become more intense; *sich ausweiten*
uprooted people people wo have lost their homes; *entwurzelte Menschen*

A new model is now being tested, with positive results – based on equity, on justice and on humanitarian values and standards. Countries and communities need more systematic, long-term support as they take on the task of helping uprooted families. Refugees themselves need to be included in new communities, and given the chance to realise their potential. And solutions are needed – to help refugees return home when the time is right, or build new lives elsewhere. The Global Compact on Refugees – to be adopted this year – aims to make these [goals] happen.

equity fairness, (*here:*) sharing responsibility for refugees

Global Compact on Refugees a UNHCR initiative: http://www.unhcr.org/formal-consultations-on-the-global-compact-on-refugees.html

BETWEEN DESPAIR AND HOPE –
SHARING RESPONSIBILITY FOR REFUGEES

Getting laws and policies right is vital. But it is local people and communities that are on the frontlines when refugees arrive, and whose welcome makes the difference – the difference between rejection and inclusion; between despair and hope; between being left behind and building a future. Sharing responsibility for refugees starts there.

despair hopelessness; *Verzweiflung*

We see this every day – in Beirut, Lebanon; Cox's Bazar, Bangladesh; Yumbe, Uganda; Frankfurt, Germany; Lima, Peru and countless villages, towns and cities around the world. It's the men, women and children there, the local organisations and faith groups, the teachers, local business people and municipal leaders who make the difference – with humanity, compassion and solidarity.

Often, these communities are themselves on the margins – in remote border areas, or with few resources of their own. Yet, overwhelmingly, when refugees arrive, they share what they have motivated by compassion, and a sense of human dignity. And when people work together, the results are powerful.

on the margins (of society) *am Rand der Gesellschaft*

Who are these everyday heroes? People who know what it means to belong to a community – and are ready to help others belong too. By extending a helping hand directly, or working together – as part of

mosque *Moschee*

a local church or mosque, a school group, sports team, cooperative society, or youth group. Some have been refugees themselves, and know what that means. Through their generosity, they shine a light on the potential of refugees – and the endless opportunities to help them.

Helping refugees rebuild their lives needs all of us – working together so that they can achieve what most of us take for granted – education, a place to live, a job, being part of a community. Over time, the impact is enormous – for refugee families and those who welcome them.

On World Refugee Day, it's time to recognise their humanity in action – and to challenge ourselves, and others, to join them – in receiving and supporting refugees in our schools, neighbourhoods, and workplaces. This is where solidarity starts – with all of us.

ASSIGNMENTS

A) Pre-Listening and Pre-Reading Activity

word cloud / think-pair-share / inside-outside circle / share ideas / speech / evaluation

1. *Think:* Look at the word cloud. What do you think the speech might be about?
2. *Pair:* Talk to your partner about your ideas and prepare a two-minute-speech using at least ten words from the word cloud below.
3. *Share:* Share your ideas with another pair and give your speech to the class.
4. *Evaluate* one of the best photos of the year 2018: A child sleeps in a bag in the village of Beit Sawa, Ghouta, Syria, March 15, 2018. Photographer: Omar Sanadiki
https://www.reuters.com/news/picture/pictures-of-the-year-2018-idUSRTS27NNG

B) Comprehension

1. Watch the video of Filippo Grandi's speech here: https://www.youtube.com/watch?v=189JvQqWEAI
   The speech transcript is available to download here: http://www.unhcr.org/news/press/2018/6/5b28bef94/statement-un-high-commissioner-refugees-filippo-grandi-world-refugee-day.html
2. Highlight the significant statements in your speech transcript.
3. Sum up Filippo Grandi's main arguments.
4. Point out the significance of World Refugee Day.

C) Analysis

1. Analyse the structure of Grandi's speech.
2. Examine some of the rhetorical devices Grandi uses to emphasise his message.
3. Analyse Grandi's appeal to the audience at the end of his speech.

D) Evaluation, Comment, Creative Activities

▶ *role play / discussion / speech / cooperation with Social Sciences class / cross-curricular connections*

1. Send an email to Filippo Grandi in response to his speech.
2. "Given the right environment, our experience is that refugees bring solutions, not problems." Discuss and describe your own experiences with refugees in your local community.
3. "Integration is an opportunity, for both refugees and the communities in which they settle." Discuss this statement and add your own response to it.
4. What can your school, your town, and your local community do to support the refugees who live in your local area?
5. Set up a project or an exhibition in your school to make people aware of World Refugee Day.

E) More Information and Further Projects

▶ *flipped classroom / research / WebQuest / presentation / discussion / speech / cooperation with Social Sciences classes / cross-curricular connections / video recording / SOLO taxonomy / evaluation*

UNHCR Global Trends Report 2018: printed by UNHCR / June 2019
https://www.unhcr.org/5d08d7ee7.pdf
UNHCR GLOBAL Appeal 2018-2019: UNHCR / June 2018
http://www.unhcr.org/publications/fundraising/5a0c05027/unhcr-global-appeal-2018-2019-full-report.html
The UNHCR Global Trends Report is published every year to analyse the changes in populations of concern, and to deepen public understanding of ongoing crises. The UNHCR counts and tracks the numbers of refugees, internally displaced people, people who have returned to their countries or areas of origin, asylum-seekers, stateless people, and other populations of concern to the UNHCR.

Tasks:

1. What are the aims of the Global Trends Report?
2. How many people are forcibly displaced worldwide?
3. "Children below 18 years of age constitute about half of the refugee population." Find out if this statement is correct or incorrect.
4. Where do refugees come from? Which countries do most refugees come from? Make a list of them.
5. Where are refugees being hosted? What are the major refugee-hosting countries? Make a list.

"A Day Full of Emotions for Me."

António Guterres, the UN Secretary-General, on World Refugee Day, on June 20, 2017

RELATED TOPICS

ASYLUM-SEEKERS · COMPASSION · CONFLICT · DIGNITY · DISPLACEMENT · DIVERSITY · FEAR · FUTURE GENERATIONS · HOPE · HUMAN RIGHTS · INCLUSION · INTEGRATION · INTERNATIONAL PEACEMAKING · MULTICULTURALISM · PERSECUTION · POPULISM · RACISM · REFUGEES · RESPONSIBILITY · SOLIDARITY · THE UNITED NATIONS · VIOLENCE · WAR

António Guterres, the ninth Secretary-General of the United Nations, took office on January 1, 2017. Having witnessed the suffering of the most vulnerable people on earth, in refugee camps and in war zones, the Secretary-General is determined to make human dignity the core of his work, and to serve as a peace broker, a bridge-builder and a promoter of reform and innovation.

Prior to his appointment as UN Secretary-General, António Guterres served as the United Nations High Commissioner for Refugees from June 2005 to December 2015, leading one of the world's foremost humanitarian organizations during some of the most serious displacement crises in decades. The conflicts in Syria and in Iraq, and the crises in South Sudan, in the Central African Republic, and in Yemen, led to a huge rise in the UNHCR's activities, as the number of people displaced by conflict and persecution rose from 38 million in 2005 to over 60 million by 2015.

Before joining the UNHCR, Guterres spent more than 20 years in government and public service. He served as the Prime Minister of Portugal from 1995 to 2002, during which time he was heavily involved in the international effort to resolve the crisis in East Timor.

From: *United Nations* https://www.un.org/sg/en/content/sg/biography

UN Secretary General António Guterres:

Ladies and gentlemen,
Thank you very much for your presence.

Section 1 */ Give this section a heading.* ______________________________

Today, World Refugee Day, is, as you can imagine, a day full of emotions for me. It is impossible to spend ten years as High Commissioner for Refugees, doing my best to try to help the most vulnerable of the vulnerable, without changing your life. And, indeed, not only witnessing the suffering of people but also learning about the extraordinary courage, resilience and capacity to permanently generate hope for refugees is something that has changed my perspective of the world and, to a large extent, changed my life. And this was the reason why I became candidate for Secretary-General of the United Nations.

Now, we are witnessing the largest number of refugees ever. But it is important to say that refugee protection is not a matter of solidarity or generosity, refugee protection is an obligation under international law – the '51 Convention and many regional instruments of binding nature. And, as a matter of fact, during the ten years in which I was High Commissioner for Refugees, I have to say that, by and large, international law was respected. Borders were, in general, open, [there were] very few situations where refugees were rejected or sent back to their countries of origin, where they might face persecution.

The number of resettlement opportunities offered by developed countries for refugees living in camps and other dramatic situations in the developing world has doubled during those ten years and there was, in general, a strong acceptance by Member States that refugee protection was something that was needed and had to be granted. The situation has considerably changed now. It's true that we are still witnessing a very large number of countries doing an enormous effort to provide protection to refugees in very dramatic circumstances. I'll be flying tonight to Uganda. Uganda has been receiving, very generously, refugees from neighbouring countries – it has now more than 1.3 million refugees, 950,000 from South Sudan alone – and providing them not only with protection, but even with plots of land and the capacity to live not in camps, but in society, in a way that is much more humane but, of course, that requires a much stronger solidarity from the country itself.

We are still witnessing many remarkable examples of solidarity in today's world. But at the same time, we are seeing more and more borders being closed, we are seeing more and more refugees being rejected, and, namely in countries of the developed world, we are seeing the opportunities for resettlement in richer countries of refugees coming from the global South being in decreasing number at the present moment.

***Section 2** / Give this section a heading.* ______________________________

And this is particularly worrying, especially when associated with forms of political populism, xenophobia, racism, in which refugees become a target, many times being accused of being part of the terror threat when refugees are not terrorists – they are the first victims of terror, they are fleeing terror; that is why they are refugees. And this is the reason why I believe it is important to make today five very strong appeals to the international community. Five very strong appeals that I believe are absolutely necessary for the right of refugees to be again fully respected.

First: I call Member States that are not doing it, to re-establish the integrity of the International Protection for Refugees Regime, which means to have the right, obviously, to manage their borders in a responsible way, but managing them also in a protection-sensitive way, and not refusing entry to those seeking asylum and deserving protection, which means asking countries not to send back people to where they might face persecution, which means asking countries to increase their resettlement quotas and to grant protection to a larger number of refugees that are living in very dramatic circumstances in crowded camps or in the slums of cities in abject poverty.

Second: Recognizing that there is no humanitarian solution for the refugee's plight, the solution is political and it is related to the solution to the conflicts that generate refugees in large numbers; to ask all parties in different conflicts in the world, and all countries that have an influence on the parties in each conflict, to come together and understand that all those conflicts are now conflicts that are causing tremendous suffering in which nobody is winning, everybody is losing, that are becoming a threat, not only to the refugees themselves, but a threat to the whole world, as those conflicts are becoming also more and more interlinked to problems of global terrorism.

Third: Humanitarian support for refugees is still largely underfunded. I believe that, *grosso modo*, appeals made are funded at about 50%. That means that the majority of refugees live below the poverty line – that many cannot bring their children to school, that many cannot guarantee adequate nutrition for their children, that many have no adequate health support, that most of them have no jobs and no hopes or perspectives to have a dignified life. It is absolutely crucial that humanitarian appeals are fully funded and that international solidarity is expressed in relation to refugees, not forgetting that 80% of the world's refugees live in the developing world.

Fourth: I appeal to countries in the developed world to be able to express a much stronger solidarity with countries of first asylum in the global South; those that host, as I mentioned, 80% of the world's refugees, and sometimes with a dramatic impact on their economy, on their society, not to mention the impact on their security, with the conflict next door.

Section 3 */ Give this section a heading.* ______________________________

If one looks at countries like Lebanon, where one third of the population is refugees, if one looks at countries like Uganda or Kenya or Ethiopia – they have now more than one million refugees- in societies that are poor, that lack resources, that have huge development gaps and huge development problems; it is absolutely crucial not only to support refugees but to support those communities. And that requires effective development cooperation with these countries. […]

But the truth is that at the same time, countries are asking those in the developing world that host the largest number of refugees to keep them but are not providing the necessary support for that to be possible. Stronger solidarity with refugee-hosting countries in the global South is absolutely a must.

And finally [Fifth]: I ask countries in the developed world to increase their resettlement quotas, at least to the levels that we had two or three years ago, to be able to offer an effective responsibility-sharing with those that are hosting millions of refugees in the deep South.

Just to give you an idea about the differences between the global North and the global South, I'm going to Uganda, as I mentioned. Uganda, last year, received three times more refugees from South Sudan than those crossing the central Mediterranean, and you all know the enormous impact in public opinion and in political debates that the movement through the central Mediterranean caused last year. Well, Uganda received three times more, and Uganda is a tiny country with a relatively small economy and with an enormous generosity in the hearts of the people and the decisions of the Government.

I'd also like to remind you that, beyond those that are able to cross the border to seek protection outside their country, we have an even larger number, probably about double, of people that are displaced within the borders of their own country, internally displaced people. And those are under the authority either of their governments or of different non-state actors that occupy parts of the territory. And they have been systematically, in many parts of the world, victims of dramatic violations of international humanitarian law and human rights law.

And so, I also would like to make a very strong appeal to all actors in all the conflicts to respect international humanitarian law and to respect human rights law and for the international community to be able to implement those methods of accountability to make sure that those that are responsible for the worst atrocities to be effectively accountable and to be punished for what they are doing, because that's probably the only way to stop the kind of tragic impact we are having on the life and dignity of, now, more than 65 million people around the world.

***Section** 4 / Give this section a heading.* ______________________________

I also think it's important to underline that the difficulties faced by refugees are also linked to the fact that the migration debate has become quite irrational in today's world. We are talking about two different situations: refugees crossing borders, fleeing conflict or prosecution, and economic migrants who aspire legitimately to have a better life and move from one country to another, aiming at a better future for them and their children. They do not have the same rights as refugees, countries are not forced to grant them protection, but they also have human rights that also need to be respected and their dignity needs to be respected. […]

And so my strong appeal in relation to migration is that a rational debate become possible about migration, that of course countries have the right to apply their own migration policies, but that they do that in full respect of human rights, that at the same time, development cooperation policies are able to address the problems of human mobility, to create opportunities in countries of origin for migration to be out of choice, not out of necessity, and much stronger cooperation of states among themselves to crack down on smugglers and traffickers, but also a much bigger offer of opportunities of legal, regular migration. I think if migration can be discussed in a rational way that will create a much better environment in our societies that are all multi-ethnic, multicultural, multi-religious, and at the same time that will also help refugees benefit more easily from the protection rights they are entitled to receive.

We will have two very important debates in the General Assembly next year: on migration and refugees. And my appeal to all member states is to engage positively in those debates and to allow for the international community to be able to define, both in terms of refugees and migrants, adequate policies that are assumed by the whole of the international community, respecting human rights, taking into account the legitimate interests of States, but also the opportunities that are generated by human mobility in our world.

ASSIGNMENTS

A) Comprehension

think - pair – share / jigsaw activity step 2: students work in "mixed groups", they help and teach each other, and create/build the complete jigsaw puzzle, the whole speech, together / evaluation

1. Look up the words you don't know which you need to understand the speech.
2. Then highlight and summarise António Guterres's main arguments.

B) Analysis

1. Analyse the structure of the speech.
2. How does Guterres try to convince the international community of his arguments?

C) Evaluation, Comment and Creative Activities

1. Do you think António Guterres's ideas and his five appeals to the international community help them to deal with the global and local refugee situations?

2. "The migration debate has become quite irrational in today's world." Discuss and explain your own opinion of this statement.
3. Imagine you are a journalist taking part in the next UNHCR press conference. What questions would you like to ask Guterres? What possible answers might he give you?
4. Prepare and give a speech on the importance of the UNHCR in today's world.

D) Ideas for Further Projects

▶ *internet research / WebQuest / tablet / whiteboard or smartboard / audio or video recording / speech*

A child is a child: Protecting children on the move from violence, abuse and exploitation
May 17, 2017, published by UNICEF: https://www.unicef.org/children-uprooted
Millions of children are on the move across international borders – fleeing violence and conflict, disaster or poverty, in pursuit of a better life. Hundreds of thousands move on their own. Deprived, unprotected, and often alone, children on the move can become easy prey for human traffickers and others who abuse and exploit them.
Tasks:
1. Read the latest UNICEF report. Highlight the most important facts.
2. Work in pairs or in small groups:
   a) Why are millions of children on the move across international borders?
   b) Alarming numbers of children are moving on their own. Explain why.
   c) How can these children be protected from violence, abuse and exploitation?
3. Interview some refugee children in your local community and at your school. Making an audio or video recording might be an effective way of presenting your interview(s) to your peers.

Children in Danger
"The water filled the boat up to my knees. I was sitting on a man's lap, and afraid for my mother, knowing the back pain she suffers from. I was afraid the boat might collapse in the middle and we would sink into the sea and die. I was afraid for my mother, and my mother was afraid for me." Malak, aged 7.
From the UNICEF website: https://www.unicef.org/children-uprooted

E) UNICEF: Acts of Humanity and Agenda For Action
Tasks:
1. Choose and watch one of the UNICEF videos and describe the contents of the video you have chosen.
2. Talk about the cinematic devices used in the video you have chosen:
   a) Camera shots, camera angles, and camera perspective play an important role when analysing a film scene.
   b) Analyse the film techniques: the script, the setting, the use of lighting, the sound design, the music, the editing, the cinematography/the camerawork and the narration.
   c) What kind of emotional message is created through the use of these techniques?
3. Watch one of the UNICEF videos or choose and read one of the texts and documents, explain its main ideas briefly, and respond with a three-minute-speech to your class.
4. Visit the UNICEF website and spread the word by sharing stories about acts of humanity to inspire others. You are welcome to produce a short video clip titled "Act of Humanity".

F) A History Project: The Great Migration in the USA
Go online and view Jacob Lawrence's famous painting series about the mass movement of African Americans from the rural South to the urban North from about 1916 to 1970. Report your findings to your History and Art classes. Further information:
https://www.moma.org/interactives/exhibitions/2015/onewayticket/

"What Would You Do If You Were Forced to Leave Your Home?"

António Guterres, the UN Secretary-General, on World Refugee Day, on June 20, 2018

RELATED TOPICS

ASYLUM SEEKERS · COMPASSION · DISPLACEMENT · DIVERSITY · FEAR · FUTURE GENERATIONS · HOPE · HUMAN RIGHTS · INCLUSION · INTEGRATION · PEACE · PERSECUTION · REFUGEES · RESPONSIBILITY · SOLIDARITY · THE UNITED NATIONS · VIOLENCE · WAR

UN Secretary General António Guterres:

What would you do if you were forced to leave your home?

Today, more than 68 million people around the world are refugees or internally displaced as a result of conflict or persecution. That is equivalent to the population of the world's 20th largest country.

Last year, someone was displaced every two seconds, mostly in poorer countries.

On World Refugee Day, we must all think about what more we can do to help. The answer begins with unity and solidarity.

I am deeply concerned to see more and more situations where refugees are not receiving the protection they need and to which they are entitled.

We need to re-establish the integrity of the international refugee protection regime. In today's world, no community or country providing safe refuge to people fleeing war or persecution should be alone and unsupported.

We stand together, or we fail.

This year, a Global Compact on Refugees will be presented to the UN General Assembly. It offers a way forward and recognizes the contributions that refugees make to the societies hosting them.

As long as there are wars and persecution, there will be refugees. On World Refugee Day, I ask you to remember them.

Their story is one of resilience, perseverance and courage. Ours must be of solidarity, compassion and action.

Speech transcript taken from: *United Nations*
http://www.un.org/en/events/refugeeday/messages.shtml

displaced uprooted; *heimatvertrieben*
persecution oppression, discrimination; *Verfolgung*
that is equivalent to *das entspricht*

to be entitled to *einen Anspruch haben*

regime (*here:*) regulation

hosting giving shelter and support to them

resilience *Belastbarkeit, Widerstandskraft*
perseverance determination; *Durchhaltewille*
courage bravery; *Mut, Courage*
compassion empathy, kindness; *Mitgefühl*

ASSIGNMENTS

A) Listening and Reading Comprehension

think – pair – share / peer support and feedback / dramatized reading / poster / presentation

1. Watch the documentary video clips and listen to António Guterres's speech here: http://www.un.org/en/events/refugeeday/messages.shtml
2. Outline Guterres's main ideas and arguments.
3. Create a poster to present the main facts from Guterres's speech to your class and school community.

B) Analysis

paired work / peer support and feedback / tablet or laptop / presentation / writing an analysis

1. Analyse some of the rhetorical devices which support Guterres's message.
2. Analyse the video clips in detail; examine the cinematic devices which are used to support the message.

C) Evaluation, Comment, Creative Activities

flipped classroom / share ideas / discussion / creative writing / podcast / video / speech / evaluation

1. Evaluate the effectiveness of António Guterres's speech and the accompanying video clips.
2. Choose one of the following tasks:
   a) Write a response to Guterres's speech for your school newspaper.
   b) Write an article for the Newspaper Project "Texthelden".
   c) "What would you do if you were forced to leave your home?"
   Write a fictional or non-fictional text in response to this question.
   d) Create a podcast or a speech accompanied by video clips for the next World Refugee Day.

D) United Nations: Global Compact for Migration

Marrakech, Morocco, December 11, 2018. Read the Preamble of the UN Global Compact for Safe, Orderly and Regular Migration, especially sections 1-15. Work in pairs or in groups and summarise and evaluate the main concepts.

United Nations: https://refugeesmigrants.un.org/sites/default/files/180711_final_draft_0.pdf

The UN Compact on Global Migration is highly controversial across Europe. Supporters of the agreement say it will foster co-operation and improve the handling of millions of migrants, but critics fear it will encourage more illegal migration. What do you think? Organize a class debate.

E) For Thought and Discussion: World Press Photo of the Year 2018

Crying Girl on the Border, Texas, USA, June 12, 2018. Photographer: John Moore

https://www.worldpressphoto.org/collection/photo/2019/38262/1/John-Moore-(2)

Donald J. Trump ✓ Follow
@realDonaldTrump

Illegal immigration affects the lives of all Americans. Illegal Immigration hurts American workers, burdens American taxpayers, undermines public safety, and places enormous strain on local schools, hospitals and communities...

The White House – November 1, 2018

"The Beauty of Human Skin in Every Colour."

Angélica Dass, TED Talks in Vancouver, British Columbia, Canada, on April 19, 2016

RELATED TOPICS

DIGNITY · DISCRIMINATION · DIVERSITY · ETHNICITY · FUTURE GENERATIONS · WORLD HISTORY · HUMAN RIGHTS · IMMIGRATION · IDENTITY · INEQUALITY · INJUSTICE · JUSTICE · LIBERTY · MIGRATION · NATIONHOOD · PREJUDICE · RACE RELATIONS · REFUGEES · SEGREGATION · SLAVERY · SOCIAL SECURITY · TOLERANCE · UNALIENABLE RIGHTS · UNESCO · UNICEF · UNITED NATIONS

Angélica Dass, born in Brazil in 1979, is a famous photographer who is currently living in Spain.

She created the portrait project *Humanae* to challenge our perceptions of skin colour and ethnicity, seeking to counter the formation of intolerance, cliché and prejudice. She started the project back in 2012, and has now photographed more than 2,500 people from all over the world.

Once Angélica Dass has taken a picture of someone, her technique is to match their skin tone to a 'Pantone shade' by taking an 11-by-11 pixel square from their face. The portrait is placed on a background of that same colour, and the Pantone shade number is then added to the bottom of the image.

Angélica Dass sees it as vitally important that the imagery does not attempt to draw any form of contradistinction between subjects, be that race, gender, age, social class or other – she simply shows the wide range of different human skin tones and the diversity and beauty encapsulated within.

Her ultimate goal is for *Humanae* to act as a discussion platform on ethnic identity, skin colour and cultural prejudices.

Speech transcript taken from the *TED Talks* website:
https://www.ted.com/talks/angelica_dass_the_beauty_of_human_skin_in_every_color/transcript

Angélica Dass:

It has been 128 years since the last country in the world abolished slavery, and 53 years since Martin Luther King pronounced his "I Have a Dream" speech. But we still live in a world where the color of our skin not only gives a first impression, but a lasting one that remains.

color (*AmE*), colour (*BrE*); *Farbe*

I was born in a family full of colors. My father is the son of a maid, from whom he inherited an intense dark chocolate tone. He was adopted by those who I know as my grandparents. The matriarch, my grandma, has a porcelain skin and cotton-like hair. My grandpa was somewhere between a vanilla and strawberry yogurt tone, like my uncle and my cousin. My mother is a cinnamon-skin daughter of a native Brazilian, with a pinch of hazel and honey, and a man [who is] a mix of coffee with milk, but with a lot of coffee. She has two sisters. One in a toasted-peanut skin and the other, also adopted, more on the beige side, like a pancake. (*Laughter*)

to inherit *erben, vererben*
matriarch the female head of the family; *Matriarchin*
cinnamon-skin *zimtbraune Haut*
pinch touch

COLOR HAD MANY OTHER MEANINGS

Growing up in this family, color was never important for me. Outside home, however, things were different soon. Color had many other meanings.

I remember my first drawing lessons in school as a bunch of contradictory feelings. It was exciting and creative but I never understood the unique [why there was only one] flesh-colored pencil. I was made of flesh but I wasn't pink. My skin was brown, and people said I was black. I was seven years old with a mess of colors in my head.

unique single, one and only

Later, when I took my cousin to school, I was usually taken for the nanny. By helping in the kitchen at a friend's party, people thought I was the maid. I was even treated like a prostitute just because I was walking alone [unaccompanied] on the beach with European friends. And many times, visiting my grandma or friends in upper class buildings, I was invited not to use the main elevator. Because in the end, with this color and this hair, I cannot belong to some places.

taken for (*here:*) presumed to be; *als Kindermädchen gelten*
nanny babysitter

In some way, I get used to it and accept part of it. However, something inside of me keeps revolving and struggling. Years later I married a Spaniard. But not [just] any Spaniard. I chose one with the skin color of a lobster when sunburnt. (*Laughter*)

Since then, a new question started to chase me. What will be the color of your children? As you can understand, this is my last concern. But thinking about it, with my previous background, my story led me to make my personal exercise as a photographer. And that is how *Humanae* was born.

Humanae photography portrait project

HUMANAE IS A PURSUIT TO HIGHLIGHT OUR TRUE COLORS

Humanae is a pursuit to highlight our true colors, rather than the untrue white, red, black or yellow associated with race. It's a kind of game to question our codes. It's a work in progress from a personal story to a global history.

pursuit quest

I portray the subjects in a white background. Then I choose an 11-pixel square from the nose, paint the background, and look for the corresponding color in the industrial palette, Pantone.

I started with my family and friends, then more and more people joined the adventure, thanks to public calls coming through the social media.

I thought that the main space to show my work was the Internet because I want an open concept that invites everybody to push the share button in both the computer and their brain.

The snowball started to roll. The project had a great welcome – invitations, exhibitions, physical formats, galleries and museums ... just happened. And among them, my favorite: when *Humanae* occupies public spaces and appears in the street, it fosters a popular debate and creates a feeling of community.

to foster (*here:*) to encourage, to stimulate, to promote

I have portrayed more than 3,000 people in 13 different countries, 19 different cities around the world. Just to mention some of them – from someone included in the Forbes list, to refugees who crossed the Mediterranean by boat. In Paris, from the UNESCO Headquarters to a shelter. And students both in Switzerland and favelas in Rio de Janeiro.

favelas (the Brazilian Portuguese word for) slums

All kinds of beliefs, gender identities or physical impairments, a newborn or terminally ill. We all together build *Humanae.*

impairment disability

Those portraits make us rethink how we see each other. When modern science is questioning the race concept, what does it mean for us to be black, white, yellow, red? Is it the eye, the nose, the mouth, the hair? Or does it have to do with our origin, nationality or bank account?

This personal exercise turned out to be a discovery. Suddenly, I realized that *Humanae* was useful for many people. It represents a sort of mirror for those who cannot find themselves reflected in any label.

It was amazing that people started to share their thoughts about the work with me. I have hundreds of that, I will share with you, too. A mother of an 11-year-old girl wrote me: "Very good for me as a tool to work on her confidence, as this past weekend one of her girlfriends argued with her that she does not belong and should not be allowed to live in Norway. So your work has a very special place in my heart and it's very important for me."

A woman shared her portrait on Facebook and wrote: "All my life, people from across the globe had difficulties to place me in a group, a stereotype, a box. Perhaps we should stop. Instead of framing, ask the individual: 'How would you label yourself?' Then I would say, 'Hi. I'm Massiel. I'm Dominican-Dutch, I grew up in a mixed family and I'm a bisexual woman.' "

Besides these unexpected and touching reactions, *Humanae* finds a new life in a different variety of fields. Just to show you some examples, illustrators and art students using it as a reference for their sketches and their studies. It's a collection of faces. Researchers in the fields of anthropology, physics, and neuroscience use *Humanae* with different scientific approaches related to human ethnicity, optophysiology, face recognition or Alzheimer's.

optophysiology the science of how neural pathways within and across brain areas influence physical behaviour
Alzheimer's disease is the most common form of dementia (*Demenz*); the term dementia is used to define brain diseases related to memory loss and diminished cognitive skills.
purpose reason, intention, aim; *Absicht, Zweck*
to encourage sb. to do sth. to inspire sb. to do sth.; *jemanden ermutigen etwas zu tun*

One of the most important impacts of the project is that *Humanae* was chosen to be the cover of *Foreign Affairs*, one of the most relevant political publications. And talking about foreign affairs, I found the perfect ambassadors for my project ... teachers. They are the ones that use *Humanae* as a tool for educational purposes. Their passion encourages me to go back to drawing classes, but this time as a teacher myself. My students, both adults and kids, paint their self-portraits, trying to discover their own unique color.

WORK HARD TO ABOLISH DISCRIMINATION

As a photographer, I realize that I can be a channel for others to communicate. As an individual, as Angélica, every time I take a picture, I feel that I am sitting in front of a therapist. All the frustration, fear and loneliness that I once felt ... becomes love. The last country – the last country in the world which abolished slavery is the country where I was born, Brazil. We still have to work hard to abolish discrimination. That remains a common practice worldwide, and that will not disappear by itself. Thank you. (*Applause*)

to abolish to get rid of, to bring an end to; *abschaffen*

ASSIGNMENTS

A) Comprehension

individual work / paired work / peer support and feedback / share results of innovative projects

1. Point out the main ideas behind the *Humanae* Photography Project created by Angélica Dass.
2. *Humanae* is an endeavour "to highlight our true colors, rather than the untrue white, red, black or yellow associated with race." Explain what Angélica Dass means.
3. Explain the photographic techniques used in the *Humanae* Project.
4. What are Angélica Dass's message and intentions?

B) Analysis

1. Watch her speech on YouTube and analyse her tone of voice, accent, appearance, and body language: https://www.youtube.com/watch?v=NiMgOklgeos&61025D278419FD47A2D97DF4199F8A8F=or on the *TED Talks* website: https://www.ted.com/talks/angelica_dass_the_beauty_of_human_skin_in_every_color#t-35863
2. How does Dass use her personal experiences and her family history to illustrate her message?

C) Evaluation, Response, Creative Writing

project work / group work / WebQuest / tablet / smartboard / presentation / discussion / evaluation

1. What do you think of this project?
2. "We still have to work hard to abolish discrimination." Could this project make people aware of discrimination and racism?
3. Could this *Humanae* Photography Project help to abolish prejudice and discrimination?

D) Creative Activity

1. Angélica Dass's project forces us to reconsider what we think we know about skin color and ethnic identity. Write an imaginary interview with Angélica Dass. Work with a partner and perform your interview to the class.
2. Translate the following text into English; then organise a class debate and discuss the statements and intentions of the exhibition.
   „Unabhängig von Hautfarbe, Religion, Sprache, ethnischer Identität und kultureller Prägung hat jeder Mensch Migrationshintergrund. In einer Welt, die im Zuge der Globalisierung immer mehr zusammenrückt, sollten wir Migration als natürlichen Bestandteil unseres Lebens akzeptieren und sie als Chance begreifen, sowohl persönlich, als auch im gesellschaftlichen und politischen Leben zu wachsen. Ohne Wandel entsteht Stillstand. Ohne Bewegung kann es kein Gleichgewicht geben." *Leitgedanke der internationalen Wanderausstellung* „2 Millionen Jahre Migration" *des Neanderthal Museums, Mettmann* www.neanderthal.de

E) Further Projects for Thought and Discussion

research / WebQuest / idea lab / cooperation with Social Sciences, Music and Art classes / cross-curricular connections / presentation / discussion / speech training / podcast / video recording

1. Michael Jackson's song "*Black or White*" issues a message of equality. People can be friends with each other no matter what their skin colour is. The whole song is summed up in the chorus: "*It don't matter if you're black or white.*" The song "*They Don't Care About Us*" highlights the issue of racial discrimination. The photographer Angélica Dass emphasises the huge variety of skin colours across the world today – our appearances are different but we are all equal. Consider the message and intentions behind Michael Jackson's songs, and Angélica Dass's *Humanae* Photography Project, then prepare and give a three-minute speech in which you compare and connect the songs and the photography project.

2. Choose songs (*Best Songs about Racism and Discrimination*) or poems (*Poetry about Racism*) or photos (*World Press Photos of the Year*) or graphic narratives (*cartoons, paintings, graphic novels, sequential storytelling, narrative illustration*) that were designed to prevent racism and discrimination. Present your choice to the class, explaining why you have chosen it.
3. **Renewed Sense of Dignity and Self-Respect**
   German artist and photographer Can Kalvelage's latest exhibition, „Menschen machen Kleider," consists of before and after photographs of homeless people, which depict their transformation after Kalvelage's help. The first black and white photos depict the stark, squalid living conditions in which Kalvelage found them, and the second, full-colour photographs were taken after Kalvelage gave them some new clothes and a makeover, as well as other vital forms of support, such as assistance finding accommodation off the streets. The photographs really do show that the person makes the clothes, not the other way round.
   Kalvelage's intention was to help the homeless people he worked with to gain a renewed sense of dignity and self-respect. Crucially, Kalvelage has also brought the often stigmatized and forgotten problem of homelessness back into the public eye. The *Westdeutsche Zeitung* published an article on this amazing project, which they say could help to combat discrimination and prejudice against homeless people, and to support their integration into society. In the article, journalist Juliane Kinast writes: "Der Essener Künstler gibt den Menschen, die er anzieht und ablichtet, einen neuen Blick auf sich selbst - und ein neues Spiegelbild in den Augen der Anderen."
   Further Information: *Westdeutsche Zeitung*, September 4, 2018, page 3: https://www.wz.de/panorama/gesellschaft/menschen-machen-kleider-kuenstler-kleidet-obdachlose-schick-ein_aid-32701693

Tasks:
1. Research the "Menschen machen Kleider" exhibition in more detail.
2. What do you think of this photography project? Do you think it will help to reduce discrimination against homeless people?
3. Imagine you are a photographer. What kind of project would you set up to combat discrimination, racism and prejudice?

F) For Thought and Discussion
1. "My Homeless Years": The British Rapper *Speech Debelle* talks and writes about her homeless years, on BBC, on May 28, 2012. She is a British hip-hop artist who won the Mercury Music Prize in 2009.
   BBC, May 28, 2012, https://www.bbc.com/news/magazine-18145323
2. "Dead dogs are treated better than dead homeless people. It's a disgrace. Some 440 people died homeless in the UK in the last 12 months." Tamsen Courtenay in: *The Guardian*, October 11, 2018, https://www.theguardian.com/commentisfree/2018/oct/11/dead-dogs-treated-dead-homeless-people-government-count

G) Let's Fight Racism and Discrimination
Some suggestions for thought, debate, discussion and action:
- What are the reasons for discrimination and racism?
- Study the stories and contributions of some famous people from all parts of the world who have fought against discrimination and racism.
- How can education raise awareness and foster tolerance?
- Why is it important to preserve, develop and appreciate different cultures?
- How can your class, your school and your community encourage respect for the culture of minority groups?
  Further Information: *United Nations* http://www.un.org/en/letsfightracism/classroom.shtml

"A Boat Carrying 500 Refugees Sunk at Sea. The Story of Two Survivors."

Melissa Fleming is the Head of Communications and the Public Information Service at UNHCR, the UN Refugee Agency. She is Senior Advisor to and Spokesperson for the UN Secretary-General, António Guterres. She presented her TED talk in May 2015.

RELATED TOPICS

ABUSE · ASYLUM SEEKERS · COMPASSION · CONFLICT · COURAGE · DIGNITY · DISPLACEMENT · DIVERSITY · EXILE · EXPLOITATION · FEAR · FREEDOM · FUTURE GENERATIONS · HOPE · HUMAN RIGHTS · INCLUSION · INTEGRATION · PEACE · PERSECUTION · REFUGEES · RESPECT · RESPONSIBILITY · SAFETY · SOLIDARITY · THE UNITED NATIONS · THE UNHCR · VIOLENCE · WAR

Melissa Fleming delivers a gut-wrenching speech on the inhumane circumstances in which refugees find themselves in as they cross the Mediterranean Sea and the invariable disasters which often occur during the voyage.
She tells the tragic story of a brave young woman who performed heroics when one journey across the sea had catastrophic consequences for the 500 refugees crammed on board. Whereas the media often provide us with a statistical view of the migrant crisis, Fleming's powerful words manage to provide the reader with the opportunity to follow a single refugee closely – to see them as a person, primarily – as they strive to escape violence and danger at home. Perhaps the most shocking element of Fleming's speech is the detail she provides of the continuing dangers which refugees face on their journeys: this is not merely left behind in their own country. The migrants face many challenges to reach the safety and freedom of Europe.
In 2017, Melissa Fleming published her book *A Hope More Powerful than the Sea*.

Speech transcript and video available here: https://www.ted.com/talks/melissa_fleming_a_boat_carrying_500_refugees_sunk_at_sea_the_story_of_two_survivors/transcript

Melissa Fleming:

Every day, I listen to harrowing stories of people fleeing for their lives, across dangerous borders and unfriendly seas. But there's one story that keeps me awake at night, and it's about Doaa.

harrowing distressing, heartbreaking; *erschütternd*

grinding oppressive, difficult; *zermürbend*
working day wages *als Tagelöhnerin arbeiten*
thriving business flourishing business; *florierender Betrieb*
weary *überdrüssig*
aspiring hopeful, ambitious

A Syrian refugee, 19 years old, she was living a grinding existence in Egypt working day wages. Her dad was constantly thinking of his thriving business back in Syria that had been blown to pieces by a bomb. And the war that drove them there was still raging in its fourth year. And the community that once welcomed them there, had become weary of them. And one day, men on motorcycles tried to kidnap her. Once an aspiring student thinking only of her future, now she was scared all the time.

to struggle to battle/to fight for one's existence

But she was also full of hope, because she was in love with a fellow Syrian refugee named Bassem. Bassem was also struggling in Egypt, and he said to Doaa: "Let's go to Europe; seek asylum, safety. I will work, you can study – the promise of a new life." And he asked her father for her hand in marriage.

DOAA WAS TERRIFIED OF THE WATER. SHE ALWAYS HAD BEEN. SHE NEVER LEARNED TO SWIM.

notorious *berüchtigt*

But they knew, to get to Europe, they had to risk their lives, traveling across the Mediterranean Sea, putting their hands in smugglers', notorious for their cruelty. And Doaa was terrified of the water. She always had been. She never learned to swim.

consented agreed
life savings (*here:*) *sämtliche Ersparnisse*

It was August that year, and already 2,000 people had died trying to cross the Mediterranean, but Doaa knew of a friend who had made it all the way to Northern Europe, and she thought: "Maybe we can, too." So she asked her parents if they could go, and after a painful discussion, they consented, and Bassem paid his entire life savings – 2,500 dollars each – to the smugglers.

crammed crowded, jammed; *zusammengepfercht*

It was a Saturday morning when the call came, and they were taken by bus to a beach, hundreds of people on the beach. They were taken then by small boats onto an old fishing boat, 500 of them crammed onto that boat, 300 below, 200 above. There were Syrians, Palestinians, Africans, Muslims and Christians, 100 children, including Sandra – little Sandra, six years old – and Masa, 18 months. There were families on that boat, crammed together shoulder to shoulder, feet to feet. Doaa was sitting with her legs crammed up to her chest, Bassem holding her hand.

Day two on the water, they were sick with worry and sick to their stomachs from the rough sea.

premonition a feeling that something, especially something unpleasant, is going to happen; *Vorahnung*

Day three, Doaa had a premonition. And she said to Bassem, "I fear we're not going to make it. I fear the boat is going to sink." And Bassem said to her: "Please be patient. We will make it to Sweden, we will get married and we will have a future."

Day four, the passengers were getting agitated. They asked the captain: "When will we get there?" He told them to shut up, and he insulted them. He said: "In 16 hours we will reach the shores of Italy." They were weak and weary. Soon they saw a boat approach – a smaller boat, 10 men on board, who started shouting at them, hurling insults, throwing sticks, asking them to all disembark and get on this smaller, more unseaworthy boat. The parents were terrified for their children, and they collectively refused to disembark. So the boat sped away in anger, and a half an hour later, came back and started deliberately ramming a hole in the side of Doaa's boat, just below where she and Bassem were sitting. And she heard how they yelled: "Let the fish eat your flesh!" And they started laughing as the boat capsized and sank.

agitated nervous, stressed, disturbed; *aufgewühlt*

to insult *beschimpfen*

to disembark to get off

unseaworthy *seeuntauglich*

deliberately on purpose, intentionally

to capsize to turn over; *kentern*

SOME PEOPLE GAVE UP HOPE

The 300 people below deck were doomed. Doaa was holding on to the side of the boat as it sank, and watched in horror as a small child was cut to pieces by the propeller. Bassem said to her: "Please let go, or you'll be swept in and the propeller will kill you, too." And remember – she can't swim. But she let go and she started moving her arms and her legs, thinking: "This is swimming." And miraculously, Bassem found a life ring. It was one of those child's rings that they use to play in swimming pools and on calm seas. And Doaa climbed onto the ring, her arms and her legs dangling by the side. Bassem was a good swimmer, so he held her hand and tread water. Around them there were corpses. Around 100 people survived initially, and they started coming together in groups, praying for rescue. But when a day went by and no one came, some people gave up hope, and Doaa and Bassem watched as men in the distance took their life vests off and sank into the water.

were doomed did not stand a chance

TED.com is a non-profit organisation devoted to spreading ideas, usually in the form of short, powerful talks (18 minutes long or less). TED covers almost every topic — from science to business to global issues — with subtitles in over 100 languages. Meanwhile, independently run TEDx events help share ideas in communities around the world.
For more information, please visit: https://www.ted.com/

One man approached them with a small baby perched on his shoulder, nine months old – Malek. He was holding onto a gas canister to stay afloat, and he said to them: "I fear I am not going to survive. I'm too weak. I don't have the courage anymore." And he handed little Malek over to Bassem and to Doaa, and they perched her onto the life ring. So now they were three, Doaa, Bassem and little Malek.

perched sitting

to stay afloat *über Wasser halten*

And let me take a pause in this story right here and ask the question: why do refugees like Doaa take these kinds of risks? Millions of refugees are living in exile, in limbo. They're living in countries fleeing from a war that has been raging for four years. Even if they wanted to return, they can't. Their homes, their businesses, their towns and their cities have been completely destroyed. This is a UNESCO World Heritage City, Homs, in Syria. So people continue to flee into neighboring countries, and we build refugee camps for them in the desert.

in limbo *in der Schwebe, im Ungewissen*

World Heritage City *Weltkulturerbestadt*

overwhelmed *überfordert*

influx large numbers; *Zustrom*

hosting accommodating; *aufnehmen*

temporary limited, a short-term solution; *vorübergehend*

to drown *ertrinken*

agitated distressed; *erregt, aufgewühlt*

Quran *Koran*

bloating swelling; *aufgedunsen*

Hundreds of thousands of people live in camps like these, and thousands and thousands more, millions, live in towns and cities. And the communities, the neighboring countries that once welcomed them with open arms and hearts are overwhelmed. There are simply not enough schools, water systems, sanitation. Even rich European countries could never handle such an influx without massive investment. The Syrian war has driven almost four million people over the borders, but over seven million people are on the run inside the country. That means that over half the Syrian population has been forced to flee. And back to those neighboring countries hosting so many. They feel that the richer world has done too little to support them. And days have turned into months, months into years. A refugee's stay is supposed to be temporary.

"MY LOVE, PLEASE HOLD ON TO HOPE, TO OUR FUTURE. WE WILL MAKE IT."

Back to Doaa and Bassem in the water. It was their second day, and Bassem was getting very weak. And now it was Doaa's turn to say to Bassem: "My love, please hold on to hope, to our future. We will make it."

And he said to her: "I'm sorry, my love, that I put you in this situation. I have never loved anyone as much as I love you." And he released himself into the water, and Doaa watched as the love of her life drowned before her eyes.

Later that day, a mother came up to Doaa with her small 18-month-old daughter, Masa. This was the little girl I showed you in the picture earlier, with the life vests. Her older sister Sandra had just drowned, and her mother knew she had to do everything in her power to save her daughter. And she said to Doaa: "Please take this child. Let her be part of you. I will not survive." And then she went away and drowned.

So Doaa, the 19-year-old refugee who was terrified of the water, who couldn't swim, found herself in charge of two little baby kids. And they were thirsty and they were hungry and they were agitated, and she tried her best to amuse them, to sing to them, to say words to them from the Quran. Around them, the bodies were bloating and turning black. The sun was blazing during the day. At night, there was a cold moon and fog. It was very frightening. On the fourth day in the water, this is how Doaa probably looked on the ring with her two children.

A woman came on the fourth day and approached her and asked her to take another child – a little boy, just four years old. When Doaa took the little boy and the mother drowned, she said to the sobbing child: "She just went away to find you water and food." But his heart soon stopped, and Doaa had to release the little boy into the water.

Later that day, she looked up into the sky with hope, because she saw two planes crossing in the sky. And she waved her arms, hoping they would see her, but the planes were soon gone.

But that afternoon, as the sun was going down, she saw a boat, a merchant vessel. And she said: "Please, God, let them rescue me." She waved her arms and she felt like she shouted for about two hours. And it had become dark, but finally the searchlights found her and they extended a rope, astonished to see a woman clutching onto two babies.

merchant vessel *Handelsschiff*

They pulled them onto the boat, they got oxygen and blankets, and a Greek helicopter came to pick them up and take them to the island of Crete.

Crete *Kreta*

But Doaa looked down and asked: "What of Malek?" And they told her the little baby did not survive – she drew her last breath in the boat's clinic. But Doaa was sure that as they had been pulled up onto the rescue boat, that little baby girl had been smiling.

Only 11 people survived that wreck, of the 500. There was never an international investigation into what happened. There were some media reports about mass murder at sea, a terrible tragedy, but that was only for one day. And then the news cycle moved on.

wreck (*here:*) shipwreck; *Schiffbruch*
the news cycle moved on *die Medien wandten sich einem anderen Thema zu*

Meanwhile, in a pediatric hospital on Crete, little Masa was on the edge of death. She was really dehydrated. Her kidneys were failing. Her glucose levels were dangerously low. The doctors did everything in their medical power to save them, and the Greek nurses never left her side, holding her, hugging her, singing her words. My colleagues also visited and said pretty words to her in Arabic. Amazingly, little Masa survived.

pediatric hospital *Kinderkrankenhaus*
on the edge of death *zwischen Leben und Tod*
dehydrated *dehydriert*
glucose levels *Blutzuckerwerte*

And soon the Greek press started reporting about the miracle baby, who had survived four days in the water without food or anything to drink, and offers to adopt her came from all over the country.

to adopt *adoptieren*

And meanwhile, Doaa was in another hospital on Crete, thin, dehydrated. An Egyptian family took her into their home as soon as she was released. And soon word went around about Doaa's survival, and a phone number was published on Facebook. Messages started coming in.

"Doaa, do you know what happened to my brother? My sister? My parents? My friends? Do you know if they survived?"

One of those messages said: "I believe you saved my little niece, Masa." And it had this photo. This was from Masa's uncle, a Syrian refugee who had made it to Sweden with his family and also Masa's older sister. Soon, we hope, Masa will be reunited with him in Sweden, and until then, she's being cared for in a beautiful orphanage in Athens.

reunited united, brought together again
orphanage *Waisenhaus*

And Doaa? Well, word went around about her survival, too. And the media wrote about this slight woman, and couldn't imagine how she could survive all this time under such conditions in that sea, and still save another life.

slight small, thin

The Academy of Athens, one of Greece's most prestigious institutions, gave her an award of bravery, and she deserves all that praise, and she deserves a second chance.

award of bravery *Auszeichnung für besonderen Mut*

But she wants to still go to Sweden. She wants to reunite with her family there. She wants to bring her mother and her father and her younger siblings, away from Egypt, there as well, and I believe she will succeed. She wants to become a lawyer or a politician or something that can help fight injustice. She is an extraordinary survivor.

But I have to ask: What if she didn't have to take that risk? Why did she have to go through all that? Why wasn't there a legal way for her to study in Europe? Why couldn't Masa have taken an airplane to Sweden? Why couldn't Bassem have found work? Why is there no massive resettlement program for Syrian refugees, the victims of the worst war of our times? The world did this for the Vietnamese in the 1970s. Why not now? Why is there so little investment in the neighboring countries hosting so many refugees? And why, the root question, is so little being done to stop the wars, the persecution and the poverty that is driving so many people to the shores of Europe? Until these issues are resolved, people will continue to take to the seas and to seek safety and asylum.

resettlement program *Umsiedlungsprogramm*
persecution oppression, discrimination; *Verfolgung*
issues are resolved solutions to problems are found

And what happens next? Well, that is largely Europe's choice. And I understand the public fears. People are worried about their security, their economies, and the changes of culture. But is that more important than saving human lives? Because there is something fundamental here that I think overrides the rest, and it is about our common humanity. No person fleeing war or persecution should have to die crossing a sea to reach safety. (*Applause*)

to override *Vorrang haben*

A WORLD IN WHICH EVERY LIFE MATTERS

One thing is for sure, that no refugee would be on those dangerous boats if they could thrive where they are. And no migrant would take that dangerous journey if they had enough food for themselves and their children. And no one would put their life savings in the hands of those notorious smugglers if there was a legal way to migrate.

if they could thrive *wenn es ihnen gut gehen würde*

So on behalf of little Masa, and on behalf of Doaa, and of Bassem, and of those 500 people who drowned with them, can we make sure that they did not die in vain? Could we be inspired by what happened, and take a stand for a world in which every life matters? Thank you. (*Applause*)

to take a stand *Stellung beziehen, sich einsetzen für*

One of the Photos of The Year 2017:
Refugees from a capsized boat off Lampedusa, Italy / Chris McGrath/Getty Images
May 24, 2017 I did a month with the Migrant Offshore Aid Station (MOAS) and each rescue took weeks. When we reached the migrants, they were not in the water – the rescue workers gave out lifejackets and tried to find out more about the situation on board. I didn't see the boat capsize – but it was so full, I think there were about 600 on the boat, which should hold 50. Once everyone ended up in the water, it was really a different assignment. I went from trying to take the best picture to being part of the rescue crew. I had people coming over with their arms outstretched – you can't take a photo and not pull them in.
From: *The Guardian*
https://www.theguardian.com/media/2017/dec/28/the-best-photographs-of-2017-by-the-people-who-shot-them

ASSIGNMENTS

A) Comprehension

self-immersion / paired work / group work / peer support and feedback / share ideas and results

1. Watch the video and read the transcript of Melissa Fleming's powerful, impressive and moving speech.
2. Highlight important statements which emphasise the situation faced by refugees.
3. What do we learn about the Syrian refugees Doaa and Bassem?
4. What information is given about the other refugees and about the smugglers?
5. How did other countries and the media react to the deaths of the 500 refugees who drowned in the Mediterranean Sea when Doaa's boat sank?
6. What possible solutions does Melissa Fleming suggest in order to avoid future tragedies?
7. Summarise Melissa Fleming's speech.

B) Analysis

paired work / group work / tablet or laptop presentation / podcast / writing an analysis / feedback

1. Analyse the structure of Melissa Fleming's speech.
2. Examine some of the rhetorical devices which Fleming uses to emphasise her message.
3. Watch the video and analyse how Melissa Fleming delivers her speech.
4. Explain how the photos accompanying the speech illustrate her message.
5. What makes Fleming's speech so powerful?
6. What do the individual tragedies described by Fleming reveal about the wider situation faced by refugees today?
7. Millions of people have watched Melissa Fleming's speech online, on YouTube. Why has Fleming's speech become so popular? Give your own opinion.

C) Evaluation, Comment, Creative Activities

work in groups / peer support and feedback / creative writing / discussion / speech training

1. Send an email to Melissa Fleming in response to her speech.
2. "Could we be inspired by what happened, and take a stand for a world in which every life matters?" Prepare and give a speech to your English class in which you respond to Melissa Fleming's speech. Use rhetorical devices to convince your class of your ideas and arguments.
3. Imagine you are a journalist reporting on the refugee tragedies in the Mediterranean Sea. Write an article for an English or American newspaper that deals with the tragedy recounted by Melissa Fleming.
4. She points out: "Only 11 people survived that wreck, of the 500. There was never an international investigation into what happened. There were some media reports about mass murder at sea, a terrible tragedy, but that was only for one day. And then the news cycle moved on." Prepare and give a two-minute-speech in response to this statement.
5. Do the weekly refugee tragedies in the Mediterranean Sea still affect people, move people, touch people, tug at people's heartstrings, and encourage them to have empathy for refugees? Explain your own opinion. Write an essay or give a short speech.
6. Compare and evaluate Chris McGrath's Photo of the Year and Melissa Fleming's speech.
7. "And why, the root question, is so little being done to stop the wars, the persecution and the poverty that is driving so many people to the shores of Europe? Until these issues are resolved, people will continue to take to the seas and to seek safety and asylum." Discuss this statement and explain your own opinion.

D) Creative Projects

▶ *self-immersion / research / WebQuest / cooperation with Social Sciences class / cross-curricular connections / presentation / discussion / speech / podcast / audio or video clip production / feedback*

1. *Interviewing refugees:* Ask your city council if you could go into a home for refugees and asylum seekers to interview them about their home countries, why they had to leave their countries, when they came to Germany, and what their hopes and future goals are. Present your interviews to your English class. Please bear in mind: Many refugees and asylum seekers will not disclose HOW they came to Europe, because they think that disclosing any illegal activity could potentially endanger their asylum claims.
2. *Inviting refugees to your English class:* You could also invite some refugees to your English class and speak to them about their past and present situations, the current problems they are confronted with, and about their hopes, goals and future plans.
3. *Contact a local refugee aid organisation:* Interview some volunteers and experts about the situation faced by refugees in your city or local community. Present your findings to your English class. Produce a short video that can be played in your next school assembly.
4. *Contact a national or international refugee aid organisation:* Interview some experts about the situation faced by refugees worldwide. Produce a video on the subject.
5. *Find out more information about:* the UN Refugee Agency, the United Nations High Commissioner for Refugees, the UNHCR, and present your findings to your English class.
6. *Prepare a four-minute speech:* Explain your point of view regarding the plight of refugees. Present your speech to the class. Your audience should then give you feedback on the content, structure, and style of your speech.
7. Imagine you are taking part in a panel discussion on *Visions of Future Africa*. Your task is to write an opening statement. Refer to the Marshall Plan in your speech, as well as to the work you have already done in class. Information: *Bundesministerium für wirtschaftliche Zusammenarbeit und Entwicklung (BMZ)* http://www.bmz.de/de/laender_regionen/marshallplan_mit_afrika/ [July 25, 2018].

E) Creative Writing

„Bitte lassen Sie sich auf ein Gedankenexperiment ein:
Stellen Sie sich vor, Sie leben im Bürgerkrieg einer faschistischen Diktatur: Menschen werden von den Machthabern erniedrigt, gefoltert. Menschenrechte werden mit Füßen getreten. Jede Form von Menschlichkeit wird durch Giftgas und Fassbomben weggefegt. Städte werden ausradiert, Krankenhäuser und Schulen skrupellos und grausam bombardiert. Soziale und materielle Lebensgrundlagen sind durch Gewalt und Ausbeutung zerstört. Sie versuchen, dem Terror und Inferno zu entkommen. Auf dem langen und beschwerlichen Fluchtweg erleben Sie menschliche Tragödien. Nach langer und beschwerlicher Flucht erreichen Sie schließlich mit Ihrer Familie ein sicheres Land. Sie versuchen dort, Asyl zu finden und ein neues Leben aufzubauen.“

Taken from: Dieter Smolka: *Integration als Leitungsaufgabe.* Carl Link Verlag, Wolters Kluwer Deutschland 2017.

Imagine this kind of “science-fiction” situation and choose one of the following tasks:

a) Write a literary text, a creative short story, a poem or a radio play, or produce a video.
b) Write a non-fictional text, an article for a newspaper, or an essay for your school newspaper.
c) Prepare and give a short speech to your class.

F) Practical Ways to Help Refugees

Melissa Fleming shares some ways of helping refugees. Read her ideas here:
http://ideas.ted.com/8-practical-ways-to-help-refugees/ (accessed: Sept. 10, 2019)

Answer the following questions:

1. How many people are refugees across the world today?
2. How do people in Europe react to refugees and migrants?
3. What are, according to Melissa Fleming, the possible ways of helping refugees?
4. What other ways of supporting refugees can you imagine?

G) Further Projects: For Thought and Discussion

1. **The music video for Roger Waters' song "The Last Refugee".** You can find the video here: http://www.rollingstone.com/music/videos/see-roger-waters-moving-new-last-refugee-video-w483188
2. **"Lifeline"-Kapitän:** Claus-Peter Reisch rettete Leben und steht jetzt vor Gericht. Der Kapitän des Rettungsschiffs "Lifeline", das über 200 Flüchtlinge vor der libyschen Küste aufnahm, erzählt in der WDR 5 Redezeit von der dramatischen Irrfahrt auf dem Mittelmeer.
   Podcast: https://www1.wdr.de/radio/wdr5/sendungen/neugier-genuegt/ng-rz-claus-peter-reisch-lifeline-100.html
3. **UNHCR Report: Desperate Journeys** https://www.unhcr.org/desperatejourneys/ (accessed March 2, 2019)
4. **Das Meer verschlingt Tausende Menschen, weil niemand hilft:** "Heute gibt es ein Wegsehen; es gibt heute die Veralltäglichung der Hilfsverweigerung. […] Die Globalisierung der Gleichgültigkeit".
   Heribert Prantl: *Süddeutsche Zeitung* v. 20.4.2019, Seite 6
   https://www.sueddeutsche.de/politik/prantl-kolumne-ostern-fluechtlinge-jona-wal-1.4415411

H) Cartoons by Talal Nayer

DID YOU KNOW?
More than **2,262** people either died or went missing at sea, attempting to reach Europe via the Mediterranean in **2018**, despite a significant reduction in the number of arrivals.
In 2017: **3,139** people dead or missing
In 2016: **5,096** people dead or missing
In 2015: **3,771** people dead or missing
In 2014: **3,538** people dead or missing

Source: UNHCR https://www.unhcr.org/news/press/2018/12/5c2a0e364/day-2018-unhcr-urges-rapid-solution-refugees-stranded-mediterranean-sea.html

Talal Nayer is a famous international cartoonist. He studied civil engineering in Sudan, and 3D video-game design in Tunisia. His journalistic career started in 2003. He is the president of the Sudanese Cartoonists Association and has lived in Germany since 2017. He took part in three film projects as a script-writer, a cameraman and a 2D animator. He is famous for his political cartoons, his international exhibitions and his articles on culture and politics.

Task: Describe, analyse and evaluate the two cartoons.

"The European Refugee Crisis: Help Those Who Need Us."

Yvette Cooper MP: Speech at the Centre for European Reform, on September 1, 2015

RELATED TOPICS

ASYLUM SEEKERS · COMPASSION · CONFLICT · DIGNITY · DISPLACEMENT · DIVERSITY · EXILE · EXPLOITATION · FEAR · FUTURE GENERATIONS · HOPE · HUMAN RIGHTS · INCLUSION · INTEGRATION · PERSECUTION · REFUGEES · RESPECT · RESPONSIBILITY · SOLIDARITY · THE UNITED NATIONS · VIOLENCE · WAR

Yvette Cooper, MP (born March 20, 1969) is a British Labour Party Politician and Member of Parliament (MP).
She studied Politics, Philosophy, and Economics at the University of Oxford.
In 1991, she won a Kennedy scholarship to study at Harvard University. She was an advisor to Bill Clinton during his 1992 presidential campaign.
She was an Economics columnist and leading journalist for the *Independent* from 1995 to 1997, when she ran for Parliament for the first time. Although she did not run for leadership of the Labour Party in 2010, citing a desire to spend more time with her children, she did serve as the Shadow Home Secretary from 2011 to 2015.
She is tipped by some to be a future Prime Minister.
Here are some excerpts taken from her exceptional speech.

From: *BBC* http://www.bbc.co.uk/programmes/profiles/4hHkzyPDQvxFZxY2f1BlKt5/rt-hon-yvette-cooper-mp
Speech transcript: https://www.cer.eu/in-the-press/speech-european-refugee-crisis-yvette-cooper-shadow-home-secretary

Yvette Cooper:

By the side of an Austrian road, a lorry.
A logo on the side. Designed to transport "original Slovenian products" – ham, and chicken. In a sealed fridge.
Inside 71 bodies. 71 people.
It looks like they came from Syria. Families. Children. A little girl just 2 years old.
They must have travelled through Turkey or Greece, through the Balkans, Hungary.
Many days journey by road. Maybe they came from Homs, where just a few weeks ago 200 innocent men, women and children were kidnapped by ISIL.
Maybe they came from camps where thousands are living in desert tents without running water, proper schooling or medical care.

Who knows how much they paid the traffickers who put them in the lorry, sealed the fridge door and drove off while they suffocated to death. A truly terrible story.

And all the more terrible because it isn't unique.
Just two days later, three children were found close to death from dehydration in the back of a crowded minivan. 52 people were found dead in the hull of a boat. Beaten by the smugglers into an airless hold. Required to pay money to come up to breathe. Those that couldn't pay suffocated to death. 100 people drowned locked in the hold of a capsized boat.
Even on our own doorstep, nine people have died in the last three months trying to cross from Calais to Dover – trapped in the wheel arches of lorries, crushed jumping onto fast moving trains or electrocuted on power lines. Terrible stories of tragedy, torture, desperation.
But the tragic stories are not just of those who have died. They are of millions more who have lost their homes and are now desperately seeking sanctuary, or stability, and to rebuild their lives.

A Humanitarian Crisis
The exhausted mother desperately holding her baby's head above the waves.
The children who have had no schooling for months.
The former teachers, office workers, shop owners, business people – now refugees, sleeping in bus stations, paying gangs to ferry them by night.
This has become a humanitarian crisis on a scale we have not seen on our continent since the Second World War. Yet we seem paralysed to respond. [...]

What are we doing now?
Our country has refused to take in any refugees from the Mediterranean. Has refused to take more than a couple of hundred vulnerable Syrian refugees directly from the camps as part of the UN programme. Just 240 have come. And our country has even returned Syrian refugees to other European countries who are already taking far more refugees, simply because they passed through those countries first. Germany has given more sanctuary to Syrians in a month than we have in a year. Germany has had twelve times more. How can we be proud of our history helping those who fled conflict if our generation turns its back [on them].

Bringing Britain Together
So it's time for us to do more. Yes, the politics are difficult. But not if we do this together. It's time for the Government to pull together an urgent national conference to work with communities and councils to see how many places we can offer to refugees from Syria and the Mediterranean.
Time to ask cities, towns, and local communities how much they each can do to help.
If every city took 10 refugee families, if every London borough took 10 families, if every county council took 10 families, if Scotland, Wales, and every English region played their part, then in a month we'd have nearly 10,000 more places for vulnerable refugees fleeing danger, seeking safety. 10,000 instead of 200.
It's time to ask the Scottish and Welsh Governments for their support.
It's time for the Home Office to give councils better and longer-term support if they can offer Syrian refugees sanctuary – be it temporary support or a permanent home.
It's time for faith groups, community organisations, campaign groups– 38 degrees, Citizens UK – trade unions, businesses, all to come together to build a new consensus to help refugees.
It's time for local councils to follow the example set by Sheffield and Birmingham and sign up to become "Cities of Sanctuary".
It's time for the media to rise to the occasion, bringing truth to people's homes, not giving in to easy headlines which sell papers by playing to fear.

And it's time for all political parties to play their part. […] And all parties need to avoid exploiting a refugee crisis for their short term political campaigns on Europe. […]
We need to be able to look our grand-parents in the eye and say we faced up to the challenges and responsibilities of our time, just as they did theirs. And we need to be able to look our grand-children in the eye and say we did not turn our backs.

This Crisis Is Not Going Away.
In the recession of the 1930s, Britain didn't just open its hearts to the 10,000 children of the Kindertransport, but also our homes. It is that strength of compassion that makes Britain great.
So that is why today I am asking the Home Secretary to change policy.
I'm asking the Prime Minister to show leadership and pledging my support if he does.
I'm asking parliament to back him.
I'm asking Scotland and Wales to agree.
I'm asking councils to offer places.
I'm asking communities to offer help.
I'm asking faith groups and charities to show the way.
I'm asking campaigning organisations to mobilise support.
I'm asking everyone to do their bit, however large or small.
The truth is, I'm not really asking very much at all.
I'm asking us to do something we've done before. Something we will do again.
To help those who need us.
I'm asking Britain to be Britain.

ASSIGNMENTS

A) Comprehension

interactive classroom / listening / self-immersion / reading aloud / think-pair-share / group work / peer support and feedback / share your findings / presentation / writing a summary

1. Work in groups. Read the excerpts of Yvette Cooper's speech.
2. Look up any words you don't know which you need to understand the speech.
3. Explain Cooper's most significant statements.
4. Sum up Yvette Cooper's main arguments.

B) Analysis

1. Analyse the structure of Yvette Cooper's speech.
2. Examine some rhetorical devices which Cooper uses to support and emphasise her message.
3. Present your findings to your class.

C) Evaluation, Comment and Creative Activities

paired work / writing competence / interview / discussion / speech competition / cooperation with a Social Sciences class / cross-curricular connections / team building / debate / feedback

1. "This has become a humanitarian crisis on a scale we have not seen on our continent since the Second World War." Discuss and explain your opinion of this statement. You may organise a debate or speech competition for your English class to take part in.
2. Write a response to or give a speech about one of the following statements:

a) "We need all European countries to sign up to take those agreed to be in need of refuge or asylum. All European countries."
b) "We need to be able to look our grandparents in the eye and say we faced up to the challenges and responsibilities of our time just as they did theirs. And we need to be able to look our grandchildren in the eye and say we did not turn our backs."

3. Imagine you are a journalist who has been given the opportunity to interview Yvette Cooper. What questions would you like to ask her? What possible answers might she give you?

D) Mediation (German = > English) "Europa macht dicht"

Von Heribert Prantl, Süddeutsche Zeitung v. 7. Juni 2018, S. 4

Die Zeit des Flüchtlingsschutzes in Europa geht zu Ende. Siebzig Jahre nach Beginn der Arbeiten am Grundgesetz, 69 Jahre nach der Verkündung des Asylgrundrechts und 67 Jahre nach Verabschiedung der Genfer Flüchtlingskonvention ist das Bewusstsein für den Wert von Asyl und Flüchtlingsschutz verschwunden. Es ist vom Gewicht der Zahlen und der Angst vor den populistischen Extremisten erdrückt worden. Es gibt keine Regierung in Europa mehr, die das Asylrecht offensiv verteidigt. Die Flüchtlinge werden nur noch numerisch registriert; ihre Geschichte, ihr Schicksal interessiert immer weniger. [...] Die sogenannte Willkommenskultur vom Herbst 2015 soll vergessen gemacht werden. [...] Deutschland übernimmt die Führungsrolle bei der Durchsetzung dieser Zurückweisungspolitik [...]

Tasks:

1. Write an email to an exchange partner who does not speak German and convey the message of the text.
2. Email Heribert Prantl and explain why you agree or disagree with his statement.
3. Prepare and give a three-minute speech in response to Prantl's comments.

E) Story of Love amid Ghouta's Bombs

Dima Nachawi is an illustrator, clown, and founder of the Memory Initiative of Syrian Culture project (MISC). She joined Clown Me In (CMI) in February 2014, participating in several clown street performances until she traveled to London in September 2015 to complete her MA in Arts & Cultural Management. She rejoined the CMI after returning to Lebanon in February 2017. Dima's illustrations reflect her personal experiences and the human rights issues she has come across around the world. She feels a strong sense of responsibility to deliver, through art, a message to the world that Syria is a country of artists, and a home for peaceful activists eager to create civil-minded projects for a better future.

From: *Clown Me In* https://clownmein.com/about-us/dima-nachawi/

At first glance, some of Dima Nachawi's illustrations could show couples from almost anywhere in the world – but the rest of the collection tells a very different story of air strikes, injuries, and death. These pictures illustrate how real people live – and love – in Eastern Ghouta, an area of Syria, where conditions have been described as "hell on earth" by the UN Secretary General António Guterres.

By Amelia Butterly, *BBC*, March 8, 2018, http://www.bbc.com/news/world-43173323?intlink_from_url=http://www.bbc.com/news/topics/c779dqxlxv2t/100-women&link_location=live-reporting-story

Education – Can It Change the World?

"Education Is One of the Blessings of Life"

Speech given on receipt of the 2014 Nobel Peace Prize by Malala Yousafzai, in Oslo, Norway, on December 10, 2014

RELATED TOPICS

ABUSE · CHILDHOOD · CHILD LABOUR · CHILD MARRIAGE · CHILDREN'S RIGHTS · DEMOCRACY · DIGNITY · EDUCATION · FREEDOM · FUTURE GENERATIONS · GIRLS' RIGHTS · GOD · GOVERNMENT · HUMANITY · HUMAN RIGHTS · INEQUALITY · INJUSTICE · ISLAM · KIDNAPPING · LIBERTY · OPPRESSION OF CHILDREN · PEACE · POVERTY · RACE RELATIONS · SCHOOL · SEGREGATION · SLAVERY · SOCIAL SECURITY · TEACHERS · TERRORISM · UNALIENABLE RIGHTS · THE UNITED NATIONS · VIOLENCE · WOMEN'S RIGHTS

Malala Yousafzai was born on July 12, 1997 in Mingora, Pakistan. However, upon receiving the Nobel Peace Prize in 2014, she was living in Birmingham in the United Kingdom. The award recognised her hugely significant fight for young people to live without oppression and to have access to education.

To achieve peace and prosperity across the world, it is particularly important that the rights of young people and children, who form the basis of the population in some developing countries, are respected. If our young people are subjected to maltreatment or suffering, they will most likely keep hold of the resentment that has plagued the previous generations.

Yousafzai started to campaign for girls' rights to education when she was just eleven years old. Her drive for change has never diminished despite Taliban gunmen attempting to kill her in 2012. She made a miraculous full recovery and went on to become a leading advocate for girls' rights.

Today, in her role as a UN Messenger of Peace, Malala Yousafzai continues to highlight the way in which education can better communities and lead to social mobility. She still emphasises the importance of this for girls, especially. In March 2018, Yousafzai returned to her homeland for the first time since the assassination attempt was made on her. She was hosted by Pakistani Prime Minister Shahid Khaqan Abbasi where she exclaimed that it had been her dream to return to Pakistan and later visited the Swat Valley where she had grown up.

Malala Yousafzai:

Bismillah ir-Rahman ir-Rahim an Arabic expression from the Quran, which Muslims often recite before beginning an important task. Its rough English translation is: "In the name of God, most Gracious, most Compassionate."

Bismillah ir-Rahman ir-Rahim.
In the name of God, the most merciful, the most beneficent.

Your Majesties, Your Royal Highnesses, distinguished members of the Norwegian Nobel Committee.
Dear sisters and brothers, today is a day of great happiness for me. I am humbled that the Nobel Committee has selected me for this precious award.

unconditional love love that has no conditions, love no matter what; *bedingungslose Liebe*

brave courageous, fearless, self-confident

Pashtun a member of the Pashtuns, an ethnic group native to Afghanistan and Pakistan

Thank you to everyone for your continued support and love. Thank you for the letters and cards that I still receive from all around the world. Your kind and encouraging words strengthen and inspire me. I would like to thank my parents for their unconditional love. Thank you to my father for not clipping my wings and for letting me fly. Thank you to my mother for inspiring me to be patient and to always speak the truth – which we strongly believe is the true message of Islam. And also thank you to all my wonderful teachers, who inspired me to believe in myself and be brave.
I am proud, well in fact, I am very proud to be the first Pashtun, the first Pakistani, and the youngest person to receive this award. Along with that, along with that, I am pretty certain that I am also the first recipient of the Nobel Peace Prize who still fights with her younger brothers. I want there to be peace everywhere, but my brothers and I are still working on that.

THIS AWARD IS NOT JUST FOR ME. IT IS FOR THOSE FORGOTTEN CHILDREN WHO WANT AN EDUCATION

Kailash Satyarthi an Indian children's rights and education advocate, and an activist against child labour. His work has been recognized through various national and international honours and awards, including the 2014 Nobel Peace Prize, which he shared with Malala Yousafzai.

I am also honoured to receive this award together with Kailash Satyarthi, who has been a champion for children's rights for a long time. Twice as long, in fact, than I have been alive. I am proud that we can work together, we can work together and show the world that an Indian and a Pakistani, they can work together and achieve their goals of children's rights.

Malalai of Maiwand a national folk hero in Afghanistan. She is also known as "The Afghan Joan of Arc" in the Western world. There are many schools, hospitals, and other institutions named after her in Afghanistan.

Joan of Arc Jeanne d'Arc (in French), a saint and a national hero in France; *Johanna/ Jungfrau von Orléans*

Dear brothers and sisters, I was named after the inspirational Malalai of Maiwand who is the Pashtun Joan of Arc. The word Malala means "grief stricken", "sad", but in order to lend some happiness to it, my grandfather would always call me: "Malala – The happiest girl in the world," and today I am very happy that we are together, fighting for an important cause.
This award is not just for me. It is for those forgotten children who want an education. It is for those frightened children who want peace. It is for those voiceless children who want change.

I am here to stand up for their rights, to raise their voice... it is not time to pity them. It is not time to pity them. It is time to take action so it becomes the last time, the last time, so it becomes the last time that we see a child deprived of an education.

a child deprived of an education *ein Kind, das keine Bildung erhält, dem Bildung entzogen wird*

SOME PEOPLE CALL ME THE GIRL WHO WAS SHOT BY THE TALIBAN. AND SOME, THE GIRL WHO FOUGHT FOR HER RIGHTS.

I have found that people describe me in many different ways. Some people call me the girl who was shot by the Taliban. And some, the girl who fought for her rights.

Some people, call me a "Nobel Laureate" now. However, my brothers still call me that annoying bossy sister. As far as I know, I am just a committed, and even stubborn person who wants to see every child getting a quality education, who wants to see women having equal rights, and who wants peace in every corner of the world.

bossy dominant; *rechthaberisch, herrisch*
committed dedicated, *engagiert*
stubborn determined, adamant; *stur, hartnäckig*

EDUCATION IS ONE OF THE BLESSINGS OF LIFE

Education is one of the blessings of life – and one of its necessities. That has been my experience during the 17 years of my life. In my paradise home, Swat, I always loved learning and discovering new things. I remember when my friends and I would decorate our hands with henna on special occasions. And instead of drawing flowers and patterns we would paint our hands with mathematical formulas and equations.

necessities requirements
Swat a valley in the Khyber Pakhtunkhwa Province in Pakistan.
equations *mathematische Gleichungen*

We had a thirst for education, we had a thirst for education because our future was right there in that classroom. We would sit and learn and read together. We loved to wear neat and tidy school uniforms and we would sit there with big dreams in our eyes. We wanted to make our parents proud and prove that we could also excel in our studies and achieve those goals, which some people think only boys can.

thirst for eagerness to, desire for
to excel in to do extremely well in/at

But things did not remain the same. When I was in Swat, which was a place of tourism and beauty, suddenly changed into a place of terrorism. When I was just ten, more than 400 schools were destroyed. Women were flogged. People were killed. And our beautiful dreams turned into nightmares.

flogged whipped; *ausgepeitscht*

EDUCATION WENT FROM BEING A RIGHT TO BEING A CRIME

Education went from being a right to being a crime.
Girls were stopped from going to school.

to speak up (*here:*) to stand up against injustice

to stand by to watch without doing anything

denying our rights *unsere Rechte leugnen, missachten*

ruthlessly cruelly, brutally

to misuse (*here:*) to pervert

unique rare

abuse *Missbrauch*

to succumb to give up, to surrender

Boko Haram a Nigerian terrorist organisation

When my world suddenly changed, my priorities changed too. I had two options. One was to remain silent and wait to be killed. And the second was to speak up and then be killed.

I chose the second one. I decided to speak up.

We could not just stand by and see those injustices of the terrorists denying our rights, ruthlessly killing people and misusing the name of Islam. We decided to raise our voice and tell them: "Have you not learnt, have you not learnt that in the Holy Quran Allah says: "If you kill one person it is as if you kill the whole of humanity?
Do you not know that Mohammed, peace be upon him, the prophet of mercy, he says, do not harm yourself or others".
"And do you not know that the very first word of the Holy Quran is the word "Iqra", which means "read"?"

I TELL MY STORY, NOT BECAUSE IT IS UNIQUE, BUT BECAUSE IT IS NOT. IT IS THE STORY OF MANY GIRLS

The terrorists tried to stop us and attacked me and my friends who are here today, on our school bus in 2012, but neither their ideas nor their bullets could win.
We survived. And since that day, our voices have grown louder and louder.
I tell my story, not because it is unique, but because it is not. It is the story of many girls.

Today, I tell their stories too. I have brought with me some of my sisters from Pakistan, from Nigeria and from Syria, who share this story. My brave sisters Shazia and Kainat who were also shot that day on our school bus. But they have not stopped learning. And my brave sister Kainat Soomro who went through severe abuse and extreme violence, even her brother was killed, but she did not succumb.

Also my sisters here, whom I have met during my Malala Fund campaign. My 16-year-old courageous sister, Mezon from Syria, who now lives in Jordan as a refugee and goes from tent to tent encouraging girls and boys to learn. And my sister Amina, from the North of Nigeria, where Boko Haram threatens, and stops girls and even kidnaps girls, just for wanting to go to school.

I AM THOSE 66 MILLION GIRLS WHO ARE DEPRIVED OF EDUCATION

Though I appear as one girl, though I appear as one girl, one person, who is 5 foot 2 inches tall, if you include my high heels. (It means I am 5 foot only) I am not a lone voice, I am not a lone voice, I am many.
I am Malala. But I am also Shazia.

I am Kainat.
I am Kainat Soomro.
I am Mezon.
I am Amina. I am those 66 million girls who are deprived of education. And today I am not raising my voice, it is the voice of those 66 million girls.

Sometimes people like to ask me why should girls go to school, why is it important for them. But I think the more important question is why shouldn't they, why shouldn't they have this right to go to school.

Dear sisters and brothers, today, in half of the world, we see rapid progress and development. However, there are many countries where millions still suffer from the very old problems of war, poverty, and injustice.

WE STILL SEE CONFLICTS IN WHICH INNOCENT PEOPLE LOSE THEIR LIVES

We still see conflicts in which innocent people lose their lives and children become orphans. We see many people becoming refugees in Syria, Gaza and Iraq. In Afghanistan, we see families being killed in suicide attacks and bomb blasts.

Many children in Africa do not have access to education because of poverty. And as I said, we still see, we still see girls who have no freedom to go to school in the north of Nigeria.
Many children in countries like Pakistan and India, as Kailash Satyarthi mentioned, many children, especially in India and Pakistan are deprived of their right to education because of social taboos, or they have been forced into child marriage or into child labour.

they do not have access to education *sie haben keine Möglichkeit einer Schulausbildung*

deprived of their right to education *ihrem Recht auf Bildung beraubt sein*

One of my very good school friends, the same age as me, who had always been a bold and confident girl, dreamed of becoming a doctor. But her dream remained a dream. At the age of 12, she was forced to get married. And then soon she had a son, she had a child when she herself was still a child – only 14. I know that she could have been a very good doctor.
But she couldn't ... because she was a girl.

to be forced *gezwungen werden*

Her story is why I dedicate the Nobel Peace Prize money to the Malala Fund, to help give girls quality education, everywhere, anywhere in the world and to raise their voices. The first place this funding will go to is where my heart is, to build schools in Pakistan – especially in my home of Swat and Shangla.

Malala Fund the official organisation, led by Malala Yousafzai, focused on helping girls go to school, and to campaign for their right to an education. For more information, visit: https://www.malala.org/

SO THAT MY FRIENDS AND MY SISTERS CAN GO TO SCHOOL

challenge *Herausforderung*

In my own village, there is still no secondary school for girls. And it is my wish and my commitment, and now my challenge to build one so that my friends and my sisters can go there to school and get quality education and to get this opportunity to fulfil their dreams. This is where I will begin, but it is not where I will stop. I will continue this fight until I see every child, every child in school.

Martin Luther King *see Additional Notes*
Nelson Mandela *see Additional Notes*
Mother Teresa *see Additional Notes*
Aung San Suu Kyi *see Additional Notes*

Dear brothers and sisters, great people, who brought change, like Martin Luther King Jr. and Nelson Mandela, Mother Teresa and Aung San Suu Kyi, once stood here on this stage. I hope the steps that Kailash Satyarthi and I have taken so far and will take on this journey will also bring change – lasting change.

My great hope is that this will be the last time, this will be the last time we must fight for education. Let's solve this once and for all. We have already taken many steps. Now it is time to take a leap. It is not time to tell the world leaders to realise how important education is – they already know it – their own children are in good schools. Now it is time to call them to take action for the rest of the world's children.

WE ASK THE WORLD LEADERS TO UNITE AND MAKE EDUCATION THEIR TOP PRIORITY

Millennium Development Goals *see Additional Notes*

We ask the world leaders to unite and make education their top priority. Fifteen years ago, the world leaders decided on a set of global goals, the Millennium Development Goals. In the years that have followed, we have seen some progress. The number of children out of school has been halved, as Kailash Satyarthi said. However, the world focused only on primary education, and progress did not reach everyone.

ambition aim, determination; *Ehrgeiz, Zielstrebigkeit*

In the year 2015, representatives from all around the world will meet in the United Nations to set the next set of goals, the Sustainable Development Goals. This will set the world's ambition for the next generation.

literacy the ability to read and write; *Fähigkeit zu lesen und zu schreiben*
sufficient enough; *ausreichend*

The world can no longer accept, the world can no longer accept that basic education is enough. Why do leaders accept that for children in developing countries, only basic literacy is sufficient, when their own children do homework in Algebra, Mathematics, Science and Physics?

Leaders must seize this opportunity to guarantee a free, quality, primary, and secondary education for every child. Some will say this is impractical, or too expensive, or too hard. Or maybe even impossible. But it is time the world thinks bigger.

POWERFUL IN CREATING WARS BUT WEAK IN BRINGING PEACE

Dear sisters and brothers, the so-called world of adults may understand it, but we children don't. Why is it that countries which we call "strong" are so powerful in creating wars but are so weak in bringing peace? Why is it that giving guns is so easy but giving books is so hard? Why is it, why is it that making tanks is so easy, but building schools is so hard?

tank *Panzer*

We are living in the modern age and we believe that nothing is impossible. We reached the moon 45 years ago and maybe, will soon land on Mars. Then, in this 21st century, we must be able to give every child a quality education.

Dear sisters and brothers, dear fellow children, we must work... not wait. Not just the politicians and the world leaders, we all need to contribute. Me. You. We. It is our duty.
Let us become the first generation to decide to be the last, let us become the first generation that decides to be the last that sees empty classrooms, lost childhoods, and wasted potentials.

Let this be the last time that a girl or a boy spends their childhood in a factory.

Let this be the last time that a girl is forced into early child marriage.

Let this be the last time that a child loses his life in a war.

Let this be the last time that we see a child out of school.

Let this end with us.

Let's begin this ending ... together ... today ... right here, right now.

Let's begin this ending now.

Thank you so much.

Speech transcript taken from: https://www.nobelprize.org/prizes/peace/2014/yousafzai/26074-malala-yousafzai-nobel-lecture-2014/

ASSIGNMENTS

A) Comprehension

SQ3R / implementing ideas / group work / enquiry-based learning / peer support and feedback / share results / posters / gallery walk / presenting results / discussion / summary writing

1. Work in groups, choose five quotations and explain their significance in the context of Malala's speech.
   a) "Thank you to my mother for inspiring me to be patient and to always speak the truth – which we strongly believe is the true message of Islam."
   b) "And also thank you to all my wonderful teachers, who inspired me to believe in myself and be brave."
   c) "I am proud that we can work together [...] and show the world that an Indian and a Pakistani, they can work together and achieve their goals of children's rights."
   d) "This award is not just for me. It is for those forgotten children who want an education. It is for those frightened children who want peace. It is for those voiceless children who want change."
   e) "I am here to stand up for their rights, to raise their voice… it is not time to pity them. [...] It is time to take action so it becomes the last time, [...] that we see a child deprived of an education."
   f) "I am just a committed and even stubborn person who wants to see every child getting a quality education, who wants to see women having equal rights and who wants peace in every corner of the world."
   g) "We had a thirst for education, [...] because our future was right there in that classroom."
   h) "We wanted to make our parents proud and prove that we could also excel in our studies and achieve those goals, which some people think only boys can."
   i) "But things did not remain the same. When I was in Swat, which was a place of tourism and beauty, suddenly changed into a place of terrorism. When I was just ten, more than 400 schools were destroyed. Women were flogged. People were killed. And our beautiful dreams turned into nightmares."
   j) "Education went from being a right to being a crime. Girls were stopped from going to school. [...] I had two options. One was to remain silent and wait to be killed. And the second was to speak up and then be killed. I chose the second one. I decided to speak up."
   k) "We could not just stand by and see those injustices of the terrorists denying our rights, ruthlessly killing people and misusing the name of Islam. We decided to raise our voice and tell them: "Have you not learnt, have you not learnt that in the Holy Quran Allah says: if you kill one person it is as if you kill the whole humanity"?"
   l) "Do you not know that Mohammed [...] says, do not harm yourself or others".
   m) "And do you not know that the very first word of the Holy Quran is the word "Iqra", which means "read"?"
   n) "The terrorists tried to stop us and attacked me and my friends who are here today, on our school bus in 2012, but neither their ideas nor their bullets could win. We survived. And since that day, our voices have grown louder and louder."
   o) "I tell my story, not because it is unique, but because it is not. It is the story of many girls."
   p) "Many children [...] are deprived of their right to education because of social taboos, or they have been forced into child marriage or into child labour."
   q) "One of my very good school friends, the same age as me, who had always been a bold and confident girl, dreamed of becoming a doctor. But her dream remained a dream. At the age of 12, she was forced to get married. And then soon she had a son, she had a child when she herself was still a child – only 14. I know that she could have been a very good doctor. But she couldn't ... because she was a girl."
   r) "We ask the world leaders to unite and make education their top priority."
   s) "Why do leaders accept that for children in developing countries, only basic literacy is sufficient, when their own children do homework in Algebra, Mathematics, Science, and Physics?"
   t) "Why is it that countries which we call "strong" are so powerful in creating wars but are so weak in bringing peace? Why is it that giving guns is so easy but giving books is so hard? Why is it that making tanks is so easy, but building schools is so hard?"
   u) "We are living in the modern age and we believe that nothing is impossible. We reached the moon 45 years ago, and maybe, will soon land on Mars. Then, in this 21st century, we must be able to give every child a quality education."

2. Write a summary outlining Malala Yousafzai's main arguments.

B) Analysis

independent learning / cooperative learning / think - pair – share / share results / idea tower / mind map / flipchart / peer support and feedback / presentation / writing an analysis

1. Analyse the structure of Malala Yousafzai's speech.
2. Examine some of the rhetorical devices which support and emphasise Malala Yousafzai's message.
3. Explain the meaning of the imagery expressed in Malala's statement: "Thank you to my father for not clipping my wings and for letting me fly."
4. Malala expresses her sense of humour in the speech. Analyse some examples.
5. Analyse the ending of Malala's speech, considering the various types of rhetorical devices she uses, and explaining her intentions in using them.

C) Evaluation, Comment and Creative Activity

interactive classroom / inspiration cards / paired work / idea tower / peer support and feedback / monologue / speech / creative writing / a role play: an interview / evaluation / SOLO taxonomy

1. "We had a thirst for education, because our future was right there in that classroom." Evaluate this quotation in the wider context of Malala's speech.
2. Choose one of your favourite quotations and give a three-minute-speech in response to it.
3. "We reached the moon 45 years ago, and, maybe will soon land on Mars. Then, in this 21st century, we must be able to give every child a quality education." How can this aim be achieved throughout the world?
4. In her speech at the United Nations on July 12, 2013, Malala Yousafzai emphasised:

   "One child, one teacher, one pen, and one book can change the world."

   "So let us wage a global struggle against illiteracy, poverty, and terrorism and let us pick up our books and pens. They are our most powerful weapons. One child, one teacher, one pen and one book can change the world. Education is the only solution. Education First." Would you agree or disagree with this statement? Give a short speech, explaining your point of view.
5. Why is education so important? Write down all the reasons you can think of.
6. Write a letter or an email to Malala to explain the effect her speech had on you, and the ideas it gave you.

D) Information and Research for Thought, Projects and Discussion

flipped classroom / independent learning / research / WebQuest / work in groups / stations learning / students teach each other / tablet or laptop / discussion / speech / collaboration with Social Sciences classes / cross-curricular connections / Speakers' Corner / talk show / press conference

1. **Islam**: Malala emphasises: "Thank you to my mother for inspiring me to be patient and to always speak the truth – which we strongly believe is the true message of Islam. [...] In the Holy Quran Allah says: if you kill one person it is as if you kill the whole of humanity." Evaluate Malala Yousafzai's message for the world today.
2. **Poverty and Injustice**: "There are many countries where millions still suffer from the very old problems of war, poverty, and injustice." Find out which countries Yousafzai might be referring to.
3. **Malala Yousafzai was appointed the youngest-ever UN Messenger of Peace:**
   Find more information here: http://www.un.org/apps/news/story.asp?NewsID=56536#.WPTRwaKkLcs
4. **Malala Yousafzai** visits Pakistan for the first time since she was shot by the Taliban:
   For more information, visit: *The Washington Post, The Associated Press*, April 2, 2018
   https://www.washingtonpost.com/world

5. **The Universal Declaration of Human Rights**: The right to education is stated in Article 26 of the Universal Declaration of Human Rights: http://www.un.org/en/universal-declaration-human-rights/
6. **UNICEF**: For more information about UNICEF and the work it does to improve the lives of children, visit: www.unicef.org
7. **UNICEF**: 75 million children in desperate need of education support, *BBC NEWS*, May 4, 2016 http://www.bbc.com/news/world-36199901
8. **UN Report: Violence against Children**: United Nations 2017
   http://srsg.violenceagainstchildren.org/story/2017-12-18_1602
   Sustainable Development Goal Target 16: End abuse, exploitation, trafficking and all forms of violence against and torture of children.
9. **UNICEF: Half of world's teens experience peer violence in and around school**
   "Physical fights and bullying disrupt the education of 150 million 13-15-year-olds worldwide."
   "Education is the key to building peaceful societies, and yet, for millions of children around the world, school itself is not safe."
   https://www.unicef.org/press-releases/half-worlds-teens-experience-peer-violence-and-around-school-unicef
10. **UNICEF: Fixing the Broken Promise of Education for All.** Findings from the Global Initiative on Out-of-School Children: https://data.unicef.org/resources/fixing-the-broken-promise-of-education-for-all-findings-from-the-global-initiative-on-out-of-school-children/
11. **UNICEF: Child marriage is a violation of human rights, but is all too common**
    Marriage before the age of 18 is a fundamental violation of human rights:
    https://data.unicef.org/topic/child-protection/child-marriage/
12. **UNITED NATIONS Sustainable Development Goal: Quality Education**
    Obtaining a quality education is the foundation to creating sustainable development.
    Further Information: *United Nations* Sustainable Development Goals
    https://www.un.org/sustainabledevelopment/education/

E) World Day Against Child Labour, June 12.

For more information about Child Labour visit: *United Nations* http://www.un.org/en/events and visit: *UNICEF* https://data.unicef.org/topic/child-protection/child-labour/

1. Read the articles, summarise the main ideas, and describe the living conditions of the children forced into child labour.
2. How could the situation be improved?

F) Mediation (German = > English)

1. Textilindustrie Jugendliche arbeiten unter grausamen Bedingungen
   Von Stefan Sauer, *Mitteldeutsche Zeitung* vom 23.06.2017 https://www.mz-web.de/wirtschaft/textilindustrie-jugendliche-arbeiten-unter-grausamen-bedingungen-27851066 (August 27, 2018)
2. KINDERARBEIT: Produktionsbedingungen bei handgeknüpften Teppichen aus Indien. ARD-Plusminus, 24.10.2018. *YouTube* https://www.youtube.com/watch?v=SkYe5H-n2gI
3. UNICEF Kinderarbeit weltweit 2018
   https://www.unicef.de/informieren/aktuelles/blog/kinderarbeit-fragen-und-antworten/166982
4. **Wachsende globale Ungleichheit: „50 'Sklaven' beschäftigt jeder von uns im Durchschnitt** – ohne es zu merken. Von Kindern geerntete Bananen, in Nähfabriken produzierte T-Shirts: Den Preis von unserem „billig" zahlen oft andere!" Rede von Bundesentwicklungsminister Gerd Müller bei der Konferenz „Global denken – lokal handeln" im Deutschen Hygiene-Museum in Dresden, 26. März 2019
   http://www.bmz.de/de/presse/reden/minister_mueller/2019/maerz/190326_rede_kommunale_ez_sachsen.html

Tasks:

1. Read the articles and the speech. Watch the video.
2. Sum up the main facts in English.
3. How can child labour be stopped?
4. How can the European Union support fair trade and fair labour conditions in all countries?

"Let Us March! Let Us Globalise Compassion, and Set Our Children Free!"

Speech given on receipt of the Nobel Peace Prize by Kailash Satyarthi in Oslo, Norway, on December 10, 2014.

RELATED TOPICS

ABUSE · CHILDREN · CHILDHOOD · CHILD LABOUR · DEMOCRACY · DIGNITY · EDUCATION · FREEDOM · FUTURE GENERATIONS · GIRLS' RIGHTS · GOD · HUMANITY · HUMAN RIGHTS · INEQUALITY · INJUSTICE · KIDNAPPING · LIBERTY · OPPRESSION · PEACE · RACE RELATIONS · SCHOOLS · SEGREGATION · SLAVERY · SOCIAL SECURITY · TEACHERS · TERRORISM · UNALIENABLE RIGHTS · THE UNITED NATIONS · VIOLENCE · WOMEN'S RIGHTS

Born on January 11, 1954, **Kailash Satyarthi** has been campaigning to bring an end to child slavery and exploitation. Having given up a successful livelihood as an electrical engineer in his homeland of India, Satyarthi became an equally successful human rights activist. In fact, his organisation Bachpan Bachao Andolan, or Save Childhood Movement, has been responsible for the removal of 83,000 children from cases of exploitation. Instead, these children are placed into a social and educational programme which educates, rehabilitates and integrates them into society.

However, Satyarthi's reach extends even further than India's borders. A worldwide group of interested parties, of which Satyarthi is part, has created the largest civil society network on the planet.

Thanks to his work, the ILO Convention 182 of 1999 was adopted by world countries to eradicate child labour and improve the circumstances of children and young people by providing them with education. Due to his unrelenting campaigning, Satyarthi was recognised with a Nobel Peace Prize alongside Malala Yousafzai in 2014. He immediately donated the prize money to foundations which lobby for children's rights and passed on his medal to the President of India's House Museum in New Delhi. This further emphasised his selfless nature as he dedicated the prize to his homeland.

Alternating between Hindi and English in his speech, Satyarthi outlines the severely negative effects that child labour, lack of opportunities and poverty can have on a person's childhood and how it can restrict their development as life progresses.

Kailash Satyarthi

My dear children of the world.

Your Majesties, Your Royal Highnesses, Excellencies, distinguished members of the Norwegian Nobel Committee, dear brother Tom Harkin, brothers and sisters, and my dear daughter Malala.

From this podium of peace and humanity, I am deeply honoured to recite a mantra from the ancient texts of wisdom, the *Vedas*.
This mantra carries a prayer, an aspiration and a resolve that has the potential to liberate humanity from all man-made crises.

The Vedas the oldest scriptures of the Hindu religion
aspiration hope, desire, ambition, aim; *Sehnsucht*
resolve determination; *Entschlossenheit*
the potential ability; *Potenzial, Leistungsvermögen*

NOT A SINGLE PERSON SHOULD BE LEFT OUT OR LEFT BEHIND IN ANY CORNER OF THE WORLD

Let's walk together. In the pursuit of global progress, not a single person should be left out or left behind in any corner of the world, from East to West, from South to North.

Let's speak together, let our minds come together! Learning from the experiences of our ancestors, let us together create knowledge for all that benefits all.

I bow to my late parents, to my motherland India, and to mother earth.

With a warm heart, I recall how, thousands of times, I have been liberated each time I have freed a child from slavery. In the first smile of freedom on their beautiful faces, I see the Gods smiling.

2) ______________________________

Give this section a heading.

I give the biggest credit of this honour to my movement's Kaalu Kumar, Dhoom Das and Adarsh Kishore from India and Iqbal Masih from Pakistan who made the supreme sacrifice for protecting the freedom and dignity of children. I humbly accept this award on behalf of all such martyrs, my fellow activists across the world, and my countrymen.
My journey from the great land of Lord Buddha, Guru Nanak, and Mahatma Gandhi; India to Norway is a connection between the two centres of global peace and brotherhood, ancient and modern.
Friends, the Nobel Committee generously invited me to deliver a "lecture." Respectfully, I am unable to do that.

martyrs people who sacrifice their lives for a good cause; *Märtyrer*

I represent here the sound of silence. The cry of innocence. And, the face of invisibility. I have come here to share the voices and dreams of our children, our children, because they are all our children.

innocence *Unschuld*

invisibility (*here:*) anonymity; *Unsichtbarkeit*

3) ______________________________

Give this section a heading.

I have looked into their frightened and exhausted eyes. And I have heard their urgent questions:
Twenty years ago, in the foothills of the Himalayas, I met a small, skinny boy. He asked me: "Is the world so poor that it cannot give me a toy and a book, instead of forcing me to take a tool or gun?"

I met with a Sudanese child-soldier who was kidnapped by an extremist militia. As his first training [exercise], he was forced to kill his friends and family. He asked me: "What is my fault?"

What is my fault? What have I done wrong?

Twelve years ago, a child-mother from the streets of Colombia – trafficked, raped, enslaved – asked me this: "I have never had a dream. Can my child have one?"

trafficked, raped, enslaved *dem Menschenhandel unterworfen, vergewaltigt, versklavt*

4) ______________________________

Give this section a heading.

There is no greater violence than to deny the dreams of our children. The single aim of my life is that every child is:
free to be a child,
free to grow and develop,
free to eat, sleep, and see daylight,
free to laugh and cry,
free to play,
free to learn, free to go to school, and above all,
free to dream.

All the great religions tell us to care for children. Jesus said: "Let the children come to me; do not hinder them, for the kingdom of God belongs to them." The Holy Quran says: "Kill not your children because of poverty."

I refuse to accept that all the temples and mosques and churches and prayer houses have no place for the dreams of our children.

mosques *Moscheen*

5) ______________________________

Give this section a heading.

I refuse to accept that the world is so poor, when just one week of global spending on armies is enough to bring all of our children into classrooms.

I refuse to accept that all the laws and constitutions, and the judges and the police are not able to protect our children.

shackles chains; *Ketten*
quest for freedom search for liberty; *Suche nach Freiheit*

I refuse to accept that the shackles of slavery can ever be stronger than the quest for freedom.

I REFUSE TO ACCEPT.

6) ____
Give this section a heading.

I am privileged to work with many courageous souls who also refuse to accept [these things]. We have never given up against any threat or attack, and we will never. Undoubtedly, progress has been made in the last couple of decades. The number of out of school children has been halved. Child mortality and malnutrition has been reduced, and millions of child deaths have been prevented. The number of child labourers in the world has been reduced by a third. Make no mistake, great challenges still remain.

child mortality *Kindersterblichkeit*
malnutrition *Mangel- bzw. Unterernährung*

Friends, the biggest crisis knocking on the doors of humanity today is intolerance.

to impart to give

We have utterly failed in imparting an education to our children. An education that gives the meaning and objective of life and a secure future. An education that builds a sense of global citizenship among the young people. I am afraid that the day is not far when the cumulative result of this failure will culminate in unprecedented violence that will be suicidal for humankind.

cumulative result end result
to culminate in to lead to
unprecedented unparalleled; *unvorstellbar*
suicidal *selbstmörderisch*

Yet, young people like Malala, are rising up everywhere and choosing peace over violence, tolerance over extremism, and courage over fear.

Solutions are not found only in the deliberations in conferences, and prescriptions from a distance. They lie in small groups and local organisations and individuals, who confront the problem every day, even if they remain unrecognised and unknown to the world
Eighteen years ago, millions of my brothers and sisters in 103 countries marched across 80,000 kilometres. And, a new international law against child labour was born. We have done this.

7) ____
Give this section a heading.

You may ask: what can one person do? Let me tell you a story I remember from my childhood: A terrible fire had broken out in the forest. All the animals were running away, including the lion, king of the forest. Suddenly, the lion saw a tiny bird rushing towards the fire. He asked the bird: "What are you doing?" To the lion's surprise, the bird replied: "I am on my way to extinguish the fire." He laughed and said: "How can you kill the fire with just one drop of water, in your beak?" The bird was adamant, and said: "But I am doing my bit."

beak *Schnabel*
adamant resolute, determined; *unnachgiebig*

8) ____________________
Give this section a heading.

You and I live in the age of rapid globalisation. We are connected through high-speed Internet. We exchange goods and services in a single global market. Each day, thousands of flights connect us to every corner of the globe.
But there is one serious disconnect. It is the lack of compassion. Let us inculcate and transform the individual's compassion into a global movement. Let us globalise compassion. Not passive compassion, but transformative compassion that leads to justice, equality, and freedom.

disconnect divide, separation
compassion kindness, empathy; *Mitgefühl*
to inculcate to instil, to encourage; *einprägen*
global movement *weltweite Bewegung*
transformative compassion (*here:*) *gestaltendes, aktives Mitgefühl*

9) ____________________
Give this section a heading.

Mahatma Gandhi said: "If we are to teach real peace in this world... we shall have to begin with the children." I humbly add, let us unite the world through compassion for our children.

Whose children are they who stitch footballs, yet have never played with one? They are our children. Whose children are they who mine stones and minerals? They are our children. Whose children are they who harvest cocoa, yet do not know the taste of a chocolate? They are all our children.

to stitch *zusammennähen*
to mine to dig for
to harvest *ernten*

10) ____________________
Give this section a heading.

Devli was born into intergenerational debt and bonded labour in India. Sitting in my car immediately after her rescue the eight-year-old girl asked: "Why did you not come earlier?" Her angry question still shakes me – and has the power to shake the world. Her question is for all of us.

intergenerational debt *generationenübergreifende Schulden*
bonded labour *in Schuldknechtschaft arbeitende Menschen, insbesondere Kinder*

Why did we not come earlier? What are we waiting for? How many more Devlis will we allow to go without rescue? How many more girls will be abducted, confined and abused? Children, like Devli across the world are questioning our inaction, and watching our actions.

abducted, confined and abused *entführt, eingesperrt, missbraucht*
inaction passivity, not doing anything to change the situation; *Untätigkeit*

urgency *Dringlichkeit*

We need collective actions with a sense of urgency. Every single minute matters, every single child matters, every single childhood matters.
I challenge the passivity and pessimism surrounding our children. I challenge this culture of silence, this culture of neutrality.

11) ______________________________
Give this section a heading.

trafficking *Menschenhandel*
illiteracy *Analphabetismus*
civilised (*BrE*), civilized (*AmE*), well organised and developed

I, therefore, call upon all the governments, intergovernmental agencies, businesses, faith leaders, the civil society, and each one of us, to put an end to all forms of violence against children. Slavery, trafficking, child marriages, child labour, sexual abuse, and illiteracy have no place in any civilised society.

to accelerate to speed up; *beschleunigen*
scattered agendas *vereinzelte Absichtserklärungen*

Friends, we can do this.
Governments must make child friendly policies, and invest in education and young people.
Businesses must be more responsible and open to innovative partnerships.
Intergovernmental agencies must work together to accelerate action.
Global civil society must rise above business-as-usual and scattered agendas.
Faith leaders and institutions, and all of us must stand with our children.
We must be bold, we must be ambitious, and we must have the will.
We must keep our promises.

12) ______________________________
Give this section a heading.

cobbler boy *Schusterjunge*
to challenge *in Frage stellen, bestreiten*

Over fifty years ago, on the first day of my school I met a cobbler boy my age sitting at the school gate, polishing shoes. I asked my teachers these questions: "Why is he working outside? Why is he not coming to school with me?" My teachers had no answer. One day, I gathered the courage to ask the boy's father. He said: "Sir, I have never thought about it. We are just born to work." This made me angry. It still makes me angry. I challenged it then, and I am challenging it today.

13) ______________________________
Give this section a heading.

dignity *Würde*

As a child, I had a vision of tomorrow. That cobbler boy was studying with me in my classroom. Now, that tomorrow has become TODAY. I am TODAY, and you are TODAY.
TODAY it is time for every child to have the right to life, the right to freedom, the right to health, the right to education, the right to safety, the right to dignity, the right to equality, and the right to peace.

TODAY, beyond the darkness, I see the smiling faces of our children in the blinking stars. TODAY, in every wave of every ocean, I see our children playing and dancing.
TODAY, in every plant, tree, and mountain, I see that little cobbler boy sitting with me in the classroom.

I want you to see and feel this TODAY inside you. My dear sisters and brothers, may I ask you to close your eyes and put your hand close to your heart for a moment? Can you feel the child inside you? Now, listen to this child. I am sure you can!
Today, I see thousands of Mahatma Gandhis, Martin Luther Kings, and Nelson Mandelas marching forward and calling on us. The boys and girls have joined. I have joined in. We ask you to join too.

14) ____
Give this section a heading.

Let us democratise knowledge.
Let us universalise justice.
Together, let us globalise compassion, for our children!
I call upon you in this room, and all across the world.
I call for a march from exploitation to education, from poverty to shared prosperity, a march from slavery to liberty, and a march from violence to peace.
Let us march from darkness to light.
Let us march from mortality to divinity.
Let us march!

to democratise knowledge when people are educated, everyone can share knowledge
to universalise justice justice should be a common and global goal
exploitation *Ausbeutung*
prosperity *Wohlstand*
mortality *Vergänglichkeit, Sterblichkeit*
divinity *Göttlichkeit*

From: *Nobel Peace Prize*
https://www.nobelprize.org/prizes/peace/2014/satyarthi/26070-kailash-satyarthi-nobel-lecture-2014/

ASSIGNMENTS

A) Comprehension

active listening / reading dramatization / enquiry-based learning / individual work / paired work / peer support and feedback / share ideas / presenting results / summary writing

1. Watch the video of Kailash Satyarthi's speech here: https://www.youtube.com/watch?v=PfOcEeimTAA
2. Read the transcript of Satyarthi's speech and highlight any significant statements.
3. The text is divided into different sections. Give a heading to each section.
4. Point out what Satyarthi says about the importance of protecting the freedom and dignity of children.
5. What kind of global challenges do we face, according to Kailash Satyarthi?
6. "Let us globalise compassion." What exactly does Satyarthi mean when he says this?
7. Write a summary of Kailash Satyarthi's main arguments.

B) Analysis

cooperative learning / share ideas / peer support and feedback / mind map / presentation of results

1. Kailash Satyarthi uses several rhetorical devices in his famous and inspiring speech. Choose five paragraphs and examine their rhetorical devices.
2. Analyse the ending of his speech; analyse the rhetorical devices he uses to support his message.
3. Kailash Satyarthi gives some examples from his own experience. Explain the significance of these examples in the context of his Nobel Peace Prize acceptance speech.

C) Evaluation, Comment, Creative Writing

flipped classroom / research / group work / creative writing / recording an interview / Skype interview / discussion / debate / speech / collaboration with Social Sciences or History classes / cross-curricular connections / presenting results / self-immersion / creative writing / feedback

1. Write an email to Kailash Satyarthi explaining your opinion of his Nobel Prize speech.
2. Kailash Satyarthi calls for "a march from exploitation to education, [...] and a march from violence to peace." Can his speech ultimately make the world a better place for children? Give your own opinion.
3. Satyarthi criticizes all forms of violence against children, such as slavery, human trafficking, child marriage, child labour, sexual abuse, and illiteracy, which have no place in any civilised society. The reality in different parts of the world looks grim and desperate.
   How can Satyarthi's goals be achieved in the world today? You can choose to:
   a) prepare and give a speech to the class on this topic, or
   b) write an essay pointing out the problems, and possible solutions to these problems, or
   c) contact UNICEF and interview an expert; then present this interview to your English class;
   d) write a creative short story, or the first chapter of a novel about these issues.

D) Recommended Book and Film: "LION – A Long Way Home"

The five-year-old Indian boy Saroo gets lost on the streets of Calcutta, thousands of kilometers from his rural home. Saroo struggles to survive as a street urchin [*Straßenkind*] until he is sent to an orphanage. He survives many dangerous challenges before being adopted by an Australian couple, the Brierley's, and moves to their home in Hobart, Tasmania. 25 years later, he sets out to find his lost family in India. The film is based on a true story.

a) *Official trailer of LION:* https://www.youtube.com/watch?v=tTpM3jHLDBI
b) *Talk Show on Channel 10 with Saroo Brierley,* The Family Behind 'Lion', Saroo Brierley's Incredible Story https://www.youtube.com/watch?v=J1Fzj8EFHuw
c) *Recommended Book: Saroo Brierley's autobiography: "Lion – A Long Way Home"*

Here is an excerpt from the "Prologue", page 1:

"They've gone. I've been thinking about this day for twenty-five years. Growing up half a world away, with a new name and a new family, wondering whether I would ever see my mother and brothers and sister again. And now here I am, standing at a door near the corner of a run-down building in a poor district of a small, dusty town in central India – the place I grew up – and no one lives there. It's empty. The last time I stood on this ground, I was five years old. [...]"

Tasks:

1. Describe the situation Saroo faces in this extract. You should consider the role of time, both the past and the present, as well as Saroo's age, the setting, and his thoughts, fears, and hopes.
2. Analyse the narrative perspective and evaluate its impact on the reader.
3. Evaluate the function of the prologue in the wider context of the book.
4. Write a possible ending to the "Prologue".

E) Recommended Film: "Capernaum", directed by *Nadine Labaki*. It is about a boy who sues his parents for giving him life in a chaotic world. It is a universal story about kids not receiving their most fundamental rights.

"Men and Women Should Have Equal Rights and Opportunities."

Speech by UN Women Goodwill Ambassador, Emma Watson, at the launch of the *HeForShe* campaign, at the United Nations Headquarters, in New York, on September 20, 2014.

RELATED TOPICS

DEMOCRACY · DIGNITY · DISCRIMINATION · EDUCATION · FEMINISM · FREEDOM · FUTURE GENERATIONS · GENDER EQUALITY · GENDER ROLES · HUMANITY · HUMAN RIGHTS · JUSTICE · LIBERTY · OPPRESSION · SCHOOL · SOCIAL SECURITY · SOLIDARITY · UNALIENABLE RIGHTS · WOMEN'S RIGHTS

Born in 1990, **Emma Watson** burst into the film industry as a child actress when she played Hermione Granger in the eight Harry Potter films, starting in the year 2001.

She was schooled in Oxford and later juggled her acting career with a degree in English Literature at Brown University in the United States.

For a long time, Watson has been a vocal advocate for humanitarian causes. She has represented the clothing brand People Tree which encourages fair trade and organic clothing. In addition, she is an ambassador of Camfed International, a charity which promotes access to education for girls in rural Africa. Watson has become a leading figure amongst women involved in the arts who are utilising their privilege and status to better other women's lives.

Since 2014, she has also held the position of a U.N. Goodwill Ambassador which offers another perfect platform to use her status to promote United Nations initiatives and programmes. More specifically, Watson is responsible for HeForShe, a campaign aiming to endorse gender equality.

The programme is being led by the U.N.'s Elizabeth Nyamayaro and Phumzile Mlambo-Ngcuka and strives to improve the status of women. Namely, it targets men and boys and asks them to show their support for their female counterparts' rights. The ambition is to make gender equality a reality. The following speech was made as part of Emma Watson's work as the U.N. Women Goodwill Ambassador.

https://www.thoughtco.com/transcript-of-emma-watsons-speech-on-gender-equality-3026200

Emma Watson:

to launch to start
HeForShe the UN campaign for gender equality across the world
to mobilize (*here:*) to activate, to set in motion; *mobilisieren*
advocate supporter, campaigner
tangible real, concrete

Today we are launching a campaign called HeForShe. I am reaching out to you because we need your help. We want to end gender inequality, and to do this, we need to get everyone involved. This is the first campaign of its kind at the UN. We want to try to mobilize as many men and boys as possible to be advocates for change. And, we don't just want to talk about it. We want to try and make sure that it's tangible.

to appoint as ambassador *zum Botschafter ernennen*
synonymous with the same as; *gleichbedeutend*

I was appointed as Goodwill Ambassador for UN Women six months ago. And, the more I spoke about feminism, the more I realized that fighting for women's rights has too often become synonymous with man-hating. If there is one thing I know for certain, it is that this has to stop.

MEN AND WOMEN SHOULD HAVE EQUAL RIGHTS AND OPPORTUNITIES

for the record *für das Protokoll, damit das klar und deutlich ist*

For the record, feminism by definition is the belief that men and women should have equal rights and opportunities. It is the theory of political, economic, and social equality of the sexes.

assumption supposition; *Vermutung, Annahme*
bossy dominant; *rechthaberisch, herrisch*
muscly muscular

I started questioning gender-based assumptions a long time ago. When I was 8, I was confused about being called bossy because I wanted to direct the plays that we would put on for our parents, but the boys were not. When at 14, I started to be sexualized by certain elements of the media. When at 15, my girlfriends started dropping out of sports teams because they didn't want to appear muscly. When at 18, my male friends were unable to express their feelings.

I decided that I was a feminist, and this seemed uncomplicated to me. But my recent research has shown me that feminism has become an unpopular word. Women are choosing not to identify as feminists. Apparently, I'm among the ranks of women whose expressions are seen as too strong, too aggressive, isolating, and anti-men. Unattractive, even.

counterpart (*here:*) colleague

Why has the word become such an uncomfortable one? I am from Britain, and I think it is right I am paid the same as my male counterparts.

I think it is right that I should be able to make decisions about my own body. I think it is right that women be involved on my behalf in the policies and decisions that will affect my life. I think it is right that socially, I am afforded the same respect as men.

But sadly, I can say that there is no one country in the world where all women can expect to have these rights. No country in the world can yet say that they achieved gender equality. These rights, I consider to be human rights, but I am one of the lucky ones.

human rights see ADDITIONAL NOTES

My life is a sheer privilege because my parents didn't love me less because I was born a daughter. My school did not limit me because I was a girl. My mentors didn't assume that I would go less far because I might give birth to a child one day. These influences were the gender equality ambassadors that made me who I am today. They may not know it, but they are the inadvertent feminists that are changing the world today. We need more of those.

my school did not limit me my school did not restrict my chances and opportunities
to assume to think, to expect
inadvertent unintentional; *unbeabsichtigt*

And if you still hate the word, it is not the word that is important. It's the idea and the ambition behind it, because not all women have received the same rights I have. In fact, statistically, very few have.

ambition drive, desire; *Ehrgeiz, Zielsetzung*

In 1997, Hillary Clinton made a famous speech in Beijing about women's rights. Sadly, many of the things that she wanted to change are still true today. But what stood out for me the most was that less than thirty percent of the audience were male. How can we effect change in the world when only half of it is invited or feels welcome to participate in the conversation?

to participate in to take part in; *teilnehmen an*

Men, I would like to take this opportunity to extend your formal invitation. Gender equality is your issue, too. Because to date, I've seen my father's role as a parent being valued less by society, despite my need of his presence as a child, as much as my mother's. I've seen young men suffering from mental illness, unable to ask for help for fear it would make them less of a man.

issue (*here:*) problem
to date until now

In fact, in the UK, suicide is the biggest killer of men between 20 to 49, eclipsing road accidents, cancer and coronary heart disease. I've seen men made fragile and insecure by a distorted sense of what constitutes male success. Men don't have the benefits of equality, either.

eclipsing even bigger than
fragile *anfällig*
distorted sense *verzerrte bzw. verfälschte Wahrnehmung*

We don't often talk about men being imprisoned by gender stereotypes, but I can see that they are, and that when they are free, things will change for women as a natural consequence. If men don't have to be aggressive in order to be accepted, women won't feel compelled to be submissive. If men don't have to control, women won't have to be controlled.

compelled forced, obliged
submissive compliant, obedient; *unterwürfig, gefügig*

Both men and women should feel free to be sensitive. Both men and women should feel free to be strong. It is time that we all perceive gender on a spectrum, instead of two sets of opposing ideals. If we stop defining each other by what we are not, and start defining our-

to perceive see, notice, recognize; *erkennen, einsehen* selves by who we are, we can all be freer, and this is what *HeForShe* is about. It's about freedom.

to take this mantle (*here:*) to campaign for this cause
vulnerable *verletzlich, verwundbar*
to reclaim to get back
to abandon to give up
more true and complete version of themselves authentic and real version of themselves

I want men to take up this mantle so that their daughters, sisters, and mothers can be free from prejudice, but also so that their sons have permission to be vulnerable and human too, reclaim those parts of themselves they abandoned, and in doing so, be a more true and complete version of themselves.

You might be thinking: "Who is this Harry Potter girl, and what is she doing speaking at the UN?" And, it's a really good question. I've been asking myself the same thing.
All I know is that I care about this problem, and I want to make it better. And, having seen what I've seen, and given the chance, I feel it is my responsibility to say something.

Edmund Burke was an Anglo-Irish philosopher and statesman (born January 12, 1729, in Dublin, Ireland - died July 9, 1797, in Beaconsfield, Buckinghamshire, England), and prominent in public life from 1765 to about 1795. He is an important figure in the history of political theory.

Statesman Edmund Burke said: "All that is needed for the forces of evil to triumph is for good men and women to do nothing."

"IF NOT ME, WHO? IF NOT NOW, WHEN?"

In my nervousness for this speech, and in my moments of doubt, I told myself firmly: "If not me, who? If not now, when?" If you have similar doubts when opportunities are presented to you, I hope those words will be helpful.

Because the reality is that if we do nothing, it will take seventy-five years, or for me to be nearly 100, before women can expect to be paid the same as men for the same work. Fifteen and a half million girls will be married in the next 16 years as children. And at current rates, it won't be until 2086 before all rural African girls can have a secondary education.

If you believe in equality, you might be one of those inadvertent feminists that I spoke of earlier, and for this, I applaud you. We are struggling for a uniting word, but the good news is, we have a uniting movement. It is called *HeForShe*. I invite you to step forward, to be seen and to ask yourself: "If not me, who? If not now, when?"
Thank you very, very much.

ASSIGNMENTS

A) Listening Comprehension

independent learning / individual work / intensive listening and reading / skimming / think-pair-share / kwl reading method / peer support and feedback

a) Listen to Emma Watson's UN speech 2014 here: https://www.youtube.com/watch?v=p-iFl4qhBsE
b) This video has subtitles: https://www.youtube.com/watch?v=w0CWe93dXjo

1. True or false?

	True	False
a) Emma Watson is launching a UN campaign called HeForShe.		
b) She wants to stop gender inequality.		
c) According to Emma Watson, this is the second campaign of its kind at the UN.		
d) Emma Watson was appointed as the UN Women Goodwill Ambassador.		
e) Emma Watson supports the belief that men and women should have equal rights and opportunities.		
f) When she was eight years old, she was confused about being called bossy because she wanted to direct the plays that she and her classmates would put on for their parents.		
g) According to Emma Watson, some countries in the world can say that they have achieved gender equality.		
h) She considers gender quality to be part of our human rights.		
i) Emma Watson points out that gender equality is an issue that only applies to women.		
j) Emma Watson emphasises that, if we do nothing, it will take 75 years, or for her to be nearly 100, before women can expect to be paid the same amount as men for doing the same work.		
k) The speech focuses on gender inequality around the world, and the important role that men and boys must play in fighting for equality for women and girls.		

2. "Mind the Gap": Fill in the gaps with words from Emma Watson's speech.

My life is a sheer __________ because my parents didn't love me __________ because I was born a __________. My school did not __________ me because I was a girl. My mentors didn't __________ that I would go less __________ because I might give __________ to a child one day. These __________ were the gender equality __________ that made me who I am today. They may not know it, but they are the inadvertent __________ that are __________ the world today. We __________ more of those.
In fact, in the UK, __________ is the biggest __________ of men between 20 to 49, eclipsing road __________, cancer and coronary heart __________. I've seen men made __________ and insecure by a __________ sense of what constitutes male __________. Men don't have the __________ of equality, either.

B) Comprehension

1. Watch the video, read the transcript and highlight any important statements.
2. Point out the general ideas of the *HeForShe* campaign.
3. Outline Emma Watson's main arguments and her final appeal to the audience.

C) Analysis

▶ *group work / peer support and feedback / posters / gallery walk / evaluation / discussion*

1. Analyse the structure of the speech.
2. What examples does Emma Watson use to illustrate the problem of gender inequality?
3. Examine some rhetorical devices Emma Watson uses to emphasise her message. Consider the use of: enumeration, allusion, repetition, rhetorical questions, forms of appeal, her tone of voice etc.
4. How does she try to make the audience believe her when she says that everyone is capable of promoting gender equality?
5. Point out the significance of Edmund Burke's quotation in the wider context of Emma Watson's speech.
6. Analyse Emma Watson's final appeal to the audience.

D) Evaluation, Comment, Creative Activities

▶ *speaking skills training / inspiration cards / research / laptops / group work / interview / role play / optimist – pessimist / discussion / speech competition / formative assessment / evaluation*

1. "No country in the world can yet say that they achieved gender equality." Would you agree or disagree with this statement? Explain your point of view.
2. Emma Watson delivered her speech in 2014. Explain whether the speech is still relevant today.
3. Email Emma Watson and respond to her speech.
4. Write an interview with Emma Watson and act it out in your English class.
5. Write and give a speech for the next International Women's Day.
6. Find out some more information about the campaign on the *HeForShe* website: http://www.heforshe.org/en. Present your findings to your class.

E) Information for Thought and Discussion

According to the United Nations:

- Globally, 750 million women and girls were married before the age of 18.
- At least 200 million women and girls in 30 countries have undergone Female Genital Mutilation (FGM).
- In 18 countries, husbands can legally prevent their wives from working; in 39 countries, daughters and sons do not have equal inheritance rights; and 49 countries lack laws protecting women from domestic violence.
- One in five women and girls, including 19 per cent of women and girls aged 15 to 49, have experienced physical and/or sexual violence by an intimate partner within the last 12 months. Yet, 49 countries have no laws that specifically protect women from such violence.
- Only 52 per cent of women married or in a union freely make their own decisions about sexual relations, contraceptive use and health care. [...]

From: *United Nations* https://www.un.org/sustainabledevelopment/gender-equality/ (accessed on Dec. 27, 2018)

F) For Thought and Discussion: Great Movies about Extraordinary Women

Hidden Figures tells the authentic story of three African-American women working at NASA who served as brilliant scientists behind the launch into orbit of astronaut John Glenn.

Suffragette – The Time is Now is an outstanding British historical film about the British Suffragette Movement, fighting for gender equality and women's right to vote.

The Iron Lady tells the story of Margaret Thatcher, Britain's first female prime minister.

Erin Brockovich is a young woman fighting for justice.

Go online and find great films about gender equality and extraordinary women.

"Education Is the Key to Real and Lasting Freedom."

First Lady Michelle Obama: Commencement Address at Dillard University, UNO Lakefront Arena, New Orleans, Louisiana, on May 10, 2014

RELATED TOPICS

THE AMERICAN DREAM · COLLEGE · COMMENCEMENT · DEMOCRACY · DIGNITY · DISCRIMINATION · EDUCATION · EQUALITY · THE FOUNDING CREED · FREEDOM · FUTURE GENERATIONS · GRADUATION · HISTORY · HUMAN RIGHTS · IMMIGRATION · JUSTICE · LEARNING · LIBERTY · LIFE CHANCES · RACE RELATIONS · SCHOOL · SEGREGATION · SLAVERY · SOCIAL SECURITY · UNALIENABLE RIGHTS

Michelle Obama is a former First Lady of the United States and the wife of President Obama. Her background consists of work as a lawyer and a Chicago city administrator. She was also a community-outreach worker.

Michelle Obama was born in Chicago, Illinois in 1964. She completed her Bachelor's degree at Princeton University in 1985, majoring in Sociology and also focusing on African-American Studies. She added to this with another degree from Harvard Law School which she earned in 1988. Finally, she holds an Honorary Doctorate of Letters from Dillard University.

Subsequently, she began working for a law firm in Chicago, where she met her future husband and the future President, Barack Obama. The two were married in 1992. Michelle Obama excelled in her role as First Lady, where she endeavoured to improve lives and raise awareness of social issues like poverty, health and education.

She once passionately offered the following advice to young Americans: "I want our young people to know that they matter, that they belong. So don't be afraid. You hear me, young people? Don't be afraid. Be focused. Be determined. Be hopeful. Be empowered. Empower yourself with a good education. Then get out there and use that education to build a country worthy of your boundless promise. Lead by example with hope; never fear."

In an effort to promote further progress, Michelle Obama requested that the graduates of Dillard University – to whom she delivered the speech below – made the most of their opportunities and used their skills to help future generations.

Speech transcript taken from: *Obama White House Archives* https://obamawhitehouse.archives.gov/the-press-office/2014/05/10/remarks-first-lady-commencement-address-dillard-university

Michelle Obama:

Oh, my goodness! Good morning!

AUDIENCE: Good morning.

MRS. OBAMA: I am so happy to be here with you all. I'm proud to be here in the Big Easy. Look at you all! (*Applause.*) You look good.

Big Easy nickname for the city of New Orleans

STUDENT: You do too!

MRS. OBAMA: Thank you. (*Laughter.*) I want to start by thanking Nicole for that very kind introduction and for sharing her story, which is not too unfamiliar to me – because they told me I couldn't be where I am, too. So I want to thank Nicole. I'm proud of her. Thank you for the selfie; I think that's the first selfie I've done at a commencement. So, Nicole, you're my first. (*Laughter.*)

And of course, I want to thank the Dillard University Choir. Oh, oh, oh! (*Applause.*) Oh! That's all I can say. It's like you want to start something up in here, right? (*Laughter.*) It's like, now we got a commencement going on up in here. (*Laughter.*) That was beautiful, beautiful. Thank you so much.

Dillard University Since 1869, Dillard University has been committed to providing students with a high quality four-year liberal arts education. Dillard is a fully accredited, private, historically black university. In 2010, the U.S. News & World Report ranked Dillard among the nation's Top 10 HBCUs (Historically Black Colleges and Universities).

to recognize (*AmE*), recognise (*BrE*), (*here:*) to acknowledge; *lobend anerkennen*

I also want to recognize Senator Mary Landrieu, who is here. Let's give her a hand. (*Applause.*) She has been a strong supporter of this university.

I want to thank the Dillard University Board of Trustees. I want to thank the faculty, the staff, and, of course, your tremendous president, Dr. Walter Kimbrough. (*Applause.*) Now, my husband has been called a few things over the years, but he has never had the honor of being referred to as the "Hip Hop President." (*Applause.*)

I also want to thank all the folks from the University of New Orleans for hosting us here today. And I know they're hosting the folks at Southern University at New Orleans for their commencement later on today as well, so we wish them a wonderful day. And thank you for having us. (*Applause.*)

And of course, I've got to give a big shout-out to all the family members in the crowd, all of the family members – (*Applause*) – especially to the mothers, because it is the day before Mother's Day. To all the mothers, Happy Mother's Day. (*Applause.*) [...]

YOU HAVE SEEN THEM THROUGH THEIR UPS AND DOWNS, AND YOU HAVE POURED YOUR HEARTS AND SOULS INTO THESE MEN AND WOMEN

In all seriousness, to all the moms out there – as well as the dads, and the grandparents, the uncles, the aunts, the brothers, the sisters, all of you who have helped raise these graduates – you have seen them through their ups and downs, and you have poured your hearts and souls into these men and women. So today is your day, too, and you should be very proud. You really should. (*Applause.*)

And finally, most of all, I want to congratulate the beautiful and handsome men and women of the Dillard University Class of 2014. Yay! (*Applause.*) You all have come so far, I know, to make it to this day – from all those early days when the girls were sneaking out of Williams Hall to go see the boys over at the Duals – oh yeah, I did my research – (*laughter*) – to all those tests you crammed for, to the plans you're making now for your careers, to go on to graduate school.

You all have seen so much. You've witnessed this school's rebirth after the devastation of Hurricane Katrina – the new buildings that replaced the ones you lost, the classrooms that started filling back up again, the service projects that you all have done to help this community bounce back.

And I know, along the way, that each of you has written your own story of resilience and determination to make it here to this day.

For example, as you heard, Nicole was told back in high school that she just wasn't college material. But now she is your class president, and she's headed off to Yale for her graduate degree. So there. (*Applause.*) That's it.

And I know that some of you may come from tough neighborhoods; some of you may have lost your homes during Katrina. Maybe you're like DeShawn Dabney, a graduate who was raised by his grandmother – (*Applause*) – maybe – that's your grandmother, isn't it, DeShawn? Raised by his grandmother while some of his family members were dealing with issues. Maybe just like him, you've been working part-time jobs since you were a teenager to make your dream of going to college come true. And now, today, you're all here ready to walk across this stage and get that diploma.

YOU FOUGHT THROUGH EVERY CHALLENGE YOU ENCOUNTERED

And no matter what path you took to get here, you all kept your hearts set on this day. You fought through every challenge you en-

tests you crammed for tests you revised for at the last minute; *Test für die Ihr (schnell noch) gepaukt habt*

devastation destruction
Hurricane Katrina *see* *Additional Notes*

bounce back to recover; *wieder auf die Beine kommen*

resilience *persönliche Belastbarkeit, Widerstandskraft*
determination willpower, resolve, motivation
she just wasn't college material she just was not good enough to go to college
class president *Jahrgangssprecher*
Yale University one of the most prestigious colleges in the USA
tough (*here:*) rough, underprivileged

were dealing with issues had their own problems to cope with; *mit sich selbst zu tun haben* countered, and you earned that degree from this fine university. And in doing so, you are following in the footsteps of all those who came before you, and you have become an indelible part of the history of this school – a history that, as you all know, stretches back to well before the Civil War, back to 1826, the year a child named Emperor Williams was born.

Now, Emperor was born into slavery. But as he grew up, he managed to teach himself to read and write well enough to create a pass that allowed him to come and go around the city without getting hassled. But one day, his master saw the pass and he said: "Where did you learn to write like that?" Now, just imagine the fear Emperor must have felt when he heard that question – because remember, back then it was illegal for a slave to learn to read or write. So who knows what kind of punishment he may have gotten – a beating, a whipping, or even worse.

We don't exactly know what happened on that day, but we do know that when Emperor turned 32, after more than three decades in bondage, he became a free man. He decided to stay in New Orleans, and he went on to become a minister – even founded a church right here in town. And in 1869, when abolitionists, missionaries, black folks and white folks came together to create a school for freed slaves here in New Orleans, Emperor was one of the original signers of the charter.

They decided to name the school New Orleans University, because even though most of the classes would be taught at a high school level or below, oh, their aspirations were much higher than that. And when they laid the cornerstone for that university's first building down on St. Charles Avenue, Emperor got a chance to speak.

He said – and these are his words – he said: "For twenty years I was a slave on these streets. It was a penitentiary offense to educate a Negro. I have seen my fellow-servants whipped for trying to learn; but today here I am, speaking where a building is to be erected for the education of the children of my people." He goes on to say: "I wonder if this is the world I was born in."

GETTING AN EDUCATION COULD OPEN UP A WHOLE NEW WORLD OF OPPORTUNITY

See, in the course of his short lifetime, Emperor saw education go from being a crime for black folks to being a real possibility for his kids and grandkids. So no wonder he was asking whether this was the same world he'd been born into. See, for a man like Emperor, getting an education could open up a whole new world of opportunity. An education meant having real power. It meant you could manage your own money. It meant you couldn't get swindled out of land or

indelible unforgettable, memorable

Emperor Williams was born a slave in 1826; he was freed in 1858, he founded a church in New Orleans and started a school for freed slaves.

getting hassled without anyone bothering him; *belästigt werden*

bondage (*here:*) slavery

minister preacher; *Pastor*

abolitionists people who campaigned for slavery to be abolished; the abolitionist movement was a social and political movement for the immediate emancipation of all slaves, and the end of racial discrimination and segregation.

charter founding document

penitentiary offense, felony, crime; *strafbare Handlung*

grandkids grandchildren; *Enkelkinder*

get swindled get cheated; *beschwindelt, übervorteilt werden* possessions when somebody told you to just sign on the dotted line; sometimes even determined whether or not you could vote.

to sign on the dotted line *auf der punktierten Linie unterschreiben*

So most folks back then saw education as the key to real and lasting freedom. That's why, when New Orleans University and the other African American college in town, Straight University, first opened their doors, one of the biggest problems they faced was too many students. That's right – too many students. Many of these students barely spoke English; they'd grown up speaking Creole or French. Few had ever seen the inside of a classroom or even been taught their ABCs.

But let me tell you, those students were hungry – you hear me? Hungry. They studied like their lives depended on it. They blazed through their lessons. And that hunger for education lasted for generations in the African American community here in New Orleans.

blazed through their lessons were desperate to learn, they were fully motivated

When an arsonist set fire to the school's library in 1877, they built a new one. When those two original schools ran into financial troubles years later, they started making plans to build an even bigger and better university. And in the 1930s, when white folks complained that this new school would mean too many black students on their buses, the folks at the school got the city to add a bus line just for their students, because nothing – nothing – was going to stop them from achieving the vision of those early founders. (*Applause.*)

arsonist *Brandstifter*

And finally, in May of 1934, they broke ground for this school, Dillard University – (*Applause*) – a university that would go on to produce some of the leading thinkers and achievers in our country. And the day the cornerstone was laid for your library, the President of Howard University spoke these words: He said, "There lies in this Southland today, buried in unmarked graves, many a black genius who would have blessed this city and this section of our country, if only his parents could have had before them the Dillard University you are now building."

to break ground for *den Weg ebnen*

And in the years since then, through segregation and depression, through threats of violence and the floodwaters of a devastating storm, students like you have come here to study and to learn, and to carry forward those hopes and dreams. And today, I stand before a sea of young geniuses. Oh, yeah. (*Applause.*)

WHAT ABOUT ALL THOSE GENIUSES
WHO NEVER GET THIS CHANCE?

So, graduates, I hope that you understand that this day is not just the culmination of your own dreams, but the realization of the dreams of so many who came before you. And you should be so proud, and

culmination climax, end result

so happy, and so excited about your futures. But what you shouldn't be is satisfied. (*Applause.*) See, because while it is a wonderful thing that all of you are here today, we have to ask ourselves, what about all those geniuses who never get this chance?

I'm talking about the young people from right here in New Orleans and across the country who aren't part of a commencement like this one today, kids no different from all of us, kids who never made it out of high school. The fact is that today, the high school graduation rate for black students is improving, but it is still lower than just about any other group in this country. And while college graduation rates have risen for nearly every other demographic, including African American women, the college graduation rate for African American men has flatlined.

flatlined plateaued, stagnated; *stagniert*

See, and the thing is, when our young people fall behind like that in school, they fall behind in life. Last year, African Americans were more than twice as likely as whites to be unemployed. They were almost three times as likely to live in poverty. And they were far more likely to end up in prison or be the victims of violent crimes.

more than twice as likely as whites to be unemployed *die Gefahr arbeitslos zu werden, ist bei Schwarzen im Vergleich zu den Weißen doppelt so groß*

Now, perhaps when you hear these statistics, you might think to yourself, well, those numbers are terrible, but I'm not part of the problem. And you might be thinking that since you're not one of those statistics, and you're sitting here wearing that nice black robe today, you can go on your way and never look back.

But folks like you and me, we can't afford to think like that – never. See, because we're the lucky ones, and we can never forget that we didn't get where we are today all on our own.

We got here today because of so many people who toiled and sweat and bled and died for us – people like our parents and grandparents and all those who came before them, people who never dreamed of getting a college education themselves but who worked, and saved, and sacrificed so that we could be here today. We owe them. (*Applause.*) We owe them.

to toil to work hard

we owe them we should be grateful to them; *wir sind ihnen zu Dank verpflichtet*

And the only way to pay back that debt is by making those same kinds of sacrifices and investments for the next generation. And I know sitting here right now, that task could seem a bit overwhelming. I know it could seem like the deck is stacked way too high against our young people. And the truth is that some of the problems we face – structural inequality, schools that lag behind, workplace and housing discrimination – those problems are too big for one person to fix on their own.

the deck is stacked way too high against our young people the expectations to solve all these problems seem to be too high for young people to meet

EDUCATION IS STILL THE KEY TO REAL AND LASTING FREEDOM

But that's still no excuse to stand on the sidelines. Because we know that today, education is still the key to real and lasting freedom – it is still true today. So it is now up to us to cultivate that hunger for education in our own lives and in those around us. And we know that hunger is still out there – we know it.

to stand on the sidelines not to get involved (in solving the problems); *sich aus allem heraushalten*
to cultivate to encourage, to nurture, to support

We see it in students like DeShawn and Nicole and all of you who scraped and clawed so you could make it to this day. We see it in the single moms who work three jobs so their kids might have a shot at earning a degree like yours. (*Applause.*) We see that hunger all around the world – in that young woman named Malala who was shot on her school bus in Pakistan just for speaking out in support of girls getting an education, and the more than 200 girls kidnapped from their own school in Nigeria for wanting an education – (*Applause*) – young people who are knowingly risking their lives every day just to go to school.

single moms single mothers; *alleinerziehende Mütter*
to have a shot at earning a degree to stand a chance of getting a degree
Malala Yousafzai winner of the 2014 Nobel Peace Prize

And in fact, you've seen that hunger right here at Dillard: your valedictorian, three salutatorians are all from Nigeria. (*Applause.*) They studied hard at an early age, earned scholarships to come here to this university, achieved 4.0 GPAs. And now they are off pursuing master's degrees, work in software development, teaching math and science to young people here in the United States.

See, now, that's the kind of hunger for education that we have to reignite in all of our communities. It's the same hunger that gave life to this university, the same hunger that defined so many of our parents and grandparents – including my own. You see, my parents never went to college, but they were determined to see me and my brother, and all the kids in our neighborhood get a good education. (*Applause.*)

valedictorian the student who gives a speech on behalf of all the students at the commencement ceremony; *Abschiedsredner/in*
salutatorian the student who delivers the salutatory address (greetings) at the commencement ceremony *(zweit-)bester Absolvent des Jahrgangs, der eine Rede auf der Abschlussfeier hält*
GPA: Grade Point Average; the most common form of GPA is based on a 0 to 4.0 scale
4.0 GPA excellent, the highest mark awarded in the USA for a degree
pursuing doing, achieving
to reignite reactivate, to rekindle, to start up

So my mother volunteered at my school – helping out every day in the front office, making sure our teachers were doing their jobs, holding their feet to the fire if she thought they were falling short. I'd walk by the office and there she'd be. (*Laughter.*) I'd leave class to go to the bathroom, there she'd be again, roaming the halls, looking in the classrooms. And of course, as a kid, I have to say, that was a bit mortifying, having your mother at school all the time.

holding their feet to the fire if she thought they were falling short (*here:*) making sure they did their best as teachers
mortifying embarrassing

But looking back, I have no doubt that my classmates and I got a better education because she was looking over those teachers' shoulders. (*Applause.*) You see, my mom was not a teacher or a principal or a school board member. But when it came to education, she had that hunger. So she believed that our education was very much her business.

And we need more people who think and act like my mother, and all those mothers out there, because the education of our young people is all of our business. That's what Emperor Williams thought. That's what the folks here in New Orleans thought as they worked to rebuild this campus after Katrina. And as graduates of Dillard University, that's how we need you to think every single day for the rest of your lives.

YOU CAN INSPIRE THOSE AROUND YOU TO REACH HIGHER AND COMPLETE THEIR OWN EDUCATION

impact influence

You all have opportunities and skills and education that so many folks who came before you never could have dreamed of. So just imagine the kind of impact that you're going to make. Imagine how you can inspire those around you to reach higher and complete their own education.

congregation a group of people who attend the same church; *Kirchengemeinde*

And you can start small. Start by volunteering at an after-school program, or helping some high school kids fill out their college applications. Show them the path that you took. Or you can think a little bigger – you can get your entire congregation or your community to start a mentoring program; maybe convince your new employer to sponsor scholarships for underprivileged kids. Or maybe you could think a little higher – maybe you could run for school board or Congress, or, yes, even President of the United States. (*Applause.*)

And then maybe you could build preschools for every single one of our kids. Maybe you could help turn that pipeline to prison into a highway to college; help give every child in America an education that is truly worthy of their promise. Those are the kind of big dreams that the folks who founded this university reached for. That is how high they set their bar.

NO DREAM IS TOO BIG, NO VISION IS TOO BOLD;
AS LONG AS WE STAY HUNGRY FOR EDUCATION

audacity boldness, courage

And so we owe it to those folks – the folks who had the audacity to call their little schools "universities" and name their baby boys "Emperor" – we owe it to them to reach as high as they did, and to bring others along the way. As the history of this school has taught us, no dream is too big, no vision is too bold; as long as we stay hungry for education and let that hunger be our North Star, there is nothing, graduates, nothing that we cannot achieve.

LET THE NEXT GENERATION KNOW THAT THERE IS NO GREATER INVESTMENT THAN A GOOD EDUCATION

So, graduates, that is your mission. This is your obligation. I want you to keep reaching higher. I want you all to keep raising your bars. Let the next generation know that there is no greater investment than a good education. And if you do all of this, then I am confident that you will uphold that duty and write your own chapter into the legacy of this great university. And let me tell you something, I cannot wait to see the world that your children will be born into.

to keep raising your bars to set your goals higher

legacy heritage, history

Congratulations. I love you all. I am honored to be here. I am proud of you. God bless you. And thank your families. (*Applause.*)

ASSIGNMENTS

A) Listening and Reading Comprehension

SQ3R / think - pair - share / idea tower / mind map / peer support / feedback / summary writing

1. Listen to Michelle Obama's speech.
2. Then highlight any significant keywords and her main arguments on your speech transcript.
3. Draw a mind map illustrating Michelle Obama's concept of education.
4. Summarise Michelle Obama's main arguments and concepts.

B) Analysis

think - pair - share / peer support and feedback / tablet presentation / discussion / SOLO taxonomy

1. Analyse the structure of Michelle Obama's speech.
2. How does she start her speech?
3. How does she try to convince the students of her arguments? Examine some rhetorical devices which support her message.
4. "You fought through every challenge you encountered." The First Lady gives some examples to illustrate the challenges which some students have encountered. Analyse some of these examples and explain what these examples reveal about contemporary American society.
5. Michelle Obama is urging graduates of Dillard University to continue "to fuel their hunger for education" and to use it to guide in their lives, and to inspire the "next generation of geniuses." What is she trying to get the students to do and how is she encouraging them to do it?
6. Why is the story of Emperor Williams significant in the wider context of Michelle Obama's speech?
7. Analyse Michelle Obama's appeal to the audience at the end of her speech.

C) Evaluation, Comment and Creative Activities

flipped classroom / independent learning / paired work / group work / tablet or laptop presentation / discussion / audio or video recording / feedback / Speakers' Corner / talk show

1. Explain why Dillard University is a significant location for Michelle Obama's speech.
2. "Education is still the key to real and lasting freedom." Discuss this statement, giving reasons for your own point of view.
3. "Maybe you could help turn that pipeline to prison into a highway to college." Discuss the significance of this statement. Prepare and give a three-minute speech in response to it.

4. Write a creative interview with Michelle Obama and act it out in your English class.
5. Michelle Obama emphasises that: "As long as we stay hungry for education and let that hunger be our North Star, there is nothing, graduates, nothing that we cannot achieve." Write and give a speech in response to this statement.
6. "I want you to keep reaching higher, I want you all to keep raising your bars, let the next generation know that there is no greater investment than a good education." Respond to this appeal by giving your own opinion of what "a good education" entails.
7. Imagine you had to give a presentation on education at the next "Abiturfeier". Work in a team of four students and find ways of making it both interesting and amusing for listeners by using cartoons, diagrams, films and any other creative means as part of your presentation.

D) Further Projects for Thought and Discussion

▶ *cooperative learning / research / WebQuest / interview / tablet or laptop presentation / creative writing / audio or video report for a TV or radio station / discussion / speech / creative video clip*

1. "While it is a wonderful thing that all of you are here today, we have to ask ourselves, what about all those geniuses who never get this chance?" What exactly does Michelle Obama mean?
2. The UNHCR has pointed out that, in quite a few countries, young people do not have the opportunity to go to school to get a good education. Find out about young people anywhere in the world who have been denied their right to an education. Use the internet, encyclopedias, newspapers, and journals to conduct your research.
3. "Now, perhaps when you hear these statistics, you might think to yourself, well those numbers are terrible, but I'm not part of the problem." [...]. "And you might be thinking that since you're not one of those statistics, and you're sitting here wearing that nice black robe today, you can go on your way and never look back." Evaluate Michelle Obama's message and respond to it with a three-minute speech.
4. Michelle Obama encourages the graduates to start small, such as through volunteering as a tutor or by rallying their local communities to start a mentor program. She also mentions the possibility of making larger contributions, such as serving on a school board, in Congress, or even as US president. What are the possible options available to young people? Evaluate these options and explain which option(s) you would choose. Write an essay or give a five-minute speech.
5. "No dream is too big, no vision is too bold; as long as we stay hungry for education and let that hunger be our North Star, there is nothing, graduates, nothing that we cannot achieve." Produce a video clip to illustrate this message.
6. **Kinderarmut und Bildungschancen in Deutschland**:
   „Jedes fünfte Kind in Deutschland lebt in Armut. Diese zeigt sich meist in schlechten Bildungschancen, einer mangelhaften Gesundheit, dem Gefühl der Scham und wenig Selbstvertrauen. Wir tun viel, um Kindern ein würdevolles Leben mit fairen Chancen zu ermöglichen."
   Vgl. *Bildungsreport des Deutschen Kinderhilfswerks 2018* https://www.dkhw.de/
7. **„Wie Armut unsere Kinder belastet"**
   Von Armin Himmelrath, *Der SPIEGEL* vom 14.11.2018 http://www.spiegel.de/lebenundlernen/schule/studie-soziale-risiken-fuer-kinder-und-jugendliche-in-deutschland-a-1238344.html (accessed on December 27, 2018)
8. What should we teach a young person that will help him or her to succeed in life? What kind of skills, knowledge, competencies and values will he or she need in the world of 2030? Write an essay for your school newspaper or prepare and give a speech to your English class.

United Nations: Peacekeeping in a World of Conflicts

H

"We Are Responsible for Each Other's Security and Welfare"

Kofi Annan delivered his final speech as UN Secretary General at the Harry S. Truman Presidential Museum in Independence, Missouri, on Monday, December 11, 2006.

RELATED TOPICS

CIVILISATION · CONFLICT · DEMOCRACY · DIGNITY · EQUALITY · FREEDOM · GLOBAL SOLIDARITY · HUMANITY · HUMAN RIGHTS · MULTILATERALISM · OPPRESSION · PEACEKEEPING · POVERTY · RESPONSIBILITY · SECURITY · SUSTAINABLE DEVELOPMENT GOALS · THREATS · TRUST · THE UNITED NATIONS · SHARED VALUES

Kofi Annan comes from Kumasi, Gold Coast – now known as Ghana – where he was born on April 8, 1938. A prominent figure within the U.N., Annan became the seventh Secretary-General in 1997 and served until 2006. While in office, he set about implementing reforms to the U.N. which aimed to make the organisation more efficient and more effective. He was a vocal supporter of upholding people's human rights and the rule of law. He encouraged the adoption of the Millennium Development Goals and aimed to improve prospects on his home continent of Africa.

An especially major setback to Annan's career came in 1994 when the U.N. failed to act decisively to prevent the Rwandan genocide of the Tutsi minority. Due to his background, Annan faced criticism for not recognising the boiling of tensions. Nonetheless, the Ghanaian strived to learn from such tragic events. He even acknowledged his own failings in regards to Rwanda in his autobiography, *A Life in War and Peace*, outlining what he could have done to thwart the tragedy.

Subsequently, the U.N. peacekeeping programme was bolstered to improve its scope and operational capabilities. Additionally, Annan also demanded that Member States launch a pair of governmental bodies, namely: the Peacebuilding Commission and the Human Rights Council. He also played his part across a whole range of issues. He established a Global Fund to combat AIDS, Tuberculosis and Malaria. He implemented the U.N.'s first counter-terrorism strategy and he secured the acceptance of Member States to protect people from genocide, war crimes, ethnic cleansing and crimes against humanity. Annan also impacted cooperate enterprises: his 'Global Compact' initiative prompted businesses to be more aware of their effects on society.

His immense portfolio of humanitarian work led to him receiving a Nobel Peace Prize, in association with the United Nations, in 2001. Annan's achievements have also been recognised on numerous occasions leading to a number of honorary degrees and international honours. He died in Bern, Switzerland at the age of 80 on August 18, 2018.

UN Secretary General Kofi Annan:

exhilarating exciting, inspiring

[...] Today, I want to talk particularly about five lessons I have learnt in the last 10 years, during which I have had the difficult but exhilarating role of Secretary-General.

genocide slaughter, massacre; *Völkermord*
ethnic cleansing mass killing of an ethnic group; *ethnische Säuberung*
solemnly seriously; *feierlich*

shield protection, defence (*here:*) excuse
intent on with the intention of, planning to
massacring slaughtering, killing
heinous terrible, monstrous

My first lesson is that, in today's world, the security of every one of us is linked to that of everyone else. [...]
It also includes our shared responsibility to protect populations from genocide, war crimes, ethnic cleansing, and crimes against humanity – a responsibility solemnly accepted by all nations at last year's UN summit.
That means that respect for national sovereignty can no longer be used as a shield by governments intent on massacring their own people, or as an excuse for the rest of us to do nothing when such heinous crimes are committed.

prosperity *Wohlstand, Erfolg*

to derive benefits from to get advantages from; *Vorteile erlangen*

abject hopeless, miserable; *erbärmlich, elend*

My second lesson is that we are not only all responsible for each other's security. We are also, in some measure, responsible for each other's welfare. Global solidarity is both necessary and possible. It is necessary because without a measure of solidarity, no society can be truly stable, and no one's prosperity truly secure.
That applies to national societies – as all the great industrial democracies learned in the 20th century – but it also applies to the increasingly integrated global market economy we live in today.
It is not realistic to think that some people can go on deriving great benefits from globalization while billions of their fellow human beings are left in abject poverty, or even thrown into it. We have to give our fellow citizens, not only within each nation but in the global community, at least a chance to share in our prosperity. [...]

My third lesson is that both security and development ultimately depend on respect for human rights and the rule of law. Although increasingly interdependent, our world continues to be divided – not only by economic differences, but also by religion and culture.
That is not in itself a problem. Throughout history, human life has been enriched by diversity, and different communities have learnt from each other. But if our different communities are to live together in peace we must stress also what unites us: our common humanity, and our shared belief that human dignity and rights should be protected by law. [...]

governments must be accountable for their actions governments must be able to justify their actions; *Regierungen müssen sich für ihre Handlungen verantworten*

My fourth lesson – closely related to the last one – is that governments must be accountable for their actions in the international arena, as well as in the domestic one. Today, the actions of one state can often have a decisive effect on the lives of people in other states.

As things stand, accountability between states is highly skewed. Poor and weak states are easily held to account, because they need foreign assistance. But large and powerful states, whose actions have the greatest impact on others, can be constrained only by their own people, working through their domestic institutions.

That gives the people and institutions of such powerful states a special responsibility to take account of global views and interests, as well as national ones. The fact is that states can no longer – if they ever could – confront global challenges alone. Increasingly, we need to enlist the help of these other actors, both in working out global strategies, and in putting those strategies into action, once agreed. [...]

My fifth and final lesson derives inescapably from those other four. We can only do all these things by working together through a multilateral system, and by making the best possible use of the unique instrument bequeathed to us by Harry Truman and his contemporaries, namely the United Nations.

In fact, it is only through multilateral institutions that states can hold each other to account. And that makes it very important to organize those institutions in a fair and democratic way, giving the poor and the weak some influence over the actions of the rich and the strong. [...]

And it also applies to the UN Security Council, whose membership still reflects the reality of 1945, not of today's world. [...] The other, perhaps even more important, is that all Council members, and especially the major powers who are permanent members, must accept the special responsibility that comes with their privilege. [...]

These five lessons can be summed up as five principles, which I believe are essential for the future conduct of international relations: collective responsibility, global solidarity, the rule of law, mutual accountability, and multilateralism. [...]

But much remains to be done to put those five principles into practice. My friends, our challenge today is not to save Western civilisation – or Eastern, for that matter. All civilisation is at stake, and we can save it only if all peoples join together in the task. [...]

More than ever today, Americans, like the rest of humanity, need a functioning global system through which the world's peoples can face global challenges together. [...]

The speech transcript is taken from: *The BBC*
http://news.bbc.co.uk/2/hi/americas/6170089.stm

accountability responsibility for one's actions; *Verantwortlichkeit, Rechenschaft*
skewed *einseitig, unausgewogen*

constrained *eingeschränkt*

to take account of to consider; *beachten, berücksichtigen*

multilateralism an alliance of multiple countries pursuing a common goal
a multilateral system a system with cooperating members from several different countries
unique extraordinary; *einzigartig*
bequeathed given, handed down, entrusted; *als Vermächtnis hinterlassen*
Harry S. Truman born on May 8, 1884 and died on December 26, 1972; he was the 33rd President of the United States
to hold each other to account *einander zur Rechenschaft ziehen*
UN Security Council see Additional Notes

at stake in danger

ASSIGNMENTS

A) Comprehension

listening for gist and detail / think – pair – share / posters / presentation / article for a newspaper

1. Watch Kofi Annan's speech on YouTube: https://www.youtube.com/watch?v=z9wwvHan9wA
2. Kofi Annan discusses "five lessons" that he has learned as Secretary-General of the United Nations. Sum up each lesson briefly.
3. What are the challenges and achievements of the United Nations, according to Kofi Annan?
4. According to Kofi Annan, what reforms are needed at the United Nations?
5. Write a summary of Kofi Annan's Farewell Address for your school newspaper.

B) Analysis

Individual and paired work / peer support / writing an analysis / presentation / evaluation

1. Analyse some rhetorical devices which Annan uses to support his message.
2. Is Annan's final appeal effective and convincing?

C) Evaluation, Comment, Creative writing

individual and cooperative learning / presentation / discussion / speech / SOLO taxonomy

1. Evaluate one of the principles Kofi Annan talked about that you agree or disagree with.
2. Kofi Annan emphasises that "some people can go on deriving great benefits from globalization while billions of their fellow human beings are left in abject poverty, or even thrown into it." Prepare and give a three-minute speech in response to Annan's statement.
3. "The fact is that states can no longer – if they ever could – confront global challenges alone." Write a response in which you explain why you agree or disagree with Annan's statement.
4. "All civilisation is at stake, and we can save it only if all peoples join together in the task." Prepare and give a two-minute speech in response to this statement from Annan's speech.

D) Further Information and Research Ideas for Thought and Discussion

research / group work / WebQuest / tablet or laptop / presentation / speech / video clip production

1. *Reforming the Security Council:* In his speech, Kofi Annan called for a reform of the Security Council, saying its membership "still reflects the reality of 1945, not of today's world." He suggested adding new members to represent parts of the world who are not currently members of the Security Council.
2. *The Responsibility of the Security Council:* Kofi Annan said that the permanent members of the Security Council, the world powers, "must accept the special responsibility that comes with their privilege." Are world powers acting responsibly at the moment?
3. Find out more information about the United Nations: The history of the UN, the UN Charter, the Universal Declaration of Human Rights, the General Assembly, the Security Council, current and former Secretary-Generals, Specialized Agencies, Member States. Please visit the website: http://www.un.org
4. *The United Nations and The 2001 Nobel Peace Prize:* The 2001 Nobel Peace Prize was jointly awarded to Kofi Annan, and to the United Nations "for their work for a better organized and more peaceful world." Do you think that Kofi Annan and the UN deserved the award? Give a three-minute speech.
5. Who should win the next Nobel Peace Prize? Write a letter of recommendation to the Nobel Committee.

"Put Peace First."

UN Secretary-General António Guterres: Appeal for Peace on January 1, 2017, in New York, USA

RELATED TOPICS

COMPASSION · CONFLICT · DEMOCRACY · DESTRUCTION · DIGNITY · EXPLOITATION · FEAR · FUTURE GENERATIONS · HEALTH · HOPE · HUMANITARIAN DISASTERS · HUMANITY · MISTRUST · PEACE · POVERTY · REFUGEES · RESPECT · RESPONSIBILITY · SOLIDARITY · SUFFERING · TERRORISM · TRUST · UNITED NATIONS

António Guterres addressed the world on the first day of January 2017 and appealed to all people on the planet to make the pursuit of peace their target for the year. The U.N. Secretary-General, who was formally appointed on October 13, 2016, began his five-year term with this request and will serve until the final day of December 2021. Between 1995 and 2002, Guterres had been Prime Minister of Portugal and had also taken on the role of U.N. High Commissioner for Refugees from June 2005. He remained in this position for ten years until December 2015.
Guterres highlighted the importance of peace by including it in his first message as Secretary-General. He requested that the whole world buy into a single shared New Year's resolution – to 'put peace first'.

UN Secretary General António Guterres:

On my first day as Secretary-General of the United Nations, one question weighs heavily on my heart.

How can we help the millions of people caught up in conflict, suffering massively in wars with no end in sight?

Civilians are pounded with deadly force. Women, children and men are killed and injured, forced from their homes, dispossessed and destitute. Even hospitals and aid convoys are targeted.

No one wins these wars, everyone loses.

Trillions of dollars are spent destroying societies and economies, fuelling cycles of mistrust and fear that can last for generations.

civilians are pounded with deadly force *Zivilpersonen werden von tödlicher Gewalt getroffen;*
to pound to beat, to hurt; *schlagen*
dispossessed and destitute deprived of everything and impoverished; *besitzlos und notleidend*
targeted marked out for attack

fuelling cycles of mistrust and fear the ongoing dangerous development of suspicion and anxiety; *ein Kreislauf von Misstrauen und Furcht wird geschürt*

to destabilize (*AmE*), destabilise (*BrE*), to weaken, to undermine; *destabilisieren*
in making one shared New Year's resolution *einen gemeinsamen Neujahrsvorsatz fassen*
resolution promise, commitment; *Vorsatz zum Neuen Jahr*
to resolve to to decide to
to strive to to try hard to
dialogue and respect across political divides *Dialog und Respekt über politische Grenzen hinweg*
ceasefire agreement to stop fighting; *Waffenstillstand*
negotiating table *Verhandlungstisch*
to negotiate to discuss, to talk; *verhandeln, aushandeln*
join me in committing to peace *setzen Sie sich mit mir zusammen für den Frieden ein*

Whole regions are destabilized and the new threat of global terrorism affects us all.

On this New Year's Day, I ask all of you to join me in making one shared New Year's resolution:

Let us resolve to put peace first.

Let us make 2017 a year in which we all – citizens, governments, leaders – strive to overcome our differences.

From solidarity and compassion in our daily lives, to dialogue and respect across political divides...

From ceasefires on the battlefield, to compromise at the negotiating table to reach political solutions.

Peace must be our goal and our guide.

All that we strive for as a human family – dignity and hope, progress and prosperity – depends on peace. But peace depends on us.

I appeal to you all to join me in committing to peace, today and every day. Let us make 2017 a year for peace. Thank you.

ASSIGNMENTS

A) Pre-Listening and Pre-Reading activity

cooperative learning / speaking skills training / TED questions / brainstorming / enquiry-based learning / market place / walking and talking / idea tower / placemat / flipchart

1. How can peace be achieved in the world today?
2. What is – in your opinion – the most important Sustainable Development Goal (SDG)?
3. What other Sustainable Development Goals are important?

B) Comprehension

think - pair - share / peer support and feedback / writing a summary / presentation

1. Appeal for Peace: Watch the appeal for peace by U.N. Secretary-General António Guterres upon becoming the head of the United Nations on January 1, 2017.
2. Take notes while watching the video.
   https://www.un.org/sg/en/content/sg/statement/2017-01-01/appeal-peace-un-secretary-general-antonio-guterres
3. Read the transcript of his speech and highlight the main keywords and important statements.
4. Outline António Guterres's main arguments.

C) Analysis

posters / flipchart / cue cards / mind mapping / word cloud / presentation / gallery walk / evaluation

1. Analyse the structure of the speech.
2. Examine and analyse the rhetorical devices Guterres uses in the speech and explain how they underline the speaker's intentions, and the overall message of the speech.

D) Evaluation, Comment, Creative Writing

think - pair - share / creative writing / interview / speech competition / discussion / feedback

1. Write an email to António Guterres in response to his speech.
2. Can this speech contribute to a more peaceful world? Explain your opinion. Write an article or prepare and give a speech on the present situation in the world today.
3. If you had the chance to interview António Guterres, what questions would you like to ask him? Please consider and write down the possible answers that he might give you.
4. If you were the UN Secretary-General, what would you tell the global community in your next speech? Prepare and give a four-minute speech as if you were the UN Secretary-General.

E) Ideas for Further Projects: For Thought and Discussion

flipped classroom / group work / research / collaboration with History and Social Sciences classes / cross-curricular connections / laptop, tablet / speech / discussion / evaluation

1. **How did the United Nations come into being?**
   Research its history and describe some of its most important aims in your own words.
2. **Building peaceful, sustainable and inclusive societies**
   "In a time of complex developmental challenges, the investments we make today in women's, children's and adolescents' health and wellbeing will help build the peaceful, sustainable and inclusive societies we have promised to achieve through the Sustainable Development Goals (SDGs)," affirmed António Guterres. "Peace cannot exist without development and development cannot exist without health and wellbeing, for healthy and empowered women, children and adolescents can bring about the change needed to create a better future for all," he added.
   United Nations News Service: http://www.un.org/apps/news/story.asp?NewsID=56605#.WPykEKKkLcs
3. **The United Nations' Sustainable Development Goals (SDGs)**
   On September 25, 2015, UN member states adopted a set of goals to end poverty, to protect the planet, and to ensure prosperity for all as part of a new sustainable development agenda. Each goal has specific targets to be achieved over the next 15 years. For the goals to be reached, everyone needs to do their bit: governments, the private sector, civil

society, and people like you. Do you want to get involved? You can start by telling everyone you know about the Sustainable Development Goals. Have a look at the United Nations' website:
http://www.un.org/sustainabledevelopment/sustainable-development-goals/

Tasks:

a) Write down the United Nations' 17 Sustainable Development Goals.
The Sustainable Development Goals are the blueprint to achieve a better and more sustainable future for all. They address the global challenges we face, including those related to poverty, inequality, climate, environmental degradation, prosperity, and peace and justice. It ís important that we achieve each Goal and target by 2030.
From: *United Nations* https://www.un.org/sustainabledevelopment/sustainable-development-goals/

The United Nations' Sustainable Development Goals

Goal	Heading	Aim / Intention	Info & Progress
Goal 1	**No Poverty**	end of poverty in all its forms everywhere	social protection systems are fundamental to preventing and reducing poverty and inequality at every stage of people's lives
[...]	[...]	[...]	[...]

b) Choose one of the 17 Sustainable Development Goals, find out some more information about it on the U.N. website, and then tell your partner and your group what you have found out about it.

c) What do you think are the most important Sustainable Development Goals? Write an article or prepare and give a three-minute-speech in response to this question.

d) How can these goals be accepted by all nations?

e) How can these goals be achieved in the near future?

f) How can governments, the private sector, civil society, and people like you contribute to the achievement of these Sustainable Development Goals?

F) Mediation (German = > English)

Die 2030-Agenda für Nachhaltige Entwicklung, die am 25. September 2015 beim UNO Nachhaltigkeitsgipfel der Staats- und Regierungschefs verabschiedet worden ist, stellt einen Meilenstein der internationalen Zusammenarbeit dar. Mit den 17 Nachhaltigkeitszielen, den Sustainable Development Goals (SDGs), hat sich die Weltgemeinschaft erstmals auf einen universalen und alle drei Nachhaltigkeitsdimensionen einschließenden Katalog von festen Zeitzielen geeinigt, der die internationale Zusammenarbeit in zentralen Politikbereichen in den nächsten Jahrzehnten maßgeblich prägen wird. Zielsetzung der 2030-Agenda ist es, die globale Entwicklung sozial, ökologisch und wirtschaftlich nachhaltig zu gestalten. [...] Klimawandel, Verlust von Biodiversität, Armut, Hunger und häufig mit hohem Ressourcenverbrauch verbundenes Wirtschaften zeigen, dass weltweit umgesteuert werden muss. Die 2030-Agenda folgt hierbei dem Grundsatz, auch die Schwächsten und Verwundbarsten der Welt mitzunehmen ("leave no one behind"), und hat den Anspruch, auch kommenden Generationen die Chance auf ein erfülltes Leben zu sichern.
Quelle: *Bundesministerium für Umwelt*
https://www.bmu.de/themen/nachhaltigkeit-internationales/nachhaltige-entwicklung/2030-agenda/

G) Good Practices and Success Stories in SDG Implementation

Sustainable Development Goals (SDGs): What are the inspiring breakthroughs, the good practices and success stories that are showing promising results and sustainable impacts? What are the gaps, the problems and limitations? Looking ahead, what steps should be taken to support and accelerate progress? Share your ideas and concepts with partner schools in our globalized world and present creative and sustainable concepts in your school and in your local community. You can also send your good practice examples to the United Nations.
For further information, visit: United Nations' Sustainable Development Goals (SDGs)
https://sustainabledevelopment.un.org/sdgs/goodpractices

"A Red Alert for the World."

António Guterres, UN Secretary-General, New Year Video Speech, January 1, 2018

RELATED TOPICS

THE COLD WAR · CONFLICT · DIGNITY · DISPLACEMENT · FEAR · FUTURE GENERATIONS · HOPE · HUMAN RIGHTS · PEACE · PERSECUTION · REFUGEES · RESPECT · RESPONSIBILITY · SOLIDARITY · THE UNITED NATIONS · UNITY · SHARED VALUES · VIOLENCE · WAR

António Guterres

In his 2018 New Year's message, United Nations' Secretary-General, António Guterres, called for unity across the global community to tackle overwhelming challenges, and to defend shared values.
"On New Year's Day 2018, I am not issuing an appeal. I am issuing an alert – a red alert for our world," said the Secretary-General.
Read his impressive speech to his "friends around the world".

Source: *United Nations* https://news.un.org/en/story/2017/12/640812-un-chief-issues-red-alert-urges-world-come-together-2018-tackle-pressing

UN Secretary General António Guterres:

Dear friends around the world. Happy New Year.

When I took office a year ago, I appealed for 2017 to be a year for peace.

Unfortunately, in fundamental ways, the world has gone in reverse.

On New Year's Day 2018, I am not issuing an appeal, I am issuing an alert, a red alert for our world.

Conflicts have deepened and new dangers have emerged.

Global anxieties about nuclear weapons are the highest since the Cold War.

And climate change is moving faster than we are.

Inequalities are growing, and we see horrific violations of human rights. Nationalism and xenophobia are on the rise.

And, as we begin 2018, I call for unity.

I truly believe we can make our world more safe and secure.

to appeal for to ask for; *dringend um etwas bitten*

to go in reverse to go in the opposite direction; *in die umgekehrte Richtung gehen*

to issue an appeal *eine Aufforderung aussprechen*
alert warning
red alert *Alarmstufe Rot*
to emerge to appear

anxiety fear, worry
the Cold War the period of geopolitical tension after World War II between powers in the Eastern Bloc (the Soviet Union and its satellite states) and powers in the Western Bloc (the United States, its NATO allies and others), roughly covering the period between 1947 and 1991
xenophobia racism, hatred of foreigners; *Fremdenfeindlichkeit*

to settle conflicts to resolve conflicts
overcome hatred *Hass überwinden*

to urge to encourage, to demand; *mahnen, auffordern*

trust faith, belief, confidence; *Vertrauen*

Shokran. Xie Xie. Merci. Spasiba. Gracias. Obrigado Thank you in different languages. The first is Arabic, the second is Mandarin Chinese, the third is French, the fourth is Russian, the fifth is Spanish, and the last one is Portuguese.

We can settle conflicts, overcome hatred, and defend shared values.

But we can only do that together.

I urge leaders everywhere to make this New Year's resolution.

Narrow the gaps. Bridge the divides.

Rebuild trust by bringing people together around common goals.

Unity is the path. Our future depends on it.

I wish you peace and health in 2018.

Thank you. Shokran. Xie Xie. Merci. Spasiba. Gracias. Obrigado.

ASSIGNMENTS

A) Comprehension

▶ *cooperative learning / think - pair - share / reading dramatization / word cloud arrangement*

1. Create a word cloud featuring the most significant words from António Guterres's speech.
2. Read the speech aloud to your partner.
3. Briefly summarise Guterres's main arguments.

B) Analysis

▶ *cooperative learning / group work / peer support and feedback / writing an analysis / presentation*

1. Analyse the structure of the speech.
2. Examine the rhetorical devices which support Guterres's message.
3. Analyse the documentary clips in the video in some detail; examine the cinematic devices which are used to support António Guterres's message.

C) Evaluation, Comment, Creative Activities

▶ *group work / peer support and feedback / interview / creative writing / audio or video recording*

1. António Guterres addresses his speech to his "friends around the world". Is his speech powerful and effective? Explain your opinion.
2. Write an email to António Guterres in response to his speech.
3. Write an imagined interview with the United Nations' Secretary-General.
4. Create your own video addressed to your "friends around the world".
5. Write a fictional or non-fictional text - a poem, a short story, an essay, a speech to "Friends Around the World".
6. Poetry Slam: "Alert to the World"
   Organise a Poetry Slam Competition in response to António Guterres's speech.
7. António Guterres received the Charlemagne prize (Aachener Karlspreis) on May 30, 2019. Go online and read his speech: https://www.un.org/sg/en/content/sg/speeches/2019-05-30/address-international-charlemagne-prize-of-aachen-for-unity-of-europe

"At This Moment We All Face a Choice."

President Barack Obama's final UN Assembly address on September 20, 2016

RELATED TOPICS

ACHIEVEMENTS · THE COLD WAR · COMPASSION · CONFIDENCE · CONFLICT · DEMOCRACY · DIGNITY · DIPLOMACY · ECOLOGY · ECONOMY · EDUCATION · EXPLOITATION · FUTURE GENERATIONS · GLOBALIZATION · HEALTH · HOPE · HUMANITY · LIBERALISM · NATIONALISM · PEACE · POPULISM · POVERTY · REFUGEES · RESPONSIBILITY · STABILITY · TERRORISM · TRUST · THE UNITED NATIONS

President Barack Obama delivered his final address to the United Nations' General Assembly, calling on leaders to work together, and criticizing those who seek a "simple rejection of global integration." Speaking at the General Assembly at the United Nation's Headquarters in New York, outgoing US president Barack Obama made his last address in front of leaders and dignitaries from all over the world, and spoke out in favour of democracy, open market economies, and international law as "the firmest foundation for human progress in this century."
Barack Obama warned that the world faced an urgent choice between striving for fairer open markets and democracies, or falling prey to the lure of populist demagogues, xenophobia, and division.
"There appears to be a growing contest between authoritarianism and liberalism right now," Obama said. "Given the difficulty in forging true democracy in the face of these pressures, it's no surprise that some argue the future favours the strongman, a top-down model, rather than strong, democratic institutions." Read the inspirational excerpts from Barack Obama's speech.

Source: *The Guardian*
https://www.theguardian.com/world/2016/sep/20/barack-obama-final-un-assembly-address-democracy-liberalism

THE PRESIDENT Barack Obama:

Mr. President, Mr. Secretary General, fellow delegates, ladies and gentlemen: As I address this hall as President for the final time, let me recount the progress that we've made these last eight years.

to recount to report on

From the depths of the greatest financial crisis of our time, we coordinated our response to avoid further catastrophe, and to return the global economy to growth. We've taken away terrorist safe havens, strengthened the non-proliferation regime, and resolved the Iranian nuclear issue through diplomacy. We opened relations with Cuba, and we welcome a democratically elected leader of Myanmar to this Assembly. Our assistance is helping people to feed themselves, to care for the sick, to empower communities across Africa, and to promote models of development rather than dependence.

non-proliferation *Nicht-Weitergabe von Atomwaffen*
to resolve to find a solution to; *klären*
dependence *Abhängigkeit*

And we have made international institutions like the World Bank and the International Monetary Fund more representative, while establishing a framework to protect our planet from the ravages of climate change.

ravages destruction; *Verwüstung, verheerende Auswirkungen*

to expose to uncover
fault lines disturbances; *Verwerfungen*

in flight from to escape from
financial disruption financial breakdown, crisis; a reference to the financial crisis of 2008, and its consequences
to weigh upon *belasten*
vast swaths large areas
to muzzle (*here:*) to oppress
to quash to crush, to suppress
dissent opposition
to censor *zensieren*
to prey upon (*here:*) to manipulate; *einwirken auf*
to endanger to put at risk; *gefährden*
to spur *erzeugen/anfachen*
to contest (*here:*) to protest against
constraint restriction
by many measures *in vielerlei Hinsicht*
unease discomfort; *Unbehagen*
strife conflict, discord
to become quicker to develop openly and faster

to retreat into to return to

accountable governance *verlässliches Regierungshandeln*
to forge to build; *schmieden*

to enhance to strengthen

irreducible (*here:*) clear; *nicht reduzierbar, unverzichtbar*

This is important work. It has made a real difference in the lives of our people. And it could not have happened had we not worked together. And yet, around the globe, we are seeing the same forces of global integration that have made us interdependent also expose deep fault lines in the existing international order.

We see it in the headlines every day. Around the world, refugees flow across borders in flight from brutal conflict. Financial disruptions continue to weigh upon our workers and entire communities. Across vast swaths of the Middle East, basic security, basic order has broken down. We see too many governments muzzling journalists, and quashing dissent, and censoring the flow of information. Terrorist networks use social media to prey upon the minds of our youth, endangering open societies and spurring anger against innocent immigrants and Muslims. Powerful nations contest the constraints placed on them by international law.

This is the paradox that defines our world today. A quarter century after the end of the Cold War, the world is by many measures less violent and more prosperous than ever before, and yet our societies are filled with uncertainty, and unease, and strife. Despite enormous progress, as people lose trust in institutions, governing becomes more difficult and tensions between nations become more quick [*quicker*] to surface.

And so I believe that, at this moment, we all face a choice. We can choose to press forward with a better model of cooperation and integration. Or we can retreat into a world sharply divided, and ultimately in conflict, along age-old lines of nation and tribe, and race and religion.

I want to suggest to you today that we must go forward, and not backward. I believe that, as imperfect as they are, the principles of open markets, and accountable governance, of democracy, and human rights, and international law that we have forged remain the firmest foundation for human progress in this century. I make this argument not based on theory or ideology, but on facts – facts that all too often, we forget in the immediacy of current events. [...]

My own family is a made up of the flesh and blood, and traditions and cultures, and faiths from a lot of different parts of the world – just as America has been built by immigrants from every shore.

And in my own life, in this country, and as President, I have learned that our identities do not have to be defined by putting someone else down, but can be enhanced by lifting somebody else up. They don't have to be defined in opposition to others, but rather by a belief in liberty and equality, and justice and fairness. [...]

This is what I believe: that all of us can be co-workers with God. And our leadership, and our governments, and this United Nations, should reflect this irreducible truth. Thank you very much. (*Applause.*)

From: *The White House Archives*
https://obamawhitehouse.archives.gov/the-press-office/2014/09/24/remarks-president-obama-address-united-nations-general-assembly

ASSIGNMENTS

cooperative learning / think-pair-share / peer support and feedback / research / presentation / interview / pros and cons debate / speech / audio, video recording / SOLO taxonomy

A) Comprehension
1. Read the excerpts of Barack Obama's UN speech aloud to your partner.
2. Then highlight any significant keywords, and Obama's main arguments, on your speech transcript.
3. Summarize Barack Obama's main arguments.

B) Analysis
1. Analyse some of the rhetorical devices which Obama uses to support his message.
2. Examine Barack Obama's final appeal to the audience at the end of his speech.
3. Share your ideas, results and findings with the other groups.

C) Evaluation, Comment, Creative Writing
Choose one of the following assignments.
1. Write an article for an English newspaper in response to Obama's speech.
2. Imagine that you are Ambassador and Permanent Representative of Germany to the United Nations. Write a speech for the next UN Conference about peacekeeping in a world of conflicts.
3. Imagine you have been given the chance to interview the former US President Barack Obama. Ask him about current affairs across the world, and the role of the United Nations in them.
4. Compare Barack Obama's UN speech with Donald Trump or Theresa May's UN speeches.

D) Further Project: The United Nations – Its Purpose, Aims, Conflicts, Problems and Significance
1. What are the aims of the United Nations?
2. Can the United Nations get closer to achieving the promise of its founders: to make the world a better, more peaceful place?
3. Analyse the significance of the roles of the General Assembly and the UN Security Council.

E) Controversial Opinions About the United Nations

Ban Ki-Moon: "From the beginning of my time as Secretary-General, I have sought to advance a practical, action-oriented vision of the U.N. as the voice of the voiceless and the defender of the defenceless." [...] "Whether the issue is climate change – peace, security and human rights – or humanitarian relief – the United Nations has never been so needed. I believe we are at an inflection point in history. All is changing. The old rules are breaking down. We do not know what new order will emerge. Yet we can be confident: the United Nations will be at the fore."

Ban Ki-Moon, the eighth Secretary-General of the United Nations (2007–2016): Opening remarks at the end-of-year press conference on December 14, 2011. From *United Nations* website:
https://www.un.org/sg/en/content/sg/speeches/2011-12-14/opening-remarks-end-year-press-conference

John R. Bolton: In 1994, John R. Bolton remarked about the United Nations' Headquarters:
"The Secretariat Building in New York has 38 stories [*Stockwerke*]. If it lost 10 stories, it wouldn't make a bit of difference." In that same speech, he said: "There's no such thing as the United Nations."

https://www.democracynow.org/2005/3/31/john_bolton_in_his_own_words

John R. Bolton is a former ambassador to the United Nations. He is President Donald Trump's National Security Adviser.

Tasks:
1. Start a pros and cons debate or prepare and give a speech about the future role of the United Nations in response to Barack Obama, Ban Ki-Moon, and John R. Bolton's remarks.
2. Produce a video or podcast about the significance of the United Nations' role in current affairs across the world.

I Technology and the Digital Age: Will They Change Our Lives?

"You Are Graduating into a World That Needs Purpose. It's Up to You to Create It."

Mark Zuckerberg's speech at the Harvard University Commencement Ceremony on May 25, 2017

RELATED TOPICS

AUTOMATION · CITIZENS OF THE WORLD · COMMENCEMENT DAY · COMPUTERS · DEMOCRACY · THE DIGITAL AGE · DIGITALISATION · EDUCATION · ENTREPRENEURSHIP · EQUALITY · FACEBOOK · FUTURE GENERATIONS · HUMAN RIGHTS · INNOVATION · INVENTION · OPTIMISM · SOCIAL MEDIA · TECHNOLOGY · VISION

Mark Zuckerberg told graduating students at the Harvard University Commencement Ceremony on May 25, 2017 – the university he dropped out of to create Facebook – to create a purpose for today's world. In his speech, Zuckerberg promoted Facebook's mission of social connection, while also calling on the graduates to "create a world where everyone has a sense of purpose."
Mark Zuckerberg, who is the sixth richest person in the world, with an estimated wealth of $63.4 billion, dropped out of Harvard in 2005 to create Facebook. What started as a dorm room project to connect Harvard students is now a giant global company with a $446 billion market cap.
Now 33, Zuckerberg received an Honorary, "Doctor of Laws" degree from Harvard University before giving his speech. He posted a photo on Facebook of himself holding his degree certificate with his parents standing proudly behind him with the diploma with the caption: "Mom, I always told you I'd come back and get my degree."
"My top priority has always been our social mission of connecting people, building community, and bringing the world closer together." But Mark Zuckerberg conceded that Facebook didn't do enough until recently to police hate speech on the social media site, but he said that it has made progress and has heard the message "loud and clear".
Mark Zuckerberg appeared before the House Energy and Commerce Committee of the US Congress on April 11, 2018 for his second day of questioning on Capitol Hill to face a number of important issues around privacy, security, and democracy: "And you will rightfully have some hard questions for me to answer," he said. Watch the Commencement Address and read the speech transcripts.

Based on: https://www.biography.com/business-figure/mark-zuckerberg; https://www.thefamouspeople.com/profiles/mark-zuckerberg-6075.php; https://www.britannica.com/biography/Mark-Zuckerberg; https://www.theguardian.com/technology/mark-zuckerberg; https://www.independent.co.uk/life-style/gadgets-and-tech/features/facebook-15-birthday-social-network-online-media-platform-internet-mark-zuckerberg-a8758846.html; https://news.harvard.edu/gazette/story/2017/05/make-a-difference-zuckerberg-tells-harvard-graduates/

Mark Zuckerberg:

President Faust, Board of Overseers, faculty, alumni, friends, proud parents, members of the ad board, and graduates of the greatest university in the world,

I'm honored to be with you today because, let's face it, you accomplished something I never could. If I get through this speech, it'll be the first time I actually finish something at Harvard. Class of 2017, congratulations!

I'm an unlikely speaker, not just because I dropped out, but because we're technically in the same generation. We walked this yard less than a decade apart, studied the same ideas, and slept through the same Ec10 lectures. We may have taken different paths to get here, especially if you came all the way from the Quad, but today I want to share what I've learned about our generation, and the world we're building together.

But first, the last couple of days have brought back a lot of good memories.

How many of you remember exactly what you were doing when you got that email telling you that you got into Harvard? I was playing *Civilization* and I ran downstairs, got my dad, and for some reason, his reaction was to video me opening the email. That could have been a really sad video. I swear getting into Harvard is still the thing my parents are most proud of me for.

What about your first lecture at Harvard? Mine was Computer Science 121 with the incredible Harry Lewis. I was late so I threw on a T-shirt and didn't realize until afterwards it was inside out and backwards with my tag sticking out the front.

I couldn't figure out why no one would talk to me – except one guy, KX Jin, he just went with it. We ended up doing our problem sets together, and now he runs a big part of Facebook. And that, Class of 2017, is why you should be nice to people.

But my best memory from Harvard was meeting Priscilla. I had just launched this prank website Facemash, and the ad board wanted to "see me". Everyone thought I was going to get kicked out. My parents came to help me pack. My friends threw me a going away party. As luck would have it, Priscilla was at that party with her friend. We met in line for the bathroom in the Pfoho Belltower, and in what must be one of the most romantic lines of all-time, I said: "I'm going to get kicked out in three days, so we need to go on a date quickly."
Actually, any of you graduating can use that line.

alumni former students; *Ehemalige*

ad board administrative board

to accomplish to achieve; Zuckerberg famously dropped out of Harvard in 2005 to work on Facebook full time. On May 25, 2017, 12 years later, he received an Honorary Degree from Harvard

unlikely speaker someone who you wouldn't have thought would be chosen to speak at the event

to drop out *vorzeitig ausscheiden*

Quad a quadrangle (or colloquially, a quad) is a courtyard

to realize (*AmE*), realise (*BrE*), to notice, to become aware of; *bemerken, merken*

tag *Etikett*

KX Jin Kang-Xing Jin studied Computer Science at Harvard, where he met Mark Zuckerberg; Jin and Zuckerberg took several classes together. Zuckerberg left Harvard in 2005 to focus on growing Facebook; Jin stayed to complete his degree, graduating *summa cum laude* in 2006.

he just went with it he didn't mind, he just got on with it

Priscilla Priscilla Chan, who is now Mark Zuckerberg's wife

Facemash was a Harvard version of "Hot or Not" that used photos from students' school profiles (called facebooks) and ranked users based on their attractiveness. Zuckerberg faced disciplinary action for creating Facemash.

I didn't end up getting kicked out – I did that to myself. Priscilla and I started dating. And, you know, that movie made it seem like Facemash was so important to creating Facebook. It wasn't. But without Facemash I wouldn't have met Priscilla, and she's the most important person in my life, so you could say it was the most important thing I built in my time here.

that movie a reference to the 2010 film *The Social Network*, in which Zuckerberg was played by Jesse Eisenberg. The film showed Facemash as the precursor [*Vorgänger*] of Facebook. Zuckerberg has said, that the film was "hurtful".

We've all started lifelong friendships here, and some of us even families. That's why I'm so grateful to this place. Thanks, Harvard.

THE CHALLENGE FOR OUR GENERATION IS CREATING A WORLD WHERE EVERYONE HAS A SENSE OF PURPOSE

Today, I want to talk about purpose. But I'm not here to give you the standard commencement about finding your purpose. We're millennials. We'll try to do that instinctively. Instead, I'm here to tell you finding your purpose isn't enough. The challenge for our generation is creating a world where everyone has a sense of purpose.

purpose meaning, significant aim , sense of life
millennials a term used to describe people reaching young adulthood by the early 21st century. Zuckerberg is 33, the youngest person ever to deliver a Harvard Commencement speech. Many of the Harvard students graduating will be 22. So instead of giving advice from one generation to the next, he's explaining how young people (like him) should live their lives.
janitor caretaker; *Hausmeister*

One of my favorite stories is when John F Kennedy visited the NASA space center, he saw a janitor carrying a broom and he walked over and asked what he was doing. The janitor responded: "Mr. President, I'm helping put a man on the moon."

Purpose is that sense that we are part of something bigger than ourselves, that we are needed, that we have something better ahead to work for. Purpose is what creates true happiness.

You're graduating at a time when this is especially important. When our parents graduated, purpose reliably came from your job, your church, your community. But today, technology and automation are eliminating many jobs. Membership in communities is declining. Many people feel disconnected and depressed, and are trying to fill a void.

void *Leere*

As I've traveled around, I've sat with children in juvenile detention, and opioid addicts, who told me their lives could have turned out differently if they just had something to do, an after-school program, or somewhere to go. I've met factory workers who know their old jobs aren't coming back and are trying to find their place.

juvenile detention *Jugendstrafanstalt*
opioid addicts people who are addicted to opioids, i.e. morphine, hydrocodone, oxycodone, heroin (an illegal opioid drug), etc.; Zuckerberg is referring to certain areas of the country that have been "left behind" by the modern job market and globalization which tend to be hit the hardest by the opioid addiction epidemic.

To keep our society moving forward, we have a generational challenge – to not only create new jobs, but to create a renewed sense of purpose.

generational challenge a challenge that a particular generation has to deal with, a challenge that defines a certain generation

I remember the night I launched Facebook from my little dorm in Kirkland House. I went to Noch's with my friend KX. I remember

dorm a colloquial abbreviation of dormitory; *Studentenwohnheim* telling him I was excited to connect the Harvard community, but one day someone would connect the whole world.

The thing is, it never even occurred to me that that someone might be us. We were just college kids. We didn't know anything about that. There were all these big technology companies with resources. I just assumed one of them would do it. But this idea was so clear to us – that all people want to connect. So we just kept moving forward, day by day. I know a lot of you will have your own stories just like this. A change in the world that seems so clear you're sure someone else will do it. But they won't. You will.

BUT IT'S NOT ENOUGH TO HAVE PURPOSE YOURSELF. YOU HAVE TO CREATE A SENSE OF PURPOSE FOR OTHERS.

But it's not enough to have purpose yourself. You have to create a sense of purpose for others. I found that out the hard way. You see, my hope was never to build a company, but to make an impact. And as all these people started joining us, I just assumed that's what they cared about too, so I never explained what I hoped we'd build.

to make an impact to have an influence (on the world)

A couple years in, some big companies wanted to buy us. I didn't want to sell. I wanted to see if we could connect more people. We were building the first News Feed, and I thought if we could just launch this, it could change how we learn about the world.

a couple [of] years in a few years after [we launched/started Facebook]; *nach ein paar Jahren*

Nearly everyone else wanted to sell. Without a sense of higher purpose, this was the start-up dream come true. It tore our company apart. After one tense argument, an advisor told me if I didn't agree to sell, I would regret the decision for the rest of my life. Relationships were so frayed that within a year or so every single person on the management team was gone. That was my hardest time leading Facebook. I believed in what we were doing, but I felt alone. And worse, it was my fault. I wondered if I was just wrong, an imposter, a 22 year-old kid who had no idea how the world worked.

everyone else wanted to sell Zuckerberg rejected multiple offers from people who wanted to buy his company but some of his co-workers wanted to sell it

frayed (*here:*) damaged, shattered, tense

imposter poser, phony, pretender

Now, years later, I understand that *is* how things work with no sense of higher purpose. It's up to us to create it so we can all keep moving forward together. Today, I want to talk about three ways to create a world where everyone has a sense of purpose: by taking on big meaningful projects together, by redefining equality so everyone has the freedom to pursue purpose, and by building community across the world.

First, let's take on big meaningful projects.

Our generation will have to deal with tens of millions of jobs being replaced by automation like self-driving cars and trucks. But we have the potential to do so much more together.

Every generation has its defining works. More than 300,000 people worked to put a man on the moon – including that janitor. Millions of volunteers immunized children around the world against polio. Millions of more people built the Hoover dam and other great projects. These projects didn't just provide purpose for the people doing those jobs, they gave our whole country a sense of pride that we could do great things.

to immunize (*AmE*), to immunise (*BrE*), to vaccinate; *immunisieren, impfen*
polio polio is an infectious disease commonly associated with children, though it can affect people of any age; polio has been eradicated across most of the world through vaccination programmes, which are recommended to this day; *Kinderlähmung*
the Hoover Dam is a concrete dam in the Black Canyon of the Colorado River, on the border between the U.S. states of Nevada and Arizona

Now it's our turn to do great things. I know, you're probably thinking: I don't know how to build a dam, or how to get a million people involved in anything.

IDEAS DON'T COME OUT FULLY FORMED. THEY ONLY BECOME CLEAR AS YOU WORK ON THEM.

But let me tell you a secret: no one does when they begin. Ideas don't come out fully formed. They only become clear as you work on them. You just have to get started.

If I had understood everything about connecting people before I began, I never would have started Facebook.

Movies and pop culture get this all wrong. The idea of a single eureka moment is a dangerous lie. It makes us feel inadequate since we haven't had ours. It prevents people with seeds of good ideas from getting started. Oh, you know what else movies get wrong about innovation? No one writes math formulas on glass. That's not a thing.

eureka moment or eureka effect refers to the experience of suddenly understanding a complex (previously incomprehensible) problem
formulas on glass one of the scenes in *The Social Network* features a scene in which Facebook co-founder Eduardo Saverin is writing the algorithm for Facemash on a window.

ANYONE WORKING ON A BIG VISION WILL GET CALLED CRAZY, EVEN IF YOU END UP RIGHT.

It's good to be idealistic. But be prepared to be misunderstood. Anyone working on a big vision will get called crazy, even if you end up right. Anyone working on a complex problem will get blamed for not fully understanding the challenge, even though it's impossible to know everything upfront. Anyone taking initiative will get criticized for moving too fast, because there's always someone who wants to slow you down.

to criticize (*AmE*), to criticise (*BrE*); *kritisieren*

WE'RE SO AFRAID OF MAKING MISTAKES

In our society, we often don't do big things because we're so afraid of making mistakes that we ignore all the things wrong today and we do nothing. The reality is, anything we do will have issues in the future. But that can't keep us from starting.

issues (*here:*) consequences

So what are we waiting for? It's time for our generation defining public works. How about stopping climate change before we destroy the planet by getting millions of people involved manufacturing and installing solar panels? How about curing all diseases and asking volunteers to track their health data and share their genomes? Today we spend 50x more treating people who are sick than we spend finding cures so people don't get sick in the first place. That makes no sense. We can fix this. How about modernizing democracy so everyone can vote online, and personalizing education so everyone can learn?

to modernize (*AmE*), modernise (*BrE*); *modernisieren*
to personalize (*AmE*), personalise (*BrE*), to individualize; *personalisieren*

These achievements are within our reach. Let's do them all in a way that gives everyone in our society a role. Let's do big things, not only to create progress, but to create purpose.

So taking on big meaningful projects is the first thing we can do to create a world where everyone has a sense of purpose.

The second is redefining equality to give everyone the freedom they need to pursue purpose.

Many of our parents had stable jobs throughout their careers. Now we're all entrepreneurial, whether we're starting projects or finding our role. And that's great. Our culture of entrepreneurship is how we create so much progress.

entrepreneurial enterprising, exploring new ideas, business models and opportunities
entrepreneurship enterprise, new business development; *Unternehmertum*

Now, an entrepreneurial culture thrives when it's easy to try lots of new ideas. Facebook wasn't the first thing I built. I also built games, chat systems, study tools, and music players. I'm not alone. JK Rowling got rejected 12 times before publishing *Harry Potter*. Even Beyoncé had to make hundreds of songs to get *Halo*. The greatest successes come from having the freedom to fail.

to thrive to flourish, to succeed, to boom

But today, we have a level of wealth inequality that hurts everyone. When you don't have the freedom to take your idea and turn it into a historic enterprise, we all lose. Right now our society is way over-indexed on rewarding success and we don't do nearly enough to make it easy for everyone to take lots of shots.

our society is way over-indexed on rewarding success our society focuses on rewarding success
to take lots of shots to try lots of times

Let's face it. There is something wrong with our system when I can leave here and make billions of dollars in 10 years while millions of students can't afford to pay off their loans, let alone start a business.

loans *Studiendarlehen*

Look, I know a lot of entrepreneurs, and I don't know a single person who gave up on starting a business because they might not make

entrepreneurs people who start their own business

cushion (*here:*) safety net

enough money. But I know lots of people who haven't pursued dreams because they didn't have a cushion to fall back on if they failed.

We all know we don't succeed just by having a good idea or by working hard. We succeed by being lucky too. If I had had to support my family growing up instead of having time to code, if I didn't know I'd be fine if Facebook didn't work out, I wouldn't be standing here today. If we're honest, we all know how much luck we've had.

NOW IT'S OUR TIME TO DEFINE A NEW SOCIAL CONTRACT FOR OUR GENERATION

New Deal, the domestic program of the administration of President Franklin D. Roosevelt between 1933 and 1939; *see* ADDITIONAL NOTES
Great Society a political slogan used by US President Lyndon B. Johnson (served 1963–69) to define his legislative program of national reform.
GDP gross domestic product; *Bruttoinlandsprodukt*
universal basic income the establishment of an unconditional basic income; *bedingungsloses Grundeinkommen*
locking us up putting us in prison
to stigmatize (*AmE*), stigmatise (*BrE*), to label somebody, to judge somebody, *brandmarken, stigmatisieren*

Every generation expands its definition of equality. Previous generations fought for the vote and for civil rights. They had the New Deal and the Great Society. Now it's our time to define a new social contract for our generation.

We should have a society that measures progress not just by economic metrics like GDP, but by how many of us have a role we find meaningful. We should explore ideas like universal basic income to give everyone a cushion to try new things. We're going to change jobs many times, so we need affordable childcare to get to work and healthcare that aren't tied to one company. We're all going to make mistakes, so we need a society that focuses less on locking us up or stigmatizing us. And, as technology keeps changing, we need to focus more on continuous education throughout our lives.

And yes, giving everyone the freedom to pursue purpose isn't free. People like me should pay for it. Many of you will do well and you should too.

The Chan Zuckerberg Initiative a project started by Mark Zuckerberg and Priscilla Chan, which focuses on science, education and engineering, on advancing human potential, and on promoting equal opportunities: https://chanzuckerberg.com/

That's why Priscilla and I started the Chan Zuckerberg Initiative and committed our wealth to promoting equal opportunity. These are the values of our generation. It was never a question of if we were going to do this. The only question was when.

Millennials are already one of the most charitable generations in history. In one year, three of four US millennials made a donation and seven out of ten raised money for charity.

But it's not just about money. You can also give time. I promise you, if you take an hour or two a week – that's all it takes to give someone a hand, to help them reach their potential.

Maybe you think that's too much time. I used to. When Priscilla graduated from Harvard she became a teacher, and before she'd do education work with me, she told me I needed to teach a class. I complained: "Well, I'm kind of busy. I'm running this company." But she insisted, so I taught a middle school program on Entrepreneurship at the local Boys and Girls Club.

I taught them lessons on product development and marketing, and they taught me what it's like feeling targeted for your race and having a family member in prison. I shared stories from my time in school, and they shared their hope of one day going to college too. For five years now, I've been having dinner with those kids every month. One of them threw me and Priscilla our first baby shower. And next year they're going to college. Every one of them. First in their families.

our first baby shower a reference to the American custom of throwing a party for expectant parents where they are given gifts of clothing, equipment etc., which the baby will need when it's born

We can all make time to give someone a hand. Let's give everyone the freedom to pursue their purpose – not only because it's the right thing to do, but because when more people can turn their dreams into something great, we're all better for it.

Purpose doesn't only come from work.

The third way we can create a sense of purpose for everyone is by building community. And when our generation says "everyone", we mean everyone in the world.

Quick show of hands: how many of you are from another country? Now, how many of you are friends with one of these folks? Now we're talking. We have grown up connected.

CITIZENS OF THE WORLD

In a survey asking millennials around the world what defines our identity, the most popular answer wasn't nationality, religion or ethnicity, it was "citizen of the world". That's a big deal. Every generation expands the circle of people we consider "one of us". For us, it now encompasses the entire world.

ethnicity ethnic origin

We understand the great arc of human history bends towards people coming together in ever greater numbers – from tribes to cities to nations – to achieve things we couldn't on our own. We get that our greatest opportunities are now global – we can be the generation that ends poverty that ends disease. We get that our greatest challenges need global responses too – no country can fight climate change alone or prevent pandemics. Progress now requires coming together not just as cities or nations, but also as a global community.

the great arc of the broad narrative of

pandemic epidemic (of disease)

But we live in an unstable time. There are people left behind by globalization across the world. It's hard to care about people in other places if we don't feel good about our lives here at home. There's pressure to turn inwards.

This is the struggle of our time. The forces of freedom, openness and global community against the forces of authoritarianism, isolationism and nationalism. Forces for the flow of knowledge, trade, and immigration against those who would slow them down. This is not a battle of nations, it's a battle of ideas. There are people in every country for global connection and good people against it.

This isn't going to be decided at the UN either. It's going to happen at the local level, when enough of us feel a sense of purpose and stability in our own lives that we can open up and start caring about everyone. The best way to do that is to start building local communities right now. We all get meaning from our communities. Whether our communities are houses or sports teams, churches or music groups, they give us that sense that we are part of something bigger, that we are not alone; they give us the strength to expand our horizons.

That's why it's so striking that, for decades, membership in all kinds of groups has declined as much as one-quarter. That's a lot of people who now need to find purpose somewhere else. But I know we can rebuild our communities, and start new ones, because many of you already are. I met Agnes Igoye, who's graduating today. Where are you, Agnes? She spent her childhood navigating conflict zones in Uganda, and now she trains thousands of law enforcement officers to keep communities safe.

I met Kayla Oakley and Niha Jain, graduating today, too. Stand up. Kayla and Niha started a non-profit that connects people suffering from illnesses with people in their communities willing to help. I met David Razu Aznar, graduating from the Kennedy School today. David, stand up. He's a former city councilor who successfully led the battle to make Mexico City the first Latin American city to pass marriage equality – even before San Francisco.

marriage equality the term for giving same-sex couples equal marriage rights

This is my story too. A student in a dorm room, connecting one community at a time, and keeping at it until one day we connect the whole world. Change starts local. Even global changes start small – with people like us. In our generation, the struggle of whether we connect more, whether we achieve our biggest opportunities, comes down to this – your ability to build communities and to create a world where every single person has a sense of purpose.

Class of 2017, you are graduating into a world that needs purpose. It's up to you to create it. Now, you may be thinking: Can I really do this? Remember when I told you about that class I taught at the Boys and Girls' Club? One day after class I was talking to them about college, and one of my top students raised his hand and said he wasn't sure he could go because he's undocumented. He didn't know if they'd let him in. Last year I took him out to breakfast for his birthday. I wanted

undocumented lacking immigration papers

to get him a present, so I asked him and he started talking about students he saw struggling and said: "You know, I'd really just like a book on social justice."

I was blown away. Here's a young guy who has every reason to be cynical. He didn't know if the country he calls home – the only one he's known – would deny him his dream of going to college. But he wasn't feeling sorry for himself. He wasn't even thinking of himself. He has a greater sense of purpose, and he's going to bring people along with him.

I was blown away I was very surprised

It says something about our current situation that I can't even say his name because I don't want to put him at risk. But if a high school senior who doesn't know what the future holds can do his part to move the world forward, then we owe it to the world to do our part too.

Before you walk out those gates one last time, as we sit in front of Memorial Church, I am reminded of a prayer, Mi Shebeirach, that I say whenever I face a challenge that I sing to my daughter when thinking about her future when I tuck her into bed. It goes:

Mi Shebeirach a Jewish prayer or blessing for an individual or group, most often recited in a synagogue when the Torah is being read; there is a lot of room for improvisation regarding whom to bless or how they can be blessed

"May the source of strength, who blessed the ones before us, help us *find the courage* to make our lives a blessing."

I hope you find the courage to make your life a blessing.
Congratulations, Class of '17! Good luck out there.

Facebook CEO, Harvard Dropout Mark Zuckerberg posted the speech he delivered for the Harvard University graduation on May 25, 2017 to his Facebook page. https://www.facebook.com/notes/mark-zuckerberg/harvard-commencement-2017/10154853758606634/

ASSIGNMENTS

A) Pre-Listening and Pre-Reading Activities

▶ *warm-up / inside-outside circle / market place: milling around / walking & talking / speed debating*

Discuss the following statements with different partners. Use the "inside-outside circle" brainstorming technique or the "market place: milling around / walking & talking" method.

1. "Global changes start small."
2. "Social media supports global communication."
3. "Technology and automation eliminate jobs."
4. "Facebook is a social network, not a diary."

B) Comprehension

paired work / peer support and feedback / mind map / writing a newspaper report / presentation

1. Watch the video of Mark Zuckerberg's speech on YouTube: https://www.youtube.com/watch?v=7KO-4t_v2to
2. Read the speech transcript and highlight the important keywords and statements.
3. How does Mark Zuckerberg start his speech?
4. Explain the three "senses of purpose" Zuckerberg emphasises. Present his ideas in a mind map.
5. Write a comprehensive report on his speech for your school newspaper.

C) Analysis

1. Analyse the structure of Mark Zuckerberg's speech.
2. Point out the function of the introduction of Zuckerberg's speech.
3. Examine the most important rhetorical devices Zuckerberg uses and their intended effects.
4. Analyse the tone of the speech.
5. Point out the significance of the ending of Mark Zuckerberg's speech.

D) Evaluation, Comment, Creative Writing

individual work / group work / peer support and feedback / research / debate / role play / hot seat / interview / speech / essay writing / Speakers' Corner / evaluation / SOLO taxonomy

1. Mark Zuckerberg remarks that "purpose is what creates true happiness." Comment on his statement and give your own opinion of it.
2. "Let's face it. There is something wrong with our system when I can leave here and make billions of dollars in 10 years while millions of students can't afford to pay off their loans, let alone start a business." What do you think about his suggestion to tax rich people more?
3. "Change starts local. Even global changes start small. In our generation, the struggle of whether we connect more, whether we achieve our biggest opportunities, comes down to this – your ability to build communities and create a world where every single person has a sense of purpose." What kind of local project would you start? Prepare and give a three-minute speech on it.
4. "Ideas don't come out fully formed. They only become clear as you work on them. You just have to get started. [...] The idea of a single eureka moment is a dangerous lie." What do you think of this statement?
5. "Our generation will have to deal with tens of millions of jobs replaced by automation like self-driving cars and trucks. But we have the potential to do so much more together." Experts believe that one in three jobs will be replaced by robots over the next two decades. Most people would fear this, but Zuckerberg is trying to present it as an opportunity. What is your opinion of this prediction?
6. "It's good to be idealistic. But be prepared to be misunderstood. Anyone working on a big vision will get called crazy, even if you end up right. [...] Anyone taking initiative will get criticized for moving too fast, because there's always someone who wants to slow you down." Evaluate the validity of these statements and give an example from your own personal experience.
7. "And as technology keeps changing, we need a society that focuses more on continuous education throughout our lives." Why is continuous education and life-long learning so important?
8. "This is the struggle of our time. The forces of freedom, openness and global community against the forces of authoritarianism, isolationism and nationalism. [...] This is not a battle of nations, it's a battle of ideas." Prepare and give a three-minute speech in which you explain your own opinion of this statement.
9. "Some people need to realize that Facebook is a social network, not a diary." Prepare and give a three-minute speech in response to this statement.

10. "The Internet is the largest tattooing machine, and, unfortunately for people who are learning this the hard way, there is no rewind button on the Internet, either." Prepare and give a three-minute speech in response to this statement.
11. "A Facebook drama": Invent and write a creative, imaginative, inspiring short story or a one-act play using "a Facebook drama" as your prompt.

E) Further Project: For Thought and Discussion

paired work / peer support and feedback / debate / discussion / speech / writing a comment

Tasks:

1. Go online and find out how Mark Zuckerberg commented on the topic of hate speech. Take notes and share your notes with a partner.
2. Imagine that you are Mark Zuckerberg. Prepare and give a speech entitled "Hate speech has no place on Facebook".
3. Watch the speech Mark Zuckerberg gave at Berlin, Townhall (Q&A, Berlin), on February 26, 2016.
   Short version: https://www.theguardian.com/technology/2016/feb/26/mark-zuckerberg-hate-speech-germany-facebook-refugee-crisis
   Long version: https://www.youtube.com/watch?v=FLauyFMf6og Please select some interesting Q&A parts.
4. Compare your speech to Mark Zuckerberg's speech and describe their similarities and differences.

F) "We didn't take a broad enough view of our responsibility, and that was a big mistake."

1. Information: [...] Zuckerberg has faced rising pressure to account for how Cambridge Analytica obtained data on millions of users, with a whistleblower alleging that the consulting firm put that information to use for Donald Trump's presidential campaign in seeking to [...] target and sway voters. Cambridge Analytica denies such information was used during the presidential campaign. [...] Zuckerberg [said] that the scandal was a "breach of trust" between the platform and its users. [...]
From: *Independent*, March 21, 2018, https://www.independent.co.uk/news/world/americas/mark-zuckerberg-statement-response-cambridge-analytica-a8267551.html

2. Mark Zuckerberg appeared before the House Energy and Commerce Committee of the US Congress on Wednesday, April 11, 2018 for his second day of questioning on Capitol Hill. Here is a transcript of Zuckerberg's introductory statement.
Transcript courtesy of Bloomberg Government April 11, 2018.
From: *The Washington Post*, April 11, 2018, https://www.washingtonpost.com/news/the-switch/wp/2018/04/11/transcript-of-zuckerbergs-appearance-before-house-committee/?utm_term=.1b3c8c8f7101

Mark Zuckerberg:

"Chairman Walden [*Representative Greg Walden, member of the Republican Party – Oregon*], Ranking Member [*Frank*] Pallone [*U.S. Representative for New Jersey and member of the Democratic Party*] and members of the committee, we face a number of important issues around privacy, security, and democracy. And you will rightfully have some hard questions for me to answer.

Before I talk about the steps we're taking to address them, I want to talk for a minute about how we got there. Facebook is an idealistic and optimistic company. For most of our existence, we focused on all the good that connecting people can bring.

And, as Facebook has grown, people everywhere have gotten a powerful new tool for staying connected to the people they care about most, for making their voices heard, and for building community and businesses.

Just recently, we've seen the "Me Too" movement and the March for Our Lives organized, at least in part,

on Facebook. After Hurricane Harvey, people came together and raised more than $20 million for relief. And there are more than 70 million small businesses around the world that use our tools to grow and create jobs.
But it's clear now that we didn't do enough to prevent these tools from being used for harm, as well. And that goes for fake news, foreign interference in elections and hate speech, as well as developers and data privacy. We didn't take a broad enough view of our responsibility, and that was a big mistake.
It was my mistake, and I am sorry. I started Facebook, I run it, and, at the end of the day, I am responsible for what happens here. So, now, we have to go through every part of our relationship with people to make sure that we're taking a broad enough view of our responsibility.
It's not enough to just connect people. We have to make sure those connections are positive. It's not enough to just give people a voice. We need to make sure that voice isn't used to harm other people or to spread misinformation. And it's not enough to just give people control of their information. We need to make sure that the developers that they share it with protect their information too. Across the board, we have a responsibility to not just give people tools, but to make sure that those tools are used for good. [...]
My top priority has always been our social mission of connecting people, building community, and bringing the world closer together. Advertisers and developers will never take priority over that for as long as I am running Facebook. I started Facebook when I was in college. We've come a long way since then. We now serve more than 2 billion people around the world, and, every day, people use our services to stay connected with the people that matter to them most. I believe deeply in what we're doing, and I know that, when we address these challenges, we'll look back and view helping people connect, and giving more people a voice as a positive force in the world. [...]

Tasks:

A) Comprehension

1. Read the transcript and highlight any important statements.
2. Outline Mark Zuckerberg's view of Facebook and the challenges it faces.

B) Analysis

1. Analyse how Mark Zuckerberg expresses his opinions. Focus on his use of rhetorical devices and communicative strategies.
2. *Cartoons on Facebook:* Work in small groups, go online and find an interesting and thought-provoking cartoon on the topic of "Facebook / Social Media". Describe, analyse and evaluate the cartoon.
3. Analyse the way the cartoonist (you have chosen), and Mark Zuckerberg try to convince their audiences of their respective views.

C) Evaluation, Comment, Creative Writing

1. Mark Zuckerberg points out: "My top priority has always been our social mission of connecting people, building community and bringing the world closer together." Would you agree or disagree with this statement? Explain your own point of view.
2. Discuss Zuckerberg's views concerning social media and the digital age. Refer to his speech, and to the work you have already done in class.
3. Imagine you were a member of the US Congress questioning Mark Zuckerberg in the hearing. What questions would you ask him? What answers would you expect him to give you?
4. Evaluate the significance of social media in a digital world. Consider your own experiences.
5. Imagine you are taking part in a panel discussion on visions for the digital future.

D) Further Projects: For Thought and Discussion

individual work / paired work / research / presentation / interview / role play / discussion / speech

1. How can personal data be protected in the digital age?
2. "Facebook and other social media providers take privacy issues seriously now." Would you agree or disagree with this statement? Explain your own point of view.
3. How can schools teach young people to use social media more responsibly? Prepare and give a three-minute speech in which you respond to this question.
4. Evaluate Mark Zuckerberg's statements in the context of the General Data Protection Regulation (GDPR) within the EU. How might the GDPR change the dynamic of how Facebook handles its users' data?
5. "Digitisation means being connected. Democracy, however, means being conjoined. In a democracy, we need each other in a deeper, a more political sense than merely by "likes" or "dislikes"." Federal President Frank-Walter Steinmeier at re:publica 2019, in Berlin on May 6, 2019, https://www.bundespraesident.de/SharedDocs/Downloads/DE/Reden/2019/05/190506-Republica-Englisch.pdf?__blob=publicationFile

E) Mediation (German = > English)

Der Billionen-Club: The "Big Five" – Freunde oder Feinde?

Von Catherine Hoffmann, *Süddeutsche Zeitung* vom 4./5. August 2018, Seite 1
https://www.sueddeutsche.de/wirtschaft/internet-konzerne-freunde-oder-feinde-1.4080496

Apple ist als erstes amerikanisches Unternehmen an der Börse mehr als eine Billion Dollar wert. Das ist eine Zahl mit zwölf Nullen und deutlich mehr, als die zehn größten deutschen Dax-Unternehmen zusammen wert sind. Der iPhone-Hersteller führt damit einen Boom von Technologie-Firmen an, deren Produkte aus dem täglichen Leben nicht mehr wegzudenken sind.

2008 hießen die größten US-Konzerne Exxon Mobil, General Electric, Microsoft, Walmart und Procter & Gamble. Zehn Jahre später ist die Welt eine andere: Apple, Amazon, die Google-Mutter Alphabet, Microsoft und Facebook sind die fünf wertvollsten US-Firmen. In den USA werden sie „Big Five" genannt. Das passiert immer dann, wenn eine Branche so groß wird, dass sie politischen Druck auf die Gesellschaft ausüben kann, etwa um Steuerzahlungen zu optimieren. [...]

Doch bislang konnten weder eine strengere Regulierung noch abschätzige Bemerkungen einstiger IT-Manager die Faszination mindern, die iPhones, Online-Shopping und soziale Netzwerke bei Konsumenten und Anlegern auslösen.

Dabei ist das Sündenregister der Big Five lang. Sie werden beschuldigt, den Wettbewerb zu unterdrücken, Steuern zu vermeiden, in die Privatsphäre einzudringen und die Demokratie zu untergraben. Die bloße Größe der digitalen Quasi-Monopole ist ebenso beängstigend wie das beispiellose Ausmaß und die Geschwindigkeit, mit der sie persönliche Daten sammeln und in Vorhersage-Algorithmen umwandeln.

So schaffen sie eine allwissende, undurchsichtige Maschinerie, die das Fundament der Demokratie zu erodieren drohe, wie die amerikanischen Wissenschaftler Moran Cerf, Sandra Matz und Guy Rolnik befürchten. Sie warnen davor, dass die fünf einen Großteil der Aufmerksamkeit kontrollieren, diktieren, welche Nachrichten wahrgenommen werden, und durch Werbung Verhaltensweisen beeinflussen.

Dennoch sind Apple, Google und Facebook äußerst beliebt, die Menschen kommen nicht los von den schicken Handys, der sensationell guten Suchmaschine, dem Klatsch auf Netzwerken. Selbst Experten sind verwirrt. Sind diese Firmen unsere Freunde oder Feinde?

Ökonomen wie David Dorn ("Der Aufstieg der Superstar-Firmen") haben in ihren Studien dokumentiert, wie stark die Marktmacht der großen Konzerne gewachsen ist. Ergebnis: Die Dominanz der Tech Five ist erdrückend. Sie beherrschen die wichtigsten Zukunftsmärkte mit Marktanteilen von teils mehr als 90 Prozent. Amazon kontrolliert zwei Drittel des Online-Buchhandels, Google 90 Prozent des Suchmaschinenmarktes, Facebook 75 Prozent der mobilen Kommunikation.

Tasks:

1. Point out the main arguments in English.
2. A Role Play: Work in groups.
   a) Imagine that you are "Big Five" Managing Directors defending the companies' policy.
   b) Imagine that you are journalists criticizing the threats of digital monopolies and the dominance of the "Big Five".
3. The "Big Five" – our friends or our foes?

"The Foothills of the Digital Age."

Matt Hancock MP, Secretary of State for Digital Culture, Media and Sport: Speech at *The Times* and *The Sunday Times*' Tech Summit on November 15, 2017

RELATED TOPICS

ARTIFICIAL INTELLIGENCE · COMPUTER SCIENCE · CHANGE · CYBER CRIMES · DATA PROTECTION · DIGITALISATION · THE DIGITAL AGE · DIGITAL MEDIA · DIGITISED SERVICES · DIGITAL STRATEGY · EDUCATION · ENTREPRENEURS · THE FUTURE · FUTURE GENERATIONS · THE GLOBAL ECONOMY · INNOVATION · INTERNET SAFETY · LEARNING · SCHOOLS · TECHNOLOGY · SHARED VALUES

Matt Hancock MP (born October 2, 1978) is a British Conservative Party politician. He was first elected as the Member of Parliament for West Suffolk in the 2010 General Election.

He was appointed Secretary of State for Digital Culture, Media and Sport (DCMS) on January 8, 2018. He was previously the State Minister for Digital Culture from July 2016 to January 2018, a role in which he was responsible for broadband, broadcasting, creative industries, cyber security and the tech industry.

Before entering politics, Matt Hancock worked for his family business, as an economist at the Bank of England, and as Chief of Staff to the Shadow Chancellor of the Exchequer. He has a Bachelor's degree in Politics, Philosophy, and Economics (PPE) from the University of Oxford, and a Master's degree in Economics from the University of Cambridge.

The Secretary of State for Digital Culture, Media and Sport has overall responsibility for strategy and policy across the Department for Digital Culture, Media and Sport.

The department's main policy areas are: culture and the arts, broadcasting, creative industries, cultural property, heritage and historical sites/monuments, libraries, media ownership, museums and galleries, sport, telecommunications, online services, and tourism.

In his speech at *The Times* and *The Sunday Times*' Tech Summit, Matt Hancock describes the challenges of the digital age.

From: *GOV.UK 7* https://www.gov.uk/government/people/matthew-hancock
Speech at The Times and The Sunday Times Tech Summit 2017
https://www.gov.uk/government/speeches/the-foothills-of-the-digital-age (published November 15, 2017)
From: *Department for Digital, Culture, Media & Sport* and *The Rt Hon Matt Hancock MP*
Delivered on: November 15, 2017 (Transcript of the speech, exactly as it was delivered)

Matt Hancock:

Section 1 / Group 1 / heading: ______________________________

Thank you for inviting me to this Tech Summit.

The word summit of course has two popular meanings. There's a gathering such as this, and then there's the peak – the zenith, the apex, the apogee - the highest point that can be reached. When it comes to tech, and to digital technology, we are very far from the summit of what can be achieved. Indeed, we are only beginning to even glimpse the potential of where digital technologies might take us, and how much they will transform our world.

These are very much the foothills, and now we must be ready for the climb. Policy making is always as much about anticipating and preparing for the future as it is with addressing current issues. Our Digital Strategy, published in March of this year, set out how we intend to make the UK the best place to establish and grow a digital business and the safest place for citizens to be online. That means today, but also in the future, so we are ready for the changes ahead. It established seven pillars that underpin the changes we need to see and I'd like to update you now on the impressive progress that, just eight months in, we have already made.

The first pillar, and central to everything, is infrastructure. In the Digital Strategy we committed to building a world-class digital infrastructure for the UK. That means ubiquitous coverage, so no one is left out, and with sufficient capacity not only for today's needs but in readiness for tomorrow. [...]

Section 2 / Group 2 / heading: ______________________________

The second pillar of the digital strategy is skills. At every level, from getting people online for the first time, to attracting and training the world's top coding talent, Britain needs stronger digital skills if we are to thrive in the years ahead.

Government can't address this shortfall alone. So when we launched the Digital Strategy in March, we committed to establish a new Digital Skills Partnership, between Government, businesses, charities and voluntary organisations. The aim was to bring greater coherence to the provision of digital skills training at a national level. And at the launch we promised to create more than four million digital training places. Just eight months in, we and our partners - including Barclays, Lloyds, Google, and many others - have impressively over-delivered, with more than two million places made available, in everything from basic online skills through to cybersecurity and coding. These skills will be crucial to our country's future prosperity, so we intend to keep up the pace.

The third pillar is to make the UK the best place in the world to start and grow a digital business. Make no mistake, Britain is already a global tech powerhouse, with more than 1.4 million people working in digital tech and new jobs being created at twice the rate of other sectors. In the first half 2017 there was a record £5.6 billion invested in tech in the UK - including from Microsoft, Amazon, Apple, IBM, and Google - and the sector has an annual turnover of £118 billion. All impressive figures, but we can still push further.

Section 3 / Group 3 / heading: ______________________________

So today we are unveiling a £21 million investment to create a new national network of regional tech hubs, across the country, from Belfast to Edinburgh, Cardiff to Birmingham. The funding will also help entrepreneurs in emerging technologies, such as Artificial Intelligence and FinTech, by connecting them to peers and potential investors in other hubs across the country, as well as by offering tailored development programmes. [...]

The fourth pillar of the Digital Strategy is that every UK business should be, to some extent, a digital business. In July, we launched the Productivity Council, which was developed through discussions with UK business leaders, the Confederation of British Industry, and the Institute of Directors, and designed to encourage and support UK businesses to go digital. Analysis suggests that only a modest improvement across a broad base of firms could unlock billions of Gross Value Added every year.

The fifth pillar is to make the UK the safest place in the world to live and work online. Our Internet Safety Strategy, published last month, is a substantial step towards that goal. The Strategy sets out how we all must play our role in tackling online harm [dangers]. We want to bring together groups from across our whole society and hear from people of all backgrounds – including technology firms, schools, the voluntary sector, and citizens young and old as we turn ambition into reality.

Section 4 / Group 4 / heading: ______________________________

We will bring in a statutory code of practice for social media companies, and are consulting on an industry levy to support educational programmes and technical solutions. We also want to see more transparency, to help inform future policy. Ensuring the internet is safe means cyber security too, and our National Cyber Security Strategy, funded to the tune of £1.9bn, sets out what we are doing to help improve Britain's cyber security. One of the programme's many aims is to find, finesse and fast-track tomorrow's online security experts. Over 6000 young people - between 14 and 18 years old - are now being invited to test their skills in online cyber and problem solving challenges, via a £20 million training programme. They might then win a place on the Cyber Discovery scheme, where they can learn cutting-edge skills from cyber security experts. But keeping citizens safe online means more than protecting them against cyber-crime. It means ensuring that the norms of behaviour online match those we have always valued offline.
The Digital Strategy is now complemented by the Digital Charter, as introduced in the Manifesto. The Charter will reinforce the work we started with the Strategy but will further consider how we apply the liberal values we value offline to the online world, so we can seize the opportunities that unprecedented connectivity provides, while also mitigating the harm [dangers] it creates. Throughout, we will be guided by three core principles. First, what is considered unacceptable offline should not be accepted online. Secondly, all users should be empowered to manage their own online risks. Lastly, technology companies have a responsibility to their users to develop and protect safe online communities.

Section 5 / Group 5 / heading: ______________________________

And we are committed to bringing about a sustainable business model for high quality journalism. I welcome Google's movement towards this, not least removing the one click free policy, but there is much more to do to ensure we find a genuinely sustainable business model for high quality journalism, as we have, for example, for the music industry, that's been through a similar radical disruption but found a way to a model that seems to be working.
The sixth pillar of the Strategy is to digitise Government. Since the creation of Government Digital Services in 2011, Britain has been a world leader in such work. From applying for a passport, to applying for lasting power of attorney, dozens of Government services have been digitised. The massive project to make tax digital is proceeding carefully, and the feedback from those who use the new digitised service is encouraging. Our G-cloud procurement system is being copied around the world, as it allows and encourages contracts to go to small innovative companies, not the traditional main players. In February this year, we had 3,947 suppliers on the Digital Marketplace, of which 93% were SMEs. And, as a result, our GovTech market is booming.
And so we arrive at **the final pillar**: data. The Digital Strategy has also committed to unlocking the power of data in the UK economy, and improving public confidence in its use. Research shows that, currently, more than 80 percent of people feel that they do not have complete control over their data online, and that is too high.

Section 6 / Group 6 / heading: ______________________________

So we are strengthening our data protection laws through the new Data Protection Bill, making UK law consistent with the EU's GDPR. Under its proposals, individuals will have more control over their data, through the right to be forgotten and to ask for their personal data to be erased. They will also be able to ask social media channels to delete information they posted in their childhood.

We want to end the existing reliance on default opt-out or pre-selected 'tick boxes', to give consent for organisations to collect personal data. We all know these are largely ignored. The Data Protection Bill will make it simpler to withdraw consent for the use of personal data and require explicit consent to be necessary for processing sensitive personal data. It also expands the definition of 'personal data' to include IP addresses, internet cookies, and DNA.
New criminal offences will be created to deter organisations from creating situations – be it through pure recklessness or deliberate intent – where someone could be identified from anonymised data. The data protection regulator, the Information Commissioner's Office, will be given more power to defend consumer interests and issue higher fines for the most serious data breaches.
So there you have it. We may be in the foothills of this digital age but we are well-equipped for the climb, and remain alert to any obstacles ahead. Much remains to do but I am confident the measures I've just outlined will continue to ensure our good progress.

ASSIGNMENTS

A) Pre-Listening and Pre-Reading Activity: "The Future of the Digital Age"

word cloud / work in pairs, then in groups and share your ideas with your classmates / collaboration with Art classes / cross-curricular connections / peer support and feedback / speech

Tasks:

1. Take a look at the word cloud. From these words, what do you think are the main ideas in Matt Hancock's speech?
2. Prepare and give a two-minute speech about the digital age using at least 10 words from the word cloud.
3. The Digital Age: Create a picture, a photo, a graphic design in your Art classes, which are visually, psychologically and intellectually stimulating.

B) Reading Comprehension

Group work suggested: the class can be divided into six groups / group work (assignments B and C) / group 1: section 1 / group 2: section 2 etc. / jigsaw activity / share ideas and results

1. Work in groups. Read your assigned excerpt of Matt Hancock's speech.
2. Look up any words you don't know which are important to understand the speech.
3. Word field: digitalisation/digital media. In your groups, make a list of important words and phrases about digitalisation and digital media which Matt Hancock uses in his speech.
4. Explain the important statements featured in your excerpt.

5. Sum up Matt Hancock's main arguments.
6. Present your findings to the other groups. Share results so that everybody has an overview of the whole speech.

C) Analysis

1. How does Matt Hancock organise his speech? Analyse the structure of the speech briefly and point out the significance of your excerpt in the wider context of the whole speech.
2. Examine some rhetorical devices Hancock uses in your assigned excerpt and point out their intended effects.
3. Present your findings to the other groups.

D) Evaluation, Comment and Creative Activities

▶ *paired work / group work / peer support / interview / debate or discussion / discussion / speech*

1. "When it comes to tech, and to digital technology, we are very far from the summit of what can be achieved. Indeed, we are only beginning to even glimpse the potential of where digital technologies might take us, and how much they will transform our world." Discuss and explain your own opinion of this statement. You may organise a debate or speech competition in class.
2. "We want to bring together groups from across our whole society and hear from people of all backgrounds – including technology firms, schools, the voluntary sector, and citizens young and old as we turn ambition into reality." Consider the current situation in Britain and in Germany. How could this goal be achieved in these countries?
3. "But keeping citizens safe online means more than protecting against cyber-crime. It means ensuring that the norms of behaviour online match those we have always valued offline." What could schools in Germany do to achieve this goal?
4. "Research shows that, currently, more than 80 percent of people feel that they do not have complete control over their data online, and that is too high." Write a response to this statement in which you argue and explain what kind of data protection laws should be put in place or strengthened.
5. "We may be in the foothills of this digital age but we are well-equipped for the climb, and remain alert to any obstacles ahead." In small groups, discuss what kind of challenges have to be met in the digital age.
6. Imagine you are a journalist who has been given the opportunity to interview Matt Hancock. What questions would you like to ask him? What possible answers might he give you?

E) Further Research and Creative Activities

▶ *research / tablet or laptop presentation / interview / optimist-pessimist / debate or discussion / speech*

1. Imagine you are spending a school year as an exchange student at your partner school in the United Kingdom. You are asked to outline the role of digital media in Germany. Make some notes, then give a speech to your class on this topic.
2. What are the benefits and the potential drawbacks of using digital media in schools? Organise a class debate on this subject.

F) Further Information, Research and Controversial Ideas

▶ *individual work / paired work / creative writing / organise a controversial TV-debate*

"Social media is harming the mental health of teenagers."

By June Eric Udorie, *The Guardian,* last modified on Wednesday, September 20, 2017

https://www.theguardian.com/commentisfree/2015/sep/16/social-media-mental-health-teenagers-government-pshe-lessons

The digital landscape has put increased pressure on teenagers today, and we feel it. There are so many social media channels: Facebook, Twitter, Instagram, Snapchat, Tumblr, you name it. I made a conscious decision to avoid Snapchat and Instagram because of the social pressure I saw them putting on my 14-year-old little sister. If my mum turned off the WiFi at 11pm, my sister would beg me to turn my phone into a hotspot. She always needed to load her Snapchat stories one more time, or to reply to a message that had come in two minutes ago because she didn't want her friend to feel ignored. If I refused, saying she could respond in the morning, I'd get the "You're ruining my social life" speech. Even as a teenager as well, I sometimes find this craze a little baffling.

A new study has found that teenagers who engage with social media during the night could be damaging their sleep, and increasing their risk of anxiety and depression. Teenagers spoke about the pressure they felt to make themselves available 24/7, and the resulting anxiety if they did not respond immediately to texts or posts. Teens are so emotionally invested in social media that a fifth of secondary school pupils will wake up at night and log on, just to make sure they don't miss out.

Perhaps the worst thing about this is that teenagers need more sleep than adults do, so night-time social media use could be detrimental to their health. Research has shown that teenagers need 9.5 hours of sleep each night but on average only get 7.5 hours. A lack of sleep can make teenagers tired, irritable, depressed, and more likely to catch colds, flu, and gastroenteritis. [...]

During the summer holidays, I lost my phone. And for the week that I was phoneless, it felt like a disaster. I love my phone. It gives me quick access to information, and allows me to be constantly looped in with my friends, to know exactly what is going on in their lives. So when I didn't have my phone for a week, I felt a fear of missing out. By the end of the week, I'd got used to not having a phone, and I'd quite enjoyed the break from social media. But there was still a lingering sense of sadness at the back of my mind that there would be conversations I had missed, messages that had been sent, funny videos shared, and night-time chats that I would probably never get to see.

A separate study by the National Citizen Service found that, rather than talking to their parents, girls seek comfort on social media when they are worried. The survey also suggests that girls are likely to experience stress more often than boys – an average of twice a week.

It's becoming more and more obvious how the pressures of social media disproportionately affect teenage girls. I can see it all around me. Pressure to be perfect. To look perfect, to act perfect, to have the perfect body, to have the perfect group of friends, and the perfect amount of likes on Instagram. Perfect, perfect, perfect. And if you don't meet these ridiculously high standards, then the self-loathing and bullying begins.

What is really worrying is that time and time again, these studies pop up and demonstrate that the mental health of teenagers, especially teenage girls, is on the line. We know this. We know the perils of the internet, we've heard about online bullying, and we know the slut-shaming that goes on in our schools. We know these things. We know that these studies demonstrate that we have to make personal, social and health education (PSHE) statutory in schools and ensure it covers a range of issues from healthy eating and sleeping to consent. So I ask: what are we waiting for? Inaction on these issues is harming the physical and emotional well-being of young people in this country. What has to happen before we do something?

June Eric Udorie (born in Nigeria on June 18, 1998) is a writer and feminist campaigner who grew up in Ireland and Great Britain, and is now based in the USA, and in Great Britain. She is a journalist and blogger for *The Guardian* and the *New Statesman* as well as *Cosmopolitan*. In 2016, the BBC included her in the list of 100 "inspirational and influential women for 2016".

Tasks:

1. Outline June Eric Udorie's article.
2. Analyse the structure of the article and the stylistic devices June Eric Udorie uses to support her message.
3. Write a letter to the Editor of *The Guardian* in response to Udorie's article.
4. Write an email to June Eric Udorie in response to her article.
5. Organise a lively and controversial debate in response to the following question: "Is social media harming the mental health of teenagers?"
6. Prepare and give a four-minute speech on the topic: "Social Media - Blessing or Curse?"

"Artificial Intelligence: How We Can Build AI to Help Humans, Not Hurt Us."

Margaret Mitchell, Senior Research Scientist on Artificial Intelligence (AI): TED Talk, in Milan, Italy, in October 2017

RELATED TOPICS

ARTIFICIAL INTELLIGENCE · COMPUTERS · COMMUNICATION · THE DIGITAL AGE · DIGITALIZATION · THE DIGITAL DIVIDE · DIGNITY · EDUCATION · THE ENVIRONMENT · EQUALITY · FUTURE GENERATIONS · HEALTH · INNOVATION · INVENTION · OPTIMISM · RESPONSIBILITY · SCIENTISTS · SOCIAL SECURITY · TECHNOLOGICAL DEVELOPMENTS · TECHNOLOGY

Margaret Mitchell, a Senior Research Scientist for Google's Research & Machine Intelligence group, is responsible for the research and development of artificial intelligence. Particularly, her research centres on the generation of vision-language and grounded language and, particularly, how this can be used to supplement, and indeed improve, people's lives. This requires her to take computer vision, natural language processing, social media, insights from cognitive science and to use statistical data. These elements are all brought together to help advance knowledge of the technology.

Mitchell was previously a founding member of Microsoft Research's Cognition group which had placed her in a similar role. Prior to that, she had formed part of the Natural Language Processing Group at the same company. She is very much an expert in her field.

In her role as a Research Scientist, Mitchell effectively communicates with computers in an effort to see what they can see and understand. Despite her enthusiasm and excitement towards the research, she displays an element of caution towards a future with artificial intelligence. She states, 'All that we see now is a snapshot in the evolution of artificial intelligence […] If we want AI to evolve in a way that helps humans, then we need to define the goals and strategies that enable that path now.'

Video, screenshot and speech transcript taken from the following TED Talk:
https://www.ted.com/talks/margaret_mitchell_how_we_can_build_ai_to_help_humans_not_hurt_us#t-6307

Margaret Mitchell:

I work on helping computers communicate about the world around us. There are a lot of ways to do this, and I like to focus on helping computers to talk about what they see and understand.

Given a scene like this, a modern computer-vision algorithm can tell you that there's a woman, and there's a dog. It can tell you that the woman is smiling. It might even be able to tell you that the dog is incredibly cute. I work on this problem thinking about how humans understand and process the world. The thoughts, memories, and stories that a scene like this might evoke for humans. All the interconnections of related situations.

cute adorable

Maybe you've seen a dog like this one before, or you've spent time running on a beach like this one, and that further evokes thoughts and memories of a past vacation, past times to the beach, times spent running around with other dogs. One of my guiding principles is that, by helping computers to understand what it's like to have these experiences, to understand what we share and believe and feel, then we're in a great position to start evolving computer technology in a way that's complementary with our own experiences.

to evolve to develop
complementary *ergänzend, komplementär*

So, digging more deeply into this, a few years ago, I began working on helping computers to generate human-like stories from sequences of images. So, one day, I was working with my computer to ask it what it thought about a trip to Australia. It took a look at the pictures, and it saw a koala. It didn't know what the koala was, but it said it thought it was an interesting-looking creature.

to generate to create

Then I shared with it a sequence of images about a house burning down. It took a look at the images and it said: "This is an amazing view! This is spectacular!" It sent chills down my spine. It saw a horrible, life-changing and life-destroying event and thought it was something positive. I realized that it recognized the contrast, the reds, the yellows, and thought it was something worth remarking on positively. And part of why it was doing this was because most of the images I had given it were positive images. That's because people tend to share positive images when they talk about their experiences. When was the last time you saw a selfie at a funeral?

to realize (*AmE*), to realise (*BrE*), to notice, to become aware of; *bemerken, merken*
to recognize (*AmE*), to recognise (*BrE*), to notice, to see; *erkennen*

I WORKED ON IMPROVING AI TASK BY TASK

I realized that, as I worked on improving AI task by task, dataset by dataset, that I was creating massive gaps, holes, and blind spots in what it could understand. And while doing so, I was encoding all kinds of biases. Biases that reflect a limited viewpoint, limited to a single dataset – biases that can reflect human biases found in the

AI artificial intelligence; künstliche Intelligenz, *see* ADDITIONAL NOTES
to encode *kodieren, verschlüsseln*
bias one-sided opinion, limited viewpoint, prejudice

data, such as prejudice and stereotyping. I thought back to the evolution of the technology that brought me to where I was that day – how the first color images were calibrated against a white woman's skin, meaning that color photography was biased against black faces. And that same bias, that same blind spot continued well into the '90s. And the same blind spot continues even today in how well we can recognize different people's faces in facial recognition technology.

to calibrate against to adjust to

I thought about the state of the art in research today, where we tend to limit our thinking to one dataset and one problem. And that in doing so, we were creating more blind spots and biases that the AI could further amplify.

to amplify to increase; *verstärken*

DISCUSS WHAT THE TECHNOLOGY OF TODAY WILL MEAN FOR TOMORROW

I realized then that we had to think deeply about how the technology we work on today looks in five years, in ten years. Humans evolve slowly, with time to correct for issues in the interactions of humans and their environment. In contrast, artificial intelligence is evolving at an incredibly fast rate. And that means that it really matters that we think about this carefully right now – that we reflect on our own blind spots, our own biases, and think about how that's informing the technology we're creating, and discuss what the technology of today will mean for tomorrow.

CEOs and scientists have weighed in on what they think the artificial intelligence technology of the future will be. Stephen Hawking warns that: "Artificial intelligence could end mankind." Elon Musk warns that it's an existential risk and one of the greatest risks that we face as a civilization. Bill Gates has made the point: "I don't understand why people aren't more concerned." But these views – they're part of the story. The math, the models, the basic building blocks of artificial intelligence are something that we can all access, and all work with. We have open-source tools for machine learning and intelligence that we can contribute to. And beyond that, we can share our experience.

have weighed in on have considered

civilization (*AmE*), civilisation (*BrE*), a society which is well organised and developed

open-source tools Open-Source-Software

We can share our experiences with technology and how it concerns us and how it excites us. We can discuss what we love. We can communicate with foresight about the aspects of technology that could be more beneficial or could be more problematic over time.

how it excites us *wie die Technologie uns begeistert/herausfordert*
with foresight *mit Weitblick*
beneficial advantageous; *vorteilhaft*

If we all focus on opening up the discussion on AI, with foresight towards the future, this will help create a general conversation, and awareness, about what AI is now, what it can become, and all the things that we need to do in order to enable that outcome that best suits us. We already see and know this in the technology that we use today.

We use smart phones and digital assistants and Roombas. Are they evil? Maybe sometimes. Are they beneficial? Yes, they're that, too. And they're not all the same. And there you already see a light shining on what the future holds. The future continues on from what we build and create right now. We set into motion that domino effect that carves out AI's evolutionary path.

domino effect a situation in which something happens that causes other similar events to happen
to carve out a path *einen Weg freilegen*

In our time right now, we shape the AI of tomorrow.

Technology that immerses us in augmented realities bringing to life past worlds.
Technology that helps people to share their experiences when they have difficulty communicating.
Technology built on understanding the streaming visual worlds, used as technology for self-driving cars.
Technology built on understanding images, and generating language, evolving into technology that helps people who are visually impaired be better able to access the visual world.

to immerse *eintauchen (in ein Thema)*
augmented reality technology that adds digital elements to the real world
visually impaired a term used for partially sighted (*sehbehindert*) and blind people

And we also see how technology can lead to problems.
We have technology today that analyzes physical characteristics we're born with – such as the color of our skin or the look of our face – in order to determine whether or not we might be criminals or terrorists.
We have technology that crunches through our data, even data relating to our gender or our race, in order to determine whether or not we might get a loan.

to analyze (*AmE*), analyse (*BrE*), to examine
to crunch through to examine; *durchforsten*
loan *Kredit*

WHAT WE DO NOW WILL AFFECT WHAT HAPPENS DOWN THE LINE, AND IN THE FUTURE

All that we see now is a snapshot in the evolution of artificial intelligence. Because where we are right now, is within a moment of that evolution. That means that what we do now will affect what happens down the line, and in the future.

If we want AI to evolve in a way that helps humans, then we need to define the goals and strategies that enable that path now. What I'd like to see, is something that fits well with humans, with our culture, and with the environment.

to enable to facilitate

Technology that aids and assists those of us with neurological conditions or other disabilities in order to make life equally challenging for everyone. Technology that works regardless of your demographics or the color of your skin.

equally challenging the same difficulty level
demographics population statistics; *Demografiedaten*

And so today, what I focus on is the technology for tomorrow, and for 10 years from now. AI can turn out in many different ways. But in this

destination *Zielort*

outcomes effects

case, it isn't a self-driving car without any destination. This is the car that we are driving. We choose when to speed up and when to slow down. We choose if we need to make a turn. We choose what the AI of the future will be.

There's a vast playing field of all the things that artificial intelligence can become. It will become many things. And it's up to us now, in order to figure out what we need to put in place to make sure the outcomes of artificial intelligence are the ones that will be better for all of us. Thank you. (*Applause*)

ASSIGNMENTS

A) Pre-Listening and Pre-Reading Activity

▶ *innovative projects / inside-outside circle or milling around / brainstorming warm-up / idea lab and sharing ideas / group work / mind map / digital narratives / storytelling / discussion*

Tasks:

1. Watch the trailer or the opening scenes of Steven Spielberg's science fiction film *A.I. Artificial Intelligence*.
2. Record your first impressions of the film or your ideas of what the film might be about on a placemat or mind map.
3. Describe and analyse Sheila.
4. Look at the photo (*on the right*) and meet Sophia: The robot who smiles and frowns just like us.
   a) Describe, analyse and evaluate the photo of Sophia.
   b) Fun or fake, science fiction or reality?
   c) Write an essay or give a speech in response to the following statements:
   - Sophia, a robot developed by Hanson Robotics, can generate an astounding number of human-like facial expressions.
     Source: *CNN* https://edition.cnn.com/videos/design/2018/10/31/sophia-robot-artificial-intelligence-smart-creativity-vision-style-orig.cnn/video/playlists/business-tech/
   - "**Sophia is a chatty A.I. android** born of the Hanson Robotics lab, in Hong Kong. Sophia processes speech and, above all, she learns constantly." Source: Avi Steinberg, *The New Yorker*, November 13, 2017
     https://www.newyorker.com/tech/annals-of-technology/can-a-robot-join-the-faith
   - **Elon Musk's Crusade to Stop the A.I. Apocalypse**: Elon Musk is famous for his futuristic gambles, but Silicon Valley's latest rush to embrace artificial intelligence scares him. And he thinks you should be frightened too. Source: Maureen Dowd, Vanity Fair, March 26, 2017
     https://www.vanityfair.com/news/2017/03/elon-musk-billion-dollar-crusade-to-stop-ai-space-x

A.I. is a science fiction film directed by Steven Spielberg. The screenplay is based on the short story "Supertoys Last All Summer Long" by Brian Aldiss. The story is set in a futuristic society. *A.I.* tells the story of David, a childlike robot programmed with the ability to love.

Sophia - the smiling robot

B) Reading and Listening Comprehension

enquiry-based learning / paired work / peer support and feedback / writing a summary and a report / using tablets or laptops / presenting results / giving feedback / video report

1. Listen to Margaret Mitchell 's speech. Watch the video here: https://www.ted.com/talks/margaret_mitchell_how_we_can_build_ai_to_help_humans_not_hurt_us#t-6307
2. Highlight any important statements in your speech transcript.
3. What are Mitchell's aims as a scientist and expert in artificial intelligence?
4. What are the benefits and risks associated with artificial intelligence that Mitchell tells us to consider?
5. "In our time right now, we shape the AI of tomorrow." What exactly does Mitchell mean?
6. What are the future challenges posed by artificial intelligence, according to Mitchell?
7. Write a summary of Mitchell's speech for your school newspaper, and for the *Texthelden* newspaper project.
8. Imagine you are a TV reporter. Produce and record a video report about artificial intelligence.

C) Analysis

think – pair – share / writing an analysis / using tablets or laptops / presentation / feedback

1. Analyse the structure of Mitchell's speech.
2. Examine some of the rhetorical devices Mitchell uses.
3. Do you think that Mitchell's arguments are convincing?
4. Is Mitchell's final appeal to the audience clear and convincing enough?

D) Evaluation, Comment, Creative Writing

idea lab / research competition / group work / using tablets or laptops / discussion / speech competition / optimist – pessimist / evaluation / future workshop / feedback / SOLO taxonomy

1. Choose one of Mitchell's arguments and explain why you agree or disagree with it.
2. Mitchell says: "There's a vast playing field of all the things that artificial intelligence can become. It will become many things. And it's up to us now, in order to figure out what we need to put in place to make sure the outcomes of artificial intelligence are the ones that will be better for all of us." Do you agree or disagree with this statement? Give reasons for your opinion.
3. "We can build AI to help humans, not hurt us." Prepare and give a three-minute speech in response to this statement from Mitchell's speech.
4. What do you think of Mitchell's argument that research into artificial intelligence must take ethics into account?
5. Evaluate the importance of AI research. Could AI change the world? Write an article or prepare and give a speech on the subject.
6. Will artificial intelligence change our lives for better or for worse over the next twenty years? Discuss this question in groups. Then write an article or prepare and give a speech in response to this question.
7. Great advances both in artificial intelligence and in genetics and genetic engineering have opened up a wide scope of applications, such as DNA data storage and the prospect of precision medicine and medical therapy. What are scientists allowed to do? What do you think?
8. On her website Margaret Mitchell points out that her research generally involves "vision-language and grounded language generation, focusing on how to evolve artificial intelligence towards positive goals." This includes research on projects that support assistive and clinical technology. For more information, please visit: http://www.m-mitchell.com/

E) Further Projects for Thought and Discussion

SQ3R / individual work / paired work / student interaction / group work / presentation / discussion

Artificial Intelligence and the Future

1. Myths about artificial intelligence

Artificial intelligence is the future. Google, Microsoft, Amazon and Apple are all making big bets on AI. From health care to transportation to national security, AI has the potential to improve lives. But it comes with fears about economic disruption and a brewing "AI arms race." Like any transformational change, it's complicated. Perhaps the biggest AI myth is that we can be confident about its future effects. [...] AI is also producing "deep fake" videos – from invented speeches by politicians to pornography featuring celebrities' computer-generated faces – that many people think are real. These rapid advances present significant concerns, shaking the public's confidence in what they see and hear.
Bill LaPlante and **Katharyn White** *The Washington Post*, April 27, 2018
https://www.washingtonpost.com/outlook/five-myths/five-myths-about-artificial-intelligence/2018/04/27/76c35408-4959-11e8-827e-190efaf1f1ee_story.html?utm_term=.5bdd9cc7cfdc

2. Information superiority of AI – truth or fake news?

"AI-enhanced forgery of audio and video media is rapidly improving in quality and decreasing in cost. In the future, AI-generated forgeries will challenge the basis of trust across many institutions. [...] The existence of widespread AI forgery capabilities will erode social trust, as previously reliable evidence becomes highly uncertain. [...] That world of truth – where seeing is believing – is about to be upended by artificial intelligence technologies."
Greg Allen and **Taniel Chan** Artificial Intelligence and National Security. *Harvard Kennedy School, Belfer Center for Science and International Affairs* 2017, pages 2/30/32
https://www.belfercenter.org/sites/default/files/files/publication/AI%20NatSec%20-%20final.pdf (accessed March 15, 2019)

3. The potential perils of AI

"The genie is out of the bottle. We need to move forward on artificial intelligence development but we also need to be mindful of its very real dangers. I fear that AI may replace humans altogether. If people design computer viruses, someone will design AI that replicates itself. This will be a new form of life that will outperform humans."
Stephen Hawking in: *Wired Magazine*, December 17, 2017 http://www.wired.co.uk/article/stephen-hawking-interview-alien-life-climate-change-donald-trump

4. Elon Musk: "A.I. is far more dangerous than nukes"

Tesla and SpaceX boss Elon Musk has doubled down on his dire warnings about the danger of artificial intelligence. The billionaire tech entrepreneur called AI more dangerous than nuclear warheads and said there needs to be a regulatory body overseeing the development of super intelligence. [...] Based on his knowledge of machine intelligence and its developments, Musk believes there is reason to be worried. "And mark my words, AI is far more dangerous than nukes."
Catherine Clifford, *CNBC*, March 13, 2018 https://www.cnbc.com/2018/03/13/elon-musk-at-sxsw-a-i-is-more-dangerous-than-nuclear-weapons.html (accessed: March 15, 2019)

5. Artificial intelligence is not good or bad – it's how we use it that matters

AI is a general-purpose technology. AI is neither good nor bad. It is instead an enabling technology that creates opportunities. How individuals, corporations and governments handle these opportunities will define the future, rather than the technology itself. [...] If AI is to become socially acceptable in the long run, it is essential that its applications are as transparent as possible – and, ideally, independently evaluated. In healthcare, for example, we could insist that AI is not just safe to use, but that it is effective and improves patient outcomes compared with the alternatives. [...] We can create a positive social agenda for AI that ensures that the whole of society shares in the potential opportunities and benefits.
Geraint Rees *The Times*, November 27, 2018 https://www.thetimes.co.uk/article/artificial-intelligence-is-not-good-or-bad-its-how-we-use-it-that-matters-w33jnrl2d (accessed: March 16, 2019)

6. Our soft skills can keep robots in their place

Artificial intelligence will wipe out many jobs but not those that need judgment and empathy. Anyone want to be a billionaire? Well I have just the business idea for you. It's an app which, in the absence of any better name, I'm planning to call "Big Brother". [...] Simply install Big Brother on your smartphone, give it access to your camera and it will sit there, watching, listening and, most importantly of all, judging. Big Brother will use its artificial intelligence (AI) algorithms to rate your behaviour and tell you when you need to be more charming, more delicate, more stubborn. It is the ultimate life coach. [...]

The great irony is that our education systems are taking us in precisely the wrong direction to confront this challenge. For all sorts of understandable reasons, they prioritise the teaching of STEM skills: science, technology, engineering and maths. Yet jobs related to these skills are the very occupations most at risk of being taken by robots. The controversial suggestion is that, in future, education should put more emphasis on teaching students "soft" skills: interpersonal relationships, working in groups, showing empathy, being ethical. Less brain, more heart. [...] Social interaction will remain the one area in which humans are likely to trump robots for years to come.
Ed Conway *The Times*, January 18, 2019 https://www.thetimes.co.uk/article/our-soft-skills-can-keep-robots-in-their-place-hzzp609hl (accessed: March 16, 2019)

7. **Artificial intelligence used to detect women with deadliest ovarian cancer**

The deadliest forms of ovarian cancer have been detected using AI, offering hope for more precise life-saving treatments. Scientists have created a tool that seeks out clusters of tumour cells with unusually shaped nuclei – the control centres at the heart of each cell. "Using this new test gives us a way of detecting tumours with hidden weaknesses in their ability to repair DNA that wouldn't be identified through genetic testing," explained Dr Yinyin Yuan, who led the study at the Institute of Cancer Research. [...] Besides choosing the best treatment, the research by Dr Yuan's team also opened new potential immunotherapy avenues. Immunotherapies consist of treatments that give the body's own immune system a boost in its fight against cancer cells.
Josh Gabbatiss *The Independent*, January 12, 2019 https://www.independent.co.uk/news/health/ovarian-cancer-ai-artificial-intelligence-deadly-tumours-research-study-a8724611.html (accessed: March 16, 2019)

8. **Artificial intelligence turns brain activity into speech**

For many people who are paralyzed and unable to speak, signals of what they'd like to say hide in their brains. No one has been able to decipher those signals directly. But three research teams recently made progress in turning data from electrodes surgically placed on the brain into computer-generated speech. Using computational models known as neural networks, they reconstructed words and sentences that were, in some cases, intelligible to human listeners. [...] People who have lost the ability to speak after a stroke or disease can use their eyes or make other small movements to control a cursor or select on-screen letters. But if a brain-computer interface could re-create their speech directly, they might regain much more: control over tone and inflection, for example, or the ability to interject in a fast-moving conversation.
Kelly Servick *Science*, Jan. 2, 2019 https://www.sciencemag.org/news/2019/01/artificial-intelligence-turns-brain-activity-speech (accessed: March 15, 2019)

9. **Machines are not our masters**

OpenAI, a US-based nonprofit organisation, decided that its new AI model, GPT2, is so good at generating articles from just a few words and phrases that the model could not be released until OpenAI better understood how it might be used. GPT2's database is so sophisticated and its algorithms so smart that it has gone far beyond text prediction to writing readable and plausible text.

The good news is that this means that computers, for example, could speed-read articles on our behalf, summarise them and answer our questions. Those chatbots that come to your aid when you are lost on some website could become really helpful. If you wear a watch that monitors your health, GPT2 could spell out warnings and diagnoses quickly in plain English. Interesting books in foreign languages will be translated more effectively.

The bad news is that in the wrong hands the likes of GPT2 could flood every social media site on a grand scale with fake news or troubling comment. Similarly, hackers who get into your computer could feed GPT2 the content of emails from your closest friends to form a database and then perfectly simulate an email to you when they go "spear phishing" – looking for personal data – tricking you into making a reply. The scope for malevolence is endless.

The task is not to throw up our hands warning that the machines are coming – it is to design a world in which we are their master, not their servant.
Will Hutton in *The Guardian*, February 17, 2019 https://www.theguardian.com/commentisfree/2019/feb/17/machines-not-our-masters-but-sinister-side-ai-demands-smart-response (accessed: March 16, 2019)

F) Further Research

individual learning / paired work / cooperative learning / research / WebQuest / fishbowl discussion / hot seat interview / debate / speech / creative writing / storyboard / podcast / video clip production

Can AI be dangerous?

Most researchers agree that a super intelligent AI is unlikely to exhibit human emotions like love or hate, and that there is no reason to expect AI to become intentionally benevolent or malevolent. Instead, when considering how AI might become a risk, experts think two scenarios most likely:

1. **The AI is programmed to do something devastating:** Autonomous weapons are artificial intelligence systems that are programmed to kill. In the hands of the wrong person, these weapons could easily cause mass casualties. Moreover, an AI arms race could inadvertently lead to an AI war that also results in mass casualties. To avoid being thwarted by the enemy, these weapons would be designed to be extremely difficult to simply "turn off," so humans could plausibly lose control of such a situation. This risk is one that's present even with narrow AI, but grows as levels of AI intelligence and autonomy increase.

2. **The AI is programmed to do something beneficial, but it develops a destructive method for achieving its goal:** This can happen whenever we fail to fully align the AI's goals with ours, which is strikingly difficult. If you ask an obedient intelligent car to take you to the airport as fast as possible, it might get you there chased by helicopters and covered in vomit, doing, not what you wanted, but literally what you asked for. If a super intelligent system is tasked with an ambitious geoengineering project, it might wreak havoc with our ecosystem as a side effect, and view human attempts to stop it as a threat to be met.

3. **Because AI has the potential to become more intelligent than any human**, we have no surefire way of predicting how it will behave. We can't use past technological developments as much of a basis because we've never created anything that has the ability to, wittingly or unwittingly, outsmart us. The best example of what we could face may be our own evolution. People now control the planet, not because we're the strongest, fastest, or biggest, but because we're the smartest. If we're no longer the smartest, are we assured to remain in control? From: Future of Life Institute (FLI) https://futureoflife.org/background/benefits-risks-of-artificial-intelligence/ (accessed: March 16, 2019)

Tasks:
1. Write down and explain the advantages and disadvantages of artificial intelligence.
2. Create a WebQuest to present your findings.
3. Organise a class discussion, debate, or speech competition about AI's advantages and disadvantages.

G) Creative Activities: "We can build AI to help humans, not hurt us."

Respond to this statement from Mitchell's speech in a creative way. Please choose one of these tasks:
1. Write a story board for a film about AI's advantages and disadvantages.
2. Produce a trailer for a film about AI.
3. *Hot Seat Interview:* Write and act out an interview between AI experts and journalists.

H) Artificial Intelligence: Projects For Thought and Discussion
1. What is artificial intelligence?
2. What are the benefits and dangers of artificial intelligence technology?
3. What are the differences between artificial intelligence and human intelligence?
4. Do we need artificial intelligence?
5. Will artificial intelligence ever be smarter than human intelligence?
6. Will artificial intelligence kill jobs?
7. How is artificial intelligence helping us today?
8. How would you like artificial intelligence to help you?
9. What movies have you seen about artificial intelligence?
10. Discuss the future impact artificial intelligence will have on our lives.
11. ZDF Doku – Claus Kleber: „Schöne neue Welt" June 19, 2016: https://www.youtube.com
12. **Deepfakes:** AI-generated fake videos that show a person's face on another's body are called "deepfakes". As the technology progresses, they're becoming easier to make, more realistic and extremely dangerous weapons and tools for manipulating and deceiving people.
13. Could robots help kids learn second languages faster? Scientists and researchers are testing a robot language tutor that will give children one-on-one attention.
14. Due to the learning function of Artificial Intelligence, the performance of translation software has improved considerably over the past few years. Do we still have to learn foreign languages?

School Shootings and Gun Control in the USA: An Urgent Problem Revisited

“We Are Going to Be the Kids You Read about in Textbooks.”

Emma González’s passionate anti-gun speech in Fort Lauderdale, Florida, on February 17, 2018

RELATED TOPICS

THE AMERICAN DREAM · THE CONSTITUTION · THE BILL OF RIGHTS · DEMOCRACY · DIGNITY · EDUCATION · THE FOUNDING CREED · FREEDOM · FUTURE GENERATIONS · THE GOVERNMENT · GUN CONTROL · HISTORY · HUMAN RIGHTS · INJUSTICE · LIBERTY · MASS SHOOTINGS · NATIONHOOD · SAFETY · SCHOOL · THE SECOND AMENDMENT · SECURITY · VIOLENCE

From the survivors of the Marjory Stoneman Douglas High School shooting, **Emma González** emerged into a large media spotlight. At an anti-gun rally, shortly after a lone shooter killed 17 people and injured 14 more at the school, Emma González spoke out against the gun lobby and the situation in the United States which all centres on the Second Amendment.

Her speech was part of a swift movement formed by young people in Florida who were outraged by the fact that an ex-student could acquire a weapon and turn it on defenceless children. The group would not be held back. They took part in conversations with politicians as well as demonstrations to demand changes to America’s famous gun laws and freedoms. It was in Fort Lauderdale, near to the school, which was affected by the shooting, that Emma González captivated an audience with her passionate speech. She recounted the events of February 15, when the shooting occurred and recalled her initial feeling that the alarm was a mere drill as she sat on the floor in her school’s auditorium. Quickly realising the severity of the situation, González moved to help her frightened peers until help was at hand.

Two days later, she was heard calling out those in positions of power, like the President, lawmakers and the gun lobby for doing little more than offering empty words to victims of gun crime. She demanded that this inaction was replaced by new measures to ensure that such crimes would not happen. Throughout her speech, González emerges from tragic circumstances with a rousing speech which reflects the growing sentiment of her and her peers to fight for tighter gun laws in America.

Speech transcript taken from: https://hellogiggles.com/news/emma-gonzalez-full-speech/

Emma González:

We haven't already had a moment of silence in the House of Representatives, so I would like to have another one. Thank you.

THE GUNS HAVE CHANGED BUT OUR LAWS HAVE NOT

Every single person up here today, all these people should be home grieving. But instead we are up here standing together because if all our government and President can do is send thoughts and prayers, then it's time for victims to be the change that we need to see. Since the time of the Founding Fathers, and since they added the Second Amendment to the Constitution, our guns have developed at a rate that leaves me dizzy. The guns have changed but our laws have not.

We certainly do not understand why it should be harder to make plans with friends on weekends than to buy an automatic or semi-automatic weapon. In Florida, to buy a gun you do not need a permit, you do not need a gun license, and once you buy it, you do not need to register it. You do not need a permit to carry a concealed rifle or shotgun. You can buy as many guns as you want at one time.

I read something very powerful to me today. It was from the point of view of a teacher. And I quote: "When adults tell me I have the right to own a gun, all I can hear is my right to own a gun outweighs your students' right to live. All I hear is mine, mine, mine, mine."

Instead of worrying about our AP Gov chapter 16 test, we have to be studying our notes to make sure that our arguments based on politics and political history are watertight. The students at this school have been having debates on guns for what feels like our entire lives. AP Gov had about three debates this year. Some discussions on the subject even occurred during the shooting while students were hiding in the closets. The people involved right now, those who were there, those posting, those tweeting, those doing interviews and talking to people, are being listened to for what feels like the very first time on this topic that has come up over 1,000 times in the past four years alone.

I found out today there's a website shootingtracker.com. Nothing in the title suggests that it is exclusively tracking the USA's shootings and yet does it need to address that? Because Australia had one mass shooting in 1999 in Port Arthur (and after the) massacre introduced gun safety, and it hasn't had one since. Japan has never had a mass shooting. Canada has had three, and the UK had one, and they both introduced gun control, and, yet, here we are, with websites dedicated to reporting these tragedies so that they can be formulated into statistics for your convenience.

grieving mourning; *trauern*

Founding Fathers *Gründerväter der Vereinigten Staaten*

The Second Amendment is one of ten amendments that form the Bill of Rights, ratified in 1791 by the U.S. Congress; it gives the American population "the right to bear arms".

dizzy (*here:*) puzzled, disturbed

gun license *Waffenschein*

permit a document that gives you permission to do something

concealed hidden

at one time (*here:*) all at once, at the same time

to outweigh *wiegt schwerer als*

AP Gov chapter 16 test a section of a test about the American government

AP Gov is short for Advanced Placement United States Government and Politics, a college-level course and examination offered to high school students in which students learn about the structure and function of the American government, and about US politics

closet *Einbauschrank*

shootingtracker.com an online gun violence archive

for your convenience that can easily be accessed whenever you like

IF YOU ACTIVELY DO NOTHING, PEOPLE CONTINUALLY END UP DEAD, SO IT'S TIME TO START DOING SOMETHING.

I watched an interview this morning and noticed that one of the questions was: Do you think your children will have to go through other school shooter drills? And our response is that our neighbors will not have to go through other school shooter drills. When we've had our say with the government – and maybe the adults have gotten used to saying: 'It is what it is,' but if us students have learned anything, it's that if you don't study, you will fail. And in this case, if you actively do nothing, people continually end up dead, so it's time to start doing something.

We are going to be the kids you read about in textbooks. Not because we're going to be another statistic about mass shootings in America, but because, just as David said, we are going to be the last mass shooting.

Just like Tinker v. Des Moines, we are going to change the law. That's going to be Marjory Stoneman Douglas in that textbook, and it's going to be due to the tireless effort of the school board, the faculty members, the family members, and, most of all, the students. The students who are dead, the students still in the hospital, the students now suffering from PTSD, the students who had panic attacks during the vigil because the helicopters would not leave us alone, hovering over the school for 24 hours a day.

There is one tweet I would like to call attention to. So many signs that the Florida shooter was mentally disturbed, even expelled for bad and erratic behavior. Neighbors and classmates knew he was a big problem. [That they] must always report such instances to authorities again and again. We did, time and time again. Since he was in middle school, it was no surprise to anyone who knew him to hear that he was the shooter. Those talking about how we should have not ostracized him, you didn't know this kid. OK, we did. We know that they are claiming mental health issues, and I am not a psychologist, but we need to pay attention to the fact that this was not just a mental health issue. He would not have harmed that many students with a knife.

And how about we stop blaming the victims for something that was the student's fault, the fault of the people who let him buy the guns in the first place, those at the gun shows, the people who encouraged him to buy accessories for his guns to make them fully automatic, the people who didn't take them away from him when they knew he expressed homicidal tendencies, and I am not talking about the FBI. I'm talking about the people he lived with. I'm talking about the neighbors who saw him outside holding guns.

Tinker v. Des Moines a decision made by the United States Supreme Court that defined the constitutional rights of students in U.S. public schools. The Tinker test is still used by courts today to determine whether a school's disciplinary actions violate students' rights.

PTSD stands for post-traumatic stress disorder, which is an anxiety disorder that can develop after a person is exposed to a traumatic event; *Posttraumatische Belastungsstörung PTBS*

vigil *Mahnwache*

expelled excluded (from school); *vom Unterricht ausgeschlossen*

erratic unpredictable; *unberechenbar*

to ostracize *ausgrenzen*

accessories extras, added features

homicidal murderous, violent; *gemeingefährlich, mit Tötungsabsichten*

If the President wants to come up to me and tell me to my face that it was a terrible tragedy, and how it should never have happened, and maintain telling us how nothing is going to be done about it, I'm going to happily ask him how much money he received from the National Rifle Association.

National Rifle Association (NRA) the NRA is among the most powerful special interest lobby groups in the US that advocates for gun rights. The organization has been the focus of intense criticism in the aftermath of high profile shootings, such as the Marjory Stoneman Douglas High School shooting.

TO EVERY POLITICIAN WHO IS TAKING DONATIONS FROM THE NRA, SHAME ON YOU

You want to know something? It doesn't matter because I already know. Thirty million dollars. And divided by the number of gunshot victims in the United States in the one and one-half months of 2018 alone, that comes out to being $5,800 [per victim]. Is that how much these people are worth to you, Trump? If you don't do anything to prevent this from continuing to occur, that number of gunshot victims will go up, and the number that they are worth will go down. And we will be worthless to you.

donation financial aid/contributions; *Spende*

To every politician who is taking donations from the NRA, shame on you.

(Audience chants) Shame on you.

If your money was as threatened as us, would your first thought be: How is this going to reflect on my campaign? Which should I choose? Or would you choose us, and if you answered us, will you act like it for once? You know what would be a good way to act like it? I have an example of how to not act like it. In February of 2017, one year ago, President Trump repealed an Obama-era regulation that would have made it easier to block the sale of firearms to people with certain mental illnesses.

to repeal to abolish, to get rid of; *abschaffen*
regulation *Verordnung*

From the interactions that I had with the shooter before the shooting, and from the information that I currently know about him, I don't really know if he was mentally ill. I wrote this before I heard what Delaney said. Delaney said he was diagnosed. I don't need a psychologist, and I don't need to be a psychologist, to know that repealing that regulation was a really dumb idea.

currently now; *[jetzt]* gerade

dumb foolish

Republican Senator Chuck Grassley of Iowa was the sole sponsor on this bill that stops the FBI from performing background checks on people adjudicated to be mentally ill and now he's stating for the record: 'Well, it's a shame the FBI isn't doing background checks on these mentally ill people.' Well, duh. You took that opportunity away last year.

sole sponsor on this bill (*here:*) he was the only person who advocated introducing the regulation to stop the FBI from conducting background checks on potential gun owners
background checks *Hintergrund-Check, Überprüfung der Vergangenheit*
adjudicated (*here:*) diagnosed; *diagnostiziert*
for the record (*here:*) in public; *zum Mitschreiben*

The people in the government who were voted into power are lying to us.

And us kids seem to be the only ones who notice and our parents to call BS.

BS an abbreviation of "bullshit"

Companies trying to make caricatures of teenagers these days, saying that all we are self-involved, and trend-obsessed, and they hush us into submission when our message doesn't reach the ears of the nation, we are prepared to call BS.

POLITICIANS WHO SIT IN THEIR GILDED HOUSE AND SENATE SEATS FUNDED BY THE NRA TELLING US NOTHING COULD HAVE BEEN DONE TO PREVENT THIS, WE CALL BS.

Politicians who sit in their gilded House and Senate seats funded by the NRA telling us nothing could have been done to prevent this, we call BS.

gilded gold-plated
The House of Representatives The *House of Representatives* and the Senate are the two houses of Congress. The House of Representatives has 435 members, and the Senate has 100 members. Both of these houses meet in the Capitol Building in Washington, D.C.
funded by sponsored by
tougher stricter
to decrease to reduce

They say tougher guns laws do not decrease gun violence. We call BS.

They say a good guy with a gun stops a bad guy with a gun. We call BS.

They say guns are just tools like knives, and are as dangerous as cars. We call BS.

They say no laws could have prevented the hundreds of senseless tragedies that have occurred. We call BS.

That us kids don't know what we're talking about, that we're too young to understand how the government works. We call BS.

If you agree, register to vote. Contact your local congress people. Give them a piece of your mind.

give them a piece of your mind tell them what you think (about introducing stricter gun controls)

(Audience chants: "Throw them out.")

ASSIGNMENTS

A) Pre-Listening and Pre-Reading Activity

▶ *interactive classroom / paired work / brainstorming / self-immersion / group work / mind mapping / idea tower / set up a project / implementing ideas / enquiry-based learning*

1. Work in pairs, then in groups: Read the headlines below. What ideas come to mind when you read headlines such as these?
2. Why are there so many mass shootings in US schools? Share your ideas with your classmates.

February 14, 2018 - Marjory Stoneman Douglas High School – in Parkland, Florida. 19-year-old former student, Nikolas Cruz, opened fire with an AR-15 rifle, killing at least 17 people, and injuring at least 14 others. According to law enforcement, the suspect activated a fire alarm to draw people outside to increase casualties. Cruz was arrested and charged with 17 counts of premeditated murder.
October 24, 2014 - Marysville-Pilchuck High School – in Marysville, Washington. Freshman Jaylen Fryberg shot five people in the school cafeteria, killing one. Fryberg died of a self-inflicted gunshot wound at the scene. A second victim died of her injuries two days later, and a third died on October 31. A fourth victim died on November 7, bringing the total number of fatalities to five, including the gunman.
December 14, 2012 - Sandy Hook Elementary School – in Newtown, Connecticut. 20-year-old Adam Lanza gunned down 20 children, aged 6 and 7, and six adults, including school staff and faculty, before turning the gun on himself. Investigating police officers later found Nancy Lanza, Adam's mother, dead from a gunshot wound. There were 28 fatalities in total, including the shooter.
February 27, 2012 – Chardon High School – in Chardon, Ohio. 16-year-old student Daniel Parmertor was killed and four others were wounded when 17-year-old student T.J. Lane opened fire at the school. On February 28, 16-year-old Demetrius Hewlin died as a result of his injuries, and 17-year-old Russell King Jr. was declared brain dead. In March 2013, Lane was sentenced to life in prison. On September 11, 2014, Lane escaped from prison. He was captured early the next morning.
October 2, 2006 - Georgetown Amish School – in Nickel Mines, Pennsylvania. 32-year-old Charles Roberts IV went to a small Amish school and took at least 11 girls hostage. Five girls were killed and six others were wounded. Roberts then turned the gun on himself.
March 5, 2001 - Santana High School – in Santee, California. 15-year-old Charles "Andy" Williams killed two of his classmates, a 14-year-old and a 17-year-old, and injured a further 13 people. In 2002, Williams was sentenced to serve at least 50 years in prison.
April 20, 1999 – Columbine High School – in Littleton, Colorado. 18-year-old Eric Harris and 17-year-old Dylan Klebold killed 12 fellow students and one teacher before committing suicide in the school library.

Taken from: *CNN*, February 19, 2018
https://edition.cnn.com/2013/09/19/us/u-s-school-violence-fast-facts/index.html

B) Reading and Listening Comprehension

cooperative learning / think – pair – share / listening and reading / dramatised reading / taking notes / writing conference / posters / gallery walk

1. Watch Emma González's speech here:
   a) Video: https://hellogiggles.com/news/emma-gonzalez-full-speech, or on:
   b) *CNN*: https://edition.cnn.com/2018/02/17/us/florida-student-emma-gonzalez-speech/index.html.
2. While watching the speech, highlight any striking keywords and important statements on your speech transcript.
3. "The guns have changed but our laws have not." Explain what Emma González means.
4. "And, in this case, if you actively do nothing, people continually end up dead, so it's time to start doing something." Explain González's criticism of inaction in this appeal to the audience.
5. "Politicians who sit in their gilded House and Senate seats funded by the NRA telling us nothing could have been done to prevent this, we call BS." Explain what Emma González means when she says this.
6. Summarize Emma González's main arguments.

C) Analysis

independent learning / work in groups / peer support / posters / presentations / feedback / discussion

1. Analyse the structure of González's speech and explain why it has been organised in this way.
2. Examine some stylistic and rhetorical devices from the speech and explain how these devices support Emma González's emotional message.
3. Analyse and evaluate González's final appeal to the audience and the effect it has.

D) Evaluation, Comment, Creative Activities

writing conference / posters / tablet or laptop presentation / discussion / speech / role play / press conference / evaluation / writing a comment or an editorial for a newspaper / feedback

1. Work with a partner or in a small group. Compare and evaluate your first impressions of Emma González's speech.
2. "That us kids don't know what we're talking about, that we're too young to understand how the government works. We call BS." Explain your own point of view regarding this statement.
3. Write an email to Emma González in which you give your opinion of her speech.
4. Role Play: Prepare and arrange a press conference with Emma González and her classmates. Journalists from different countries attend the conference and ask questions.

E) Further Projects for Information, Thought and Discussion

research / WebQuest / tablet or laptop presentation / discussion / speech / role play / press conference

1. Go online and find out some more information about the National Rifle Association (NRA) in the US. Make a list of the most important facts about it.
2. Gather the most important information about weapon laws in Germany, and in the U.S. Discuss your findings in class.
3. Emma González cites Wayne LaPierre, the National Rifle Association's Executive Vice President, who said: "The only thing that stops a bad guy with a gun is a good guy with a gun." Prepare and give a three-minute speech in your group, then in class, in response to LaPierre's statement, and González's opinion of it.
4. **The year 2018 was by far the worst on record for gun violence in US schools.** The NPS Center for Homeland Defense and Security counted 95 school shooting incidents in 2018. The School Shooting Database Project is conducted as part of the Advanced Thinking in Homeland Security program at the Naval Postgraduate School's Center for Homeland Defense and Security (CHDS). Source: https://www.chds.us/ssdb/about/

F) Further Information: The Second Amendment

1. **The Second Amendment is one of 10 amendments that form the Bill of Rights,** ratified in 1791 by the U.S. Congress. Differing interpretations of the amendment – often referred to as "the right to bear arms" – have fueled a long-running debate over gun control legislation, and the right of individual citizens to buy, own, and carry firearms. The text of the Second Amendment reads in full: *"A well-regulated Militia, being necessary to the security of a free State, the right of the people to keep and bear Arms, shall not be infringed."*
   Practically since its ratification, Americans have debated the meaning of the Second Amendment, with vehement arguments being made on both sides.
   The crux of the debate is whether the amendment protects the right of private individuals to keep and bear arms, or whether it instead protects a collective right to bear arms that should be exercised only through formal military units. Those who argue it is a collective right point out the "well-regulated Militia" clause in the Second Amendment. They argue that the right to bear arms should be given only to organized groups, like the National Guard.
   On the other side are those who argue that the Second Amendment gives all citizens, not just militias, the right to own guns in order to protect themselves. The National Rifle Association (NRA), founded in 1871, and its supporters, have been the most visible proponents of this argument, and have pursued a vigorous campaign against gun control measures at local, state, and federal levels.

Those who support stricter gun control legislation have argued that limits are necessary on gun ownership, including who can own them, where they can be carried, and what type of guns should be available to purchase.
From: *History* https://www.history.com/topics/2nd-amendment

2. **The Second Amendment: Scientific Research**
„Der zweite Verfassungszusatz hatte zunächst gar nicht das individuelle Recht der amerikanischen Bürger im Sinn, sondern sprach von Waffen für eine Bürgerwehr, erklärt Manfred Berg, Professor für Amerikanische Geschichte. An der Uni Heidelberg befasst er sich mit der Verfassungsgeschichte der USA. Berg sagt: "Es ging den Gründervätern um das Recht des Volkes, sich in Milizen zu organisieren. Das bewaffnete Volk galt ihnen als Gegengewicht gegen tyrannische Regierungen."
http://www.t-online.de/nachrichten/ausland/usa/id_83310970/waffengesetze-in-den-usa-warum-die-amerikaner-waffen-so-lieben.html (March 25, 2018)

Tasks:

1. Outline the historical context of the Second Amendment.
2. Evaluate the significance of the Second Amendment in the United States today.

G) "Dear National Rifle Association: We Won't Let You Win."

By Darcy Schleifstein, Zachary Dougherty and Sarah Emily Baum
The New York Times, March 13, 2018
https://www.nytimes.com/2018/03/13/opinion/nra-shooting-marjory-stoneman-douglas.html
The killings of 17 people at [...] Douglas High School [...] may be the massacre that finally gets [...] governments to enact common-sense gun control laws. [...] Our parents and grandparents did not succeed in ensuring our safety at school. So we must do it ourselves. [...] We have to [...] end senseless killing, not just for our sakes, but for the sakes of future generations [...].
***Darcy Schleifstein** is a sophomore at Randolph High School, **Zachary Dougherty** is a junior at Toms River North High School and **Sarah Emily Baum** is a senior at Marlboro High School, all in New Jersey.*

Tasks:

1. Go online and visit the NYT website: Read the students' *Letter to the NRA* and summarise the main ideas.
2. Write an email to the students in response to their letter to the NRA.
3. Give a speech and explain your opinion.

H) Further Reading for Thought and Discussion:

1. **"How right-wingers attacked Parkland students with lies, hoaxes and smears"**
This group [*March for Our Lives*] of idealistic young people has officially become the right's leading hate figures. No issue unites the American right more than their opposition to gun control. The first and most repugnant strategy was to directly attack high-profile campaigners, especially students David Hogg and Emma González. [...]
Jason Wilson in: *The Guardian,* March 26, 2018 / https://www.theguardian.com/us-news/2018/mar/26/emma-gonzalez-david-hogg-attacks-rightwing-constitutions-hoaxes
2. **The American College of Physicians (ACP)** "firmly believes that firearms-related injuries and deaths can be prevented by implementing common-sense restrictions to keep guns from people who pose a threat to themselves or others, including requiring universal background checks [...] ."
Go online and visit the ACP website: https://www.acponline.org/acp-newsroom/acp-reaffirms-urgent-need-for-policies-to-reduce-gun-violence-in-light-of-recent-mass-shootings (accessed: March 21, 2019)
3. **North Carolina proposes laws allowing teachers to carry guns in schools:**
North Carolina is planning controversial new laws that allow teachers to carry weapons while on school grounds and even provide a financial incentive for educators to arm themselves. Rachel Chernaskey in: *The Guardian,* March 20, 2019
https://www.theguardian.com/us-news/2019/mar/20/north-carolina-proposes-laws-allow-teachers-carry-guns-schools
4. **Fake News and Conspiracy Theory:** The Sandy Hook mass shooting has become synonymous with the most macabre and vicious case study in conspiracy theory. From the day after the shooting the inhuman suggestions that the murders had been "staged" by the American "deep state" or "the anti-gun lobby", that the grieving parents were "crisis actors", and that their children had not been murdered at all, has been fuelled and spread across social media.
Tim Adams in: *The Guardian,* March 31, 2019
https://www.theguardian.com/us-news/2019/mar/31/sandy-hook-shooting-suicide-parents-fake-news-conspiracy

"They Hate Individual Freedom."

Wayne LaPierre is the Executive Vice President of the National Rifle Association (NRA) in the USA. He gave this speech during the Conservative Political Action Conference (CPAC) at the National Harbor in Oxon Hill, Prince George's County, Maryland, on February 22, 2018.

RELATED TOPICS

THE AMERICAN DREAM · THE CONSTITUTION · THE BILL OF RIGHTS · THE FOUNDING CREED · FREEDOM · THE GOVERNMENT · GUN CONTROL · HISTORY · HUMAN RIGHTS · INJUSTICE · LIBERTY · MASS SHOOTINGS · RIGHT WING POLITICS · SCHOOLS · THE SECOND AMENDMENT · SECURITY · VIOLENCE

Some of the most powerful people in American politics are members of the gun lobby, including **Wayne LaPierre**. His position as a supporter of lax gun controls and the Second Amendment faces ever more scrutiny, particularly due to mass school shootings. LaPierre's approach to these challenges is often very defensive. He retorts that it is the 'elites' and 'socialists' who are most likely to want stricter gun controls implemented. This is something which he feels compromises the very constitution of the United States.

Speaking to the Political Action Conference (CPAC) in Maryland, Wayne LaPierre discussed what he believes are the political motivations of these 'elites'. As far as he is concerned, the right approach would be for the authorities to offer more protection for places, such as schools. Instead, their approach of requesting stricter controls strikes LaPierre as a simple means of gaining more power and control by leaving the population unarmed. He claims, 'They hate the National Rifle Association (NRA), they hate the Second Amendment and they hate individual freedoms.'

LaPierre's high-level position within the gun lobby has naturally seen him become one of the most well-known gun rights advocates in the United States. In fact, he has been involved with the administration of the NRA for many years, starting in 1977, and having since held the positions of Executive Vice President and Chief Executive Officer since 1991. His reputation as a leading supporter of gun rights places him right in the middle of campaigners on both sides of the argument. Those who support the Second Amendment adore his work while those who are working to achieve stricter laws naturally see people like him as the biggest problem.

Speech transcript and video available on *CNN* http://edition.cnn.com/TRANSCRIPTS/1802/22/cnr.03.html

Wayne LaPierre:

Thank you very much. I appreciate this opportunity. We have serious discussions ahead and serious issues that impact each and every one of us.

Just a week ago, we were all horrified by another terrible tragedy at an American school. Each and every member of the National Rifle Association mourns the loss of the innocent and continues to keep their families and that community in our prayers. We share a goal of safe schools, safe neighborhoods, and a safe country.

As usual, the opportunists wasted not one second to exploit tragedy for political gain. Saul Alinski would have been proud. The break back speed of calls for more gun control laws and the breathless national media eager to smear the NRA.

THEY HATE THE NRA. THEY HATE THE SECOND AMENDMENT. THEY HATE INDIVIDUAL FREEDOM.

Think about that, in the midst of genuine grief, and a very understandable passion, as millions of Americans searched for meaningful solutions, what do we find? Chris Murphy, Nancy Pelosi, and more, cheered on by the national media, eager to blame the NRA and call for even more government control. They hate the NRA. They hate the Second Amendment. They hate individual freedom.

In the rush of calls for more government [controls], they also revealed their true selves. The elites don't care, not one wit about America's school system. And school children. If they truly cared, what they would do is they would protect them. For them, it is not a safety issue. It is a political issue. They care more about control, and more of it. Their goal is to eliminate the Second Amendment and our firearms freedoms, so they can eradicate all individual freedoms. (*Applause*)

What they want are more restrictions on the law abiding. Think about that, their solution is to make you, all of you, less free. They want to sweep right under the carpet the failure of school security, the failure of family, the failure of America's mental health system, and even the unbelievable failure of the FBI. (*Applause*)

They fantasize about more laws, stopping what other laws failed to stop. The truth is, laws succeed only when people obey them. That's what the law-abiding majority in this country practices. But once again, so many existing laws were ignored.

Their laws don't stop illegal criminals from crossing our borders every single day.

to appreciate to be grateful for
to impact to affect; *Auswirkung haben auf, beeinflussen*

an American school (*here:*) a reference to Marjory Stoneman Douglas High School in Fort Lauderdale, Florida
to mourn to grieve; *trauern*
goal aim

opportunist if you describe someone as an opportunist, you are critical of them, arguing that they take advantage of any situation in order to gain power/influence, without considering whether their actions are right or wrong
to exploit tragedy for political gain *die Tragödie für den politischen Vorteil missbrauchen*
to smear to tarnish, to damage the reputation of; *jemandes Ruf beschädigen*
genuine honest, sincere
grief sorrow, misery
Chris Murphy Following the tragic shooting at Sandy Hook elementary school in 2012, Senator Murphy became one of the leading proponents of common sense reforms to reduce gun violence; he is a member of the Democratic Party.
Nancy Pelosi is a member of the Democratic Party who has served as the Minority Leader of the House of Representatives since 2011; she previously served as the 52nd House Speaker from 2007 to 2011, the only woman ever to do so.
not one wit not at all, not one iota; *kein bisschen, um keinen Deut*
to eliminate to abolish, to get rid of; *abschaffen*
The Second Amendment is one of ten amendments that form the Bill of Rights, ratified in 1791 by the U.S. Congress. It gives the American population "the right to bear arms."
to eradicate to destroy, to get rid of
the law-abiding majority *gesetzestreue Mehrheit der Bürger*
to sweep right under the carpet *unter den Teppich kehren*
to fantasize *phantasieren*
to obey to follow orders, to do what one is told to do; *befolgen*

Their laws don't stop the scourge of gang violence and drug crime that savages Baltimore, Chicago, and every major American community.

scourge horror; *Geißel, Übel*

Their laws haven't stopped the plague of opioids, and Chinese fentanyl from Mexico, that floods American streets, and kills victims every single day in this country.

opioids drugs; *Opioide*
Chinese fentanyl (*here:*) deadly Chinese narcotics/drugs

No wonder law-abiding Americans, all over this country, revere their Second Amendment freedom to protect themselves more than ever. [...]

to revere to cherish, to appreciate; *verehren*

They don't care if their laws work or not. They just want to get more laws, to get more control over people.

But the NRA, the NRA does care. We – (*Applause*) We at the NRA are Americans who continue to mourn and care and work every day at contributing real solutions to this very real problem. Real practical action to truly protect our children.

to contribute (*here:*) to come up with; *beitragen, sich ausdenken*

Think about it. It is a bizarre fact that in this country our jewelry stores, all over this country, are more important than our children. Our banks, our airports, our NBA games, our NFL games, our office buildings, our movie stars, our politicians, they're all more protected than our children at school. Does that make any sense to anybody? Do we really love our money and our celebrities more than we love our children? Can we answer that question honestly? Any of us? Can we answer that question honestly? Knowing that we surround and protect so much with armed security while we drop our kids off at school that are so-called gun free zones, that are wide open targets for any crazy mad man bent on evil to come there first.

celebrities famous people; *Berühmtheiten*
to be bent on evil *entschlossen sein, Böses zu tun*

In every community in America, school districts, PTAs, teachers' unions, local law enforcement, moms and dads, they all must come together to implement the very best strategy to harden their schools, including effective trained armed security that will absolutely protect every innocent child in this country. (*Applause*)

A Parent-Teacher Association (PTA) is an organization composed of parents, teachers, and staff that is intended to facilitate parental participation in a school
to implement to put in place; *umsetzen*
to harden to strengthen, (*here:*) to protect
innocent *unschuldig*

And that has to happen now. Evil walks among us. And God help us if we don't harden our schools and protect our kids. The whole idea from some of our opponents that armed security makes us less safe is completely ridiculous. If that's true, and just think about this, if that's true, armed security makes us less safe, let's just go ahead and remove it from everywhere. Let's remove it from the White House, from Capitol Hill, and remove it from all of Hollywood. (*Applause*)

ridiculous silly, absurd, foolish; *lächerlich*

WE WILL PROVIDE IMMEDIATE ASSISTANCE AND WE WILL ALSO PROVIDE IT ABSOLUTELY FREE TO ANY SCHOOL IN AMERICA.

Any American school that needs immediate professional consultation and help with organizing and defining these solutions should call the National Rifle Association school shield program. And we will provide immediate assistance and we will also provide it absolutely free to any school in America. (*Applause*) [...]

Obama promised a fundamental transformation of our country. And you know what, it began with his own national party. A party that is now infested with saboteurs who don't believe in capitalism, don't believe in the Constitution, don't believe in our freedom, and don't believe in America as we know it. Obama may be gone, but their utopian dream, it marches on.

That should terrify every citizen who values the American ideal in this country of individual liberty. [...] Absolute control in every corner of our government is their ultimate dream. These intellectual leads, they think they're smarter than we are. They think they're smarter than the rest of us. And they think they're better than we are. They truly believe it, and you know it. (*Applause*) [...]

There is no stronger supporter of our law enforcement than the National Rifle Association. My gosh, we're one of the largest law enforcement organizations in the United States if you look at our membership. (*Applause*)

And we're proud of that. Everywhere I go I get a police officer coming up to me, thanking me and saying I'm a member of your organization, keep up what you're doing. And there are tens of thousands of incredible men and women at the FBI. These are honorable, decent, hardworking people, and they're dedicated to keeping our country safe every single day. (*Applause*) [...]

Look, and this is really important, and you never hear this on the national media, so I want to say it to all of you now and I need your help in telling all Americans, this is the truth. The National Rifle Association originated the national instant check system, it was our bill. No one on the prohibited persons list should ever have access to a firearm. No killer, no felon, no drug dealer. (*Applause*)

And anyone that is adjudicated as mentally incompetent or a danger to society should be added to the check system and prevented from getting their hands on a gun. (*Applause*)

Look, you know, the whole discussion of the Second Amendment and the gun issue in this country has become so dishonest in the national

transformation change

infested with saboteurs *von Saboteuren befallen*

saboteur a person who makes a mess of a situation on purpose

intellectual leads (*here:*) clever leaders

law enforcement *Durchsetzung von Gesetzen*

incredible exceptional, outstanding; *außergewöhnlich engagiert*

dedicated committed, devoted; *mit Leib und Seele (für die Sicherheit unseres Landes) einsetzen*

check system gun control system

prohibited persons list a list of people who are not allowed to carry guns

to have access to (*here:*) to be able to use

felon criminal

adjudicated (*here:*) diagnosed; *diagnostiziert*

dishonest *unehrlich*

media and so dishonest among politicians that you can barely stand it.

I even heard a television pundit recently suggesting that people seeking to buy a firearm should be interviewed first. I mean, interviewed first? Who's going to conduct that interview? And what will they ask? That's the challenge we as a free society face. How do we create a step along the way called due process that protects the innocent law-abiding people of this country from being falsely accused, politically abused, and permanently stigmatized unjustly?

pundit expert, specialist

stigmatized *stigmatisiert*
unjustly unfairly

THEY LIKE ONLY LIMITED SPEECH, CONTROLLED SPEECH, CONTROLLED BY THEM.

Come on. Socialists oppose all of our most fundamental freedoms enshrined in the Bill of Rights. They don't like free speech any more than they like the Second Amendment. They like only limited speech, controlled speech, controlled by them, through safe speech zones, where they can shame the outspoken, or riot to shut them up. If you still think we have full First Amendment freedom in this country, try going right now out to Berkeley and speaking out in favor of conservative causes or even the Second Amendment. (*Applause*)

THIS GROWING SOCIALIST STATE DREAMS OF MANIPULATING SCHOOLCHILDREN

This growing socialist state dreams of manipulating schoolchildren, to squeeze and squeeze information about their parents. They'll be asking your kids if mommy and daddy spank them, or what mommy and daddy feeds them for dinner, they'll want to know what TV shows you watch, what magazines and newspapers you read, and, oh, yes, do mommy and daddy own a gun?

enshrined (*here:*) protected, preserved
The Bill of Rights amendments (created: September 25, 1789 / ratified: December 15, 1791) add to the Constitution specific guarantees of personal freedoms and rights, and clear limitations on the government's power
The First Amendment protects several basic individual liberties, such as freedom of religion, freedom of speech, freedom of the press, freedom to petition, and freedom of assembly.
Berkeley a reference to the University of California, Berkeley, in San Francisco; Berkeley is known as a liberal university.
try going right now out to Berkeley and speaking out in favor of conservative causes LaPierre claims that there is a lack of free speech on college campuses
to squeeze (*here:*) to extract; *herauspressen*
to spank to hit, to smack

And all that private information will be entered into that ultimate list, that cloud of data storage that couldn't care less about due process and constitutional freedom and your privacy as an American citizen. And then it is just a short hop to the systematic destruction of our most basic freedoms in this country. And you all know what they are, but let me say them, family, faith, individual responsibility, and self-destiny, a free market economy, patriotism, respect for our national flag and national anthem, personal liberty, and justice for all. (*Applause*)

data storage *Informationsträger, Datenspeicherung*
that couldn't care less *nicht im geringsten darauf Wert legen*
due process *rechtsstaatliches Verfahren*
privacy *Privatspäre*
hop jump

Going back a decade or more, these essential freedoms and these essential values have been increasingly and sadly ridiculed and disrespected and diminished in this country. And it won't take long if we stay on the path.

ridiculed laughed at, made fun of; *verhöhnt, lächerlich gemacht*
disrespected insulted, dishonored; *nicht geachtet, nicht geschätzt*
diminished weakened, reduced

ASSIGNMENTS

A) Reading and Listening Comprehension

cooperative learning / paired work / mind mapping / group work / peer support and feedback

1. Watch the video of Wayne LaPierre's speech here: https://www.youtube.com/watch?v=vvw3pHiWUfQ
   C-Span TV Network Video:
   https://www.c-span.org/video/?441475-3/conservative-political-action-conference-wayne-lapierre-remarks
2. Read the transcript and highlight or underline any important keywords, phrases and statements.
3. Work with a partner. Discuss LaPierre's most significant statements.
4. What does Wayne LaPierre suggest doing in order to "protect every innocent child in this country?"
5. Write a summary of Wayne LaPierre's speech and explain his main arguments.

B) Analysis

individual work / group work / students teach each other / peer support and feedback / presentation

1. Analyse a) the structure, b) the language, c) the most frequently used keywords and phrases, and d) the tone of Wayne LaPierre's speech, and explain their intended effects on the audience.
2. Watch the video and analyse a) Wayne LaPierre's body language and b) his appearance and gestures, c) his tone of voice.
3. Examine the rhetorical devices LaPierre uses and explain their intended effects on the audience. Here are some ideas to start with.
   a) "We have serious discussions [...] We share a goal [...] we were all horrified [...] in our prayers [...] every one of us [...]"
   Rhetorical Device: ____________________ Message: ______________________________
   Intended Effect: ______________________________
   b) "We share a goal of safe schools, safe neighborhoods, and a safe country. [...]"
   c) "They hate the NRA. They hate the Second Amendment. They hate individual freedom."
   d) "They fantasize about more laws [...] Their laws don't stop illegal criminals [...] Their laws haven't stopped the plague of opioids [...] Their laws don't stop the scourge of gang violence."
   e) "It is a bizarre fact that in this country our jewelry stores, all over this country, are more important than our children. Our banks, our airports, our NBA games, our NFL games, our office buildings, our movie stars, our politicians, they're all more protected than our children at school."
   f) "But the NRA, the NRA does care. We at the NRA are Americans who continue to mourn and care and work every day at contributing real solutions to this very real problem. Real practical action to truly protect our children."
   g) "Come on. Socialists oppose all of our most fundamental freedoms enshrined in the Bill of Rights. They don't like free speech any more than they like the Second Amendment. They like only limited speech, controlled speech, controlled by them."

C) Evaluation, Comment, Creative Activities

agile work / interactive classroom / writing conference / posters / gallery walk / role play / hot seat / discussion / speech / press conference / evaluation / SOLO taxonomy

1. "The elites don't care, not one wit about America's school system. And school children. If they truly cared, what they would do is they would protect them." What kind of protection does Wayne LaPierre offer? Discuss and evaluate his suggestion and explain your own point of view.

2. Wayne LaPierre criticizes his opponents, saying: "Their goal is to eliminate the Second Amendment and our firearms freedoms, so they can eradicate all individual freedoms." Prepare and give a three-minute speech in response to his remarks.
3. Go online and find controversial quotations from Wayne LaPierre's speeches. Choose one of these quotations and prepare and give a three-minute speech to your group, then to your class, in response to it.
4. *Hot Seat:* Prepare a *hot seat interview* in groups. One student takes on the role of Wayne LaPierre, the Vice President of the NRA. Then he or she is interviewed by journalists representing a wide range of political and social movements and ideas.
5. Role Play: Prepare and arrange a press conference with Chris W. Cox, the NRA Executive Director, and members of his team. Journalists from different countries attend the conference and ask questions.

D) Further Project: Dana Loesch: "Many in legacy media love mass shootings."

NRA spokeswoman Dana Loesch said that the media exploits mass shooting to capitalize on ratings. "Many in legacy media love mass shootings," Loesch said. "I'm not saying you love the tragedy, but you love the ratings. Crying white mothers are ratings gold."

Tasks:

1. Watch Dana Loesch's speech on the Huffington Post website:
   https://www.huffingtonpost.com.au/2018/02/22/nras-dana-loesch-many-in-legacy-media-love-mass-shootings_a_23368790/
2. Video: Dana Loesch, NRA SPIEGEL Online
   http://www.spiegel.de/video/nra-sprecherin-dana-loesch-und-die-politische-agenda-video-99013584.html
3. Dana Loesch says that "many in legacy media love mass shootings to capitalize on ratings".
   a) Why does Loesch use the term legacy media?
   b) Write a letter to the editor in response to Loesch's statements.
   c) Write an email to Dana Loesch in response to her video.
   d) Evaluate her statements and organise a class debate about them.

E) President Trump tweeted his support for Wayne LaPierre and the NRA:

F) Mediation (German = > English)

„NRA-Chef Wayne LaPierre. Abwiegeln, ablenken, angreifen"

Nach dem jüngsten Massaker sorgt der Chef von Amerikas mächtiger Waffenlobby für Entsetzen. Bei einem Mann kommt Wayne LaPierres Masche dagegen an: Donald Trump.

Über eine Woche hatte Wayne LaPierre geschwiegen. [...] Der Geschäftsführer der National Rifle Association (NRA),

einer der mächtigsten Lobbygruppen in den Vereinigten Staaten, wartete bis Donnerstag. Und er wählte eine für ihn weit angenehmere Umgebung für seinen Auftritt: die Conservative Political

Action Conference in Maryland – das größte Jahrestreffen der amerikanischen Konservativen.
Es hätte ein Auftritt voller Demut werden können. Ein Moment der Selbstreflexion, nachdem ein junger Mann mit einem Sturmgewehr durch die Parkland-Highschool gezogen war und 17 Schüler und Lehrer erschossen hatte. Doch nicht mit Wayne LaPierre. Der 68-Jährige machte das, was er seit Jahrzehnten tut: abwiegeln, ablenken – und vor allem attackieren. Klar beklage seine Organisation die Opfer, sagte LaPierre. Aber in Wahrheit würden doch andere jetzt den Fall instrumentalisieren: die "Eliten", die Demokraten. "Sie hassen die NRA", schimpfte LaPierre. "Sie hassen die individuelle Freiheit."
Nach dem Massaker hatte die Kritik an der Lobbygruppe wieder deutlich zugenommen. Schülerproteste fanden weltweit Beachtung. LaPierre sprach nun von "Sozialisten im europäischen Stil" und "Saboteuren", die bei den Demokraten die Kontrolle übernommen hätten. Seine Rede war ein Rundumschlag: gegen die "Mainstreammedien", gegen Liberale, gegen das FBI.
Bei einem Mann kommt so etwas gut an. US-Präsident Donald Trump nahm LaPierre und seine Leute in Schutz. Was viele nicht verstehen wollen, twitterte Trump, Wayne und die Leute, "die so hart bei der NRA arbeiten, sind großartige Menschen und großartige amerikanische Patrioten". [...]
SPIEGEL ONLINE, Kevin Hagen, 23.02.2018, https://www.spiegel.de/politik/ausland/usa-nra-geschaeftsfuehrer-wayne-lapierre-der-scharfmacher-a-1195108.html

Tasks:
1. Translate the author's main ideas and arguments into English.
2. Discuss and explain your own opinion on the issue of gun control.
3. Write and act out an imagined discussion between Sarah Emily Baum, Chris W. Cox, Zachary Dougherty, Emma González, David Hogg, Wayne LaPierre, Dana Loesch, and Darcy Schleifstein.

G) Cartoons about "Gun Control" and "School Mass Shootings"
Go online and find cartoons about "gun control" and "school mass shootings".

Tasks:
1. Describe and analyse one of the cartoons you have found.
2. Evaluate how the cartoon portrays current issues surrounding gun control and school mass shootings.
3. Evaluate how well the cartoonist gets his or her message across.
4. Set up a gallery featuring the most impressive and inspiring cartoons.
5. Contact a cartoonist and tell them your opinion of the significance of the cartoon(s).

H) For Thought and Discussion
1. "All we are asking is to be safe. We don't want any more guns in our schools. We want to live, learn and prosper – not run, fight and hide." Lauren Hogg and Ryan Deitsch, Miami Herald, May 2, 2019, https://www.miamiherald.com/opinion/op-ed/article229969154.html Lauren Hogg is a student and Ryan Deitsch is a graduate of Marjory Stoneman Douglas High School. They are co-founders of *March For Our Lives*.
2. „Immer mehr Tote durch Schusswaffen in den USA": ARD Tagesschau v. 14.12.2018
Audio: https://www.tagesschau.de/multimedia/audio/audio-64551.html
3. „Der Gebrauch von Schusswaffen ist Alltag in den USA. Das bedeutet pro Jahr 40.000 Tote. Die Ärzte schlagen Alarm." *Süddeutsche Zeitung* vom 30. Januar 2019, Seite 1 und 3

The Future UK – EU Relationship

K

Theresa May's Brexit Speech and the Future UK – EU Relationship

On March 2, 2018, Theresa May delivered a speech at Mansion House in London on her plans for a future UK – EU relationship after Brexit. Here is (A) the introductory part and (B) the final part of Theresa May's Brexit speech setting out her vision.

RELATED TOPICS

BREXIT · DEMOCRACY · EUROPEAN UNION · FUTURE · GOVERNMENT · GREAT BRITAIN · PARTNERSHIP · PRIME MINISTER · REFERENDUM · RELATIONSHIP WITH EUROPE · UNITED KINGDOM · VALUES

Theresa May is a leading conservative politician in the United Kingdom. She was elected the MP for Maidenhead in 1997. Since she took office, May has played a major role in a number of administrations and cabinets. Until the coalition government of 2010, May served as part of a Conservative Shadow Cabinet for around 11 years. Often one to break down boundaries, May was the first Conservative Party Chairwoman, a role which she held between 2002 and 2003. In 2010, she joined the Conservative and Liberal Democrats coalition cabinet as the Home Secretary. She remained in this role as the Conservatives won the election outright in 2015, until 2016, when she became the Prime Minister herself.

Theresa May is the daughter of a vicar and during her upbringing, she experienced both state and private schooling. Her education culminated with a degree in Geography from Oxford University, where she attended St Hugh's College. This gave her the foundations to launch a successful career, beginning at the Bank of England, before also working at organisations such as the Association for Payment Clearing Services (APACS) in a variety of multi-national roles.

After David Cameron resigned from his post as Prime Minister, Theresa May automatically became the new Leader of the Conservative Party when the only other candidate dropped out of the running. This resulted in her becoming the Prime Minister on July 13, 2016.

After failing to get her Brexit deal through the Houses of Parliament three times, Theresa May stepped down on the agreed date of May 24, 2019. She remains a politician for her constituency in Maidenhead.

The Prime Minister Theresa May:

A) I am here today to set out my vision for the future economic partnership between the United Kingdom and the European Union.
There have been many different voices and views in the debate on what our new relationship with the EU should look like. I have listened carefully to them all. But as we chart our way forward with the EU, I want to take a moment to look back. Eighteen months ago I stood in Downing Street and addressed the nation for my first time as Prime Minister.

I made this pledge then, to the people that I serve: I know you're working around the clock, I know you're doing your best, and I know that sometimes life can be a struggle. The government I lead will be driven not by the interests of the privileged few, but by yours. We will do everything we can to give you more control over your lives. When we take the big calls, we'll think not of the powerful, but you. When we pass new laws, we'll listen not to the mighty, but to you. When it comes to taxes, we'll prioritise not the wealthy, but you. When it comes to opportunity, we won't entrench the advantages of the fortunate few. We will do everything we can to help anybody, whatever your background, to go as far as your talents will take you.
We are living through an important moment in our country's history. As we leave the European Union, we will forge a bold new positive role for ourselves in the world, and we will make Britain a country that works not for a privileged few, but for every one of us.
That pledge, to the people of our United Kingdom is what guides me in our negotiations with the EU. And for me that means five things:
First, the agreement we reach with the EU must respect the referendum. It was a vote to take control of our borders, laws and money. And a vote for wider change, so that no community in Britain would ever be left behind again. But it was not a vote for a distant relationship with our neighbours.
Second, the new agreement we reach with the EU must endure. After Brexit both the UK and the EU want to forge ahead with building a better future for our people, not find ourselves back at the negotiating table because things have broken down.
Third, it must protect people's jobs and security. People in the UK voted for our country to have a new and different relationship with Europe, but while the means may change our shared goals surely have not – to work together to grow our economies and keep our people safe.
Fourth, it must be consistent with the kind of country we want to be as we leave: a modern, open, outward-looking, tolerant, European democracy. A nation of pioneers, innovators, explorers and creators. A country that celebrates our history and diversity, confident of our place in the world; that meets its obligations to our near neighbours and far off friends, and is proud to stand up for its values.
And fifth, in doing all of these things, it must strengthen our union of nations and our union of people. We must bring our country back together, taking into account the views of everyone who cares about this issue, from both sides of the debate.
As Prime Minister it is my duty to represent all of our United Kingdom, England, Scotland, Wales and Northern Ireland; north and south, from coastal towns and rural villages to our great cities. So these are the five tests for the deal that we will negotiate. Implementing the decision of the British people; reaching an enduring solution; protecting our security and prosperity; delivering an outcome that is consistent with the kind of country we want to be; and bringing our country together, strengthening the precious union of all our people. [...]

B) I look forward to discussing our future partnership with our European friends.
Because although we are leaving the EU – and in that regard we will become separate - we are all still European and will stay linked by the many ties and values we have in common. And because it is only by working together that we will find solutions that work for all our peoples.
Yes, there will be ups and downs in the months ahead. As in any negotiation, no-one will get everything they want. We will not be buffeted by the demands to talk tough or threaten a walk out. Just as we will not accept the counsels of despair that this simply cannot be done. We will move forward by calm, patient discussion of each other's positions. It is my responsibility as Prime Minister to provide that leadership for our country at this crucial time. By following the course I have set out today, I am confident we will get there and deliver the right outcome for Britain and the EU. A generation from now what will be remembered is not the rough and tumble of negotiation, but whether we reached an enduring solution cast in the interests of the people we are all here to serve.
So my message to our friends in Europe is clear. We know what we want. We understand your principles. We have a shared interest in getting this right. So let's get on with it.
Source: *BBC*, March 2, 2018, https://www.bbc.com/news/uk-politics-43256183

Tasks:

1. Summarise Theresa May's ideas. (*Comprehension*)
2. Analyse the rhetorical devices she uses to emphasise her message. (*Analysis*)
3. Choose one of these tasks (*Evaluation and Comment*):
   a) Write a letter to the editor of a newspaper and explain your opinion about the current relationship between Great Britain and the European Union.
   b) Write a speech about the current relationship between the United Kingdom and Germany.
4. Mediation (German = > English)
   a) Translate the following "letter", an editorial that was published in *Westdeutsche Zeitung*, into English and send it to your English-speaking partner school.
   b) Prepare and give a speech in response to this letter/editorial. Consider the current situation and the relationship between the United Kingdom and the European Union.
5. **For Thought and Discussion: EU Referendum Results: UK votes to LEAVE the EU**
   On June 23, 2016, the UK voted to leave the EU by 51,9 % to 48,1 %.
   Leave won the majority of votes in England and Wales, while every council in Scotland saw Remain majorities.
6. "To serve the country I love". Theresa May resigns as prime minister: Go online and watch her resignation speech on May 24, 2019: https://www.youtube.com/watch?v=KKt-Z5Yk2Wo

Leave: 51.9%	**REMAIN: 48.1%**
17,410,742 Votes	16,141,241 Votes

   For more information, visit:
   BBC https://www.bbc.com/news/politics/eu_referendum/results
7. On 5th September 2019, Prime Minister Boris Johnson said "he would rather be dead in a ditch" than delay Brexit. Explain, analyse and evaluate this statement.

„Ihr verrückten Briten, lasst den Brexit doch einfach“
Leitartikel, *Westdeutsche Zeitung*, Düsseldorf, 11.12.2018
Von Ekkehard Rüger

Liebe Briten, es ist Zeit für einen neuen Anlauf. Eigentlich war alles gesagt, das Tischtuch zerschnitten, die Liebe erkaltet. Aber manchmal gibt es im Leben eine zweite Chance. „Es ist. Ist es nicht?“
Seit wir uns beim Lesen von „Asterix und die Briten“ unter den Tisch gelacht haben, hattet Ihr einen klischeebeladenen, aber festen Platz in unseren Herzen: etwas spleenig vielleicht und ein bisschen zu oft auf eine Extrawurst bedacht, aber im Grunde in Eurer leicht gequälten Originalität auch irgendwie liebenswert. Von Eurem wunderbaren Land ganz zu schweigen. Wer dieses verrückte Konglomerat von Engländern, Walisern, Schotten und Iren nicht liebt, dem ist nicht mehr zu helfen. Und Eurer Queen liegt doch mittlerweile die ganze Welt zu Füßen.
Doch dann habt Ihr leider hohlen Populismus mit durchdachtem Eigensinn verwechselt und mit knapper Mehrheit den Ausstieg aus der EU erklärt. Zweieinhalb Jahre ist das jetzt her. Es gibt Menschen, die haben weniger Zeit zum Nachdenken. Wir sind sicher, Ihr habt sie genutzt. Nicht alle vielleicht, aber mehr als damals im Juni 2016.
Jetzt hat Euch der Europäische Gerichtshof noch mal eine goldene Brücke über den Ärmelkanal gebaut. Ihr könntet den Brexit mitsamt dem 600 Seiten starken Austrittsvertrag einfach in der Nordsee versenken, als wäre nichts gewesen – ohne uns noch mal zu fragen. Wenn Ihr das bringen würdet, hätte Eure Spleenigkeit endgültig Kultstatus erreicht und Eure Art, Politik zu betreiben, wäre ein Anwärter auf die Eintragung als Weltkulturerbe. Wäre das nicht ein Traum? Es ist. Ist es nicht?
Dieser Traum kostet Euch nur einen einzigen Brief an den EU-Rat. Ihr schreibt einfach, dass Ihr eindeutig und bedingungslos in der Europäischen Union bleiben wollt. Das war es. Wie Ihr das im Detail hinbekommt, ob mit einem neuen Referendum oder nicht – Eure Sache. Aber macht es. Ihr habt noch gut drei Monate Zeit.

Cartoon by Gerhard Mester

Dass in den vergangenen zweieinhalb Jahren jede Menge Geld, Nerven und Zeit in unsere Trennung gesteckt wurde – Schwamm drüber. Damals wart Ihr unter den Ersten, die dem Populismus Tür und Tor geöffnet haben. Jetzt könntet Ihr zu den Ersten gehören, die ihm wieder die Tür vor der Nase zuschlagen. Das könnte der Anfang einer neuen, besseren Zeit in Europa sein. Und Ihr vorneweg. Das müsste doch Balsam für die geschundene Empire-Seele sein.
Statt weiter mit der Brexit-Abstimmung zu taktieren und am Ende ins Chaos eines ungeregelten Austritts zu schliddern, lasst den ganzen Quatsch also einfach sein. Unseren Rückhalt habt Ihr. Und am Ende stoßen wir auf eine große gemeinsame Zukunft an – gerne mit einem Guinness.

Herzlichst,
Eure EU

Additional Material

1. Additional Notes

A) American Dream or American Nightmare?

The U.S. Constitution was signed on September 17, 1787, by delegates to the Constitutional Convention in Philadelphia, presided over by George Washington, established America's national government and fundamental laws, and guaranteed certain basic rights for its citizens.

The Great Society: A political slogan used by President Lyndon B. Johnson (served 1963–69) to describe the aim of his legislative program of national reform. In his first State of the Union message, delivered on January 4, 1965, the president proclaimed his vision of a "Great Society" and pledged to redouble the "war on poverty". He called for an enormous program of social-welfare legislation, including federal support for education, and hospital care for the elderly through an expanded Social Security program. From *Encyclopedia Britannica* https://www.britannica.com/event/Great-Society

Independence Day – Fourth of July, a great national holiday in the United States, marks the date back in 1776 when Americans broke away from British rule. Back then, America was divided up into 13 British colonies: New Hampshire, Massachusetts Bay, Rhode Island and Providence Plantations, Connecticut and New Haven, New York, New Jersey, Pennsylvania, Delaware, Maryland, Virginia, North Carolina, South Carolina and Georgia.

Those resident in these colonies were required to pay taxes to Britain, even though they were without parliamentary representation. Eventually, people were tired of British rule. In June 1776, a group called the Colonies' Second Continental Congress came together in Philadelphia, which used to be the capital of America, in order to put together a document finally cutting ties with Great Britain. The document was written and rewritten until – after 86 changes – the final version was finished on July 4, 1776, and the colonies declared themselves independent of the British Empire. The following day, the document - called the Declaration of Independence - was made public.Fighting between the Americans and the British did carry on after this date, but a few years later the British Parliament also officially recognised America's independence. The Declaration of Independence to many Americans symbolises their freedom and their sovereignty and is seen as a key artefact and national historic document in the history of the United States of America.

Main Street Suffers: In the year 2008, the world encountered the worst financial crisis since the Great Depression during the 1930s. The financial crisis impacted a large number of people across the developed world. The first sign of trouble was at the beginning of 2006, when house prices in the United States began to drop in value. This initially impacted the American financial sector, and then financial markets all over the world. The crisis was caused, in part, by the high amount of mortgages which had been offered to people who were not able to repay them. The term 'Main Street', which is derived from the term 'Wall Street' (meaning the financial sector or big business), refers to ordinary people. The terms Main Street and Wall Street are occasionally mentioned in speeches to refer to small business or big business.

The New Deal was a programme introduced by U.S. President Franklin D. Roosevelt between 1933 and 1939, which was supposed to bring about economic relief as well as reforms in industry, agriculture, finance, and labour. The term "New Deal" was taken from Roosevelt's acceptance speech for his nomination as the Democratic Party candidate for the presidency in 1932.

Patriots of 1776: Congress declared the colonies to be free and independent states in July 1776. The Patriot leadership expressed their ideological standpoint of liberalism and republicanism and the rejection of monarchy and aristocracy, and proclaimed that all men are created equal. This is often seen as a key American ideal, to this day.

Pearl Harbor attack: The Japanese attack on the U.S. Pacific naval base on Oahu Island, Hawaii, on December 7, 1941. After this attack, the United States decided to join the Allied forces in World War II.

B) Civil Rights and Human Dignity

The Berlin Wall: The Communist government of the German Democratic Republic (GDR) began constructing a wall on August 13, which they called the *Antifaschistischer Schutzwall*, but otherwise became known as the Berlin Wall, between East and West Berlin. The GDR built the wall claiming that it was supposed to prevent fascist influence on the inhabitants of East Germany which would endanger their socialist ideals, as well as the state. However, the primary objective of this wall was to prevent citizens from East Germany leaving to the West, which about 2.5 million people had already done between 1949 and 1961. The Berlin Wall stood until November 9, 1989, when Günter Schabowski, the head of the East German Communist Party, made known that citizens of the GDR could freely cross the border whenever they desired, without fear of retribution. Even today, traces of the Berlin Wall remain throughout the city. These traces exist as a monument to the Cold War and symbol of East-West confrontation.

The Bridge in Selma: The Edmund Pettus Bridge in Selma, Alabama was the location of the "Bloody Sunday"-conflict on March 7, 1965. Armed with clubs and tear gas, police attacked demonstrators as they attempted to march from Selma to Montgomery. However, this did not slow the movement and on March 21, 1965, the marchers, led by Martin Luther King Jr., crossed the bridge again this time successfully walking to the Capitol building. The Voting Rights Act was subsequently enshrined into law in that year. This key event in the Civil Rights Movement led to the bridge in Selma being declared a National Historic Landmark on March 11, 2013.

The Civil Rights Movement in the 1960s: Nearly 100 years after the Emancipation Proclamation, which effectively ended slavery, African Americans in Southern American states still lived in a world of segregation, inequality and various forms of oppression, including race-inspired violence. African Americans were excluded from classrooms, public toilets, theatres, train carriages, and from juries. Civil rights activists engaged in non-violent protest and civil disobedience in order to bring about change. The federal government started initiatives such as the Voting Rights Act of 1965 and the Civil Rights Act of 1968. During this time, many leaders from within the African American community and beyond rose to prominence, including Martin Luther King Jr., Rosa Parks, Malcolm X, Andrew Goodman and many others. They risked their lives, often facing harsh consequences – all in the name of freedom and equality.

The Civil Rights Act of 1964: This document ended segregation in public places and made it illegal to discriminate against a person on the basis of their race, skin colour, religion, sex or ethnic origin. The act was signed into law by Lyndon B. Johnson. In subsequent years, Congress oversaw expansion of the act as well as passing additional legislation aimed at giving African Americans equality, such as the Voting Rights Act of 1965.

The Emancipation Proclamation of 1863: This was an order by President Abraham Lincoln to free slaves, issued as a war measure, making Emancipation a goal of the Civil War (1861-65). Actually there were two Presidential Proclamations known as the Emancipation Proclamation, issued within 100 days apart from each other, the second and final one being issued on January 1, 1863. The proclamation declared "that all persons held as slaves" within the rebellious states "are, and henceforward shall be free".

Hoses in Birmingham: During the 1960s, Birmingham was the location of many mainly non-violent civil-rights protests led by Martin Luther King Jr. and others that were partially met with brutal police violence. (**hoses** *Wasserwerfer)*

Human Rights: These are the rights that all human beings are entitled to, regardless of their nationality, ethnicity, gender, religion, language, residence, or their status within society. Every person has human rights, which should enable them to live free from any sort of discrimination and persecution. Human rights all depend on each other, connect to one another, and cannot be divided. The foundation of international human rights law is the Principle of the Universality of Human Rights. This principle was first written into law in the Universal Declaration of Human Rights which was adopted by the United Nations General Assembly in 1948 and has been repeated in many international human rights resolutions and testimonies ever since. This declaration consists of a preamble and 30 articles.

Human rights should never be removed unless there is genuine reason to do so, but this must always be lawfully justified. If, for example, a court of law finds a person guilty of having committed a crime, their liberty may be restricted. All human rights must be universally protected. If one right is deprived, this has the concurrent effect of causing harm to another.

As the chair of the United Nations Human Rights Commission, Eleanor Roosevelt was the driving force in creating the 1948 charter of liberties: The Universal Declaration of Human Rights. Go online and visit the UN Audiovisual Library, where you can find Eleanor Roosevelt reading the Universal Declaration of Human Rights:
https://www.unmultimedia.org/avlibrary/asset/1093/1093412/

Martin Luther King Jr. was a Baptist minister and civil-rights leader, born on January 15, 1929, in Atlanta, Georgia. He played an important role in the Civil Rights Movement who peacefully sought recognition of black people's right, being influenced by his Christian beliefs and by Mahatma Gandhi's philosophy and teachings. For his efforts in combating racial inequality through non-violent methods, he received the Nobel Peace Prize in 1964. He was assassinated on April 4, 1968 in Memphis, Tennessee. His assassination caused riots in many cities of the United States.

The Montgomery bus boycott: This was a mass protest against the segregated bus system in Montgomery, Alabama, by civil rights activists alongside allies of the cause, often considered to be the first major mass mobilisation of the civil rights movement. The Montgomery bus boycott led to a Supreme Court decision in 1956 that the segregation laws on buses were unconstitutional.

Seneca Falls Declaration (1848): This declaration can be regarded as the culmination of a reformist movement with its origins in the early part of the 19th century. The declaration strove to achieve greater rights for women, most notably in the area of politics, and could be considered to be one of the catalysts for the Suffragette movement.
Stonewall (1969): This incident refers to a series of protests by members of the LGBT-community in response to a police raid that took place on June 28, 1969, at the Stonewall

Inn, a gay bar in New York City. Stonewall stands as a symbol of resistance to the discrimination of a variety of sexual minorities that would inspire solidarity among LGBT-groups for decades.

The **Women's Suffrage Movement** sought to achieve the legal right for women to vote in national and local elections. On Election Day in 1920, millions of American women exercised their right to vote for the first time. It had taken activists and reformers nearly 100 years to win that right. On August 26, 1920, the 19th Amendment to the Constitution was finally ratified. This was a watershed moment in American history as now women had the same rights as men and in this regard could be seen to be on a level playing field in terms of their responsibilities as American citizens.

E) The Earth in Danger: Climate Change

COP23 stands for the 23rd meeting of the Conference of the Parties (COP) to the United Nations Framework Convention on Climate Change (UNFCCC). On 6th November 2017, an international conference set up to converse about climate change and the issues surrounding it, met in Bonn, Germany. This was the 23rd time this group had met, and included all members of the UNFCCC. This meeting also ran concurrently with the Kyoto Protocol's 13th session.

The Green Climate Fund (GCF) was set up by 194 governments with the intention of limiting the increase in the Earth's air temperature to 2°C, or to keep it below this level. The GCF is an organization that focuses its efforts on investing in lowering emissions, sustainable development and reducing greenhouse gases, both in more economically developed nations, as well as poorer parts of the world.

Hurricane Katrina was an extremely destructive storm that hit the Gulf Coast of the United States in August 2005. It was a natural disaster and one of the five deadliest hurricanes in US history. About 90 000 square miles of land were affected. Almost 1900 people lost their lives in the storm and in the subsequent floods. Especially New Orleans and the surrounding areas were very badly damaged. Dillard University in New Orleans, for example, due to extensive flood damage in the wake of Hurricane Katrina, had to completely rebuild and refurbish more than 30 campus buildings. It is estimated that the storm displaced more than 1 million people in the whole region.

The Millennium Development Goals (MDGs): These are a set of goals spanning a wide range of topics, for example reducing poverty, eradicating HIV/AIDS and enabling all children globally to at least receive primary education. The aim was to achieve these goals by the year 2015, and they were presented as a way in which the world could develop as a whole into the new century. In addition to these goals, there has been a call to work towards a new agenda of 17 Sustainable Development Goals (SDGs) over the next 15 years. These goals are a shared vision of humanity and a better world.

National Economic Research Associates (NERA) This is a large economic consultant firm. The NERA study that the Trump Administration selectively quoted and used to leave the Paris Agreement, failed to make note of the potential economic benefits of tackling climate change. NERA did not provide a sufficient analysis of the potential uplift in domestic US employment levels as a result of the expansion of the renewable energy sector.

The Paris Climate Accord: At the Paris climate conference (COP21) in December 2015, 195 countries adopted the first-ever universal, legally binding global climate deal. The agreement sets out a global action plan to put the world on track to avoid the dangers of climate change by limiting global warming to well below 2°C. Further information: https://ec.europa.eu/clima/policies/international/negotiations/paris_en

G) Education – Can It Change the World?

Mother Teresa: a Roman Catholic nun and missionary. She was born on August 26, 1910, in Skopje, Macedonia. However, she actually spent most of her life in India, for 17 years working as a teacher before turning towards helping to care for those in need, namely the sick and poor. She created the 'Order of the Missionaries of Charity'. Her work striving to improve conditions and to alleviate suffering wherever she could eventually earned her the Nobel Peace Prize. She is remembered for her devotion towards the cause of helping others, She died in 1997 and is recognised as a saint by the Catholic Church.

Nelson Mandela was born on July 18, 1918, in South Africa. He was deeply involved in the anti-apartheid movement for much of his life. He joined the African National Congress in 1942. For 20 years, he directed a peaceful, non-violent campaign against the South African government's apartheid regime and its racist policies. For this work he was awarded the Nobel Peace Prize in 1993. In 1994, Mandela became South Africa's first black president. Mandela died on December 5, 2013, at the age of 95.

Aung San Suu Kyi: a human rights activist, Nobel Peace Prize winner and the State Counsellor of Myanmar. She founded a non-violent campaign that advocated for democracy and human rights in Myanmar. In 1989, the Burmese government placed Suu Kyi under house arrest in an attempt to silence her and to reduce her influence. She spent 15 years in custody. In 2010, she was eventually allowed to be free once more, and in turn began a career in politics. Suu Kyi has been reluctant to defend the Rohingya Muslims in her country. She also tried to play down the seriousness of the refugee crisis and has therefore become a very controversial figure in recent years.

H) United Nations: Peacekeeping in a World of Conflicts

Asylum-seekers: People who are seeking sanctuary in a country other than their own, who are waiting for a decision regarding their right to remain in that country. The legal processes related to asylum are complex and variable. When an asylum application is successful, the person is awarded refugee status.

A refugee: A person who has been forced to flee his or her country because of political or religious reasons, war, or violence. A refugee has a well-founded fear of persecution on the grounds of race, gender, religion, nationality, political opinion, health status or membership of a particular social group. Refugees are recognized under various international agreements.

The UN Security Council is tasked with the responsibility of ensuring the protection of international security and related matters such as peace and stability in regions wherein challenges may present themselves. The council seeks to reduce the possibility of conflict breaking out by always attempting diplomatic solutions.

Comprising of 15 members, a democratic system seeks to deal with perceived threats in the form of aggressive or dangerous activity, either on a macro level from states themselves or on a smaller scale in the form of regional conflicts or generalised instability which may pose a threat to wider security.

Furthermore, they also hold an extra democratic responsibility in the form of electing new members to the council, as well as the ability to vote judges into the International Court of Justice.

However, the council does possess powers to go further than the aforementioned diplomatic procedure. This will often take the form of economic sanctions or restrictions upon trade, but sometimes they may opt to use military force in order to ensure peace is maintained.

I) Technology and the Digital Age

Artificial Intelligence (AI) is the ability of a computer, or of a robot, to perform tasks commonly associated with intelligent beings (humans, and in some cases, animals). The term is frequently applied to the project of developing systems endowed with the intellectual processing characteristics of humans, such as the following abilities: reasoning, discerning meaning, generalizing, and learning from past experience.
Since the development of the digital computer in the 1940s, it has been demonstrated many times that computers can be programmed to carry out very complex tasks. Some programs have attained the performance level of human experts in performing certain specific tasks. Further information: *Encyclopaedia Britannica* https://www.britannica.com/technology/artificial-intelligence

The First Man on the Moon: Apollo 11 took off on July 16, 1969. Neil Armstrong, Edwin Aldrin and Michael Collins were the astronauts onboard. On July 20, 1969, Armstrong and Aldrin landed on the moon. Neil Armstrong became the first human to set foot on the moon. After spending 21 hours on the Moon's surface, the astronauts embarked on their journey back to planet Earth. This was not before leaving a message stating that they had been the first humans to set foot on the Moon and that their mission was of peaceful intent. On July 24, 1969, all three astronauts safely returned to Earth.

2. Teaching and Learning Methods and Cooperative Learning Strategies

Try something a bit different. Here are various teaching and learning methods to motivate cooperative learning strategies. Teachers base their lessons on a mixture of methods and approaches to meet the different needs, such as the age, experience and language competence, of learners, the different aims of lessons, as well as course objectives, expectations and resources.

acting out the speech
active learning:
  active listening
  active speaking
  active reading
  active writing
agile work methods
assessment
audience response tools
brainstorming
brain writing
chain technique:
  comment chain,
  question chain
chunking
classroom stations technique
communicative activities
conference
collaboration with:
  Social Sciences classes
  History classes
  Art and Music classes
  Drama classes
conducting a survey
cooperative learning
cross-curricular connections
creative activities
creative writing
crossover learning
cue cards
debate/debating
designing a poster
devising a (role) play
digital media production
digital narratives
digital tools
discussion
divide the speech
doing experiments
dramatisation
dramatised reading
dramatised group reading
elevator pitches: 60-second pitch/presentation
enabling innovative projects
enquiry-based learning
evaluating website content
evaluation
exchanging ideas
exchanging knowledge at stalls
extensive reading: scanning
facilitate student interaction
feedback
fishbowl discussion
flipchart
flipped classroom
formative assessment
four corners activity
future workshop
gallery walk
games
ghost writing
giving a presentation
giving a speech
group work
hot seat
idea tower
idea lab
implementing ideas
improved reading
independent learning
individual work
innovative developments
inside - outside circle
inspiration cards
intensive reading: skimming
interactive classroom
interior monologue
internet research
interview
interviewing experts
jigsaw activity
jigsaw activity: step 2
kwl reading method:
  what we know
  what we want to know
  what we learned
laptops
listening for detail
laptop presentation
listening for gist
market place
mediation
mind mapping
milling around
monologue technique
optimist – pessimist
pair share
paired work
panel discussion
paragraphing
peer assessment
peer feedback
peer support
placemat method
podcast
poetry slam
portfolio
posters
project-based learning
pre-listening activity
preparing a speech
pre-reading activity
pre-listening activity
press conference
presentation
presenting results
problem solving strategies
producing a podcast
producing a video
pros and cons debate
project work
questionnaire
quiz
radio talk
reading aloud
reading with confidence
reading dramatisation
reading for gist
research
research competition
research project
review reading strategies
rewriting a text
role play
scanning
self-immersion
send an email
serial storytelling
set up a project
share ideas
share ideas with classmates
silent writing discussion
skimming
Skype interview
smartboard use
smartphone use

social media wall: feedback
SOLO taxonomy: structure of observed learning outcomes
Speakers' Corner
speech competition
speech conference
speech training
speaking skills training
speed debating
SQ3R reading method: survey, question, read, recite, review
stations learning
students teach each other
speech writing
storyboard
storytelling
support
summary writing
tablets
tablet presentation
taking notes
talk show
teacher's presentation
teacher's lecture
team building
TED questions
think - pair - share
three-minute speech
TV talk show
TV debate
tweet summary
use smartphones, laptops, tablets
video clip production
video chat
video recording
video conferencing
visualising ideas
walking & talking
warm-up technique
warm-up discussion
warm-up speech training
WebQuest
whiteboard
word cloud
word cloud technique
work in groups
workshop
work in pairs, then in groups
writing conference
writing and giving a speech

Cartoon by
Gerhard Mester

Task:
Give this cartoon a catchy title and a speech bubble text that reflects the message.

3. Rhetorical and Stylistic Devices and Intended Effects

Rhetorical devices can be a powerful tool for any speaker. Here are some examples which might give you some help for the analysis of speeches. Please notice that the effects depend on the particular context and cannot always be generalised. If you use rhetorical devices in your own speech, then be careful and don't go overboard with too many of them.

Alliteration: this is a repetition of a sound, usually a consonant; the same sound appears at the beginning of two or more words.
Examples: "Let us go forth to lead the land we love." / "Pay any price, bear any burden." (John F. Kennedy)
Effects: Alliteration focuses the listeners' attention on a particular section of the text. Alliterative sounds can create a memorable rhythm and can have emotional associations and undertones, so that the expression can easily be remembered.

Allusion: this can be a reference to a well-known literary text or a historic event; the listeners are expected to recognise and respond to it.
Example 1: "I had a member of my family killed." (Robert F. Kennedy)
Effect: This is a reference to Robert F. Kennedy's brother, John F. Kennedy, the former U.S. President, who was assassinated on November 22, 1963. Robert F. Kennedy wants to remind the audience of common ideals and values of non-violence and peace, which the listeners understand and appreciate.
Example 2: "Five score years ago, a great American, in whose symbolic shadow we stand today, signed the Emancipation Proclamation." (Martin Luther King Jr.)
Effect: Martin Luther King Jr. is referring to the Gettysburg Address given by President Abraham Lincoln; it took place on November 19, 1863 and opened with the words "Four score and seven years ago". He wants to quote an authority of great historic significance and to create a memorable phrase that reminds the audience of common ideals.

Anaphora: repetition of a word or phrase at the beginning of successive consecutive / following phrases, clauses or lines.
Examples: "I have a dream. [...] I have a dream" (Martin Luther King) / "To those old allies... To those new states... To those people..." (John F. Kennedy)
Effects: The speaker wants to heighten the listeners' attention, so that they can understand the message clearly, it also helps listeners to remember the speech and its key points. The speaker wants to reinforce an idea and to create a memorable powerful effect.

Antithesis: a form of contrast that compares a word or idea with its opposite, often in a parallel structure; two opposite ideas are put together in a sentence to achieve a contrasting effect.
Example: "Ask not what your country can do for you, ask what you can do for your country." (John F. Kennedy)
Effects: the speaker wants to get the listeners' attention; to help the audience understand the difference between two concepts, words or events; to help the audience understand the speaker's message and/or his opinion more clearly. In this example JFK appeals to the audience to take active responsibility for the country and to show commitment to civic engagement.

Appeal: At the end of a speech, the speaker wants his audience to think about his message; he often uses a call for action, a personal request, or a strong recommendation.
Examples: "Now is the time to make justice a reality for all of God's children." (Martin Luther King Jr.) / "Unity is the path. Our future depends on it." (António Guterres) / "Let us create together a new national spirit of unity and trust." (Jimmy Carter) / "Let's begin ..." (Malala Yousafzai)
Effects: a call for action, a strong recommendation for the listeners to be more responsible and take action to change, for example, an unfair or even dangerous political or social situation. Jimmy Carter, for example, emphasises a new spirit of "unity and trust".

Contrasts: the speaker emphasises the differences between two or more ideas or concepts.
Example: "a lonely island of poverty in the midst of a vast ocean of material prosperity"/ "Now is the time to rise from the dark and desolate valley of segregation to the sunlit path of racial justice." (Martin Luther King Jr.)
Effects: Contrasts illustrate different ideas and goals and can help to focus the listeners' attention on the speaker's main arguments. The contrasts *("poverty ... prosperity" / "the dark and desolate valley of segregation" / "the sunlit path of racial justice")* visualise the depressing situation at the time and a positive vision of a promising, hopeful future.

Emotions: The speaker should be an expert on the subject; but he should not only give abstract pieces of information and lots of data. He also uses words and phrases which reveal his emotions and thus have an emotional connotation.
Examples: "For man holds in his mortal hands the power to abolish all forms of human poverty and all forms of human life." / "...its hour of maximum danger." (JFK) / "To every politician who is taking donations from the NRA, shame on you." (Emma Gonzales)
Effects: Emotions attract the audience and get them involved in the speech and in the speaker's message. If the speaker is authentic and emotional and knows what he is talking about, then the audience will be interested in what the speaker has to say. A speech is most impressive when the speaker is able to combine real and true facts, clear and logical statements and thoughtful consideration with

personal and emotional commitment.

Exaggeration: a speaker uses exaggeration as a rhetorical device to emphasise or even dramatise an important idea. *Example: "They hate the NRA. They hate the Second Amendment. They hate individual freedom." (Wayne LaPierre) / "This American carnage stops right here and stops right now." (Donald Trump) / "AMERICA will once again be a nation that thinks big, dreams bigger, and always reaches for the stars". (Donald Trump)*
Effect: the speakers use exaggeration to dramatise and give extra stress to an idea or concept which they are trying to convey without any restraint. But when facts are ignored, exaggerations can have harmful consequences in the hands of populists. Therefore the audience should be critical, if a speaker uses one-sided or exaggerated statements.

Examples, anecdotes, personal stories: Authentic and vivid, often personal examples, short and relevant personal stories, are a powerful and trustworthy communicative device.
Examples: "One man approached them with a small baby perched on his shoulder, nine months old – Malek. He was holding onto a gas canister to stay afloat, and he said to them: "I fear I am not going to survive. I'm too weak. I don't have the courage anymore." And he handed little Malek over to Bassem and to Doaa, and they perched her onto the life ring. So now they were three, Doaa, Bassem and little Malek." (Melissa Fleming) / "Growing up in this family, color was never important for me. Outside home, however, things were different soon. Color had many other meanings." (Angélica Dass) / "I've sat with children in juvenile detention, and opioid addicts, who told me their lives could have turned out differently" (Mark Zuckerberg)
Effects: The speaker wants to help listeners understand the message of the speech more clearly; her examples and short stories can be convincing, encouraging and motivating; these concrete examples or stories can move the audience; the dramatic and tragic examples make the speech very impressive and powerful and provide supporting evidence for abstract ideas and concepts. A personal story can build trust. Melissa Fleming does not talk about an abstract and detached "immigration" concept; she wants to stir the listeners' emotions and to get the audience to acknowledge the existence of a serious human problem in the real world. Angélica Dass emphasises that racism has no place in society. Mark Zuckerberg reveals that his personal account is authentic and quite significant for the young people listening to his speech.

Humour: Humour creates a sense of connection and identification between the speaker and the audience.
Example: "I am pretty certain that I am also the first recipient of the Nobel Peace Prize who still fights with her younger brothers. I want there to be peace everywhere, but my brothers and I are still working on that." (Malala Yousafzai)
Effects: Humour can make the audience smile or even laugh; humour can bring a sense of light-heartedness or cheerfulness to an otherwise serious and thoughtful speech, by providing the audience with some relief from a serious topic. A speaker should however be aware of the fact, that some kind of "forced humour" can spoil the speaker's message.

Imagery: This is the collective term for devices, such as metaphor and simile, which help the audience to understand and visualise abstract ideas and concepts.
Example: "Let us, each of us, now embrace with solemn duty and awesome joy what is our lasting birth right. With common effort and common purpose, with passion and dedication, let us answer the call of history and carry into an uncertain future that precious light of freedom." (Obama)
Effects: The speaker creates a memorable picture in the audience's minds and presents an abstract idea or goal more clearly.

Irony: This is a figure of speech in which words are used in such a way that their intended meaning is different to, and often the opposite of, the literal meaning of the words.
Effects: The speaker wants to get the listeners' attention; to force listeners to use their imagination to understand the underlying ironical meaning of the speech. But the speaker should be careful not to overuse ironical statements which can be misunderstood by the audience.

Language: Any speaker is well advised to use clear, understandable and comprehensive language.
Effects: the use of language conveys the speaker's thoughts about the issues he is talking about; clarity of speech can make a speaker appear more credible, reliable, trustworthy and confident. The speaker tries to use language that listeners will understand; he wants to help the audience understand the message of the speech more clearly. If a speaker, however, uses complex, academic words and rather complicated phrases, he may also want to present himself as intelligent, brainy, and "out of touch with the common man".

Metaphor: This is a figure of speech that makes an implicit, implied, or hidden comparison between two things that are unrelated, but which share some common characteristics.
Examples: The following examples are taken from Martin Luther King's "I Have a Dream" speech:
"a great beacon light of hope": this metaphor emphasises guidance, confidence, hope, optimism, and encouragement for a better future and a fairer society
"crippled by the manacles of segregation" / "the chains of discrimination ": these metaphors describe the cruel treatment black people experienced during the time of slavery, as manacles and chains were used to restrain black slaves.
"the sunlit path of racial justice": this metaphor illustrates justice, human rights and a fair treatment of all human beings / *"This sweltering summer of the Negro's legitimate discontent will not pass until there is an invigorating autumn of freedom and equality." / "I have a dream that one*

day even the state of Mississippi, a state sweltering with the heat of injustice, sweltering with the heat of oppression, will be transformed into an oasis of freedom and justice." King uses a metaphor and a contrast; he compares injustice and oppression to sweltering heat, freedom and justice to an oasis. King repeats the sweltering heat metaphor, referring specifically to Mississippi, a state where some of the worst offenses against blacks were carried out; he mentions an oasis that awaits even these places; King expands his message of hope to those suffering the most.
"We continue a never-ending journey to bridge the meaning of those words with the realities of our time." (Barack Obama)
Effects: A metaphor creates a memorable and impressive mental picture in the audience's minds and presents an abstract idea of freedom and equality or concept of human rights more clearly.

Paradox: a statement that seems self-contradictory yet turns out to have a rational or deeper meaning.
Example: "Only when our arms are sufficient beyond doubt can we be certain beyond doubt that they will never be employed." (JFK)
Effects: A paradox is used to illustrate concepts or ideas that are contradictory to one another, yet, when placed together, reveal a significant message; the significance of a paradox is not revealed at first glance, so that the listeners might enjoy some puzzling "food for thought".

Parallelism: the repetition of similar or identical words or phrases; some parts of a sentence or several sentences are expressed similarly.
Example: "United there is little we cannot do in a host of co-operative ventures. Divided there is little we can do..." (JFK)
Effects: Parallelism and contrast ("*United*" - "*Divided*") draw the listeners' attention to important ideas and show that JFK's ideas of cooperation, unity and solidarity are equally important.

Pauses: Any moment of stillness, in a speech, can be important. Many speakers use pauses for emphasis, suspense or dramatic effect – or simply pause for thought.
Effects: A speaker may use pauses to put emphasis on a certain point; to let a point sink in; to give the audience time to consider what the speaker has said. Pauses are used to great effect by Barack Obama.

Personal Pronouns: The deliberate choice of personal pronouns may be significant in the speech, because people tend to use first person singular personal pronouns when talking about themselves and their own experiences.
Example: "but we have never had to put a wall up to keep our people in, to prevent them from leaving us." (JFK)
Effects: The frequent use of personal pronouns, such as 'we, 'our', 'your' help to establish a personal relationship, a feeling of togetherness, closeness, common understanding, a group feeling. This might reduce the level of communicative distance between the speaker and their listeners thus making it a rather personal, individual and inclusive form of address; the speaker might even emphasise that he feels a sense of solidarity with the audience, by appealing to concepts like empathy, teamwork, optimism, inclusion, mutual respect, solidarity and support, and collective identity, such as the collective American identity and the American Dream; JFK expresses solidarity with the people in Berlin who live in a dangerous political situation; he points out that democracy and freedom would never build a wall to control or imprison its own citizens.
On the contrary, the use of personal pronouns ("they", "them") can also have a different intention:
Example: "They don't like free speech any more than they like the Second Amendment. They like only limited speech, controlled speech, controlled by them, through safe speech zones, where they can shame the outspoken, or riot to shut them up." (Wayne LaPierre)
Effect: In this example, the use of the personal pronouns *"they", "them"* has a different connotation; the speaker focuses on people who – in his opinion – want to destabilise the country – and therefore should be regarded as dangerous and antagonistic, averse, ill-disposed, dissenting and hostile people.

Personification: This is a rhetorical device in which an object, an idea or an animal or plant have human qualities or act like human beings.
Example: "The whole of Nature cries out at our mistreatment of Her." (Prince Charles)
Effect: The speaker attributes human qualities and behaviour ("cries out") to nature; this is a strong appeal to the audience not to "mistreat" and destroy nature ("*Her*"), but to support responsible global as well as regional action for achieving sustainable development goals.

References: references to past events may refer to experiences, memories, reminiscences recollections shared by the speaker and his audience.
Examples: "I have sworn before you and Almighty God the same solemn oath our forebears prescribed nearly a century and three-quarters ago." / "With a good conscience our only sure reward, with history the final judge of our deeds..." (JFK) / "With malice toward none, with charity toward all" / "all men are created equal" (Abraham Lincoln)
Effects: The Declaration of Independence contains the famous line Lincoln uses in his speech: *"We hold these truths to be self-evident, that all men are created equal, that they are endowed by their Creator with certain unalienable rights, that among these are life, liberty, and the pursuit of happiness." "The creed all men are created equal"* means that people hold certain unchangeable (inalienable) natural rights that are fundamental to (and innate in) all human beings.

Religious connotations: References to religious contexts, such as to the Bible, to God, and to religious beliefs, often employed by speakers.
Examples: "... let us go forth to lead the land we love, asking

His blessing and His help, but knowing that here on earth God's work must truly be our own." (JFK) / "We are protected by God" (Donald Trump); the words "prayers" and "may God grant us wisdom, and may He watch over the United States of America" (George W. Bush) / "That is how we will preserve our planet, commanded to our care by God." (Barack Obama) / "Thank you. God bless you, and may He forever bless these United States of America." (Barack Obama)
Effects: The speakers want to create a sense of shared identity with their audience. Religious language is used in particular in Inaugural Addresses and also in political speeches: "and may He watch over the United States of America". George W. Bush appeals to various religions by mentioning their characteristic languages "in English, Hebrew, and Arabic". Bush emphasises that it was a radical and extreme terrorist group which is responsible for the 9/11 attacks. He rejects prejudices against Muslim people. He is not blaming any religion for the act of terror. Barack Obama emphasises our respect, esteem, appreciation, thankfulness and great responsibility for *"our planet commanded to our care by God."*

Repetition: When a word or phrase is repeated two or more times.
Examples: "For man holds in his mortal hands the power to abolish all forms of human poverty and all forms of human life."(JFK) / "Who is responsible for this?" (Shalvi Shakshi) / "Our journey is not complete." [repeated several times] (Barack Obama)
Effects: The speaker wants to raise the listeners' attention so that they remember the main message of the speech more easily; the speaker wants to emphasise important points in the speech; making a lasting impression by repeating those terms or ideas that are most important and significant; to appeal to the audience's emotions, for example, to intensify a feeling of concern, hope, optimism, motivation and encouragement; and to persuade the audience.

Rhetorical question: Rhetorical questions are a feature of persuasive speeches. A rhetorical question is used in order to anticipate the questions of the audience; a question to which the answer seems to be quite obvious; therefore an answer is not actually required and not expected from the audience.
Examples: "What is the great issue between the free world and the Communist world?" (JFK) "Do we really love our money and our celebrities more than we love our children? Can we answer that question honestly? Any of us? Can we answer that question honestly?" (Wayne LaPierre) / "And why ... is so little being done to stop the wars, the persecution and the poverty that is driving so many people to the shores of Europe?" (Melissa Fleming) / "Global warming anyone?" (Donald Trump)
Effects: the speaker wants to communicate with the audience; rhetorical questions create a feeling of understanding each other. The speaker wants to emphasise a point or raise the listeners' attention and make them feel involved in his line of argumentation. Rhetorical questions are often used when the speaker wants to push the listeners to a rather logical and obvious conclusion. A rhetorical question can also imply a request or a strong appeal.

Sentence structure: Parataxis and Hypotaxis
Parataxis is characterised by successive independent clauses; phrases and clauses are placed one after another independently, without the use of conjunctions.
Example: "Day four, the passengers were getting agitated. They asked the captain: "When will we get there?" He told them to shut up, and he insulted them. He said: "In 16 hours we will reach the shores of Italy." They were weak and weary." (Melissa Fleming)
Hypotaxis: The sentences, clauses, and phrases are subordinated and linked to show the relationship between clauses; hypotaxis contains subordinate clauses that build on to the main clause in order to provide additional information that explains the main ideas of the speaker.
Effects: Paratactic sentences are useful in explaining a sequence of thoughts with equal importance; the listeners can easily understand the importance of each separate, often short sentence; parataxis helps the readers to focus on particular ideas, one after the other.
Hypotactic sentences explain and intensify the meaning of the main idea; they give some more information, so that the listeners can recognise, understand and visualise the complete and rather complex idea or concept which the speaker is trying to convey. A speaker is well advised, however, not to use too many complex hypotactic sentences in the speech, because then the audience might be rather irritated and confused.

Slogan/Refrain: This is a regularly repeated sentence or line, a catchy word or phrase.
Example: "Yes, we can!" (Barack Obama) / "I have a dream." (Martin Luther King Jr.) / "What can you do?" (Timoci Naulusala) / "America First" (Donald Trump)
Effect: The speaker wants to help the audience remember the key message or a certain aspect of the speech for a long time, after they first heard the speech itself; the speaker wants the audience to keep this slogan in mind.

Structure of the speech: The speech should be organised in a clear and logical way.
Effects: Does the speaker keep the speech simple, with a clear beginning, middle and end, so that the listeners can follow the train of thought easily?
Does the speaker prove the statements with facts, experience, knowledge and examples to support the message?
Does the speaker employ a request or recommendation, a strong appeal at the end of his speech?

Superlatives illustrate the importance and significance of an event, idea or action.
Examples: "the greatest demonstration for freedom" (Martin Luther King Jr.) / "the proudest boast" (JFK)
Effects: The use of superlatives emphasises the great sig-

nificance of an important, notable, noteworthy, particular, special, momentous, historic event, it reveals the speaker's views, priorities and his personal commitment. A speaker is well advised, however, not to overdo this and use too many superlatives, because then a critical audience might become more skeptical of being manipulated.

Symbols: Symbols signify ideas, concepts and emotions, by visualising figurative meanings which are different from their literal sense.
Example: "We have seen the unfurling of flags, the lighting of candles, the giving of blood, the saying of prayers" (George W. Bush) / symbols, i.e. "flags" / "candles" / "blood".
Effect: The flags represent American patriotism, the belief in the strength of one's own country; the candles remind the audience of the losses and of the fallen; the blood puts emphasis on the injuries and pain of the victims. The symbols are well-known and they are easily understood by the listeners.

Tone of voice: The tone of voice is made up of the speaker's intonation and the choice of words; it reflects the speaker's emotional attitude towards the topic of the speech.
Examples: the tone can be formal, informal, friendly, serious, thoughtful, humorous, comic, funny, amusing, sarcastic, ironic, satirical, sad, or cheerful, joyful.
Effect: The tone is used to refer to the implicit evaluation which the author manages to convey behind his explicit presentation; the tone of a speech is significant; on the one hand, it can convey empathy, kindness, encouragement, inspiration, support and motivation, but on the other hand, it can also convey a negative atmosphere of intimidation, pressure, rudeness, even ruthlessness, also stress, fear and anxiety.

Combination of rhetorical devices (1): Various rhetorical devices are combined to visualise certain complex images.
Example: "What is true of this city is true of Germany – real, lasting peace in Europe can never be assured as long as one German out of four is denied the elementary right of free men, and that is to make a free choice. In 18 years of peace and good faith, this generation of Germans has earned the right to be free, including the right to unite their families and their nation in lasting peace, with good will to all people." (JFK)
Effects: creating a climax / repetition of keywords *"peace", "free men", "free choice", "good faith", "good will", "true", "right"* (repetition of keywords: 3 x peace, 3 x free, 2 x good, 2 x true, 2 x right); JFK visualises the global interdependence of a more peaceful, democratic and human world; he also emphasises his message; the choice of words, the repetitions raise the listeners' attention to JFK's message of freedom, peace, and unity.

Combination of rhetorical devices (2): A variety of different rhetorical devices reveals a vivid imagery.
Examples: "You live in a defended island of freedom, but your life is part of the main. So let me ask you as I close, to lift your eyes beyond the dangers of today, to the hopes of tomorrow, beyond the freedom merely of this city of Berlin, or your country of Germany, to the advance of freedom everywhere, beyond the wall to the day of peace with justice, beyond yourselves and ourselves to all mankind." (JFK)
Effects: Many rhetorical devices are used here: the metaphor: *"island of freedom"* / the climax: *"Berlin, Germany, everywhere, all mankind"* / the repetition of keywords: *"freedom", "peace"* / the contrast: *"dangers of today versus hopes of tomorrow"* / the contrast: *"beyond the wall to the day of peace with justice"* / the climax: *"beyond yourselves and ourselves to all mankind."*
The speaker emphasises by means of various rhetorical devices his political message of encouragement, solidarity, shared democratic values, and ideals.

Combination of rhetorical devices (3):
Example: "Freedom is indivisible, and when one man is enslaved, all are not free. When all are free, then we can look forward to that day when this city will be joined as one and this country and this great Continent of Europe in a peaceful and hopeful globe." (JFK)
Many rhetorical devices are used: the metaphor *"Freedom is indivisible"* / the climax: *"this city / and this country / this great Continent of Europe / in a peaceful and hopeful globe" (JFK)*
Effects: A climax is a rhetorical device in which the speaker positions and arranges a series of words or sentences in order to intensify and increase importance, significance, or emphasis. Kennedy visualises an abstract idea *"Freedom"*, as well as the global concept of hope, unity, and peace all over the world. JFK addresses the people directly, he shows identification and sympathy, he expresses solidarity, supports encouragement and motivation and employs a strong personal appeal to the people that they should not give up hope for a better future; JFK's final conclusion expressed in German *"Ich bin ein Berliner"* sums up his personal encouraging, hopeful and positive message.

Combination of rhetorical devices (4):
Examples: *"We will bring back our jobs. We will bring back our borders. We will bring back our wealth. And we will bring back our dreams." (Trump)*
Effects: The speaker uses repetitions "We will" to demonstrate his determination; he uses the personal pronouns "we / our" to express unity, identity; he uses a paratactic sentence structure to emphasise his strong commitment to various political promises: *"jobs / borders / wealth / dreams."*

For more information, please visit:
Literary Devices. Definition and Examples of Literary Terms / https://literarydevices.net
Study Guides and Strategies: http://www.studygs.net/
ThoughtCo: Rhetorical devices / https://www.thoughtco.com/rhetorical-devices-4169905

Body Language: A Communicative Device

Cartoon by Gerhard Mester

Body Language is a significant communicative device. It is part of non-verbal communication. This includes the way a speaker talks, moves and appears on stage.
Body language is part of the message a speaker wants to give. The speaker's movement, gestures, postures, facial expressions, eye-contact with the listeners, and tone of voice reveal an important underlying or "hidden" message. Body language is not only the way you position yourself on stage. A speaker can convey positive as well as negative emotions. The speaker's body language might also reveal the confidence and self-reliance which support the speech. On the one hand, body language can support and emphasise the speaker's message, but on the other hand it can also irritate the audience or distract them from the speaker's message.
The cartoon by Gerhard Mester illustrates Donald Trump's body language in a particular context: The President's rude criticism of "fake news" media: "Fake, fake, disgusting news". Watch these examples:

1. Donald Trump attacks CNN's reporter Jim Acosta in a White House press conference: *"You are a rude, terrible person. [...] Just sit down. [...] When you report fake, which CNN does, a lot, you are the enemy of the people."* From: Press Conference on November 7, 2018
   Watch the two-minute video on: https://www.independent.co.uk/news/world/americas/trump-cnn-jim-acosta-video-midterms-white-house-sarah-sanders-press-conference-a8622656.html
2. Speaking at a rally for a Republican candidate for the Senate (on August 3, 2018), Donald Trump calls journalists "horrible, horrendous people": Watch the short video here: https://www.theguardian.com/us-news/video/2018/aug/03/fake-fake-disgusting-news-trump-launches-new-broadside-against-media-video

4. An Effective Presentation and a Good Speech – Recommended Websites

A) How to Give an Effective Presentation

Read the information in your English Course book.
For further information, go online and visit:

Top Tips for Effective Presentations:
https://www.skillsyouneed.com/present/presentation-tips.html

How to Give a Presentation:
https://www.wikihow.com/Give-a-Presentation

How to Give a Good Presentation:
https://www.princeton.edu/~archss/webpdfs08/BaharMartonosi.pdf

How to Give a Short Class Presentation Competently:
https://www.instructables.com/id/How-to-Give-a-Short-Class-Presentation-Competently/

The Only Way To Prepare To Give A Presentation:
https://www.forbes.com/sites/forbesleadershipforum/2013/06/19/the-only-way-to-prepare-to-give-a-presentation/#76781c49b84e

How to Give the Best Presentation You Possibly Can:
https://www.huffingtonpost.com/karl-gude/how-to-give-the-best-pres_b_3932280.html

How to Give a Killer Presentation:
https://hbr.org/2013/06/how-to-give-a-killer-presentation

17 Killer Presentations Tips for Students Who Want to Stand out:
https://www.powtoon.com/blog/17-killer-presentations-tips-students-stand/

B) How to give a Good Speech

Read the information in your English Course book.
For further information, go online and visit:

9 Tips to Make Your Speech Memorable:
http://sixminutes.dlugan.com/memorable-speech/#more-10150

11 Tips for Giving a Great Speech:
https://www.oxford-royale.co.uk/articles/11-tips-great-speech.html

How To Give A Great Speech:
https://www.forbes.com/sites/jacquelyn-smith/2013/08/13/how-to-give-a-great-speech-3/#64f8e63f6696

How to Prepare and Give a Speech:
https://www.wikihow.com/Prepare-and-Give-a-Speech

7 Tips for Giving a Killer Speech:
https://www.americanexpress.com/us/small-business/openforum/articles/7-tips-for-giving-a-killer-speech/

7 Things to Do When You Have to Give a Short Speech:
https://www.inc.com/bill-murphy-jr/7-things-to-do-when-you-have-to-give-a-short-speech.html

How to Prepare and Deliver a Speech Effectively:
http://www.englishmate.com/blog/how-to-prepare-and-deliver-a-speech-effectively/

Oral Presentations: Tips on How to Deliver a Speech for School or Work:
https://jerz.setonhill.edu/writing/technical-writing/oral-presentations-tips/

> "You do not know what you are able to do until you try.
> Try it in every possible way. [...]
> Be thoughtful, and painstaking. [...]
> Learn your own possibilities."
>
> *George Bellows, American painter*
> (born August 12, 1882, Columbus, Ohio – died January 8, 1925, New York, N.Y.)

Picture References

|akg-images GmbH, Berlin: John Parrot/Stocktrek Images 14; World History Archive 20. |alamy images, Abingdon/Oxfordshire: 360b 168, 233; COP21 122; Danita Delimont 71; EDB Image Archive 219; Julie Edwards 287; Kristoffer Tripplaar 242; Malcolm Park editorial 256; MediaPunch Inc 205; Richard Ellis 27, 157; SOPA Images Limited 271; White House Photo 107; ZUMA Press, Inc. 229. |Baaske Cartoons, Müllheim: Mester, Gerhard 92, 121, 151, 290, 296, 302. |ddp images GmbH, Hamburg: Arnaud Bouissou 129. |Getty Images, München: (c) 2010 Arthur Edwards - WPA Pool 87; (c) 2014 Robin Marchant 213; (c) 2017 Alex Wong 134; (c) 2017 Chris McGrath 187. |Granlund, Dave, Waconia MN: 46, 58, 60, 65, 143. |Harper Collins Publishers Ltd, London: reprinted by permission (c) Marie Colvin: On the Front line 87. |https://www.humanae.org: © Bret Hartman/TED 175. |Interfoto, München: Danita Delimont / Dennis Brack 117; Granger, NYC 37, 78; SuperStock 48. |mauritius images GmbH, Mittenwald: United Archives 56. |Mitchell, Margaret: 262. |Nachawi, Dima, Beirut: Amelia Butterly 194. |Nayer, Talal, Osnabrück: 190, 190. |PantherMedia GmbH (panthermedia.net), München: Peter Röther 6. |Picture-Alliance GmbH, Frankfurt/M.: Agencia EL UNIVERSAL/Alejandra Leyva/EVZ 195; AP 83; AP Images 279; CPA Media 93; dpa 103, 116; Eventpress Stauffenberg 181; Martin Meissner 146; Mikayla Whitmore 110; Solo Syndication/Daily Mail 191; ZUMA Wire 67. |Shutterstock.com, New York: Rich Carey / WWF 133. |Shutterstock.com (RM), New York: SERGEY DOLZHENKO/EPA-EFE/REX 266. |stock.adobe.com, Dublin: smolaw11 Titel. |Thumser, Harald, Frankfurt/M.: 36, 142, 143, 156, 174, 285. |UNHCR, Genf: Susan Hopper 164. |UNICEF Pacific, 360 Victoria Parade: Pacific/2017/Heinrich 152. |United Nations Photo Library/Department of Public Information, New York: 234.